"This book offers a breath of fresh air for a ... of women's rights in the USA. The rich c ... ... that there has been, and continues to be, ongoing, albeit uneven, revolutionary changes in attitudes toward gender equality and against sexual violence. It should be read by gender scholars, political analysts, and all others who are concerned about the future of gender justice in this country."

—**Nancy A. Naples**, *University of Connecticut*

"*Gender Revolution* is a data-based chronicle of change and a roadmap for transformation. Aronson and Fleming demonstrate that achievements for all genders in politics and culture are not just an end in themselves but a means for further progress. Despite periodic setbacks in social movements, this book provides hope for a future with true gender equality."

—**Barbara McQuade**, *University of Michigan Law School*

"*Gender Revolution*'s incisive analysis portrays both the power and the limitations of the #MeToo movement. While views about gender equality have changed dramatically, much is still contested. Aronson and Fleming's detailed research helps us understand how a social movement can bring about gendered cultural change in everyday life. While there are 'bumps' along the way, this book convinces me we are experiencing a gender cultural revolution."

—**Holly McCammon**, *Vanderbilt University*

"Aronson and Fleming, drawing on a unique combination of data, establish where we are today in politics and everyday culture with the long-sought goal of gender equality, as well as with continuing gender divisions. An important and timely read for anyone interested in how past protests and movements shape the present and influence the future."

—**Jo Reger**, *Oakland University*

"This innovative and insightful multi-method study of news media accounts of the 2017 Women's March on Washington, politicians' statements, and focus group dialogues illuminates the dynamic interdependence of macro-cultural change and micro-level psychological processes. Aronson and Fleming document in fascinating detail how politicians' self-presentations in 2018 gubernatorial and 2020 presidential primary elections exhibited both gender-traditional and innovative elements, echoed by focus group members' reactions to the candidates. Personal narratives of the meaning of sexual consent likewise show that while the gender revolution is moving forward, it remains incomplete."

—**Jeylan Mortimer**, *University of Minnesota*

GENDER REVOLUTION

Gender Revolution carefully examines the profound transformations happening in both public and private arenas of gender relations. It also draws critical attention to the simultaneous and potent challenges that have risen in response.

The authors look to large-scale phenomena in this contemporary study and address how electoral politics and the #MeToo movement are reshaping everyday life. This gender revolution has led to a culture in which women, and increasing numbers of men, refuse to accept traditional gender norms and gender inequalities. People of all genders no longer tolerate abuses of power in politics or in their interpersonal relationships. Despite vigorous resistance, women are seizing power and refusing to back down, in ways both large and small. The authors note on the one hand that people of all genders in support of these transformations are voting for progressive candidates, engaging on social media, and making their interpersonal relationships more equal. On the other hand, they document considerable backlash and contestation, as some people are resisting these changes and creating adversarial gender divisions. Probing across these issues, the book develops an analysis of gendered social and cultural change that reveals how movement ideas diffuse into broader culture.

Gender Revolution presents a vibrant and essential study for a moment marked by significant changes to attitudes, beliefs, and views surrounding gender and gender relations and will appeal to readers interested in the scholarly study of gender, society, politics, media, law, and culture.

Pamela Aronson, professor of sociology and affiliate in women's and gender studies at the University of Michigan-Dearborn, has over three dozen publications on gender inequalities, sexual misconduct, the transition to adulthood, higher education, and identities and the life course in such places as *Gender & Society*, *Contexts*, *Journal of Youth Studies*, and *Emerging Adulthood*. Her work appears in *BBC Reel* and *The Takeaway* on National Public Radio, *Salon*, and *Vox*.

Matthew R. Fleming, former research assistant at the University of Michigan-Dearborn and now attorney in the Detroit area, has publications on higher education and other works under review for publication. His work appears in *Contexts*, *Contemporary Social Science* and *Journal of Youth Studies*.

GENDER REVOLUTION

How Electoral Politics and #MeToo
Are Reshaping Everyday Life

Pamela Aronson and Matthew R. Fleming

Routledge
Taylor & Francis Group

NEW YORK AND LONDON

Designed cover image: Unsplash
First published 2024
by Routledge
605 Third Avenue, New York, NY 10158

and by Routledge
4 Park Square, Milton Park, Abingdon, Oxon, OX14 4RN

Routledge is an imprint of the Taylor & Francis Group, an informa business

Library of Congress Cataloging-in-Publication Data
Names: Aronson, Pamela, author. | Fleming, Matthew R., author.
Title: Gender revolution : how electoral politics and #MeToo are
    reshaping everyday life / Pamela Aronson and Matthew R. Fleming.
Description: First Edition. | New York : Routledge, 2023. | Includes
    bibliographical references and index. |
Summary: "Gender Revolution carefully examines the profound
    transformations happening in both public and private arenas of gender
    relations and draws critical attention to the simultaneous and potent
    challenges that have risen in response. The authors look to large scale
    phenomena in this contemporary study and address the ways electoral
    politics and the #MeToo movement are reshaping everyday life.
Identifiers: LCCN 2022060354 (print) | LCCN 2022060355 (ebook) |
    ISBN 9781032125961 (hardback) | ISBN 9781032125954 (paperback) |
    ISBN 9781003225331 (ebook)
Subjects: LCSH: Feminism—United States. | Sexual harassment of
    women—United States. | Elections—United States. | Political
    campaigns—United States. | MeToo movement.
Classification: LCC HQ1426 .A756 2023 (print) | LCC HQ1426
    (ebook) | DDC 305.420973—dc23/eng/20230224
LC record available at https://lccn.loc.gov/2022060354
LC ebook record available at https://lccn.loc.gov/2022060355

ISBN: 978-1-032-12596-1 (hbk)
ISBN: 978-1-032-12595-4 (pbk)
ISBN: 978-1-003-22533-1 (ebk)

DOI: 10.4324/9781003225331

Typeset in Bembo
by Apex CoVantage, LLC

For the trailblazing innovators who came of age in earlier eras and struggled to make the world a better place for themselves and their children;

For today's innovators, who continue to fight against inequalities with courage and tenacity;

And for future innovators, who will ardently and fearlessly continue to stand up for women's rights.

CONTENTS

ACKNOWLEDGMENTS

As with any project, this work was completed in connection with many people. We would like to thank Pamela's father, Ronald Aronson, who provided vital intellectual and emotional support in every way to this project. Ronald not only talked through all of the ideas in this book but also read multiple drafts of most of the chapters. He also provided help and critique as only a father, and a seasoned and successful book author, could do.

Tyler Bay, our editor, was enthusiastic about the book from the beginning, when all we had written was the proposal. He sensed that we were onto something important and has stuck with us this entire time, guiding us through the publication process. Tyler's faith in the project was unwavering and his enthusiasm unmatched. We would also like to thank Paige Loughlin and Charlotte Taylor at Routledge for their timely and crucial assistance, as well as our anonymous external reviewers, who provided invaluable feedback. Additionally, Basia Nowak, our independent editor, provided excellent comments and suggestions on the entire manuscript and helped guide the revisions in fruitful directions.

Additionally, many people at University of Michigan-Dearborn supported this project. Pam's writing group read chapter drafts and provided extensive critiques and suggestions, as well as motivation. As book authors themselves, they modeled a way forward. In particular, Maureen Linker helped us to clarify the overarching argument. Georgina Hickey offered a historical perspective and advice about the narrative. Patricia Smith and Jacqueline Vansant provided insightful line-by-line comments. Liz Rohan pushed us to articulate the uniqueness of our methods. We also appreciate the help of Francine Banner, who read chapter drafts and encouraged us along the way. Many others provided various types of support, including Rachel Buzzeo, Ivy Forsythe-Brown, Lisa Martin, Carmel Price, Jonathan Smith, and Rose Wellman. The University of Michigan-Dearborn's "write on site" group met virtually throughout the pandemic, and we are grateful to its organizer (Maya Barak) and frequent participants (Nick Iannarino, Michael MacDonald, Olivia Lowrey, Sarah Silverman, Autumn Canes, Hillary Mellinger, Emily Luxon, and Watoii Rabii). The late James Gruber also influenced this study. As a pioneering researcher on sexual harassment, Jim said something powerful on his deathbed that influenced this project profoundly. To paraphrase: "#MeToo will only truly make a difference when average women are able to come forward and make reports. It can't just be actresses in Hollywood but also waitresses at a diner." Our book captures transformations in expectations in the lives of ordinary women, which we hope will eventually lead to changes that fulfill Jim's vision and legacy.

Without funding or research assistants, this project would not have been possible: the College of Arts, Sciences and Letters, the Office of Research, and the Commission for Women, all at the University of Michigan-Dearborn, as well as the Institute for Research on Women and Gender, the Center for Institutional Diversity, and the Center for the Education of Women+ (CEW+), all at University of Michigan-Ann Arbor. Research assistants supported this project in innumerable ways: Leah Oldham and Destiny Flowers-Fayad helped with the initial conceptualization, data collection (including focus groups), and analysis; Emily Lucas collected and coded data on electoral politics; Grace Bradley also collected and coded data; Marshall Burns assisted with focus groups; and Phoenix DiMauro spent countless hours on the references and Appendix 2, and provided feedback on ways to employ gender-neutral language. Finally, we would like to thank our study participants, who shared their perspectives and stories with us. It is their courage and honesty that allowed us to write this book. We sincerely hope that we have captured their bravery accurately and compassionately.

Pamela

The idea for this project began on vacation, while walking on a beach. It was early in the Trump presidency and just a month before I was diagnosed with thyroid cancer. While thyroid cancer is very treatable (it is often dubbed "the best kind of cancer you can get"), it was a challenging time. This book helped me find a way out of the darkness. Although the data contained in its pages include struggle and contestation, they also contain hope for the future.

This project would not have been possible without my coauthor, Matthew. Together, we conceptualized this project, collected the data, coded and analyzed the results, and drafted and revised the pages of the book. Despite the serious nature of our topic, it was fun to work on this research together. While Matthew reduced his involvement at times while in law school, he saw this project to its fruition. I am grateful to Matthew for joining me on this journey, talking through all of my ideas, pushing me forward, and even pulling me out of rabbit holes when I dove down them. A collaboration of this magnitude requires an incredible amount of effort on both sides, and I appreciate Matthew's support and commitment.

I would also like to thank my family and friends, who deserve much of the inspiration for this book. My husband, Todd, supports all of my endeavors. Having a truly egalitarian partnership is rare in a world filled with gender inequality, but I have been lucky enough to have such a partner. Todd's love and encouragement are unfaltering and remind me every day that there is more to life than work. My parents, Phyllis and Ronald Aronson, who have spent their entire lives fighting for social justice and equality, made sure I didn't get discouraged and helped me get through many roadblocks. The book is reader-friendly and lucid because of their efforts. They were also a sounding board when I felt stressed and always advised me to relax more, which was often what I needed. My daughter, Hannah Crain, pushed me to take on research that I am passionate about. My son, Zachary Aronson-Paxton, has quietly supported this project, from understanding misogyny as a first-year student in high school to engaging in perhaps too many dinner-time conversations about sexual consent. Both Hannah and Zachary inspired me to write this book and to envision a future of true gender equality. I am proud to have played a part in the respectful and egalitarian way that they approach gender relations in their own lives. This project would have been much less fun without my furriest family member, Ollie, who sat by my side and at my feet during all of my writing and provided much-needed distraction and cuddles whenever I needed a break.

Others provided support and distraction. My graduate school "gal pals," Kimberly Simmons, Martha Easton, and Heather VanderLey, have processed most of the ideas here. They were a consistent and excellent sounding board and provided important opportunities for escape as well. People providing inspiration and diversion include: Nina, Ayden and Amira Aronson-Cruz, Claire Crain, Laurel Queen, and Lauren Hirsch. I would also like to thank my friend and workout partner, Lisa Bonello, who offered motivation. Lisa said something many years ago that was one of the jumping-off points for this project. After talking about the new affirmative consent training that her son had at college, she noted historical changes in consent with the comment, "In my day, they just called it 'you [women] had too much to drink.'" This book attempts to grapple with and explain these historical changes in definitions and practices, and her comment has stayed with me all of these years.

Matthew

This project was a challenge and a blessing that I am truly grateful for. As an undergraduate student, I was lucky enough to be noticed by my professor, Pamela Aronson, lucky enough to be invited onto this project, and lucky enough to see it to its conclusion even as my schedule at times demanded that I take short breaks from the project. Writing this book during the COVID-19 pandemic and my stint in law school was challenging, to say the least. Yet that is precisely why I am so thankful for Pam, as she provided me with encouragement, advice, and especially understanding. My first and most important "thanks" is to you, Pam.

I would also like to thank my family and friends: to my father, Mike Fleming, for instilling in me at a young age the grammar and writing habits that I use to this day (although I'm sure he will find a grammatical miscue somewhere!); to my mother, Kathy Fleming, the most caring mom and educator I know; to my sister, Maureen Nosewicz, for her endearing passion for reading that has positively influenced me in so many ways (you are next to be published, Maureen!); to my brother-in-law, Josh Nosewicz; to my good friends, including, but certainly not limited to, Ian Joachim and Aaron Miller; and to everyone else in my life who has helped me get to this point—you know who you are. Last, but certainly not least, I would also like to thank my small and loving dog, Bo, who provided me with countless smiles and necessary leisure breaks.

This book is a glaring example of the need for understanding, compassion, and kindness toward everybody in society. It is my hope that it will encourage readers to continue pushing egalitarian ideas forward into the next generation. This is why I close with the words of a sports talk radio host in the metropolitan Detroit area, "Stay safe, everybody, and treat everyone with respect."

INTRODUCTION

Three women and two men sat around a small conference room table on a cold November day. As students at a midwestern commuter university, some of them had discussed inequalities in their coursework. On this day, they were gathered as complete strangers in a focus group. Pamela, a facilitator and a professor at their university, asked, "Do you think that there's confusion about how to define sexual consent?" She and Matthew, her co-facilitator, then an undergraduate student, were surprised by the outspoken nature of their responses.

Maram,[1] a 21-year-old Middle Eastern woman, was the first to answer: "Definitely. If you're all OK with me sharing just a little bit." She took a breath and then continued, "I was assaulted a year and a half ago and I didn't realize I was assaulted until about a year ago." Maram said "the lines were so blurred" between consent and sexual assault that she didn't see it as sexual assault at first: "I was feeling all the things that a trauma victim endures, but I couldn't put my finger on why it felt that way if it wasn't assault. I couldn't find myself a clear definition of it." Maram saw parallels between her own experience and news reports about actor and comedian Aziz Ansari, who was publicly accused of sexually assaulting a woman on their first date:

> I saw how similar that was to my own story. And that's when I broke down and finally understood why I felt the way that I did. I could not look my parents in the eye. I wanted to burn my skin off in the shower.

Slowly, with the help of a therapist who validated her experiences, she began to recover.

DOI: 10.4324/9781003225331-1

The Centers for Disease Control and Prevention reported that over one-third of women have experiences of sexual violence and almost one in five have survived rape or attempted rape (Smith et al. 2017). Yet before the #MeToo movement, over half of survivors did not acknowledge their experiences as either rape or sexual assault, particularly when the circumstances were not violent stranger attacks of stereotypical "rape scripts" (Donde et al. 2018). The #MeToo movement, however, is chipping away at survivors' reluctance to define their experiences as sexual assault; it has also encouraged more survivors to speak out. Our focus groups shed light on these widespread cultural transformations taking place in people's everyday lives. The people we call "innovators" are creating new expectations of sexual consent. They are also generating a language that reflects women's growing sense of agency and empowerment. These changes are part of a larger gender revolution that is profoundly reshaping gender relations.

At the same time, the gender revolution is fiercely resisted. A week after Maram spoke out, another focus group, consisting of five men and two women, slowly filed into the conference room. Sitting together for the first time, they briefly introduced themselves by their first name. They discussed the upcoming midterm elections and then the conversation turned to the topic of sexual consent. Pamela asked, "How big a problem are sexual assault and harassment?" When Harper, a 23-year-old multiracial woman, responded by emphasizing that they are "a huge problem," several men spoke up.

Ahmad, a 21-year-old Middle Eastern man, began by agreeing that sexual assault "is a really big problem." Using the word "but" to abruptly transition to an opposing view, he swiftly contradicted Harper in a way that was typical of the majority of focus group men:

> *But*[2] this is where I'm coming from. I have family members and friends who have been accused of sexual assault, *but* they never did anything. One of my friends has a pending court case right now against him. And I believe him that he didn't do it. And there's many witnesses and a lot of evidence proving that he didn't do it.

The consequences of false accusations can be dire. According to Ahmad, "If the jury decides that he did do it, he's facing 60 years. And he's only 20 years old. And I don't think that's fair for him." He took aim at the #MeToo movement, which he believed some women use to "get back at other people" through "false" accusations. Calling women "they" in an adversarial way, Ahmad pointed out that women are in an advantageous position when they accuse men of sexual assault: "I don't want to sound offensive. *But* there's some people who abuse lack of detail in the definition of sexual assault. So *they're* at an advantage when something doesn't go *their* way." Noah, a 33-year-old multiracial man, jumped in, supporting Ahmad: "That's true. I've experienced that too." Noah described a situation when he felt he was falsely accused of sexual harassment at work and an investigation resulted in his involuntary transfer to a different job at the same company.

As we see throughout this book, although innovators are creating social and cultural change, the people we call "resisters" are pushing back. The majority of focus group men were worried about false accusations and used words like "fear," "danger," and "scary" to describe their potential career-ruining consequences. Claims of "false" accusations contest women's rising power as a result of #MeToo and reassert traditional heterosexual gender roles, in which men are the presumed initiators of sexual activity and women are gatekeepers. As people are increasingly rejecting inequalities and men's power in interpersonal relationships, some men are trying to maintain them.

. . .

The gender revolution is also taking place on the political level. Gretchen Whitmer, a white woman who first was elected governor of Michigan in the 2018 midterm elections, and then reelected in 2022, directly linked her campaigns with the Women's March, the #MeToo movement, and abortion rights. On her website and in ads in 2018, Whitmer featured images of a speech she gave at the 2017 Michigan Women's March (Whitmer 2018a), the day of the largest single-day demonstration in U.S. history, which protested Donald Trump's inauguration as president. On her 2022 campaign website, she featured a photo of her speaking to a reproductive rights rally after the U.S. Supreme Court overturned *Roe v. Wade* (Whitmer 2022). Conservatives criticized her social movement involvement, and she faced powerful opposition for being so vocal about gender issues. In both elections, Whitmer defended her stance and involvement. In 2018, in a sarcastic "Mean Tweets" ad, she read a tweet, "Michigan will elect either Bill Schuette, the current Attorney General, or pussyhat Gretchen Whitmer," referring to the pink pussyhats worn by protesters. Whitmer stared confrontationally into the camera with a smirk on her face and responded, "If you need a hat this winter, I know where to get you a pretty pink one" (Whitmer 2018b). In 2022, Whitmer defended her seat against Trump-endorsed Tudor Dixon (who is anti-abortion, even in cases of rape and incest) by aggressively focusing on abortion rights as the centerpiece of her campaign (New York Times 2022).

Whitmer faced significant resistance and misogyny, including death threats and a kidnapping plot that resulted in the conviction of several men (Vitagliano 2022). Attacks against Democratic governors for strict stay-at-home COVID-19 pandemic orders were common, but the anger and aggression against Whitmer carried gendered overtones. Images of men in battle fatigues and openly displayed firearms carried signs calling Whitmer a "witch" and "tyrant bitch" and depicting images that likened her to Adolf Hitler (Nichols 2020). One protester, James Chapman, himself a Republican candidate for the 21st Michigan House district (who lost in 2020 and 2022), carried an ax and an American flag, from which a naked doll with brunette hair hung from a noose (Dodge 2020). Violating a statewide stay-at-home order, protesters were responding directly to Trump's April 2020 tweet to "LIBERATE MICHIGAN!" (Fox 2 Detroit 2020). In 2021, the Michigan GOP leader called Whitmer and the state's other two executive leaders "witches" and joked about assassination by burning (Bridge Michigan 2021). Whitmer's responses to this misogyny were forceful. Confronting the Michigan GOP chair, Whitmer posted a photo of herself on Twitter holding the book *The Witches Are Coming* and tweeted, "Speaking of witches, I highly recommend this book! 'For a long time, a certain set of men have called women like me "witches" to silence and discredit us.'—Lindy West" (Whitmer 2021). Likewise, when Trump denounced "that woman from Michigan" for demanding more federal supplies of personal protection equipment for hospital workers (Jackson and Collins 2020) during the pandemic, "That Woman From Michigan" T-shirts were created and then proudly worn by Whitmer herself (Lofton 2020).

Additionally, in 2013, even before the birth of the #MeToo movement, Whitmer was vocal about being a rape survivor. Whitmer revealed her own private trauma in front of the Michigan Senate and connected it to women's collective experiences. While explaining her decision to vote "no" on a bill restricting women's right to an abortion because it was "misogynistic," her eyes teared up and her voice trembled as she said, "In an effort to try to give a face to the women that you are hurting by moving this forward . . . I'm about to tell you something that I've not shared with many people in my life." She then connected her experience of sexual assault with the experiences of other women: "As a mother with two girls, the thought that they would ever go through something like I did, keeps me up at night. I am not the only woman in our state that has faced that horrible circumstance" (Michigan Senate Democrats 2013). Although public accounts among politicians and candidates became more visible in the years following this 2013 revelation, Whitmer's 2018 gubernatorial Republican opponent, Bill Schuette, trivialized her account in an attack ad by using the images of Whitmer's grim facial expression during this statement (Culham 2018).

The visibility of women in politics speaking out about sexual assault influences non-activist women to come forward as well. Our voting-aged focus group interviews uncover the shifts in women's political power and culture as they are experienced on the ground, in people's everyday lives. Maram emphasized the effect of Whitmer's sexual assault: "She's part of the #MeToo movement and now we're seeing that with Whitmer or female candidates. I'm starting to identify with that movement too. And that's a really *super-empowering* thing." Maram, along with other innovators, supported women candidates *because* of their gender and political platform on women's issues.

Yet our interviews also reflected deep gender divisions in views on the role of women in electoral politics. Most focus group men emphasized that they downplayed candidates' gender when they vote and instead focused on the gender-blind

FIGURE 0.1   Campaign Lawn Signs in Michigan in 2022 Supporting Democratic
               Candidates and the Reproductive Freedom Ballot Referendum

Source: Author.

merit of individual candidates. Ahmad and Noah insisted that no one should vote
for a candidate because of their gender. Ahmad said that the most important aspect
of a candidate is: "What they're *advocating for*, that's what matters the most, *regardless of what their gender is*." Noah concurred, "I still personally would vote more on
what they say, the *individual*, base my vote more on *what I like and dislike about the
candidate, than gender*." This gender-neutral position allows men a space to support
some women candidates based on their qualifications and politics while ignoring
such issues as underrepresentation and persisting inequalities.

The 2018, 2020, and 2022 elections illustrate the gender revolution in electoral politics. In 2018, women in general, and women of color in particular, were
elected to office in record numbers, resulting in a Democratic "blue wave." Unlike
previous elections, women candidates embraced and highlighted, rather than
ignored and minimized, their gender. Women's issues were front and center in
many races, although resistance was also intense.

These changes in electoral politics continued in subsequent elections. The
2020 Democratic presidential primary, for example, was unprecedented in both
its demographic diversity and the innovative self-presentations of the candidates.
By the 2022 election, Michigan was the epicenter of a "historic blue earthquake"

FIGURE 0.2 Michigan Governor Whitmer in her 2022 Acceptance Speech with Reproductive Rights Lapel Pin That Reads "Bans Off Our Bodies"

Source: Shutterstock.

(Orner 2022) that stunned pollsters, journalists, and politicians alike, as a "red wave" and even "red tsunami" had been predicted to sweep Republicans into office. In Michigan, Whitmer defended her seat (by 11 percentage points), as did the other women in executive office (including reelected Secretary of State Jocelyn Benson, who won by 14 points, and reelected Attorney General Dana Nessel, who won by 9 points) (Orner 2022). Furthermore, Michigan voters passed (by a margin of over 13 percentage points) a ballot referendum that enshrines a "fundamental right to reproductive freedom" into the state constitution (Orner 2022). A voting rights ballot referendum also passed, and Democrats flipped both the Michigan House and Senate for the first time since the 1980s (Orner 2022). Whitmer ran on preserving reproductive freedom, even wearing a "bans off our bodies" lapel pin during her acceptance speech. In the years since Trump's election, the gender revolution has led to electoral successes for candidates who confront misogyny directly and align with women's rights movements. As we will see, these political transformations are intertwined with more deeply personal ones.

Gender Revolution: Progress and Resistance

This book examines expressions of culture and the experiences of ordinary people to paint a picture of how the #MeToo movement and electoral politics are reshaping everyday life in more egalitarian ways. Transformations in gender relations have spread throughout culture and society, influencing and connecting these political and personal realms. Changes in electoral politics and people's lives have created, reinforced, and also caused resistance to the gender revolution. Although partial and still incomplete, the gender revolution in electoral politics and everyday life has exposed a struggle for power and the deep cleavages that we see in American society and culture.

We are living through an era of dramatic and rapid social change. From Trump's election in 2016 to an explosion in social movement activism, from the pandemic's deepening of gender inequalities in the household division of labor to increased accountability for perpetrators of sexual assault, from attacks on democracy and voting rights to an unprecedented number of women and people of color attaining political power, and from the toppling of the federal right to abortion to legal and political activism to secure abortion access, we are in the midst of a hotly contested gender revolution and, simultaneously, intense contestation. Political and personal areas of social and cultural change are interrelated and together represent a revolution in which women and other marginalized groups are claiming control over their own lives as never before, rejecting inequalities, and demanding political and social power. We have also witnessed unprecedented resistance to this social change, including attacks on gender equality and self-determination.

The term "gender revolution" or "revolution" has been used before, typically to refer to limitations in the extent to which gender relations have changed. When we discuss these transformations with family, friends, and colleagues, we encounter a variety of reactions. People often wonder how, in the midst of so much opposition, we can use the term "revolution." In this context, a friend and philosopher, Maureen Linker, asked a simple but pointed question about this book in its early stages. After reading the first draft of the book proposal, she asked, "Is this story optimistic or pessimistic?" Pamela answered immediately, "Optimistic." And yet this answer is also complex; social change is always uneven and contains both progressive and contested elements. So although the term "revolution" signifies great historical change, it also captures the complexity and contradictions of our time.

Gerson (2010) argued that although young men and women define their identities in ways that defy traditional gender expectations, they remain skeptical about whether they will find a relationship that fits their ideals. Similarly, Risman (2018: 2) said that although "the gender revolution has now been in process too long for it to seem revolutionary, . . . we cannot claim victory" because significant gender inequality continues to exist. Likewise, Hochschild's (1989) classic book argued that a "stalled" gender revolution resulted from uneven historical change, in which women moved into traditionally masculine roles like paid work but men did not move into traditionally feminine roles like housework and child care. England (2010) pointed out that the gender revolution is "uneven" because women's activities continue to be devalued. In contrast, Chandra and Erlingsdóttir (2020:

13) saw the #MeToo movement as a revolution because it is "an unprecedented and historic event" that "has provided some victims of sexual violence with the survivor's absolute right to speak up (or not to speak up) in her own voice and on their own terms."

We see the current gender revolution as *simultaneously* containing both elements of "revolution" (i.e., progress toward equality) and resistance (i.e., reversal of progress). While the #MeToo movement has contributed to a revolution of individuals speaking up, this book focuses on both the *personal* level and the *political* level, and the connection between the two. Although we are optimistic that the current gender revolution has moved toward equality, we also recognize the pervasive and resilient character of gender inequalities. Although social and cultural transformations have profoundly influenced electoral politics and everyday lives, the simultaneous resistance works against a full and complete revolution. The phrase "gender revolution" should itself be understood as a complex, contradictory, and incomplete transformation.

This book explores the struggle for power in contemporary gender relations: the simultaneous profound transformations, and potent challenges, that are occurring in both the public and private arenas. We examine how electoral politics and the #MeToo movement are reshaping everyday life, including electoral politics and people's daily experiences. We ask: How have transformations in gender and elections, the #MeToo movement, and social movement activism influenced people's everyday perspectives? As women and other marginalized people increasingly reject gender inequalities and seize personal and political power, what are the challenges to these changes? How are these transformations creating new gender divides and potential bridges? Finally, what inequalities are still being left unchallenged?

Like an "irreversible tide" (Rochon 1998: 7), this gender revolution has led to a culture in which many people, including a small but increasing number of men, refuse to accept gender inequalities. People of all genders no longer tolerate abuses of power in politics or interpersonal relationships. In ways both large and small, and despite vigorous resistance, women are seizing power and refusing to back down. People of all genders who support these transformations are voting for progressive candidates, engaging on social media, and making their interpersonal relationships more equal. This book documents these transformations and their resistance and contestation.

To address these complex issues, we weave together both national-level data and local interview data. We study people's everyday lives with focus group interviews to examine a microcosm of broader changes in identity and culture. We also draw on national news media and campaign materials in key elections to supplement the focus group data. While the national-level data help us to capture broader trends, the focus group interviews are integrated throughout the book to anchor the analysis in people's everyday experiences. Triangulating these differing sources and levels of data provides a multidimensional understanding of gender relations today.

In doing so, this book explores how movement ideas diffuse into the broader culture at both the political and personal levels. Following scholars' recommendations to expand research on cultural diffusion (e.g., Van Dyke and Taylor 2018; Earl 2004), we examine social and cultural changes in two places: in the performances (or as we call it, self-presentations) of politicians and in the discourses of people in their everyday lives. Thus, we consider the diffusion of new perspectives and language "into ordinary speech," such as narratives that reveal "new collective identities" (Van Dyke and Taylor 2018: 487; see also Polletta 1999). We also examine the "signs or practices" that are "clear examples of cultural change" (Earl 2004: 510). For instance, the 2017 inauguration protesters wore homemade pink pussyhats as a symbol of resistance to Trump's infamous "grab 'em by the pussy" statement. We consider language as expressed by focus group participants and candidates to examine representations of gender divisions and a collective identity, a "we."

Gender Revolution breaks new ground in three specific ways. First, we connect personal experiences in the #MeToo era with electoral politics. The 2018 and 2020 elections began a new era of candidate self-presentations that were gender nontraditional and feminist. Candidates emphasized women's issues and embraced new language and approaches. Innovator voters pushed forward these changes in electoral politics. Second, we explore how the #MeToo movement (which spread across politics, popular culture, electronic media and social media, the workplace, and the courts) influenced electoral politics and the lives of ordinary people. The affirmative consent standard embraced by our innovator participants, and increasingly institutionalized in laws and policies, asserts a new power of self-determination. Third, we examine social movement diffusion, especially how the dissemination of innovative ideas influences people's everyday experiences. In our digital age, an awareness of gender inequalities has become rapidly widespread and has elevated women's experiences and voices. As #MeToo movement perspectives spread, many people resist these changes and reassert traditional perspectives.

Theories of Social and Cultural Transformation

When sociologists study social movements, they focus on movement activists and leaders rather than the spread of movement ideology, practices, and language throughout society and culture, leaving everyday experiences as a theoretical and empirical "black box." As feminism has become diffused into our cultural norms, it is paradoxically "everywhere and nowhere" (Reger 2012); it has profoundly influenced women's lives while simultaneously appearing to be invisible and apolitical (see Aronson 2008; Aronson 2017). With the rise of digital media and social media, feminist ideologies have spread near and far. In fact, the #MeToo movement and perspectives from the 2017 Women's March have become a part of ordinary people's everyday experiences. This book focuses on cultural artifacts and ordinary people's experiences rather than activists in order to understand how the gender revolution has become diffused into larger culture.

Culture is a "'tool kit' of symbols, stories, rituals and world-views" (Swidler 1986: 273); it has also been defined as "the logics or schemas or models with which people operate in a particular institution" (Jasper and Polletta 2018: 66). There are three types of culture within a social movement: performance (e.g., protests, individual and organizational behavior), ideations (e.g., identities, values, ideology, and social movement frames, which are the link between individual movement participants and social movement organizations' interpretative frameworks), and cultural artifacts (e.g., language and symbols) (Van Dyke and Taylor 2018). Some examples of cultural artifacts used in this book include political campaign advertisements and social movement images and symbols. For example, symbols from the Women's March were disseminated over social media in highly personalized ways (Weber et al. 2018).

Social and cultural change occurs during historical periods characterized by "crisis" (Kuhn 1962; Rochon 1998; Swidler 1986). Kuhn (1962), for example, suggested that paradigms are transformed and replaced by new ones through challenges to existing paradigms. When a new paradigm challenges an old one, sometimes through generational change, the resulting crisis leads to paradigm competition, and eventually a revolution in ideas (Kuhn 1962). Rochon (1998: 8) suggested that a crisis produces "irreversible tides of political change" when a new generation of ideas usher in new cultural values that become disseminated through social and political movements. Rochon (1998) pinpointed this process as starting with leaders who "initiate changes in cultural values that represent a truly original break from past ways of thinking" (Rochon 1998: 8–9). Movement leaders are "innovators" who introduce new values to others but fade into the background as the movement gathers steam (Rochon 1998: 89). Changes on the ground are difficult to capture with research because they take place in a "decentralized way," in "invisible settings in which individuals go about their daily lives" (Rochon 1998: 89). In our study, we adopt the term "innovators" to signify actors who push social change forward, although we apply this term to both leaders and non-leaders. Innovation does not occur only at the leadership level, as non-activists can also embrace new ideas and identities and push change forward.

During certain historical moments, social and cultural change occurs rapidly. "Cracks in the foundation" of gender relations can create "inconsistencies" and "crises" (Risman 2018: 36). Rochon (1998: 10) said that "explosive rapidity in cultural change" gives rise to new symbols and ideas. "Unsettled cultural periods" have the potential to alter existing frameworks and create social change through a "contested cultural arena" characterized by a competition in ideology (Swidler 1986: 277). Change can also occur when existing models "lose their prescriptive force" over people's lives (Jasper and Polletta 2018: 66). The result is that current frameworks ("existing institutional logics") become "delegitimized" (Jasper and Polletta 2018: 66). New worldviews, symbols, ideologies, and rituals emerge as previous ones fade away or lose legitimacy. Cultural change thus occurs when historical moments "make possible new or reorganized strategies of action" (Swidler 1986: 283). This, in turn, leads to "widespread changes in individual identities and practices, organizations and institutions, and the wider society" (Van Dyke and Taylor 2018). As we will see, the #MeToo movement has produced profound transformations in people's lives, culture, and institutions.

Yet people resist and contest new frameworks. We call these people "resisters" because they stick to traditional conceptions and challenge innovations in norms and identities. Although periods of rapid social change serve as "crystallizing agents" to produce common experiences and identities (Mannheim 1952: 310), not everyone is affected in the same way. There is often a "cultural lag," in which some people are "reluctant to abandon familiar" approaches "for which they have the cultural equipment" (Swidler 1986: 281). Cultural transformations become "complete" when new values are "no longer highly controversial" but are instead "accepted as a 'normal' part of thinking" (Rochon 1998: 17). In other words, real change happens when resistance dies down and new norms take their place.

The gender revolution is still very much in process. New and innovative approaches are being created, and yet they are still controversial and vigorously challenged by resisters. Innovators of all genders push change forward through new paradigms, ideas, ideology, language, and collective identities. Cultural transformations appear in meanings, language, symbols, and discourse. In the #MeToo movement, even being able to speak about previously private and hidden traumatic experiences illustrates cultural transformation.

Here, we examine a wide range of cultural artifacts, such as media representations; political candidates' advertisements; and language, images, and symbols in ordinary people's everyday lives. On the political level, innovators protested Trump's inauguration in 2017 and ran for political office in 2018 and 2020. On the personal level, innovators demand self-determination and affirmative consent and speak out about their own experiences with sexual violence. Resisters contest these new paradigms, ideas, ideology, language, and collective identities. Traditional cultures of masculinity influence everyday experience and resisters often seek to maintain the status quo. Since the gender revolution is still only partial, some people fuse both innovative and resistant perspectives, blending together seemingly incongruous ideologies. Our study examines how people are thinking about these issues on the ground, in their everyday lives. However, actors are not always aware of, or able to express, their motivations discursively (i.e., through language) (Giddens 1979).

These theories of social movements and social change are general and abstract but are built from studying more particular activists and movements. In this book, we examine social movements and social change, in the experiences of ordinary people. We look to the political and personal levels, and the interaction between the two, to help us understand how new ideas, such as assertions of gender equality, become diffused throughout society—into both politics and people's daily lives. As innovators spark change and call into question the basis of inequalities, resisters defend the status quo to protect their own interests. As we will see, the emerging picture of the gender revolution reveals the push and pull of progress and resistance.

Methodology

We examine the gender revolution from multiple angles: the ways that gender is reflected in the personal lives of non-activists, its representations in politics, and the interaction between the personal and political levels. To create a broad, multidimensional, national-level understanding of gender relations, we conducted a content analysis of news media data on the 2017 Women's March, which was a pivotal event for the gender revolution. In particular, we draw on ideologically diverse news outlets (the *New York Times*, *MSNBC*, *Politico*, *CNN*, and *Fox News*). This approach moves beyond typical social movement media analysis that focuses primarily on outlets like the *New York Times*. Using search terms that capture women's activism, we analyzed the content of all 150 news articles that appeared in these news outlets from November 2016 through January 2019. We also analyzed organizational website data, especially mission statements, from the 34 organizations that participated in organizing the 2017 inauguration protests. These analyses are supplemented by focus group interview discussions on topics related to the Women's March. These national-level data help to supplement the local, focus group interviews, which provide in-depth and personal understandings of the gender revolution and show how the personal and political levels are interconnected.

We also conducted a content analysis of campaign materials (including advertisements and candidate web pages) and media coverage to examine the 2018 and 2020 elections. For the 2018 election, we focused on the eight open gubernatorial races that had women candidates (Michigan, Georgia, New Mexico, South Dakota, Kansas, Maine, Wyoming, and Idaho). For the 2020 election, we examined both the Democratic presidential primary and the general election. Using the search engines Google Trends and YouTube, we identified the top stories for each candidate based on the number of views and analyzed news coverage that had the most prominent viewership. Additionally, we conducted a content analysis of the messages that came straight from the candidates (e.g., advertisements and websites). Campaign advertisements and news stories were transcribed verbatim and analyzed alongside images and tone. To analyze the interconnections between political leaders and non-activists, we supplemented these data with focus group interview discussions on topics related to women running for political office.

To shed light on how people at the micro level are personally processing, and helping to create, these large-scale cultural changes, we conducted focus group interviews with a highly diverse group (in terms of gender, age, race, and social class) of students at a midwestern commuter university. We conducted 11 focus groups with 74 participants between October 2018 and February 2019, including five mixed-gender (n = 32) and six gender-similar (n = 42) focus groups. In contrast to prior research, our sample is not based on students at elite colleges nor is it largely homogeneous in terms of racial background or age.

Recruitment of Participants

The focus groups took place in Michigan, an epicenter of the political divisions facing the country. In the 2016 primary election, Democratic voters nominated Bernie Sanders over Hillary Clinton, yet Donald Trump won the general election in the state. The area is an ideal case study as a result of its geographic, political, and racial and ethnic diversity. It has a major urban center with high-income suburbs, as well as major university towns and many rural communities. In 2018, voters in Michigan created a "pink wave" through electing women to several major offices, including governor, senator, attorney general, secretary of state, and five U.S. House of Representatives seats; the attorney general was the first openly gay person to hold a statewide elected office. And yet the state also has many Republican voters. Thus, our sample is situated in a highly diverse urban area with ideologically diverse perspectives.

Interviewees were recruited through an email list of 9,400 enrolled students at the university, received through the Information Technology Services office. There were two recruitment announcements sent to a total of 1,054 potential participants (randomly selected from the full list of enrolled students) in October 2018 and January 2019. The target number of interviewees was 75. Participants volunteered by signing up for a focus group interview date and time themselves; all open spaces filled quickly (within a few hours of the initial recruitment email).

Focus Group Procedures

Focus group interviews were conducted face to face in a university conference room. The interviews lasted about one hour and included a range of questions about recent elections; perceptions of gender differences in sexual consent, assault, and harassment; and attitudes toward the #MeToo movement. Interviewees were given a $20 Visa gift card at the conclusion of the interview. The study followed ethical standards of informed consent and confidentiality. The Institutional Review Board approved the research protocol, and human subject protections were followed. Participants consented to participate, and confidentiality of respondents has been protected. All identifying information has been removed from the quotes used in this study, and we use pseudonyms to refer to participants.

It was surmised that the gender composition of the interviewer team would be important to establish rapport on controversial gender issues. The mixed-gender focus group interviews were facilitated by Pamela and Matthew together and the gender-similar focus groups were facilitated by the gender-similar researcher. This approach was undertaken to allow space for the interviewees to feel comfortable in sharing their gender-specific experiences and perspectives. This appeared to have worked; in one of our gender-similar focus groups, for example, the participants connected with each other and the topic so much that the discussion continued long after the designated time came to an end.

All of the focus groups were audio recorded and transcribed verbatim. We also used an in-person scribe as part of the research team so that we could identify the speaker and connect their statements to their demographic information in the analytical phase. Three research assistants served as scribes, and we maintained the gender similarity of the focus groups with the selection of scribes. We also administered a survey to each participant that asked open-ended questions on demographic information, including gender; race and ethnicity; parents' education levels; annual income; and work, family, and relationship situation.

As with any study, this project has both strengths and limitations. First, as a local sample, the focus groups were bounded by the region in which they were located. The focus group study is not based on a national sample and participants were affiliated with an institution of higher education. As a result, there are limits to generalizability to other groups. At the same time, the diversity of the sample is a significant strength. The Detroit metropolitan area is highly diverse in demographics and political ideology. The sample itself was highly diverse in terms of age, social class, life experience, and racial and ethnic background. This diversity enriches what we can say about gender issues.

Additionally, as a research team, we have been able to collect and analyze focus group interview data that have eluded other researchers. Our differences in age and gender provide a unique perspective that enhances our analysis of these pressing social issues and are, in fact, part of our research method. These different standpoints and experiences significantly strengthen the analysis of the data. In particular, most of the books published on related topics have been written by women and therefore do not fully understand men's perspectives. Working together on all of the ideas presented in this book makes our analysis comprehensive and nuanced.

Interview Sample

The diversity of the sample is one of the strengths of our study and provides a window to understanding larger social transformations among a broad group of people. Of the 74 participants, 44.6 percent (n = 33) were women, 54.1 percent (n = 40) were men, and 1 person classified themselves as nonbinary. The sample had significant racial and ethnic diversity: 27 percent (n = 20) were white (non-Hispanic/Latinx and non-Middle Eastern), 13.5 percent (n = 10) were Middle Eastern or North African, 6.8 percent (n = 5) were Hispanic/Latinx, 24.3 percent (n = 18) were Black, 16.2 percent (n = 12) were Asian American, and 8.1 percent (n = 6) were multiracial. (The remainder—4.1 percent, n = 3—did not report their racial or ethnic background on their survey; see Appendix 1 for further details.) The interviewees were quite diverse in social class background, with one-third being the first in their families to attend college and about half coming from low-income households (those making under $50,000 per year; see Appendix 1). Interviewees were diverse in terms of age, relationship and family status, and employment status; the vast majority of them were registered voters. Their ages ranged from 18 to 58, with an average age of 24.5 (see Appendix 1).

In some respects, our sample may not be generalizable to other regions and populations, particularly those outside of an institution of higher education. Although the sample was drawn from a college campus, the racial, ethnic, and age diversity of the sample make it atypical of residential college campuses. Overall, the diversity of the sample is one of the strengths of our study and provides a window to understanding larger social transformations.

Data Analysis

The analysis of the data started with inductive open coding for major themes and then progressed to more fine-grained, focused coding based on emergent themes. We used a qualitative data analysis program (Atlas.ti) to enter codes, to highlight passages of text, and to examine co-occurrences of codes. This strategy sought to compare data on a given theme. The coding scheme and analytical framework were continually refined throughout the analytic process. Together, these diverse data sources illuminate multiple levels of the gender revolution and their interconnections.

The Book Ahead

In Part 1, we examine the early stages of the gender revolution. Chapter 1 sets the stage by explaining its prehistory. It also provides an overview of the wider historical context, such as changes in common understandings of sexual assault and harassment. Chapter 1 then gives an overview of the 2016 election to set the stage for Chapter 2, which uncovers the social movement activism that emerged in its shadow. The 2017 Women's March protests were the largest single-day mass protests on record, with 1 in 100 Americans participating. The slogans, signs, and "pussyhats" illustrate that the Women's March was an integral part of the #MeToo movement and the changes to follow. This chapter analyzes focus group participants' perceptions of the Women's March and their attitudes toward feminism.

Part 2 examines "the political" aspect of the gender revolution by focusing on electoral politics in the wake of Trump's election, specifically the unprecedented 2018 and 2020 elections. We start with the 2018 midterms, during which women (both candidates and voters) created a "blue wave." Chapter 3 examines key races in depth, focusing on the eight open gubernatorial seats that had women candidates. Our content analysis of candidates' campaign advertisements and media coverage documents the broad range of gender self-presentations of women candidates and transformations in women's political power.

Chapter 4 examines the 2020 Democratic presidential primary and general election, especially rising gendered political agency and contestations to these transformations. In the Democratic primary, the candidates were markedly feminist and gender nontraditional in their self-presentations. Yet the Trump-Pence campaign in the general election drew on racialized and misogynistic attacks against vice presidential candidate Kamala Harris. Thus, while women candidates broke new political ground, they also faced backlash. Ultimately, however, the large number of women candidates and particularly the pathbreaking candidacy of Harris has profoundly altered our political landscape in ways that cannot be undone. And yet the 2020 election contributed to a chasm around gender issues that will continue in the foreseeable future.

Part 3 focuses on "the personal" and the diffusion of the gender revolution into everyday lives, especially discourse and the everyday experiences of the #MeToo movement. In Chapter 5, we explore how definitions of sexual consent are changing in people's everyday lives. We begin with resisters, who espoused the most traditional gender norms around consent. These views were expressed by a majority of the focus group men. In contrast, innovators (mainly women and nonbinary interviewees) emphasized the importance of affirmative consent. This chapter provides evidence that some of the focus group men fused progressive and traditional discourses to simultaneously reject and embrace social and cultural change. These findings shed light on the incomplete and partial aspect of the gender revolution.

Chapter 6 examines resisters' discourses around sexual harassment and assault, which center on concerns about "false" accusations. Most of the men distanced themselves from "other" men, who they saw as the perpetrators of violence, in ways that allowed them to avoid taking responsibility for sexual assault as a *social* problem. In a context in which women are affirming their right to self-determination through speaking out about sexual harassment and assault, this chapter argues that resistance to "false" accusations reflects an attempt to reassert dominance. This chapter also considers the discourses of about a quarter of the focus group women, who fused some traditional perspectives with innovative views of gender relations. These women expressed some skepticism about the #MeToo movement yet simultaneously endorsed affirmative consent and appreciated #MeToo. The majority of the men resisted social and cultural changes resulting from the #MeToo movement.

Chapter 7 examines how innovators think about sexual assault and harassment. Innovators, mainly women and nonbinary participants, shared personal experiences with sexual assault and harassment and often redefined past experiences as having been inappropriate. This chapter documents the power of survivors' "voices" in the #MeToo era. This chapter also considers the views of the minority of the focus group men who are innovators. Like other innovators, these participants do not emphasize *individualized* solutions to sexual assault but instead see it as a widespread *social* problem. This chapter suggests that innovators of all genders are pushing forward cultural transformations that may develop a bridge across the gender divide. These discourses reveal how change is created not only in the media and among celebrities but also on the ground, in people's everyday lives through social movement diffusion.

The book has three appendices. Appendix 1 provides a detailed analysis of the focus group sample. Appendix 2 contains a list of our interviewees by pseudonym and includes key demographic information. Appendix 3 provides a timeline of events that are mentioned throughout this book to explain the larger historical context.

The conclusion highlights the uneven and contested cultural transitions of the gender revolution, reflects on its implications for the results of the 2022 elections, and moves toward an understanding of where we are headed in the future. We argue that social change is never complete and is rarely uncontested. Although widespread transformations have taken place in women's everyday lives as a result of the #MeToo movement and the expansion of women in politics, they have not happened uniformly. Rather, increases in women's agency and power, through both sexual self-determination and women's role in the political sphere, are chipping away at arrangements based on gender inequalities. New expectations and collective identities increasingly view patriarchy as unacceptable and see inequalities as a systemic problem. The tension between innovators and resisters results in fluctuation from progress to regress. Despite fluctuation, innovators' demands for greater equality have become diffused throughout society and culture. As we will see, although there is vigorous resistance, the gender revolution is more powerful than resisters' clamor for the status quo.

Notes

1. All names and identifying information have been changed to protect the confidentiality of interviewees.
2. Throughout this book, specific words and phrases within focus group quotes are italicized for our emphasis, to draw the reader's attention to them.

References

Aronson, Pamela. 2017. "The Dynamics and Causes of Gender and Feminist Consciousness and Feminist Identities." pp. 335–353 in *The Oxford Handbook of U.S. Women's Social*

Movement Activism, edited by Holly J. McCammon, Verta Taylor, Jo Reger, and Rachel L. Einwohner. New York, NY: Oxford University Press.

Aronson, Pamela. 2008. "The Markers and Meanings of Growing Up: Contemporary Young Women's Transition From Adolescence to Adulthood." *Gender & Society*, 22(1): 56–82.

Bridge Michigan. 2021. "Michigan GOP Chair Calls Whitmer, Nessel, Benson 'Witches' Who Should Be Burned." Retrieved November 14, 2022 (www.bridgemi.com/michigan-government/michigan-gop-chair-calls-whitmer-nessel-benson-witches-who-should-be-burned).

Chandra, Giti and Irma Erlingsdóttir. 2020. "Introduction." pp. 1–23 in *The Routledge Handbook of the Politics of the #MeToo Movement*, edited by Giti Chandra and Irma Erlingsdóttir. New York, NY: Routledge.

Culham, Devin. 2018. "Schuette's Latest Attack Ad Uses Images From Whitmer's Sexual Assault Story." *Detroit Metro Times*. Retrieved October 26, 2021 (www.metrotimes.com/news-hits/archives/2018/09/10/schuettes-latest-attack-ad-uses-images-from-whitmers-sexual-assault-story).

Dodge, Samuel. 2020. "Protester Explains Doll, Noose Demonstration at Capitol, Wants to Gift Props to Trump." *MLive*. Retrieved November 14, 2022 (www.mlive.com/news/2020/05/protester-explains-doll-noose-demonstration-at-capitol-wants-to-gift-props-to-trump.html).

Donde, Sapana D., Sally K. Ragsdale, Mary P. Koss, and Alyssa N. Zucker. 2018. "If It Wasn't Rape, Was It Sexual Assault? Comparing Rape and Sexual Assault Acknowledgment in College Women Who Have Experienced Rape." *Violence Against Women* 24(14):1718–1738.

Earl, Jennifer. 2004. "The Cultural Consequences of Social Movements." pp. 508–530 in *The Blackwell Companion to Social Movements*, edited by David A. Snow, Sarah A. Soule, and Hanspeter Kriesi. Malden, MA: John Wiley & Sons Ltd.

England, Paula. 2010. "The Gender Revolution: Uneven and Stalled." *Gender & Society* 24(2):149–166.

Fox 2 Detroit. 2020. "President Trump Tweets: 'LIBERATE MICHIGAN!'" Retrieved November 14, 2022 (www.fox2detroit.com/news/president-trump-tweets-liberate-michigan).

Gerson, Kathleen. 2010. *The Unfinished Revolution: Coming of Age in a New Era of Gender, Work, and Family*. New York, NY: Oxford University Press.

Giddens, Anthony. 1979. *Central Problems in Social Theory: Action, Structure and Contradiction in Social Analysis*. Berkeley, CA: University of California Press.

Hochschild, Arlie Russell. 1989. *Second Shift, the: Working Families and the Revolution at Home*. New York, NY: Penguin Putnam Inc.

Jackson, David and Michael Collins. 2020. "Trump to Mike Pence: 'Don't Call the Woman in Michigan,' aka Gov. Gretchen Whitmer." *USA Today*. Retrieved November 14, 2022 (www.usatoday.com/story/news/politics/2020/03/27/coronavirus-donald-trump-tells-pence-not-call-michigan-governor/2931251001/).

Jasper, James M. and Francesca Polletta. 2018. "The Cultural Context of Social Movements." pp. 63–78 in *The Wiley Blackwell Companion to Social Movements, Second Edition*, edited by David A. Snow, Sarah A. Soule, Hanspeter Kriesi, and Holly J. McCammon. Hoboken, NJ: John Wiley & Sons Ltd.

Kuhn, Thomas S. 1962. *The Structure of Scientific Revolutions*. Chicago, IL: University of Chicago Press.

Lofton, Justine. 2020. "Gov. Gretchen Whitmer Wears 'That Woman From Michigan' Shirt on Comedy Central." *Michigan Live*. Retrieved November 14, 2022 (www.mlive.com/

news/2020/04/gov-gretchen-whitmer-wears-that-woman-from-michigan-shirt-on-comedy-central.html).

Mannheim, Karl. 1952. "The Problem of Generations." pp. 276–320 in *Essays on the Sociology of Knowledge*, edited by P. Kecskemeti. London: Routledge and Kegan Paul.

Michigan Senate Democrats. 2013. Senator Whitmer Shares Personal Story in Opposition to Latest Republican Attack on Women. *YouTube*. Retrieved October 26, 2021 (www.youtube.com/watch?v=kUlKLJ1Dsvk&feature=youtu.be&t=7m53s).

New York Times. 2022. "Whitmer and Dixon Differ Sharply in Michigan Governor's Debate." Retrieved November 14, 2022 (www.nytimes.com/live/2022/10/13/us/whitmer-dixon-debate-michigan).

Nichols, Anna. 2020. "Watchdog Group: Anti-Whitmer Protests Tied to Out-of-State Conservative Outfits." *Michigan Advance*. Retrieved November 14, 2022 (https://michiganadvance.com/2020/05/20/watchdog-group-anti-whitmer-protests-tied-to-out-of-state-conservative-outfits/).

Orner, Ben. 2022. "Red Wave? No, a Historic Blue Earthquake: The Week in Michigan Politics." *MLive*. Retrieved November 14, 2022 (www.mlive.com/politics/2022/11/red-wave-no-a-historic-blue-earthquake-the-week-in-michigan-politics.html).

Polletta, Francesca. 1999. "'Free Spaces' in Collective Action." *Theory and Society* 28(1):1–38.

Reger, Jo. 2012. *Everywhere and Nowhere: Contemporary Feminism in the United States.* New York, NY: Oxford University Press.

Risman, Barbara J. 2018. *Where Will the Millennials Take Us? A New Generation Wrestles With the Gender Structure.* New York, NY: Oxford University Press.

Rochon, Thomas R. 1998. *Culture Moves: Ideas, Activism, and Changing Values.* Princeton, NJ: Princeton University Press.

Smith, S. G., J. Chen, K. C. Basile, L. K. Gilbert, M. T. Merrick, N. Patel, M. Walling, and A. Jain. 2017. "The National Intimate Partner and Sexual Violence Survey (NISVS): 2010–2012 State Report." *NISVS*. Retrieved July 19, 2022 (www.cdc.gov/violenceprevention/pdf/NISVS-StateReportBook.pdf).

Swidler, Ann. 1986. "Culture in Action: Symbols and Strategies." *American Sociological Review* 51(2):273–286.

Van Dyke, Nella and Verta Taylor. 2018. "The Cultural Outcomes of Social Movements." pp. 482–498 in *The Wiley Blackwell Companion to Social Movements, Second Edition*, edited by David A. Snow, Sarah A. Soule, Hanspeter Kriesi, and Holly J. McCammon. Hoboken, NJ: John Wiley & Sons Ltd.

Vitagliano, Brian. 2022. "3 More Men Found Guilty in Whitmer Kidnapping Plot." *CNN*. Retrieved November 14, 2022 (www.cnn.com/2022/10/26/politics/gretchen-whitmer-kidnapping-plot-michigan).

Weber, Kirsten M., Tisha Dejmanee, and Flemming Rhode. 2018. "The 2017 Women's March on Washington: An Analysis of Protest Sign Messages." *International Journal of Communication* 12:2289–2313.

Whitmer, Gretchen. 2022. Retrieved November 14, 2022 (https://gretchenwhitmer.com/meet-governor-whitmer/).

Whitmer, Gretchen. 2021. Retrieved November 14, 2022 (https://twitter.com/gretchenwhitmer/status/1375529312561070080).

Whitmer, Gretchen. 2018a. In Your Corner. *YouTube*. Retrieved October 14, 2021 (www.youtube.com/watch?v=oVUCNGo77zY&t=1s).

Whitmer, Gretchen. 2018b. Gretchen Reads Mean Tweets. *YouTube*. Retrieved October 14, 2021 (www.youtube.com/watch?v=RRrcyPju_Kk&t=14s).

PART 1

Early Stages of the Gender Revolution

1

THE HISTORY BEHIND THE GENDER REVOLUTION

"Tweet Me Your First Assaults": The 2016 Election and the Birth of #MeToo

The release of the now infamous Donald Trump conversation with Billy Bush of *Access Hollywood* propelled forward a new social movement that challenges gender inequalities and abuses of power. In the recording, Trump bragged about kissing and groping women without their consent: "I just start kissing them. It's like a magnet. Just kiss. I don't even wait. And when you're a star, they let you do it. You can do anything. . . . Grab 'em by the pussy. You can do anything" (New York Times 2016). Trump also faced nearly three dozen accusations of sexual harassment and assault spanning a period of nearly four decades (Pearson et al. 2017). Although progressives hoped that the recording would lead to his downfall, Trump drew on misogyny and racism to defeat Hillary Clinton, the first woman nominated for president by a major political party. Yet the *Access Hollywood* recording helped to light a social movement fuse and crystalized a rebellion.

The release of the recording resulted in a social media explosion when Kelly Oxford, a Canadian novelist and screenwriter, sent out a request: "Tweet me your first assaults." Within just a few days, Oxford had received 8.5 million responses (Rogers 2016). The almost daily outpouring of sexual assault and harassment accounts in the news and on social media made public what previously was hidden and largely viewed as an individual, private, and personal problem. This social media activism took place within a larger historical context that linked violence against women with male dominance and power.

This chapter considers the 2016 election, providing an overview of the election and reflections from focus group participants. We then turn to the #MeToo

DOI: 10.4324/9781003225331-3

movement, which is situated within a larger context of women's movements against gendered violence. Yet compared to the past, #MeToo spread like wildfire as a result of social media and digital activism. This digital movement pushed new ideas forward and led to the diffusion of social media ideology into people's everyday lives. Rather than influencing social movement leaders and activists, #MeToo quickly catalyzed average people to become innovators who embraced a collective identity centered on women's power and agency. The birth of #MeToo is tied to the 2016 election and itself produced widespread social and cultural change. This chapter explores how this gender revolution began.

"A Catalyst for Change": The 2016 Election and Voter Reactions

The growing awareness of women's collective interests was sparked by the 2016 presidential election, which was a shock to many voters. Pre-election polls consistently predicted a popular and electoral win for Clinton. While Clinton won the popular vote, Trump prevailed electorally. According to exit polls, the majority of white women and men (52 percent for both categories) reported voting for Trump (Washington Post 2016). Despite widespread social media posts of women voting for Clinton in clothes that idolized her legendary "pantsuits" (as opposed to more gender-traditional skirt suits) (Chittal 2016), Trump's win called into question white women's identification with gender issues. This voting pattern suggests the presence of "internalized misogyny," an unconscious disdain for, or bias against, women that results from living in a patriarchal society (Aronson 2018). As stated elsewhere, "Because subtle gender inequalities are pervasive, even people who identify as feminists may find themselves unconsciously preferring male leadership" (Aronson 2018).

Trump's campaign, like his self-presentation more generally, centered on hegemonic masculinity. At Trump rallies, it was common to see misogynistic campaign materials, such as T-shirts with the slogan "Trump That Bitch" or pins with the slogan "Finally Someone with Balls" (Aronson 2018). Journalists argued that it was men's fear of subordination to women that drove male misogyny in the election (Aronson 2018). Some women supported this perspective. For example, one Trump supporter was seen wearing a T-shirt with the words "Trump can grab this," with a downward arrow pointing toward her vagina (Ellefson 2016). Trump's self-presentations were aggressive toward Clinton; he embraced chants at rallies calling to "lock her up" and interrupted her during general election debates (over 50 times in the first debate and 37 times in the third debate, compared to Clinton's 11 and 9 interruptions [Landsbaum 2016; Wilson 2016]). As Faber et al. (2017: 6) summarized, Trump "projected a hegemonic masculinity, continuously denigrating strong and popular woman figures." He also accused Clinton of playing the "woman card"—using her gender to pander to voters.

Clinton's campaign sought to balance a focus on gender with gender-neutral or even gender-nontraditional, masculine self-presentations. Highlighting gender, for example, Clinton's campaign website released a web page that sarcastically listed some of the "perks that your Woman Card gets you," such as lower wages and no family leave (Anderson 2016). Likewise, an ad called "Mirrors" featured girls looking at themselves in a mirror while a voice-over of Trump replayed his negative statements about women, including words like "slob" and "pig" (see Aronson 2018). This ad, which was clearly focused on gender, was not aired at all immediately following the release of the *Access Hollywood* recording. Shying away from gender issues at this particular moment suggests that the Clinton campaign sought to minimize gender issues just as they were exploding in the news media and on social media (Aronson 2018).

Our focus group interviews asked voting-age participants to reflect on the role of gender in this election. These conversations acknowledged both important social changes that resulted from the election and resistance to change. These perceptions were gendered: Men participants were more likely to view Clinton's pioneering run in individualized ways, while women emphasized gendered collective identities in response to the election.

In contrast to the focus group women, a sizable number of focus group men explicitly said that they disliked Clinton. Hunter, a 22-year-old white man, said, "Hillary looked very *arrogant* and just *pompous, cocky*, just *very full of herself.*" Anthony, a 35-year-old Black man in the same focus group, agreed with Hunter and likened Trump's victory to "a vote against Hillary." Luke, a 22-year-old white man, said he heard women saying that "I want to vote for Hillary because she's a woman." Yet he disagreed with gender-based voting and thought that gender-neutral "qualifications" were more important. Luke pointed out that a focus on "who is qualified" was "how Trump got elected."

Other focus group men reported hearing a lot of negative comments about Clinton as a candidate. Although they often framed this lack of support as a perspective of *other* men and not necessarily themselves, most did not outrightly dismiss these views. Aran, a 20-year-old Asian American man, said that he heard, "Oh, she's a female, I don't want her in office." Deven, a 20-year-old Asian American man, pointed out that voters cast ballots for Trump rather than Clinton

> because she's a woman, but they probably weren't outspoken about it. They probably would've kept that to themselves. There's a lot of people, even minorities or Democrats and they separate the gender roles. They don't believe in a woman being in power. So a lot of people wouldn't speak on that but unconsciously or silently vote.

It is possible that these comments about *other* men could be a politically correct way of expressing their own ideas. Noah, a 33-year-old multiracial man, worked on Bernie Sanders's 2016 campaign team and realized firsthand that Clinton was not well liked: "The results came in and I noticed something that I hadn't picked up on, which was how much people *hated* Hillary Clinton." Although he himself did not support Clinton at first, he was surprised by the level of hatred toward her: "I still don't quite understand what the hatred was. So much hatred."

In contrast, women interviewees were more likely to call out the sexism that is inherent in the concept of "likability." Kim, a 27-year-old white woman, pointed out that likability is based on gender and that the same qualities that voters hated in Clinton are often viewed positively in men candidates. Kim defined likability as including "the way someone talks and the way they say things." Although many women voters in our focus groups expressed excitement about voting for a woman for president, Alyssa, a 29-year-old Black woman, thought the election was "disappointing" but not "surprising," given pervasive sexism and racism. She said, "The whole election was really frustrating and very exhausting." "Likability" is thus an intangible yet important factor that systematically disadvantages women candidates.

Focus group participants of all genders saw Clinton as a role model for other women. For their part, focus group men emphasized the individualized way that this might matter, as Clinton serves as a role model for *individual* women moving into politics. For example, Leo, an 18-year-old Asian American man, called Clinton a "role model" and stated that Clinton's run for president made other women "believe that I can do it, too." Gabriel, a 23-year-old Asian American man, put it similarly, "First woman running for president, that's the start of this, everyone trying to get women into government." Terrell, a 25-year-old Black man, thought that Clinton "standing up encouraged others who may have had that thought or idea." Terrell emphasized that women might now be willing to claim ideas as their own rather than asking men to represent them:

> Instead of women thinking of solutions and then trying to pass it off to some male figure, people might look up to that person. They can stand up for themselves and be that leader and go out and do something.

Thus, some of the men viewed Clinton's candidacy positively, as creating role models for individual women who want to take on leadership positions.

Focus group men also thought that Trump's victory would eventually lead to progressive social change as a result of public opinion *against* him. Yet they did not connect social change to #MeToo or the Women's March. Noah called Trump a "cultural trickster figure" and said that he was "a catalyst for change by breaking values and social norms, because people come forward as a reaction to that." Noah mused, "Maybe that's a good thing [that Trump was elected]. Architects are like tricksters, they usually bring out good through their bad." Noah concluded by labeling himself "an optimist." Although Leo did not mention Trump by name when he said that the election was "a mistake," he intimated that Trump's victory served as an impetus for people "trying to learn from that mistake, trying to improve for next time." Although these interviewees emphasized social change through resistance, they did not mention social movements in particular. This perspective is ultimately an individualized framework that viewed one man, Trump, as an impetus for change rather than viewing social change in terms of the work of millions of activists.

Although most of the men focused on the individualized effects of the elections, several took a broader perspective. Cam, an 18-year-old Asian American man, emphasized Clinton's role in "catalyzing" social change on a grand scale. Like the men above, Cam began by focusing on Clinton as a role model for individual women running for office: "The fact that a woman can run for president and it's the first time it's happened, encourages other women to step up and join the political sphere." Cam went on, stressing that the expansion of women in politics can have broad implications, including greater gender and racial equality:

> It just encourages people to see that *a woman can do just as much as a man can.* The 2016 election may have *catalyzed* the fact that putting a woman on a grand scale of political debates and whatever, *catalyzed* the fact that it can happen in smaller elections too. The country itself is *evolving*, becoming *less sexist, less racist, less traditional.*

Yet this view that Clinton's historic campaign was a catalyst for a broad range of social changes was atypical of the men.

Similarly, Khalid, a 21-year-old Middle Eastern man, thought that Trump's poor treatment of women led citizens to demand social change: "Trump always downgrades women. He treats women differently from how he treats men. And then his followers stand behind him and agree with everything he says, like the way that they view women." Khalid thought that this treatment would lead to a rise of women in politics:

> I think that women have seen a possibility to get Trump out of the way. Maybe they're getting ready for the next elections to have a bigger group for the presidential election, make a party of *women* and let them have the right to vote the same way men have a right to vote and speak out for themselves.

Khalid was careful to say that he did not see Trump's election "as a blessing" but rather "something that we can try to make the most out of." Although he refers to women as "they" several times in his statement, he ended by including himself and others who opposed Trump within a framework of collective opposition, using the words "we" and "together": "*We* are trying to build something *together.*" This identification with a collective identity was rare for the men.

The example of Khalid notwithstanding, the women interviewees more often saw the election in terms of a gendered collective identity. They were also more likely to recognize and call out sexism as responsible for the election results. As a result, they were less sanguine about the potential positive effects of the election. Christina, a 36-year-old Black woman, pointed to the double standard in how women and men are evaluated. She said that Trump "was able to get away with" saying "grab her by the vajayjay" and it was dismissed because "he's just a guy being a guy." She said that if Clinton would have said something similar, she would have been criticized for not being "a lady." People would say, "She shouldn't be talking like this. She should uphold herself this way. A politician doesn't do that."

Women participants were quick to point out that sexism on the part of voters hurt Clinton's candidacy. Kim said,

> Trump is a ridiculous person and he had no experience with politics. Clinton has a plethora of experience with politics. And if she would've been a guy, I think the distinction would've been clearer. I think she lost *because she was a woman*. People used Hillary being a woman as a reason to not vote for her. If she would've been a guy, she would've won.

Meghan, a 22-year-old white woman, tied Clinton's loss to gendered power: "Gender does play a really big role because people don't think that women in general can handle power. That's always been a problem." She said that people feared that "if things were to come down to a catastrophe, Clinton wouldn't be able to handle it." Although she disagreed, she said that voters thought that Trump "looked more powerful." Alyssa thought that Trump appealed to racial tensions: "Gender did play a bit of a role in it, but honestly, just being who I am, I think other things like race played a bigger role. It's all about who's in power and people wanting to keep the power."

Additionally, a number of focus group women pointed to sexism in the media and gendered expectations about candidates' appearance in particular. For example, Charlotte, a 23-year-old multiracial woman, said that if the election had featured "Trump versus a white male, the results might have turned out very different." Sexism influenced voting behavior among Democrats: "Just the fact that Clinton was a female caused people who would have voted Democratic to vote for Trump instead, so her gender definitely was a determining factor." Sexism in the media influenced the election as well. In contrast to Barack Obama, who was criticized only once for wearing the "wrong" color suit, Clinton faced this scrutiny constantly, said Charlotte: "For Hillary, it wouldn't have been just a one-time thing. It would've happened again and again and again. Like her clothing would have been like zoomed in on or criticized." Amelia, a 20-year-old multiracial woman, said that Trump's wife faces a similar emphasis on her clothing: "They talk about her dress and she's not even the one running the country. They're attacking her." Charlotte concluded by emphasizing gender: "Women are in general more sexualized than are men." Viewing the election within a framework of gender inequalities helped these women to embrace a collective identity around gender.

Some focus group men also recognized double standards in the election. Ahmad, a 21-year-old Middle Eastern man, said, "If a woman does what a man does, there's a double standard. Women won't be judged the way a man is judged." Referring to the outrage over Clinton's emails and comparing them to Trump's ties with Russia and dishonesty with Trump University, Noah agreed. After starting his sentence with the word "we," indicating that he placed himself among those who judge women more harshly, he backpedaled and shifted his language to focus on "culture" instead: "*We* more readily forgive, *not we,* but you know, *the culture* in general more readily forgives corruption in men than corruption in women."

Overall, the focus group voters saw the 2016 election as important for sparking social change. Yet men participants often took an individualized approach to the election, either rejecting Clinton as a candidate or seeing her as a role model for individual women. Focus group women were more aware of the broad-scale sexism that Clinton faced, suggesting that the election made gender issues salient to them. This election helped to ignite the gender revolution and provides backdrop for understanding the social movement activism that followed it.

"The Personal Is Political": How Social Movements Create Social Change

Social movements are typically understood to be groups or organizations that work outside of existing political or institutional arenas to challenge or defend existing arrangements (Snow et al. 2004). Macro-level studies examine sequences of events, mobilization of resources, or the ways political leaders and elites create policy change that in turn sparks social movement activism. Micro-level research, or research that bridges the macro and micro levels, examines social movement "frames" and the creation and mobilization of collective identity (della Porta and Diani 2015).

Frame theory, adapted from Goffman's (1974) classic work, bridges the macro and micro levels. Frame analysis considers how meaning is created through an interpretative process that is mediated by culture. Framing involves the construction of meaning by movement activists, leaders, elites, and even countermovements (Snow 2013; Snow 2004; Tan and Snow 2015; Snow and Benford 1988). Frames operate as the link between individual movement participants and social movement organizations' "interpretative frameworks"; they organize experience and guide individual or collective action (Snow et al. 1986). For example, the phrase "#MeToo" became a social movement frame with its own cultural meaning and significance. Gamson (1992: 7) identified three components of collective action frames: identity (the process by which a "we" is defined in opposition to a "they"), agency (an awareness that collective action can alter conditions or policies), and injustice (the "moral indignation" present in consciousness).

Since events and worldviews can lead to different interpretations, frames focus or refocus attention on a particular perspective (Snow 2013). Frames often have a "transformative function," such as changing the meanings associated with everyday injustices and creating new interpretations that contest old ones (Snow 2013: 1). As they do so, frames create changes in culture through reforming, reshaping, or dismantling existing cultural institutions and "fusing them together in a bricolage fashion" (Tan and Snow 2015: 526).

To become involved in a social movement, people develop a collective identity that aligns with that movement. Collective identity in turn shapes the movement. Klandermans (2004: 364) defined collective identity as "a place shared with other people." He stated that "movements offer the opportunity to act on behalf of one's group. This is most attractive if people identify strongly with their group" (Klandermans 2004: 367). Gamson's (1992) classic work similarly viewed collective identity as an enlargement on an individual's personal identity to include the collective (the "we"). These changes in personal identity can be enduring (Hunt and Benford 2004).

Collective identity is multidimensional; it includes cognitive, moral, and emotional elements that are linked to, but not identical to, ideology and personal identity (Hunt and Benford 2004). Taylor and Whittier (1992: 111) suggested three ways to understand collective identity construction: boundaries ("differences between a challenging group and dominant groups"), consciousness ("the interpretive frameworks that emerge out of a challenging group's struggle to define and realize its interests"), and negotiation ("the symbols and everyday actions subordinate groups use to resist and restructure existing systems of domination").

Boundary work is created through collective identity. As Hunt and Benford (2004: 443) stated, it consists of "constructing both a collective self and a collective other, an 'us' and a 'them.'" The second aspect of collective identity, consciousness, "imparts a larger significance to a collectivity" (Taylor and Whittier 1992: 114). According to Gamson (1992), consciousness lies at the intersection between the micro and macro levels, between individuals' meanings and larger sociocultural processes. Consciousness is the process by which the meanings that individuals attribute to social situations become a shared definition, which allows for the possibility of collective action (Gamson 1992). Flacks (1988) pointed out that collective mobilization is likely to occur when people stop tolerating the past rules and norms that previously structured their lives. This "liberation consciousness" occurs when people doubt the moral rightness of their accustomed subordination and begin to formulate new demands, often in the form of "daily assertiveness" (Flacks 1988: 77, 82). Negotiation, the third aspect of collective identity, is defined as "cultural representations," or a "set of shared meanings that are produced and reproduced, negotiated and renegotiated" (Hunt and Benford 2004: 447).

Women's movements are located within a broader cycle of protest (including other social movements of the time period and past women's movements). They arise in part because the demands of other groups help to transform previous ideological frames (Tarrow 1989). Thus, movements are interrelated and have both "generative" and "spillover" effects on each other, including creating and altering "frames, discourses, collective identity, goals, tactics, and organizational structure" (Whittier 2004: 532). The women's movement of the late 1960s and 1970s emerged in connection with the civil rights and new left movements, and in part as a critique of the gendered aspects of those movements (Evans 1980). The second-wave women's movement created new public policies and governmental bodies that created future opportunities for the movement's development (Costain 1992; Meyer and Staggenborg 1996). Women's activism during this period was not solely focused on gender and intersected with other identities, such as race and social class.

On the personal level, consciousness-raising, which Whittier (2017: 376) described as "deliberate self-reconstruction of identity, thought, and feelings related to gender," has been important for women's movements. In the late 1960s and 1970s, the small, decentralized groups that emerged coined the phrase "the personal is political"; their mission was to reinterpret women's individual experiences as something shared and connected with larger social dynamics and vice versa (Whittier 2017). This type of activism, a form of "visibility politics," is "transformative emotionally" for its participants and can also create "larger cultural change" (Whittier 2017: 386–387).

In this book, we move away from studying activists and leaders and focus instead on how movement "frames" have become diffused into non-activists' everyday lives. Although frames "legitimate and inspire social movement campaigns and activities," we know little about their diffusion to groups outside of social movement actors (Snow 2013: 1; Snow 2004). Theories on diffusion processes have been limited to understandings within and across movements (Soule and Roggeband 2018). Thus, diffusion or dispersion is understood as the "discursive processes through which frames evolve, develop, and change" (Snow 2013: 5). Diffusion is important for understanding how culture is transformed. As the current gender revolution emerged, #MeToo quickly spread through popular culture and social media; it diffused from activists and leaders to the general public.

From before "Me Too" to #MeToo: The History of Activism against Sexual Violence

The phrase "me too" was created by Tarana Burke in 2006 to raise awareness about sexual assault and promote support for victims, particularly Black women (Chandra and Erlingsdóttir 2020). As a youth worker, Burke (2022) sought to "bring resources, support, and pathways to healing where none existed before . . . to interrupt sexual violence wherever it happens." It was not until over ten years later (in 2017) that it inspired "flash activism," when celebrity and actress Alyssa Milano popularized (some say appropriated) the phrase as a hashtag.

Illustrating the effect of electronic media and social media in the digital age, the sudden public awareness and explosion of the #MeToo movement occurred as celebrities (beginning with Milano's "#MeToo" tweet) spoke out about their own exploitive experiences with former film director and convicted offender Harvey Weinstein. Awareness led to the digital sharing of experiences by women across many industries and life circumstances. As Chandra and Erlingsdóttir (2020: 1) recounted: "Within 24 hours, about half a million women had either endorsed the challenge [by tweeting #MeToo] or added their own story." By October 2018, the #MeToo hashtag had been used over 19 million times on Twitter alone (Hearn 2020). As Hurwitz (2017: 466) put it: "Women activists continue to develop new consciousness about gender inequalities online and develop new tactics to transform male-dominated media." As a result, social media has "made feminism more relevant to women's lives" (Hurwitz 2017: 466). This public discourse, new language, and symbols are evidence of the diffusion of social movement frames into people's *personal* lives in the digital age. The frame links survivors together through visibility and speaking out about previously private and hidden traumas.

The #MeToo movement is situated within a larger historical context of activism around sexual violence. In the nineteenth century, efforts challenged laws and norms of "patriarchal privilege and control" (Arnold 2017: 271). Much later, the second-wave women's movement was responsible for naming sexual harassment and linking it to workplace inequalities (Boris and Elias 2017). Catherine MacKinnon's legal scholarship altered understandings of sexual harassment starting in the late 1970s, as she defined it as a form of sex discrimination tied to gender inequalities. Exposing harassment as a form of male dominance, feminist activism and changing attitudes led to the enactment of new policies prohibiting these behaviors (Boris and Elias 2017).

In 1991, the shaming of Anita Hill in the confirmation hearings of Supreme Court Justice Clarence Thomas brought sexual harassment into public consciousness in new ways. The 1992 election that followed the hearings was called the "year of the woman," as women were elected to Congress in then-unprecedented numbers. The Violence Against Women Act, which created new governmental bodies and provided financial resources to sexual assault and domestic violence agencies, was passed in 1994 (Arnold 2017). The activists who pushed this agenda forward viewed violence against women as systemic and rooted in male dominance; they also sought to take women's experiences of violence seriously rather than dismissing them (Arnold 2017). At the same time, support from "frenemies," specifically conservative elected officials who could mobilize different constituencies, was important for the passage of the Violence Against Women Act (Whittier 2018). Movements to end violence against women were not without their critics;

women of color pointed out that new criminalization policies negatively affected communities of color; other activists were concerned about co-optation by the government (Arnold 2017).

Two decades later, the feminist activism that emerged in the mid to late 1990s drew on previous social movement frames yet extended feminism in new directions, particularly its intersections with race, ethnicity, and sexuality (Reger 2012). Many activists advanced intersectional critiques of the women's movement from a standpoint that viewed oppression within a "matrix of domination" that included other marginalized identities, such as race, class, ethnicity, and sexuality (e.g., Collins 1990). Queer theory critiquing heteronormative ideas about sexuality argues that gender exists within a "heterosexual matrix" that is itself tied to gender inequality existing within a gender binary (Butler 1990). Among those who use the feminist "wave" metaphor, this period is often labeled the "third wave," although there are controversies about this term (Reger 2017). One of the defining characteristics of this period is widespread diffusion and acceptance of feminist ideas and policies throughout dominant culture (Aronson 2003; Aronson 2008; Reger 2017).

These fluctuations and changes in activism are typical in the lives of social movements. The periods "in between" the most active feminist mobilizations are important for consolidating ideas and building policy and cultural successes (Taylor and Rupp 1993). During periods of women's movement "abeyance," three elements influence future mobilization: feminist collective identity, pre-existing networks of activists, and the existence of established goals and tactics (Taylor 1989). Periods of abeyance do not mean that the movement is irrelevant; it means that it has moved into a period of maintenance (Taylor and Rupp 1993).

In today's digital age, social movements look different than in the past. Power from traditional social movements typically originates from a small group of dedicated activists, but the rise of technology and digital culture has pushed social movements online (Earl et al. 2015; Hurwitz 2017). More people, particularly those who are marginalized, are able to participate than would normally participate using traditional tactics, such as street protests; online involvement is less time-consuming and costly (Earl et al. 2015). As a result, diffusion to a broader group of people, outside of activists and leaders, is more readily possible. Jasper and Polletta (2018: 65) pointed out that "new digital media may be changing people's everyday understandings of the boundaries between private ownership and public use in ways that affect the kinds of causes people see as worth mobilizing around." In this context, social movement diffusion to the general public is more widely possible than ever before.

The rapid viral spread of ideas was a key to #MeToo movement success. Online activism represents a new way for awareness about inequalities to spread quickly and allows for "global networking and alternative media" (Hurwitz 2017: 469). One form of protest that has proliferated in the digital age is the use of hashtags on social media websites, particularly on Twitter, which serves to link people and ideas together in robust ways (Jackson et al. 2020). Engaging on Twitter and other social media websites without "mediation by the mainstream media or other traditional sources of power" (Jackson et al. 2020: xxx) allows people to freely engage in discussions that might otherwise be restricted or censored. Thus, as a result of widespread changes in technological communication, we are witnessing a new era of social movements that has ideological diffusion at its center.

Social protest in the digital age is akin to a "flash flood" or "flash activism," with changes sparked rapidly and inspiring online protest (Earl et al. 2015). Crossley (2019: 72) described how the speed of communication has influenced organizing when she said, "In contrast to previous forms of feminism . . . the Internet allows for interaction with other activists and adversaries at unparalleled speed and frequency." In this context, images are reinterpreted as they are disseminated and contribute to a social movement's progression (Doerr et al. 2015). As we saw with #MeToo, movements form more easily and robustly in the digital age if they involve celebrities, who can reach many people quickly and easily (Earl 2018). Images and symbols used by disadvantaged groups in the digital age counterbalance traditional viewpoints, inspire collective identity, and mobilize attention toward social problems (Doerr et al. 2015).

The #MeToo movement builds on previous women's movements and influences other social movements. Although distinct in many ways, the #MeToo movement has been influenced by the historical legacy of the feminist movements that came before it: the ideology, the organizations, and previous tactics and goals. Additionally, the #MeToo movement may be influencing other emerging social movements because it reached people who were non-activists. In particular, it may have influenced Black Lives Matter mobilization, which had been in existence for many years but became mainstream during and immediately following the growth of #MeToo visibility (Simmons 2020). Earl (2018) argued that the Black Lives Matter movement was propelled forward as important recordings and links were shared and watched by large audiences. It is possible that, like the 1960s and 1970s, current mobilizations around gender and racial justice developed alongside and in connection with each other.

Participation in the #MeToo movement represents an act of solidarity among women and an effort to feel more comfortable sharing their experiences of sexual harassment and assault (Jackson et al. 2020). The #MeToo movement further advances the "the personal is political" approach of earlier decades of women's movements, as it emphasizes the way that personal experiences of sexual assault stem from systemic and political degradation of women (Jackson et al. 2020; Keller et al. 2016). In fact, the #MeToo hashtag has become so mainstream that companies have used it in marketing and advertising campaigns, as illustrated by a Gillette commercial that called attention to toxic masculinity (Jackson et al. 2020).

There are many benefits to social media protest, particularly on controversial issues like sexual assault and harassment. Although the use of protest hashtags has faced backlash (sometimes violent), social media is a "safer" place to engage in protest compared to more traditional, public places (Keller et al. 2016). Sharing accounts of sexual assault provides a space for readers to realize that previous experiences of their own might be defined as assault (Keller et al. 2016). Digital media, especially Twitter, can be used as a means of educating others about misogyny and can challenge rape culture (Keller et al. 2016).

"Hashtag feminism" and the #MeToo movement draw on visibility politics to make rape culture visible (Whittier 2017). In all of these ways, the #MeToo movement moves beyond second-wave women's movement consciousness-raising; it connects survivors together in a community, "a 'we' of solidarity and shared experience" in the public, rather than private, sphere (Chandra and Erlingsdóttir 2020: 2). As Berger (2020: 57) put it, social media is "erasing the border between the public and private spheres" and "between the 'personal' and the 'political.'" That is, although the term "sexual harassment" originated as a legal category, MacKinnon (2020: 42) argued that with #MeToo, the "first mass movement against sexual abuse in the history of the world" has taken place in society and culture rather than litigation and the law. Rather than pursuing legal recourse, the movement often focuses on restorative justice, rooted in truth-telling, with the goal of "regain[ing] political stability after a societal trauma" (Chandra and Erlingsdóttir 2020: 9).

Digital organizing also produced the 2017 Women's March, the largest single day of protest in U.S. history. As Fisher (2019: 126) described: "Technological innovation has lowered the cost of protest and facilitated engaging in collective action despite the absence of geographic proximity." Digital activism is possible as a result of three factors: the ability to organize across geographic boundaries, fluid membership, and social media networks that are loosely affiliated (Fisher 2019). Activists have been able to create online toolkits that can be disseminated to organize events in multiple locations (Fisher 2019). Together, the Women's March and #MeToo are part of the larger gender revolution.

Conclusion

This chapter provides a context for understanding the gendered changes that are unfolding in the current gender revolution. Our focus group interviewees were aware that the 2016 election catalyzed social movement activism, particularly among women and people of color. And yet gendered divisions in focus group participants' perceptions of this election are apparent. In particular, most of the men viewed the election in individualized terms. They tended to see Clinton's defeat as resulting from her unlikable particular characteristics rather than as a result of her gender. Men participants often saw Clinton's pioneering run as creating social change, but in an individualized way, as a role model for subsequent women. They also viewed Trump's election as leading to social change in an individualized way—as a cultural trickster—rather than seeing change in the context of the work of millions of activists. In contrast, women interviewees were more likely to attribute Clinton's loss to sexism, which is consistent with the gendered collective identity that they expressed on other topics. Thus, the men generally failed to recognize Trump's emphasis on hegemonic masculinity and saw the role of gender in this election in a narrow way. In contrast, the women viewed the election within a broader framework of gender inequalities.

The 2016 election was a key catalyst of the #MeToo movement. While "me too" originated earlier and built on a long history of activism surrounding eradicating violence against women, Trump's admission of sexually assaulting women on the *Access Hollywood* hot mic sparked flash activism on social media. In the digital age, celebrities coming forward with their stories of sexual harassment and assault provided a model for average people, not just activists, to engage in social media activism surrounding this issue. Electronic and social media in the digital age led to rapid diffusion of #MeToo movement frames, beyond leaders and activists and to people living in their everyday lives. The findings in this chapter lay out important groundwork for what follows; the gender differences in perceptions of the 2016 election undergird our other findings on electoral politics and the diffusion of #MeToo movement ideology into ordinary people's lives.

References

Anderson, Logan. 2016. "This Is What an Official Hillary for America 'Woman Card' Gets You." *Hillary for America*. Retrieved August 20, 2022 (www.hillaryclinton.com/feed/what-official-hillary-america-woman-card-gets-you/).

Arnold, Gretchen. 2017. "U.S. Women's Movements to End Violence Against Women, Domestic Abuse, and Rape." pp. 270–290 in *The Oxford Handbook of U.S. Women's Social Movement Activism*, edited by Holly J. McCammon, Verta Taylor, Jo Reger, and Rachel L. Einwohner. New York, NY: Oxford University Press.

Aronson, Pamela. 2018. "'I'm Not Voting for Her.' Internalized Misogyny, Feminism and Gender Consciousness in the 2016 Election." pp. 204–218 in *Nasty Women and Bad Hombres: Gender and Race in the 2016 Presidential Election*, edited by Christine Kray, Tamar Carroll and Hinda Mandell. Rochester, NY: University of Rochester Press.

Aronson, Pamela. 2008. "The Markers and Meanings of Growing Up: Contemporary Young Women's Transition From Adolescence to Adulthood." *Gender & Society* 22(1):56–82.

Aronson, Pamela. 2003. "Feminists or 'Postfeminists?': Young Women's Attitudes Toward Feminism and Gender Relations." *Gender & Society* 17(6):903–922.

Berger, Anne-Emmanuelle. 2020. "Subject of Desire/Subject of Feminism." pp. 55–64 in *The Routledge Handbook of the Politics of the #MeToo Movement*, edited by Giti Chandra and Irma Erlingsdóttir. New York, NY: Routledge.

Boris, Eileen and Allison Louise Elias. 2017. "Workplace Discrimination, Equal Pay, and Sexual Harassment." pp. 193–213 in *The Oxford Handbook of U.S. Women's Social Movement Activism*, edited by Holly J. McCammon, Verta Taylor, Jo Reger, and Rachel L. Einwohner. New York, NY: Oxford University Press.

Burke, Tarana. 2022. *Me Too*. Retrieved August 15, 2022 (https://metoomvmt.org/get-to-know-us/history-inception/).

Butler, Judith. 1990. *Gender Trouble: Feminism and the Subversion of Identity*. New York, NY: Routledge.

Chandra, Giti and Irma Erlingsdóttir. 2020. "Introduction." pp. 1–23 in *The Routledge Handbook of the Politics of the #MeToo Movement*, edited by Giti Chandra and Irma Erlingsdóttir. New York, NY: Routledge.

Chittal, Nisha. 2016. "Clinton Supporters Wear Pantsuits to the Polls." *NBCNews.com*. Retrieved August 15, 2022 (www.nbcnews.com/storyline/2016-election-day/clinton-supporters-wear-pantsuits-polls-n680101).

Collins, Patricia Hill. 1990. *Black Feminist Thought: Knowledge, Consciousness, and the Politics of Empowerment*. New York, NY: Routledge.

Costain, Anne N. 1992. *Inviting Women's Rebellion: A Political Process Interpretation of the Women's Movement*. Baltimore, MD: Johns Hopkins University Press.

Crossley, Alison Dahl. 2019. "Online Feminism Is Just Feminism: Offline and Online Movement Persistence." pp. 60–78 in *Nevertheless, They Persisted: Feminisms and Continued Resistance in the U.S. Women's Movement*, edited by Jo Reger. New York: Routledge.

della Porta, Donatella, and Mario Diani. 2015. "Introduction: The Field of Social Movement Studies." pp. 1–28 in *The Oxford Handbook of Social Movements*, edited by Donatella della Porta and Mario Diani. New York, NY: Oxford University Press.

Doerr, Nicole, Alice Mattoni, and Simon Teune. 2015. "Visuals in Social Movements." pp. 557–566 in *The Oxford Handbook of Social Movements*, edited by Donatella della Porta and Mario Diani. New York, NY: Oxford University Press.

Earl, Jennifer. 2018. "Technology and Social Media." pp. 289–305 in *The Wiley Blackwell Companion to Social Movements, Second Edition*, edited by David A. Snow, Sarah A. Soule, Hanspeter Kriesi, and Holly J. McCammon. Hoboken, NJ: John Wiley & Sons Ltd.

Earl, Jennifer, Jayson Hunt, R. Kelly Garrett, and Aysenur Dal. 2015. "New Technologies and Social Movements." pp. 355–366 in *The Oxford Handbook of Social Movements*, edited by Donatella della Porta and Mario Diani. New York, NY: Oxford University Press.

Ellefson, Lindsey. 2016. "People Are Losing It Over a Woman Whose Shirt Says Trump Can Grab Her . . . You Know." *Mediaite*. Retrieved August 15, 2022 (www.mediaite.com/online/people-are-losing-it-over-a-woman-whose-shirt-says-trump-can-grab-her-you-know/).

Evans, Sara M. 1980. *Personal Politics: The Roots of Women's Liberation in the Civil Rights Movement and the New Left*. New York, NY: Vintage Books.

Faber, Daniel, Jennie Stephens, Victor Wallis, Roger Gottlieb, Charles Levenstein, Patrick CoatarPeter, and the Boston Editorial Group of CNS. 2017. "Trump's Electoral Triumph: Class, Race, Gender, and the Hegemony of the Polluter-Industrial Complex." *Capitalism Nature Socialism* 28(1):1–15.

Fisher, Dana R. 2019. *American Resistance: From the Women's March to the Blue Wave*. New York: Columbia University Press.

Flacks, Richard. 1988. *Making History: The Radical Tradition in American Life*. New York, NY: Columbia University Press.

Gamson, William A. 1992. "The Social Psychology of Collective Action." pp. 53–76 in *Frontiers in Social Movement Theory*, edited by A. D. Morris and C. M. Mueller. Yale University Press.

Goffman, Erving. 1974. *Frame Analysis: An Essay on the Organization of Experience*. Harmondsworth, NY: Harper Colophon Books.

Hearn, Jeff. 2020. "#MeToo as a Variegated Phenomenon Against Men's Violences and Violations." pp. 65–84 in *The Routledge Handbook of the Politics of the #MeToo Movement*, edited by Giti Chandra and Irma Erlingsdóttir. New York, NY: Routledge.

Hunt, Scott A. and Robert A. Benford. 2004. "Collective Identity, Solidarity, and Commitment." pp. 433–57 in *The Blackwell Companion to Social Movements*, edited by David A. Snow, Sarah A. Soule, and Hanspeter Kriesi. Hoboken, NJ: John Wiley & Sons Ltd.

Hurwitz, Heather McKee. 2017. "From Ink to Web and Beyond: U.S. Women's Activism Using Traditional and New Social Media." pp. 462–484 in *The Oxford Handbook of U.S. Women's Social Movement Activism*, edited by Holly J. McCammon, Verta Taylor, Jo Reger, and Rachel L. Einwohner. New York, NY: Oxford University Press.

Jackson, Sarah J., Moya Bailey, and Brooke Foucault Welles. 2020. *#Hashtagactivism: Networks of Race and Gender Justice*. Cambridge, MA: The MIT Press.

Jasper, James M. and Francesca Polletta. 2018. "The Cultural Context of Social Movements." pp. 63–78 in *The Wiley Blackwell Companion to Social Movements, Second Edition*, edited by David A. Snow, Sarah A. Soule, Hanspeter Kriesi, and Holly J. McCammon. Hoboken, NJ: John Wiley & Sons Ltd.

Keller, Jessalynn, Kaitlynn Mendes, and Jessica Ringrose. 2016. "Speaking 'Unspeakable Things': Documenting Digital Feminist Responses to Rape Culture." *Journal of Gender Studies* 27(1):22–36.

Klandermans, Bert. 2004. "The Demand and Supply of Participation: Social-Psychological Correlates of Participation in Social Movements." pp. 360–379 in *The Blackwell Companion to Social Movements*, edited by David A. Snow, Sarah A. Soule, and Hanspeter Kriesi. Malden, MA: John Wiley & Sons Ltd.

Landsbaum, Claire. 2016. "Guess How Many Times Donald Trump Interrupted Hillary Clinton During the Debate." *The Cut*. Retrieved August 20, 2022 (www.thecut.com/2016/10/trump-interrupted-clinton-37-times-in-final-debate.html).

MacKinnon, Catharine A. 2020. "Global #MeToo." pp. 42–54 in *The Routledge Handbook of the Politics of the #MeToo Movement*, edited by Giti Chandra and Irma Erlingsdóttir. New York, NY: Routledge.

Meyer, David S. and Suzanne Staggenborg. 1996. "Movements, Countermovements, and the Structure of Political Opportunity." *American Journal of Sociology* 101(6):1628–1660.

The New York Times. 2016. "Transcript: Donald Trump's Taped Comments About Women." *The New York Times*. Retrieved August 15, 2022 (www.nytimes.com/2016/10/08/us/donald-trump-tape-transcript.html).

Pearson, Catherine, Emma Gray, and Alanna Vagianos. 2017. "A Running List of the Women Who've Accused Donald Trump of Sexual Misconduct." *HuffPost*. Retrieved August 15, 2022 (www.huffpost.com/entry/a-running-list-of-the-women-whove-accused-donald-trump-of-sexual-misconduct_n_57ffae1fe4b0162c043a7212).

Reger, Jo. 2017. "Contemporary Feminism and Beyond." pp. 109–128 in *The Oxford Handbook of U.S. Women's Social Movement Activism*, edited by Holly J. McCammon, Verta Taylor, Jo Reger, and Rachel L. Einwohner. New York, NY: Oxford University Press.

Reger, Jo. 2012. *Everywhere and Nowhere: The State of Contemporary Feminism in the United States*. New York, NY: Oxford University Press.

Rogers, Jenny. 2016. "What Happens When You Ask Women for Their Stories of Assault? Thousands of Replies." *The Providence Journal*. Retrieved August 15, 2022 (www.providencejournal.com/story/news/politics/2016/10/11/what-happens-when-you-ask-women-for-their-stories-of-assault-thousands-of-replies/25225943007/).

Simmons, Kimberly. 2020. Personal communication.

Snow, David A. 2013. "Framing and Social Movements." pp. 1–6 in *The Wiley-Blackwell Encyclopedia of Social and Political Movements*, edited by David A. Snow, Donatella della Porta, Bert Klandermans, and Doug McAdam. Oxford: Wiley/Blackwell.

Snow, David A. 2004. "Social Movements as Challenges to Authority: Resistance to an Emerging Conceptual Hegemony." *Research in Social Movements, Conflict, and Change* 25:3–25.

Snow, David A. and Robert D. Benford. 1988. "Ideology, Frame Resonance, and Participant Mobilization." *International Social Movement Research* 1(1):197–217.

Snow, David A., E. Burke Rochford, Steven K. Worden, and Robert D. Benford. 1986. "Frame Alignment Processes, Micromobilization, and Movement Participation." *American Sociological Review* 51(4):464–481.

Snow, David A., Sarah A. Soule, and Hanspeter Kriesi. 2004. "Mapping the Terrain." pp. 3–16 in *The Blackwell Companion to Social Movements,* edited by David A. Snow, Sarah A. Soule, and Hanspeter Kriesi. Malden, MA: John Wiley & Sons Ltd.

Soule, Sarah A. and Conny Roggeband. 2018. "Diffusion Processes Within and Across Movements." pp. 238–251 in *The Wiley Blackwell Companion to Social Movements, Second Edition*, edited by David A. Snow, Sarah A. Soule, Hanspeter Kriesi, and Holly J. McCammon. Hoboken, NJ: John Wiley & Sons Ltd.

Tan, Anna E. and David A. Snow. 2015. "Cultural Conflicts and Social Movements." pp. 513–533 in *The Oxford Handbook of Social Movements*, edited by Donatella della Porta and Mario Diani. New York, NY: Oxford University Press.

Tarrow, Sidney G. 1989. *Democracy and Disorder: Protest and Politics in Italy, 1965–1975.* Oxford: Clarendon Press.

Taylor, Verta. 1989. "Social Movement Continuity: The Women's Movement in Abeyance." *American Sociological Review* 54(5):761–775.

Taylor, Verta and Leila J. Rupp. 1993. "Women's Culture and Lesbian Feminist Activism: A Reconsideration of Cultural Feminism." *Signs: Journal of Women in Culture and Society* 19(1):32–61.

Taylor, Verta and Nancy Whittier. 1992. "Collective Identity in Social Movement Communities: Lesbian Feminist Mobilization." pp. 104–129 in *Frontiers in Social Movement Theory*. New Haven, CT, CT: Yale University Press.

The Washington Post. 2016. "2016 Election Exit Polls: How the Vote Has Shifted." *The Washington Post*. Retrieved August 20, 2022 (www.washingtonpost.com/graphics/politics/2016-election/exit-polls/).

Whittier, Nancy. 2018. *Frenemies: Feminists, Conservatives, and Sexual Violence*. New York, NY: Oxford University Press.

Whittier, Nancy. 2017. "Identity Politics, Consciousness-Raising, and Visibility Politics." pp. 376–397 in *The Oxford Handbook of U.S. Women's Social Movement Activism*, edited by Holly J. McCammon, Verta Taylor, Jo Reger, and Rachel L. Einwohner. New York, NY: Oxford University Press.

Whittier, Nancy. 2004. "The Consequences of Social Movements for Each Other." pp. 531–551 in *The Blackwell Companion to Social Movements*, edited by David A. Snow, Sarah A. Soule, and Hanspeter Kriesi. Malden, MA: Blackwell Publishing.

Wilson, Chris. 2016. "Donald Trump Interrupted Hillary Clinton and Lester Holt 55 Times in the First Presidential Debate," *Time*, September 27, 2016 (http://time.com/4509790/donald-trump-debate-interruptions/).

2

THE WOMEN'S MARCH AND ATTITUDES TOWARD FEMINISM

"Pussy Grabs Back": The 2017 Women's March

Millions of people, many dressed in pink "pussyhats" and carrying homemade signs, descended on Washington, DC, and cities around the world on January 21, 2017, to protest the inauguration of Donald Trump as president. They held signs, including one with the phrase "pussy grabs back," referring to an *Access Hollywood* clip from 2005 when Trump bragged about "grabbing 'em [women] by the pussy." There were over 673 sister marches around the world and in every U.S. state. With as many as five million participants in the United States, many of whom were first-time activists, the protest was historically the largest single-day demonstration (McKane and McCammon 2018).[1]

While drawing together a diverse coalition of protesters and organizations, the Women's March crystalized a new cultural moment that expressed the diffusion of women's movement frames into people's everyday lives. This march was historically unique, as demonstrations were only a part of movement mobilization rather than the end goal (Fisher 2019). Through digital organizing, the march created collective identity and "combined unconventional forms of contentious politics with more institutional forms of electoral politics" (Fisher 2019: 126). Signs reflected "personalized action frames"; they emphasized "women as powerful agents of resistance," reappropriated women's bodies (Weber et al. 2018), and demonstrated the diffusion of feminism (Reger 2019). In fact, Women's March activists and their supporters are innovators—pushing social change forward.

The idea for the Women's March originated from two unconnected white women—Teresa Shook (a retired attorney) and Bob Bland (a fashion designer) (Gökarıksel and Smith 2017)—and circulated throughout social media. After

DOI: 10.4324/9781003225331-4

FIGURE 2.1   The 2017 Women's March Crowd in Washington, DC

Source: Mobilus in Mobili/Retrieved through Flickr and reprinted under CC-BY-SA 2.0.

objections about the lack of attention to the concerns of people of color, three women of color activists joined Bland as co-chairs of the event (Linda Sarsour, Tamika Mallory, and Carmen Perez) (Gantt-Shafer et al. 2019). Together, the organizers were explicitly committed to intersectionality (Moss and Maddrell 2017), as they invited all women to join the march ("Black women, Indigenous women, poor women, immigrant women, disabled women, Muslim women, lesbian, queer and trans women"), as well as those who had survived sexual assault (McKane and McCammon 2018), and anyone else "regardless of gender or gender identity, who believes women's rights are human rights" (Moss and Maddrell 2017: 614). Although the march focused on issues beyond gender and represented a broad coalition of over 100 organizations (McKane and McCammon 2018), charges of white privilege marred some perceptions of the march.

The pussyhats themselves represented a site of both resistance and conflict. The Pussyhat Project was originated by Krista Suh and Jayna Zweiman (who could not attend the march as a result of injuries) and spread over social media as a way to "gift" those in attendance the hats (Hamasaki 2017). The handmade pink cat-eared hats were intended to visually illustrate "a show of solidarity and support for women's rights" (Hamasaki 2017) through "a unique collective visual statement which will help activists be better heard" (May 2020: 79). In an interview, Zweiman said that the pussyhats referred to the *Access Hollywood* video, "but it's also so much more. . . . It's reappropriating the word 'pussy' in a positive way. This is a project about women supporting women" (Hamasaki 2017). As a fiber-based craft, the hand-knitted hats drew on a long history of women's needlework (May 2020). The color pink was selected to reappropriate a color associated with femininity and weakness by reclaiming "pussy power" (May 2020: 80). As Gökarıksel and Smith (2017: 635) put it,

> The pink pussy hats accomplish so much: the hat creates a vivid and impossible to ignore visible signal that embraces and celebrates femininity while it simultaneously evokes a cheeky vulgarity through its multiple valences as a sexual symbol now proudly reclaimed against a violent record of masculine assault in which Trump unabashedly participates.

Reger (2019: 8) tied the pussyhats to the creation of a collective identity when she said, "The hats were a simple and easy way to broadcast an . . . oppositional feminist identity." The image of millions of protesters in pussyhats drew attention to gender inequalities worldwide.

Yet the pussyhats were also controversial. Gökarıksel and Smith (2017: 635) pointed out that they "infantilize" women by making them look like kittens; the

FIGURE 2.2 A Baby in a Pussyhat at the 2017 Women's March

Source: Morna Gerrard/Retrieved from Women's March on Washington Collection, Archives for Research on Women and Gender. Special Collections and Archives, Georgia State University. Reprinted with permission.

stereotypical color "feels too safe and too reductive to be an answer to the complex issues facing women today." In particular, some activists expressed concern that the hats failed as a metaphor against sexual assault and obscured the experience of trans women and women of color. For example, a subsequent Women's March conference session title proclaimed, "Not All Women Have Pussies and Not All Pussies are Pink" (Aronson 2017a). Ultimately, Gökanksel and Smith (2017: 636) concluded that the pussyhats "seek to challenge gender norms" but inadvertently "end up reiterating them." Despite these controversies, in an important way, the Women's March highlighted women's *collective* identities *as women*, which helped create "feminist solidarity" (May 2020). Likewise, the backgrounds of the organizers and participants were diverse and the march focused on issues aside from gender.

The Women's March was important for the gender revolution and its social and cultural transformations. Understanding how social movements develop and eventually create social change is important for studies of movement diffusion. The march represented and spread a social movement frame in which women demanded power and defined their own interests in relation to a gendered collective identity. Accordingly, this chapter examines the 2017 Women's March itself, drawing on organizational data and print media coverage of the event from ideologically diverse outlets. As Nicolini and Hansen (2018) found, solidarity and resistance were also reflected in the news media's coverage of the march. In contrast to the past, activity took place in electronic media, social media, and people's everyday lives. To explore the discourses in everyday conversations and debates, we also examine focus group interviewees' perceptions of the march and their attitudes toward feminism more generally.

"We Will Fight for What We Believe in": Innovators and the 2017 Women's March

On a cold January day in 2017, singer Alicia Keys spoke out at the Women's March in Washington, DC: "*We* will not allow *our* bodies to be *owned and controlled by men* in government or men anywhere for that matter" (Sanchez 2017). Senator Elizabeth Warren, who would go on to run for the 2020 Democratic nomination for president, echoed this claim for women's power:

> *We* can whimper. *We* can whine. Or *we* can *fight back*! *We* come here to stand shoulder to shoulder to make clear: *We* are here! *We* will *not be silent*! *We* will not play dead! *We* will *fight* for what we believe in! (Sanchez 2017)

In fact, famous people stood with ordinary people to speak out against Trump's election and express a collective identity *as women* (signified by the word "we" and "our" in Keys's and Warren's speeches). In claiming women's right to power and self-determination, these innovators embraced a #MeToo and social movement frame of women's collective identity and power. This frame espoused a collective identity in which women connected their identities to other women. This frame, which was diffused into the everyday lives of focus group innovators, contrasts with the more individualized approach expressed by focus group resisters.

The diffusion of these ideas can be seen in interviewees' perspectives that the 2016 election, the Women's March, and the #MeToo movement are connected. Participants viewed the rise of women's movement activism as a reaction to the 2016 election. For example, although Aran, a 20-year-old Asian American man, began by saying that these events "don't directly correlate," he also saw their interconnection: "Ever since the 2016 election, there's been a lot of women's movements. From Hollywood to politics, it's been a lot of women's involvement, the whole Women's March that happened." Aran said that the 2016 election "raised a lot of awareness for where women stand" and "sparked something in them" to propel activism forward. Leo, an 18-year-old Asian American man, saw the election as a direct impetus for activism: The election "caused a major conflict and the most activism I've ever seen, with protests and media being spread around with Twitter." Hunter, a 22-year-old white man, agreed that Trump's history of assault "gave birth to the #MeToo movement, because after he was elected, the people spoke up." Harper, a 23-year-old multiracial woman, argued that women are "fighting back" because Trump "talks so much crap." She said that Trump plans to "inhibit women from making important decisions," such as abortion, and women "want to prove him wrong, like we are able to make a difference." Harper emphasized that women are no longer timid: "They're scared, but not this year."

To study the Women's March in depth, we collected website data from each of the 34 organizations that signed on as organizers. The organizations are only a fraction of those that later were partners or supporters of the march. We collected data focusing on the history and backgrounds of the organization, current organizational information, and mission statements. These data suggest that organizational participation included gender-focused organizations, feminist organizations, and those that were focused on other concerns, such as climate change, civil rights, or racial justice. Additionally, we collected and coded all of the news articles covering the Women's March from five ideologically divergent news outlets, starting in 2016: the *New York Times*, *MSNBC*, *Politico*, *CNN*, and *Fox News* (for a total of 150 news articles). Together, these data suggest diversity in the collaborating organizations and participants themselves.

Women's March Organizations

The mission of the Women's March organization, founded in the wake of the 2016 election, is "to harness the political power of diverse women and their communities to create transformative social change." Its website states that it is "a women-led movement providing intersectional education on a diverse range of issues and creating entry points for new grassroots activists & organizers to engage in their local communities." The organization is "committed to dismantling systems of oppression through nonviolent resistance and building inclusive structures guided by self-determination, dignity and respect" (Women's March 2019).

The Women's March organization, which coordinated the inauguration protests in 2017, is located within a long history of women's activism, yet its reliance on social media allowed sister marches around the world to spread rapidly through networks. As a result, many of those who attended were first-time activists. Dow et al. (2017) found that one-third were first-time protesters and over half had not participated in a protest in over five years. As Dow et al. (2017) concluded, "The Women's March has potentially lit the political fires of a new generation of activists and reactivated the political activism of others." In fact, protesters included those who were involved in organizations, as well as "independent individuals" who were not connected with an established organization (Dow et al. 2017). Fisher (2019) explained that such activism in a digital age encouraged those who were not tightly connected through organizations to become active.

Despite the presence of many unaffiliated individuals, the Women's March protest was made up of a broad coalition of organizations. Our analysis of organizational websites suggests that the Women's March was successful at mobilizing a broad constituency of interests. Reflecting the coalition that resulted, *Fox News* (2017) said,

> The idea for the women's march took off after a number of women posted on social media in the hours after Trump's election about the need to mobilize. Hundreds of groups quickly joined the cause, pushing a wide range of causes, including abortion rights, gun control, climate change and immigrant rights.

Fisher (2019: 17) described these diverse organizations as "unlikely bedfellows."

Gender-focused organizations on the Women's March website included long-time organizations, such as the League of Women Voters. There were also established feminist organizations, including Planned Parenthood, NARAL Pro-Choice America Foundation, the National Organization for Women, the Human Rights Campaign, and Code Pink. Other organizations included the National Center for Lesbian Rights, Black Girls Rock, Catholics for Choice, Gay and Lesbian Alliance Against Defamation (GLAAD), and EMILY's List. Reproductive rights were a prominent concern (e.g., signs read "Keep your policies off my body" and "My pussy, my choice, my body, my voice") (Weber et al. 2018). Three co-organizer organizations were established in 2016, in direct response to the presidential election: the Women's March itself, Pantsuit Nation, and the Pussyhat Project. These organizations all defined themselves as advancing women's interests. For example, Libby Chamberlain created Pantsuit Nation as a "secret" Facebook group in late October 2016 (although it grew to 3.8 million members). Initially, Chamberlain invited about 30 friends to wear pantsuits (referring to Hillary Clinton's trademark clothing) to the polls on

Election Day. The group's mission was to "harness the power of collective storytelling to drive social and political change" (Pantsuit Nation 2022). One additional organization, New Wave Feminists, was listed initially but was quickly removed when the march organizers discovered that it opposes abortion rights.

These organizations, focused on gender issues, worked in coalition with others that did not have gender as their primary focus. Human rights organizations, such as the American Civil Liberties Union (ACLU), signed on, as did several large unions, including the American Federation of Teachers and the American Federation of Labor and Congress of Industrial Organizations (AFL-CIO). Progressive political organizations were also partners in the march, including MoveOn and two new groups founded in response to the election, Indivisible and Brand New Congress. Additionally, environmental organizations became involved, including Natural Resources Defense Council Platinum Sponsor, Greenpeace, and Oxfam.

Human rights and racial justice organizations also sponsored the march, including Amnesty International, Human Rights Watch, Equality Now, Black Lives Matter, National Association for the Advancement of Colored People (NAACP), Americans for Indian Opportunity, Native Organizers Alliance, and the Arab American Association. Together, this broad coalition of organizations covered many issues, helped to increase the visibility of the march, and attracted participants.

Women's March Goals and Tactics

Capturing women's anger and rising power, one Women's March sign proclaimed, "A woman's place is in the revolution." Women's assertiveness and anger breaks free from stereotypes of niceness and represents the gendered social change characteristic of the gender revolution. There was evidence of women seizing power on march signs and in journalists' interviews with protesters. In a *CNN* article, one participant emphasized strength in fighting for women's rights when she said,

> I feel really like this is "Game on." This is no joke, and we are going to be *loud*, and we are going to be *strong*, and we're going to *fight* for what we believe that we already had and now we're afraid we may lose (Wallace 2017).

Words like "loud," "strong," and "fight" do not conform to gender-traditional expressions of "niceness." Such gender-nontraditional language was common in signs, slogans, and chants. Wallace (2017) interviewed another woman who used words like "fight" and "speak up" to explain her reasons for marching: "This stuff has to be *fought for*. . . .You have to be willing to *speak up* and to step out." Likewise, a protester said that participating gave "us an enormous opportunity to be smarter and grittier and *tougher* and *more vocal* (Wallace 2017)." *Fox News* (2017) quoted comedian Chelsea Handler's speech, which echoed these themes: "The only thing you can do when you have a setback is to step forward and continue to *fight* and *use your voice.*" *Politico's* Dovere and Schor (2017) also reported interviewing a woman who focused on anger as a mobilizing force: "Immediate *outrage* and sustained *outrage* are two different things. I'm gearing up to be *mad as hell* for a long time." Weber et al.'s (2018: 2300) analysis of protest signs highlighted women's anger and power: "A woman's place is in the *resistance*," "It is time for women to stop being *politely angry*," and "I'm 83 and I'm *mad* as hell."

March activists were innovators, portraying a new style of protest that drew on gendered symbolism. In addition to pussyhats, homemade signs illustrated a reappropriation of "pussy" and other terms linked to the vagina: "Cunt touch this," "Public cervix announcement: Fuck you," and "Labia majority" (Weber et al. 2018: 2301). Other signs merged popular culture with feminist messages like "Fight like a girl" and "I got 99 problems and white heteronormative patriarchy is all of them" (Weber et al. 2018: 2305). Weber et al. (2018: 2308) concluded that these messages capture personalized politics that signify "the meanings of a new massive political moment for feminism . . . by reinterpreting existing forms of popular feminism."

News media coverage indicated that participants were drawn to the march because they were concerned about potential losses in women's power. One protester connected the march with a legacy of women's activism. She told a reporter that the pace of progress had been "small, incremental" in the 1920s with the right to vote and that there was "a lot more progress in the 1970s (Wallace 2017)." After the 2016 election, "Now women are really worried. . . . Women have seen progress, and I think they're really afraid that they're going to lose it" (Wallace 2017). Activists called Trump's election "a real wake-up call" and the march "an awakening" from complacency and "the first page of the next chapter" (Wallace 2017). Another participant said, "We've just triggered the next wave of feminism" (Wallace 2017). Likewise, another participant said the words "agency" and "control" while explaining that she was marching so her daughters would have rights in the future: "I want my daughters to have *agency* and have *control* over their bodies and feel comfortable in the country. . . . We don't agree with what is happening right now and we are taking a stand" (Hartocollis and Alcindor 2017). A reporter concluded that the march itself ushered in a new wave of feminist activism:

> I heard a number of familiar themes about why women are going and what they hope to accomplish: They want to mobilize women, end complacency surrounding women's rights and encourage a level of activism not seen since the women's movement of the 1970s (Wallace 2017).

Concern for women's rights in the future led many protesters to bring their children to the march. As Wortham (2017) reported, "By some descriptions, the turnouts were multigenerational and multiracial. And it's true that there were children everywhere, and their presence was one of the more hopeful notes of the day's events, suggesting a long future of activism." In a *CNN* article, Wallace

(2017) reported that one protester "immediately bought tickets for herself and her 12-year-old daughter to attend. Despite never having organized a march before, she reached out to one of the national organizers and offered her services." Wallace also interviewed a protester who brought her 11-year-old daughter in hopes that it would be "a stepping stone to her own activism and the activism of all the other younger girls who attend." Another protester who brought her 14-year-old daughter to the march said, "In order to feel like a part of the change, you need to be there and be present and be active in what's going on" (Wallace 2017). Hartocollis and Alcindor (2017) documented multigenerational groups of activists and highlighted the involvement of a 6-year-old:

> Plenty of children attended the march with parents and grandparents. Along the route, Annabel Lui, 6, stood on a bench proudly holding a sign that said: "Little Donald, you've been a bad boy. Now go to your room for the next four years." Passers-by stopped to watch as she chanted, "Trump has to go!"

The intergenerational presence expresses great hope for the future of women's rights.

FIGURE 2.3 A Young Girl at the 2017 Women's March Wearing a Girl Scouts USA Sash and Holding a Sign That Reads "Respect Women of Color"

Source: Clinton Edminster/Retrieved from Women's March on Washington Collection, Archives for Research on Women and Gender. Special Collections and Archives, Georgia State University. Reprinted with permission.

The Women's March was directly connected to the #MeToo movement. Pussy-hats suggest this connection, as do the content of signs. News media articles also implied these links. For example, actress Ashley Judd was quoted as saying, "They 'ain't for grabbing. . . .They are for birthing new generations of filthy, vulgar, nasty, proud, Christian, Muslim, Buddhist, Sikh, you name it, for new generations of nasty women'" (Hartocollis and Alcindor 2017). Similarly, one protester, who was 20 years old, held a "Nasty Woman" sign and said, "We're here saying, no, people do not have permission to grab women without our permission" (Hartocollis and

FIGURE 2.4   Examples of 2017 Women's March Protest Signs: "Sister Act," "This Pussy Grabs Back," and "We March On!"

Source: Ted Eytan/Retrieved through Flickr and reprinted under CC-BY-SA 2.0.

Alcindor 2017). Likewise, a 23-year-old woman told a *CNN* reporter that women should "have the right to be in this world without fear" (Fox and Mackintosh 2017). Thus, the links between the Women's March and #MeToo were evident in how protesters understood their involvement.

Tactics emphasized women's power and collective identities as women. For example, Hartocollis and Alcindor (2017) reported that signs read "You can't comb over misogyny" and "You can't comb over sexism" (accompanied by a drawing of Trump's hair). Smith-Spark (2017) documented protest chants that emphasized women's collective identities: "'Women united will never be defeated' and 'When women's rights are under attack, what do we do, *stand up, fight back*.' Some carried banners with messages such as 'Girl *Power* vs. Trump Tower' and 'Dump the Trump.'"

The Women's March energized both women candidates and supportive voters, and women increased their electoral power in the 2018 midterm elections. For example, in a *CNN* article titled "What's Next for Women's March Participants," Grinberg (2017) said that one goal was to "recruit more women for public

FIGURE 2.5 Example of 2017 Women's March Tactics: A Protester Carrying an Inflatable Penis with the Words "Only Dicks Are Scared of Empowered Chicks"

Source: Clinton Edminster/Retrieved from Women's March on Washington Collection, Archives for Research on Women and Gender. Special Collections and Archives, Georgia State University. Reprinted with permission.

service," while another was to "prepare for the [2018] Midterms." Siegfried (2017) summarized the goals of the march in terms of seizing political power: "More important, perhaps, than their message was their intent: Many saw themselves as the nucleus of a legitimate opposition movement that could have a real impact on policy and elections for years to come." The march was thus tied to other changes in the gender revolution.

Intersectionality and the Women's March

In a now classic photo from the Women's March, a Black woman named Angela Peoples held a sign that said, "Don't Forget: White Women Voted for Trump" (Wortham 2017). Protest signs analyzed by Weber et al. (2018) captured similar critiques of feminism. As we saw earlier in the controversy over pussyhats, concerns about a lack of attention to intersectionality plagued the march. Yet this concern was not universally shared; some activists and scholars have argued that intersectional concerns were woven into the march. Based on an analysis of news media coverage, we find that the march was portrayed as emphasizing diversity and intersectionality, rather than homogeneity, with the pussyhat critiques a notable exception.

Articles criticizing the march for focusing on the concerns of white women at the expense of women of color were present but rare. In advance of the protest, the *New York Times* featured an article about racial divisions in the march, quoting a Black march volunteer who "advised 'white allies' to listen more and talk less" (Stockman 2017). After reading her social media post, a white woman who had planned to attend decided to cancel her trip, telling Stockman (2017), "'This is a women's march. . . . We're supposed to be allies in equal pay, marriage, adoption. Why is it now about, 'White women don't understand black women?'"

Research has revealed that some of the racial, ethnic, and religious rifts that fractured the Women's March were intentionally created outside of the United States. Over 150 Russian accounts produced divisive social media material about march organizer Linda Sarsour, who is Muslim. Over social media, "Russia's troll factories and its military intelligence service put a sustained effort into discrediting the movement" (Barry 2022). People responsible for creating divisive social media posts have said that the goal of this initiative was to exploit divisions and shift discourse. Russia targeted feminism as a movement that seeks to break down traditional values (Barry 2022).

Racial divisions, including those that were fabricated, received media attention. News outlets reported that while women of color demanded more representation on the leadership team, some white women thought that the march should be concerned more exclusively with gender issues and labeled women of color as "divisive" (Adelman 2017). One op-ed argued that "the loudest criticism of the march has come not from Trump supporters; rather, it has come from participants who argue that women of color have hijacked the event by focusing it on themselves, instead of women more broadly" (Adelman 2017). Another example comes from an op-ed that appeared in *CNN* titled "What the Women's March Was Missing." The author, Zito (2017), critiqued the protest:

> Billed as the Women's March on Washington it was somewhat diverse, but was mostly filled with white women, many middle aged, many part of the feminist movement from the '70s who brought their daughters and granddaughters, with a serious amount of them dressed in bright pink vagina costumes, or pussycat pink knit caps.

Wortham (2017) critiqued the protest signs that were "infuriatingly lifted from moments in black culture," including "We Shall Overcomb" (referring to Trump's hair). Other signs held by white protesters offered support in infantilizing ways, such as one that read "We love our Muslim, Immigrant, L.G.B.T.Q., Latin Brothers and Sisters" (Wortham 2017).

Although the Women's March was criticized by some activists and journalists for privileging the concerns of white women, scholars have found that the protest was quite intersectional and focused on concerns of women from diverse backgrounds. There was demographic diversity among the protesters, as well as diversity in reasons for attending (Fisher et al. 2017). In one sample of participants, 85 percent were women, 23 percent were women of color, and the median age was 43 (Fisher et al. 2017). Additionally, while over half of surveyed participants attended the protest as a result of their concerns for women's rights, protesters also attended out of concern for a host of other social issues (Dow et al. 2017; Fisher et al. 2017). Over 40 percent of those surveyed cited "equality" as one of their top reasons for attending, while about a quarter referred to social welfare, reproductive rights, or the environment, and 15 to 19 percent cited racial justice, LGBTQ rights, politics/voting, or immigration as their top reasons (Fisher et al. 2017). Fisher et al. (2017: 2) also found that participants were motivated both by issues related to their identities and by issues that were not necessarily directly salient, suggesting "intersectional motivations for participating." These scholars concluded that "the Women's March was different in that its protesters were seemingly engaged in intersectional activism—a version of activism that is sensitive to how race, class, gender and sexuality complicate inequality" (Dow et al. 2017).

Our analysis of the news media also indicates that diversity and intersectionality were key components of the march. Nicolini and Hansen's (2018) analysis of key messages in media frames supported these findings. In an op-ed in the *New York Times*, Adelman (2017) said that intersectionality was central to the march's organizers: "The march [is] a chance to embrace a new model of organizing, instead of rallying around single issues." As one organizer stated, "This is a women-led march focused on the idea that women's rights are human rights. . . .

But we wanted to push that further: that women are intersectional human beings who live multi-issued lives" (Adelman 2017). Adelman (2017) concluded that "rather than dragging down social justice movements by pushing to see themselves reflected in them," women of color in the Women's March "are well positioned to lead as people who understand interconnected systems of oppression and how to fight them."

In various news outlets, protesters were quoted as expressing positive views about the focus on diversity. For example, one protester said, "I am a woman of color and I am an immigrant"; she saw the march as "completely inclusive" (Rogers 2016). Similarly, in an op-ed, a march participant Siegfried (2017) described its diversity as follows: "It was made up of women of every background—black, white and brown; moderate and radical; urban and rural; rich and poor; Christian, Muslim and Jew—united in their belief in women's rights." In an interview with *CNN*, Andrea Mercado, co-chairwoman of an immigrants' rights organization, described the march as focusing on both gender and immigrants' rights: "In this moment when we know so many actions will be taken against women, immigrants and refugees, we need to find ways to stay together" (Grinberg 2017). In another *CNN* article, a protester (who described herself as "I'm a shade of brown, and I'm a woman") summed up her multiple reasons for marching in Washington as "concerns about tolerance, misogyny, reproductive rights, climate change" (Wallace 2017). Likewise, *Politico* quoted a woman who said that she was marching to "fight" for her 9-year-old daughter, as well as "all Americans, whether you're black, white, Latino, Muslim, gay" (Schor and Conway 2017). Finally, in a letter to the editor, Freeman (2017) spoke out as a white woman concerned about racism:

> Too many of us who are white and consider ourselves progressive are silent about racism. We say we're against racism, yet we do nothing about it. I am a 76-year-old white woman from Mississippi. I am taking the bus to the Women's March on Washington because I am convinced such public actions are essential to a healthy democracy. I invite other women to march with me in Washington, and urge us to break our silence about racism.

These intersections suggest themes of unity, which were also present on protesters' signs (e.g., "Stronger TogetHER" and "We are all in this together" [Weber et al. 2018]).

Protesters outside of the United States also cited reasons for attending that focused on intersections between gender and other issues, including climate change, racial justice, disability status, sexuality, religion, and immigration status. Reporting on London's march, Fox and Mackintosh (2017) described diversity in its composition: "There were mothers, wives, sisters, daughters, husbands, fathers, brothers and sons; their ages ranged from those in strollers to people with walkers and they were united in a message of solidarity with women around the world."

FIGURE 2.6 Example Expression of Intersectionality at the 2017 Women's March: A Protest Sign Featuring Women of Different Racial and Ethnic Backgrounds in a Rosie the Riveter Stance with the Words "We Can All Do It!"

Source: Lisa Flaherty/Retrieved from Women's March on Washington Collection, Archives for Research on Women and Gender. Special Collections and Archives, Georgia State University. Reprinted with permission.

One protester in London told *CNN* that she marched as a result of her concerns "as a disabled person and an LGBT person" (Fox and Mackintosh 2017). Smith-Spark (2017) said of London's march, "Women's rights weren't the only issue on the agenda, with placards also bearing slogans to do with Brexit, nuclear weapons, workers' rights and lesbian, gay, bisexual and transgender rights." *Fox News* (2017), reporting on a march in Copenhagen, Denmark, quoted organizer Lesley-Ann Brown, who emphasized people with diverse backgrounds coming together: "Nationalist, racist and misogynistic trends are growing worldwide and threaten the most marginalized groups in our societies including women, people of color, immigrants, Muslims, the LGBT community and people with disabilities." In Cape Town, South Africa, protesters carried signs that read "climate change is a women's issue" (Smith-Spark 2017). Taken together, our analysis of the news media stories suggest that the Women's March brought together a diverse group of protesters focused on both gender issues and issues that intersected with gender, such as racism and climate change.

"Call Me a Sexist, But . . .": Resisters Object to the Women's March

Although most of the news articles supported the idea that social change was positive, some resisters attempted to dampen its effects. For example, one reporter sarcastically objected to the "disgusting signs" at the march, emphasizing that women protesters should have acted "nice" instead:

> Some of the signs and T-shirts these women wore were putrid and vulgar. "This bitch bites." "Pussy Power." "Nasty Women Make A Difference." "I Have a Vagina and I Vote." "Good Women Never Change History." (Tell that to Rosa Parks.) "Dykes Against Trump." And other such *niceties.* I even saw young girls, high school age and younger, accompanied by their parents with these *disgusting* signs (Moore 2017).

Resisting the social change that the Women's March was pushing for, some journalists rejected protesters' deviation from stereotypical, traditional gender norms. Moore (2017) critiqued the utility of swearing for undermining their own cause by resorting to the "vulgarity" that is typical of men:

> Do these women understand that the B word and the C word and the D word and the P word are terms men use in the locker room to disparage and objectify women? Do they want these terms to become part of *polite* company? Women were outraged—rightly so—when Trump used these disgraceful words. Now they retaliate against him by using the same language? The marchers seemed to believe that resorting to vulgarity is a measure of women's empowerment. They seemed to be saying: Look at me. I can cuss like a sailor. The chains are off. We are liberated, because we can be as profane as the men. *Call me a sexist, but* I hold women to higher standards of conduct than men.

This reporter resisted women's anger and use of confrontational, gender-nontraditional language.

Fox News quoted several commentators who objected to the tactics and language deployed in the protest. Zito (2017) objected to the focus on "'pussy' hats and vagina costumes," pointing out that protesters have the potential to "just become a sideshow and side story about people unhappy about election results." In another article, Erickson (2017) likened the protest to a strike among people who are "aggrieved sore losers." He said that the women are "without any actual grievances" and mocked their approach. Erickson (2017) trivialized women's work by comparing it to his own, which he implied had greater importance, as he financially supported his ill wife:

> They will call on *all women everywhere to stop making sandwiches and stay out of the kitchen* or wherever else they work, *not that all of them have real jobs.* They want the world to see what it would be like if leftwing women did not show up to work. What they will really show is what *sore losers* they continue to be and how good they really have it. These leftwing women, many of whom have already gone on strike from shaving their legs and general hygiene, will simply not show up for work.

Erickson (2017) pointed out that these women have "privilege" and are "well off." In contrast, he portrayed his own work as more important for the insurance it provided to treat his wife's cancer. These kinds of critiques suggest a growing rift between innovators and resisters.

"We Want Just to Have the Same Rights as They Do": Attitudes toward Feminism after the Women's March

Typically, social movements seek to diffuse their ideology to the general public. Historically, this diffusion has included shifts in attitudes toward women's issues and feminism more broadly. Yet the development of feminist consciousness, including the conditions that both promote and impede its development, is complex. Elsewhere, Aronson (2018) defined "gender consciousness" as an awareness of women's political and social interests as women. This awareness, and the salience of gender, can take a wide variety of forms. Some women develop a gender consciousness based on an affirmation of women's traditional roles or blend traditional and nontraditional self-conceptions or frames. Additionally, feminist consciousness, an awareness and critique of gender inequalities and patriarchy, differs from feminist identity, as some who reject gender inequality do not identify as feminists per se (Aronson 2017b). The same is true for the #MeToo movement: People may express support for the movement, its frames, and ideology without embracing a feminist identity. Thus, identification with #MeToo is not necessarily associated with identification with the ideas of feminism more broadly or with embracing feminism as an identity.

The movement itself articulates a frame that rejects inequalities; diffusion occurs as ordinary women begin to question inequalities in their own lives. Yet even if they reject inequalities, the general public may or may not explicitly embrace feminism. In the second wave, women often came to feminism as a result of their experiences with discrimination and harassment (Martin et al. 2002) or through consciousness-raising groups, which helped women to recognize oppression as a social pattern rather than an individual problem (Hercus 2005). One measure of "success" of a movement is determined by how far its ideologies extend.

From the mid-1980s to the 2000s, about 30 to 40 percent of women called themselves feminists, which is about the same percentage of people who labeled themselves as Republicans or Democrats (Ferree and Hess 1995). Yet in the four years immediately following the 2016 election and 2017 Women's March, the popularity of feminism reached an "all time high" (Watson 2020). According to a Pew Research study in 2020, the majority of women overall (61 percent), as well as the majority of those from all education levels and ages, said that "'feminist' describes them very (19 percent) or somewhat (42 percent) well" (Barroso 2020). Reflecting the political generation in which they came of age (see Aronson 2000; Aronson 2003), middle-aged women (aged 30–64) were less likely to identify with feminism when compared with women aged 18–29 or those 65 and older (Barroso 2020). There were differences by education level and political party identification, with college-educated and Democratic or Democratic-leaning women more likely to identify with feminism (Barroso 2020). Still, 42 percent of Republican and Republican-leaning women said that "feminist" described them and a majority (54 percent) of those with a high school diploma or less also agreed (Barroso 2020). Likewise, 79 percent of adults believed that gender equality is "very important" (Watson 2020). Thus, feminism became more popular among the general public after the 2016 election and the Women's March.

Yet the term "feminism" is polarizing and gender differences emerge in assessments of attitudes. Nationally, 4 in 10 men said that this term describes them at least "somewhat well," with Democratic men at 54 percent and Republican men at only 26 percent (Barroso 2020). Likewise, only 42 percent of all genders viewed feminism as inclusive and 45 percent thought that it is polarizing. As Barroso (2020) explained, these views are gendered: "Women are more likely than men to associate feminism with positive attributes like empowering and inclusive, while men are more likely than women to see feminism as polarizing and outdated."

Some women exhibit feminist consciousness but reject a feminist identity (Aronson 2017b). Historically, women of color, working-class women, and lesbians felt marginalized in the second-wave women's movement and have argued that the movement did not address their concerns (Collins 1990; Reger 2012). Additionally, due to racial segregation and economic exploitation, some women of color may emphasize racial and class oppression over gender oppression (Chow 1987). That is, for women of color, racial consciousness might be more salient and politicized than feminist consciousness. Research also has suggested that young women may exhibit an awareness of inequalities while rejecting a feminist identity (Aronson 2003).

And yet feminism is often *lived* through women's everyday experiences rather than being an ideology that one either embraces or rejects (Aronson 2008). In fact, feminist consciousness has been influenced by the simultaneous diffusion and depoliticization of feminism. Despite ambivalence about the term "feminism," themes of women's independence and self-development have infused nearly every aspect of our culture (Aronson 2008). That is, women conceptualize their future lives in ways that defy traditional gender expectations (Gerson 2010), such as expecting to have fulfilling jobs and supporting themselves financially (Aronson 2008). As a result of the way that feminism has become diffused into our cultural norms, it is paradoxically "everywhere and nowhere": Feminism has profoundly influenced women's lives while simultaneously appearing to be invisible (Reger 2012). The "semiconscious" (Stacey 1991) and "unconscious" (Reger 2012) adoption of feminist ideologies affects women's lives. In fact, women may be "living feminism" by incorporating feminist ideologies and attitudes in their life course plans and expectations (Aronson 2008).

Studying feminism as a label and identity is complex, as it is often based on stereotypes and feminism's exclusionary history. One way to capture the complexity and ambiguity associated with the term "feminism" is to view it as a continuum of identification (Aronson 2003; Aronson 2017b). While previous research has explored this continuum of identification in relation to the "postfeminist" generation (Aronson 2003) and women activists (Aronson 2017b), our focus group interviews offer insights into attitudes toward feminism for non-activists of all genders. In the analysis that follows, we examine focus group participants' responses to the question, "What are your views of feminism?" In doing so, we created a continuum of feminist identification that is modified from earlier work (Aronson 2003). These findings suggest that feminism has been diffused to non-activists, particularly women, in the post-Women's March era and, as expected, women were more supportive of feminism than were men.

"I Support Feminism"

On one end of a continuum is support for feminism without qualifications. Although time limitations did not allow space to ask each participant directly about their identities in relation to feminism, a number of the women in our focus groups stated that they identified themselves as feminists. Drawing on a collective identity with other women, Maram, a 21-year-old Middle Eastern woman, said simply, "I'm a feminist." Alyssa, a 29-year-old Black woman, immediately agreed, "I identify as a feminist as well." When asked what feminism meant to them and how they define it, Maram emphasized equality of opportunity and used the word "we" to indicate a collective identity: "Everyone should have an *equal* chance at life. The world is so full of opportunities and *we* shouldn't be discriminated against or barred from trying to pursue those opportunities." Alyssa agreed, also using the word "we," "*We* want everyone to have rights. *We* want everyone to have equal rights." She said that men often view feminism as "bashing of men." Aligning herself with the other women by using the word "we" while adversarially calling men "they," Alyssa said, "*We* want just to have the same rights as *they* do."

Interviewees who took this approach were critical of anti-feminists. For example, Alex, a 21-year-old multiracial nonbinary interviewee, explained that feminism "gets thrown around a lot without knowing the nuances of what the word means and the history it has." They pointed out that many people associated feminism with anger and activism: People "have this idea that the raging feminist, the person that yells, screams, goes to protests, that that's it, that's all there is." Alex, who identified as a feminist, distanced themself from these stereotypes. Rima, a 20-year-old Middle Eastern woman, said, "It's a really great movement." Rima thought that people who were critical of feminism need to "actually research it and look at what it is" rather than "representing it in the wrong way." She said that if "people understand what it is, then they would be a part of the movement, not criticizing it all the time."

Interviewees pointed out that stereotypes assume that feminists dislike men. For example, Isabella, a 21-year-old Latinx woman, said, "A lot of people assume 'feminist' is someone who hates men and they're anti-men. But actually it's equality between both genders." Laughing, Isabella said that she had some conflict with her "anti-feminist" father: "When it comes to feminism, he doesn't understand it at all and he has a perception that I'm anti-men." Nadine, a 20-year-old white woman, agreed that "people don't know the definition of feminism too well, because they don't think of themselves as feminists." She explained, "You don't have to be a man hater to be a feminist. Clearly, you don't know what a feminist is. I feel like more people would say, 'Oh, I'm a feminist,' if they knew what that term was." Similarly, Christina, a 36-year-old Black woman, identified with feminism but was also concerned about stereotypes:

> I consider myself a feminist. I hate the fact that men think that when we push for issues with change, men feel like they're excluded. People get this idea that, "Oh, they're bitchy and they're man haters. They don't want to take baths and they don't want to shave their legs."

Christina went on to explain that feminists like her (who she called "we") "get bad names because men think that we're trying to exclude them all together, like we want a world full of women, and women in power." She continued, emphasizing ideologies rooted in equality, "It's not that. It's just we want to be treated as equals professionally, in our relationships, our friendships. We just want to be treated equally." This emphasis on equality was an important focus for those who embraced feminism.

In one focus group, six women discussed their support of feminism and their concerns about stereotypes, which undermined equality. In the discussion, some of these women emphasized their collective identity as women ("we," italicized here) in contrast to men ("they," italicized here), whose masculinity was "in jeopardy":

Zainab: [32-year-old Middle Eastern woman] If you say that you're a feminist, it's basically like a curse word. Guys say, "Oh, you're just a feminist."

Kayla: [21-year-old Black woman] As an insult.

Zainab: Yeah, exactly. *They're* just taking it as not rational, and-

Kim: [27-year-old white woman] Man hater.

Zainab: Yeah, exactly. Man hater, not rational, very highly emotional, and just want women to take over the world. No, *we* just want to be taken seriously.

Kim: *Men* make fun of it on purpose because *they* want to delegitimize it. *They're* interpreting it as anti-man, so if I make fun of this and enough people feel embarrassed to call themselves a feminist, maybe people will stop doing it.

Zainab: Yeah, make fun of it because I don't want to be seen as a feminist. I don't want my masculinity to be in jeopardy.

Kim: Or if you're a girl and you're a feminist, and you have a lot of guy friends, suddenly you're not the cool girl anymore. You're not the laid-back girl, you're the feminazi.

Zainab: Yeah like, unshaved legs and armpit hair and no bras. Right.

Riley: [18-year-old Black woman] The extremes of a group are seen. So 99 percent of feminists don't really identify with that, but the 1 percent who do are what's heard. And that just kind of ruins the label for everyone else.

Aria: [21-year-old woman] It's just so weird how "feminist" is such a negative connotation. I had to defend myself and say, "Look, these are statistics." People think that feminism is only one way.

Jada: [18-year-old Black woman] Everyone's just focused on that stereotype for that whole group. There's all these different definitions for what feminism really is.

This focus group discussion suggests an adversarial relationship between genders, illustrates support for feminism, and recognizes that there are many stereotypes associated with the label. It also expresses concerns about those who draw on stereotypes to trivialize and undermine feminism.

There was only one focus group man who supported feminism without quali-
fication. Like the women above, Sang, a 19-year-old Asian American man, agreed
that feminism was an ideology of equality: "The way I view feminism personally is
not tearing men down, but bringing men and women equal opportunities, rights."
He distinguished his perception with how feminism "is portrayed in social media" as

> a lot more about women wanting to have more power than men, gaining the
> sort of control that men have had over females for the past years and genera-
> tions. People assume that's feminism, but I don't think that's what it is. It's just
> females trying to get the same opportunities, the same rights, same pay as men.

This perspective was atypical among the focus group men.

"I Support Feminism, But . . ."

In contrast to those who expressed unequivocal support for feminism, some interviewees were supportive but also distanced themselves from the negative connotations associated with feminism, particularly "extremism." Using the word "but" to
distinguish what she disagreed with, Amelia, a 20-year-old multiracial woman, said,
"I think feminism is good, *but* the extremist in every group, like feminism, is what
you see on the media." Amelia objected to people who said "get rid of all the men"
and "we should be running every position. We are the best gender." She concluded,
modifying her support, "Feminism itself is good, *but* the extremists that are leading
it are bad." For Caleb, a 21-year-old white man, feminism was seen as "inherently
necessary and a good thing," yet he emphasized the primacy of individual rights
over collective solutions to inequality: "I would probably label myself a feminist.
And I agree with gender equality and the rights of women." At the same time, he
expressed concern about feminism's focus on strengthening the role of government
to create change. Caleb wanted to "take a step back from feminism" at times when it
"tries to affect others outside of the individual by growing the state." In his view, the
rights of individuals took precedence over collective and governmental solutions to
gender inequality. As seen throughout our research, the focus group men tended to
view gender inequalities in an individualized (and less collective) framework than the
women. The women more often embraced collective solutions to social problems,
which is itself rooted in women's movement frame-building and collective identity.

Reflecting historical exclusion from the women's movement, some of the
women of color critiqued feminism for failing to address their concerns (see also
Aronson 2017b). Noting this history, Brianna, a 21-year-old Black woman, said,
"Historically feminism was originally for white women." Brianna was careful to
point out that she supported a particular type of feminism, "intersectional feminism," which recognized multiple oppressions. This type of feminism "is more for
all women because that includes Black women, that includes Hispanic women,

Asian women, every woman, that includes all women. Intersectionality is a major part of feminism. When you're included in intersectionality, then yes," she supported feminism. Although their reasons differed, the participants who took this modified approach supported feminism yet also distanced themselves from the label.

"I'm Not a Feminist, But . . ."

In the next place on the continuum, interviewees distanced themselves from feminism while endorsing many of the principles of feminist ideology. For example, Grayson, a 22-year-old Middle Eastern man, supported feminism but used the word "but" to qualify his support: "Feminism certainly has its place in modern society when there is systemic sexism. I think that there is value in feminism. *But* you have to understand where it starts and where it ends. It becomes murky." In this example, Grayson stops short of calling himself a feminist.

Although prior work suggested that interviewees in this category were often quite privileged in their racial and class backgrounds (Aronson 2003), the focus group participants who took this approach were often from disadvantaged racial and ethnic backgrounds. In fact, several women of color did not define themselves as feminists because they viewed it as a white women's movement. Alexandra, a 38-year-old Black woman, qualified her support with the word "but": "I can support, *but* not feminism. I'm probably *not* a feminist. *But* I'm not anti-feminist. *But* it's not for Black women." Alexandra continued, using the words "us/our/we" and "them/their/they" to distinguish between Black and white women, "Feminism is not for *us*. It's for white women. It works great for *them*, but it's not for *us* because historically *our* issues are not *their* issues. *We* never had a problem with sharing household duties" with men. Alexandra commented specifically on the 2017 Women's March to explain that Black women's concerns are often secondary:

> Actually, unfortunately, feminism has worked *against* Black women because, even with the Women's March and with women's marches historically, *they* put Black women's issues on the side. Birth control has never been our issue or being able to raise families.

Alexandra expressed concerns that "white women just wanted to bring us into the folds to support the numbers." She concluded by saying that she saw herself "as a womanist" but then immediately qualified it by tacking on the word "maybe." Kayla made similar points:

> I'm sure you have heard the term "white feminism." A lot of people who call themselves feminists don't recognize how intersectional everything is. I am Black and I am a woman. And those things aren't parallel to each other, they intersect.

Kayla continued, qualifying her support of feminism, "It's not that I don't want to say I'm a feminist, *but* I want to make sure that it's clear that I recognize the differences in the plight of a woman, depending on her circumstances." The "I'm not a feminist, but" perspective was more supportive of feminism than the remainder of the views.

"I'm a Fence-Sitter"

Next on the continuum, the fence-sitting approach reveals a paradoxical support for some feminist issues, as well as ambiguity toward the negative connotations of "feminism." This group valued some aspects of feminism yet emphasized ambivalence about, or critiques of, feminism. Jasmine, a 40-year-old Black woman, was one of the few women who took this approach:

> I want equal rights, *but* I don't want to do certain things. You know how some people say, "Well, if somebody hits, hit him back?" No, don't hit me back. I'm a woman. No, change my tire. I want to stay a woman.

This belief in traditional feminine roles led Jasmine to avoid taking a position on feminism.

Focus group men often espoused support for some aspects of equal rights. Carter, a 21-year-old Middle Eastern man, started by saying "I think it's a great movement." He then used the words "well" and "but" to explain that feminists ("they") go too far: "*Well* again, there's a bell curve. Most people who are feminists are doing the right thing. *But* there's also people who just really strongly identify with the feminist movement and *they* just take it *way over the top*." Similarly, Xiu, a 22-year-old Asian American man, said that there "should be a fine line between getting women more opportunity in order to accelerate their growth and pushing the woman forward to give them more opportunities" and "putting men down." Anthony, a 35-year-old Black man, embraced equality yet expressed negative views of feminism: "I agree with equality, a *part* of feminism, where I feel that women should actually be equal to men." Anthony's girlfriend, who he called "super feminist," wanted to see women win in political races, a perspective he called "sexist": "That's sexist to me. I feel like, 'No, I thought you were about equality.'" He described an absence of "equality rhetoric," as feminists, who he called "they," focus on "man privilege" and "toxic masculinity" while ignoring "female privilege" and "female, feminine toxic-ness or whatever." Anthony stressed that there are inherent gender differences that feminists (who he called "you" in an adversarial way) fail to recognize: "If *your* whole base is equality, *you* have to talk about both sides. Men and women are *different*. Women are better at some things and men are better at some things." The fence-sitting approach thus is careful to distinguish the parts of feminism that participants either endorse or reject.

"I Never Thought about Feminism"

At the next spot on the continuum were interviewees who had no opinion about feminism or had substantial difficulty defining the term itself. For example, Noah, a 33-year-old multiracial man, said, "I've never heard the same definition of feminism twice. So I don't even know how to comment." Jeremiah, who is 36 and multiracial, expressed positive views about feminism, then confusion: "Feminism is a pretty great concept, as far as it meaning equality for all people. And I think that we get confused on what that means." As found previously, some interviewees in this category conflated the term "feminist" with "feminine" (Aronson 2003). For example, when asked about feminism, Laila, a 43-year-old Black woman, focused on feminine and masculine gender roles: "I know a lady who can put a car together and go get her nails done. I have a friend that dresses jazzy, drives an eighteen-wheeler." These participants thus had not given feminism much thought because of the confusion surrounding its very definition.

"I Don't Agree with Feminism"

On the other end of the continuum is a rejection of feminism. Some focus group men (but not women) rejected feminism altogether or were ardently anti-feminist. For example, Jin, a 21-year-old Asian American man, believed that men and women "are different" and criticized feminists: "Some feminists, oh, my God, it becomes a headache. Sometimes feminists, extreme feminists, go a little overboard." Ethan, a 28-year-old white man, thought that feminism and the #MeToo movement hurt men: "I think feminism is a man-hating movement. I honestly think that men are being degraded a little bit as a gender by the feminist movement." He said, "We should build up women instead of tear down men," and then took aim at #MeToo: "With the #MeToo movement, instead of bringing up all these stories, those stories should be brought up in the right place and at the right time." Ethan turned the focus to an individualized solution to the social problem of sexual assault: parents' "obligation to teach their children to defend themselves and defend their chastity."

Several men questioned feminism's focus on equality. Ahmad, a 21-year-old Middle Eastern man, thought there was "definitely a double standard within feminism." In his view, the focus should be on "equity rather than equality." Likewise, Aran said that men and women are "not necessarily equal on everything. It's just whatever is fair." Luke, a 22-year-old white man, said that "feminism is supposed to be equality between men and women," while he pointed out that people distort this concept by arguing for "equality for where they see fit and not equality everywhere." Deven, a 20-year-old Asian American man, agreed, "Men don't really have representation in the movement, so it's not really equality." Aran went on to call "the extremists in the group, feminazis." Luke agreed, laughing, "The feminazis that are saying, 'All men must die,' and things like that."

As they viewed systemic inequalities in individualized terms, focus group men often questioned the need for feminism today. For example, Thiago, a 25-year-old Latinx man, argued that feminism was of limited value, "Personally, I question the need for feminism today. There are no institutional barriers against race, color, creed, I mean we killed that." Although he repeated three times that he understood "that there are social barriers that exist," Thiago ultimately took an individualized approach to addressing those barriers, calling for "understanding core values with individual human beings." He asserted that individuals can overcome barriers through equal opportunity rather than social movements that focus on systemic oppression:

> *But* we all have equal opportunity. I understand that social barriers exist *but* we have the ability to break down those barriers. I struggle with the importance of the feminist movement today, considering that there aren't any institutional barriers that exist.

In summary, gender differences were pronounced in the focus group participants' attitudes toward feminism, with women more supportive and men more likely to critique feminism and take an individualized approach to gender inequalities.

Conclusion

This chapter combines an analysis of focus group interviews with news media and organizational data to capture how the Women's March catalyzed the gender revolution. Organizational and news media data uncover its broad base. Sponsoring organizations included those that were explicitly feminist, as well as a wide range of other organizations concerned with the environment, human rights, and racial justice. March tactics illustrated a gendered social movement frame, expressing women's power through images rooted in concerns about inequalities. Women espoused a collective identity, a "we," through their language and movement tactics. News media analysis lends evidence to the intersectional nature of the march, as quoted participants stressed the diverse backgrounds of protesters and issues of concern. Protesters drew on a social movement frame that highlighted gender and women's power, emphasizing women's collective identity in ways that included an intersectional understanding of inequalities. Despite some critical articles, most of the news media overall (even conservative outlets like *Fox News*), depicted the Women's March as creating positive or neutral social change.

The impact of the march is visible in widespread, although gender-differentiated, attitudes toward feminism. In national surveys and among our participants, women are more likely to support feminism while men are more likely to critique it. This chapter thus documents the importance of the Women's March in the beginning of the gender revolution, as it propelled forward gendered social and cultural change.

Overall, the Women's March pushed forward innovative ideas and tactics that ordinary people supported and accepted. As the largest single-day march in U.S. history, the Women's March emphasized the acceptance of gender equality. It did so using confrontational tactics, including pussyhats, as well as signs and slogans that challenged existing patriarchal arrangements. Protesters all over the world connected protests to the #MeToo movement and called into question traditional gender norms of women's passivity and niceness. Protests drew on women's anger about the 2016 election and did not shy away from gender-nontraditional language. Focus group participants, especially women, expressed support for the march. Yet, intersectional critiques of the Women's March should not be dismissed, and focus group women of color were hesitant about feminism as a result of its history of exclusion.

A gendered chasm emerged between men's and women's views of the Women's March and feminism. Focus group women and our one nonbinary interviewee supported innovative ideas that rejected gender inequalities in both politics and their personal lives. However, the majority of focus group men resisted such social and cultural change; they more often qualified their identification with feminism or rejected it altogether.

As we will see, the march sowed the seeds for the 2018 and 2020 elections that followed it. The 2016 election, the rise of the #MeToo movement, and the Women's March are all part of the gender revolution. The 2016 election produced a groundswell of anger and a sense that women needed to "fight." Such gender-nontraditional and feminist discourses were common both within and beyond the Women's March context, in the self-presentations of politicians in subsequent elections, and in people's everyday lives.

Note

1. Although the Women's March retains its power as the largest single-day event, it has been eclipsed by Black Lives Matter in the total number of participants—15 million to 26 million people in the United States participated in demonstrations over the death of George Floyd in the weeks immediately following his death (Buchanan, Bui and Patel 2020).

References

Adelman, Lori. 2017. "How the Women's March Could Resurrect the Democratic Party." *The New York Times*. Retrieved August 20, 2022 (www.nytimes.com/2017/01/20/opinion/how-the-womens-march-could-resurrect-the-democratic-party.html).

Aronson, Pamela. 2018. "'I'm Not Voting for *Her.*' Internalized Misogyny, Feminism and Gender Consciousness in the 2016 Election." pp. 204–218 in *Nasty Women and Bad Hombres: Gender and Race in the 2016 Presidential Election*, edited by Christine Kray, Tamar Carroll, and Hinda Mandell. Rochester, NY: University of Rochester Press.

Aronson, Pamela. 2017a. Field notes from Women's March Conference, Detroit, Michigan October.

Aronson, Pamela. 2017b. "The Dynamics and Causes of Gender and Feminist Consciousness and Feminist Identities." pp. 335–353 in *The Oxford Handbook of U.S. Women's Social Movement Activism*, edited by Holly J. McCammon, Verta Taylor, Jo Reger, and Rachel L. Einwohner. New York, NY: Oxford University Press.

Aronson, Pamela. 2008. "The Markers and Meanings of Growing Up: Contemporary Young Women's Transition from Adolescence to Adulthood." *Gender & Society* 22(1):56–82.

Aronson, Pamela. 2003. "Feminists or 'Postfeminists?'": Young Women's Attitudes Toward Feminism and Gender Relations." *Gender & Society* 17(6):903–922.

Aronson, Pamela. 2000. "The Development and Transformation of Feminist Identities Under Changing Historical Conditions." *Advances in Life Course Research* 5:77–97.

Barroso, Amanda. 2020. "61% Of U.S. Women Say 'Feminist' Describes Them Well; Many See Feminism as Empowering, Polarizing." *Pew Research Center*. Retrieved August 20, 2022 (www.pewresearch.org/fact-tank/2020/07/07/61-of-u-s-women-say-feminist-describes-them-well-many-see-feminism-as-empowering-polarizing/).

Barry, Ellen. 2022. "How Russian Trolls Helped Keep the Women's March Out of Lock Step." *New York Times*. Retrieved September 18, 2022. (www.nytimes.com/2022/09/18/us/womens-march-russia-trump.html?smid=nytcore-ios-share&referringSource=artic leShare).

Buchanan, Larry, Quoctrung Bui, and Jugal K. Patel. 2020. "Black Lives Matter May Be the Largest Movement in U.S. History." *The New York Times*. Retrieved August 20, 2022 (www.nytimes.com/interactive/2020/07/03/us/george-floyd-protests-crowd-size.html).

Chow, Esther Ngan-Ling. 1987. "The Development of Feminist Consciousness Among Asian American Women." *Gender & Society* 1(3):284–299.

Collins, Patricia Hill. 1990. *Black Feminist Thought: Knowledge, Consciousness, and the Politics of Empowerment*. New York, NY: Routledge.

Dovere, Edward-Isaac and Elana Schor. 2017. "Will the Women's March Be Another Occupy, or a Democratic Tea Party?" *Politico*. Retrieved August 28, 2022 (www.politico.com/story/2017/01/womens-march-organizing-strategy-233973).

Dow, Dawn M., Dana R. Fisher, and Rashawn Ray. 2017. "This Is What Democracy Looks like!" *Sociological Images*. Retrieved August 20, 2022 (https://thesocietypages.org/socimages/2017/02/06/this-is-what-democracy-looks-like/).

Erickson, Erick. 2017. "Erick Erickson: A Day Without Overly Privileged Leftist Women Is a Great Idea." *Fox News*. Retrieved August 20, 2022 (www.foxnews.com/opinion/erick-erickson-a-day-without-overly-privileged-leftist-women-is-a-great-idea).

Ferree, Myra Marx and Beth Hess. 1995. *Controversy and Coalition the New Feminist Movement Across Four Decades of Change*. London: Taylor and Francis.

Fisher, Dana R. 2019. *American Resistance: From the Women's March to the Blue Wave*. New York, NY: Columbia University Press.

Fisher, Dana R., Dawn M. Dow, and Rashawn Ray. 2017. "Intersectionality Takes It to the Streets: Mobilizing across Diverse Interests for the Women's March." *Science Advances* 3(9):1–8.

Fox, Kara and Eliza Mackintosh. 2017. "London Marches for 'Hope Not Hate'." *CNN*. Retrieved August 20, 2022 (www.cnn.com/2017/01/21/europe/london-womens-march/index.html).

Fox News. 2017. "Hundreds of Thousands of Women Protest Against Trump." *Fox News*. Retrieved August 20, 2022 (www.foxnews.com/us/hundreds-of-thousands-of-women-protest-against-trump).

Freeman, Margery. 2017. "Race Issues and the Women's March on Washington." *The New York Times*. Retrieved August 20, 2022 (www.nytimes.com/2017/01/12/opinion/race-issues-and-the-womens-march-on-washington.html).

Gantt-Shafer, Jessica Cara Wallis, and Caitlin Miles. 2019. Intersectionality, (Dis)unity, and Processes of Becoming at the 2017 Women's March." *Women's Studies in Communication* 42(2):221–240. doi:10.1080/07491409.2019.1616021

Gerson, Kathleen. 2010. *The Unfinished Revolution: Coming of Age in a New Era of Gender, Work, and Family*. Oxford: Oxford University Press.

Gökarıksel, Banu and Sara Smith. 2017. "Intersectional Feminism Beyond U.S. Flag Hijab and Pussy Hats in Trump's America." *Gender, Place & Culture* 24(5):628–644.

Grinberg, Emanuella. 2017. "What's Next for Women's March Participants." *CNN*. Retrieved August 22, 2022 (www.cnn.com/2017/01/23/us/womens-march-next-steps/index.html).

Hamasaki, Sonya. 2017. "Pussyhat Project Tops off Women's March on Washington | CNN Politics." *CNN*. Retrieved August 20, 2022 (www.cnn.com/2017/01/20/politics/pussyhat-project-washington-march-trnd/index.html).

Hartocollis, Anemona and Yamiche Alcindor. 2017. "Women's March Highlights as Huge Crowds Protest Trump: 'We're Not Going Away'." *The New York Times*. Retrieved August 22, 2022 (www.nytimes.com/2017/01/21/us/womens-march.html).

Hercus, Cheryl. 2005. *Stepping Out of Line: Becoming and Being a Feminist*. New York, NY: Routledge.

Martin, Patricia Yancey, John R. Reynolds, and Shelley Keith. 2002. "Gender Bias and Feminist Consciousness Among Judges and Attorneys: A Standpoint Theory Analysis." *Signs: Journal of Women in Culture and Society* 27(3):665–701.

May, Katja. 2020. "The Pussyhat Project: Texturing the Struggle for Feminist Solidarity." *Journal of International Women's Studies* 21(3):77–89.

McKane, Rachel G. and Holly J. McCammon. 2018. "Why We March: The Role of Grievances, Threats, and Movement Organizational Resources in the 2017 Women's Marches." *Mobilization: An International Quarterly* 23(4):401–424.

Moore, Steve. 2017. "Steve Moore: What I Learned at the Women's March." *Fox News*. Retrieved August 22, 2022 (www.foxnews.com/opinion/steve-moore-what-i-learned-at-the-womens-march).

Moss, Pamela and Avril Maddrell. 2017. "Emergent and Divergent Spaces in the Women's March: The Challenges of Intersectionality and Inclusion." *Gender, Place & Culture* 24(5):613–620.

Nicolini, Kristine M. and Sara Steffes Hansen. 2018. "Framing the Women's March on Washington: Media Coverage and Organizational Messaging Alignment." *Public Relations Review* 44(1):1–10.

Pantsuit Nation. 2022. "Pantsuit Nation—Public." in *Facebook* public community page. Retrieved August 22, 2022 (www.facebook.com/pantsuitnation11.8/).

Reger, Jo. 2019. "The Making of a March: Identity, Intersectionality and Diffusion of U.S. Feminism." pp. 1–22 in *Nevertheless, They Persisted: Feminisms and Continued Resistance in the U.S. Women's Movement*, edited by Jo Reger. New York: Routledge.

Reger, Jo. 2012. *Everywhere and Nowhere: The State of Contemporary Feminism in the United States*. New York, NY: Oxford University Press.

Rogers, Katie. 2016. "Amid Division, a March in Washington Seeks to Bring Women Together." *The New York Times*. Retrieved August 22, 2022 (www.nytimes.com/2016/11/19/us/womens-march-on-washington.html).

Sanchez, Ray. 2017. "Here's What Celebrities and Activists Said in Fiery Women's March Speeches | CNN Politics." *CNN*. Retrieved August 22, 2022 (www.cnn.com/2017/01/21/politics/womens-march-speeches/index.html).

Schor, Elana and Madeline Conway. 2017. "Millions Join Trump Protest Marches Around the Globe." *Politico*. Retrieved August 22, 2022 (www.politico.com/story/2017/01/womens-march-dc-democratic-tensions-233945).

Siegfried, Evan. 2017. "What Republicans Have to Learn From the Women's March." *The New York Times*. Retrieved August 22, 2022 (www.nytimes.com/2017/01/23/opinion/what-republicans-have-to-learn-from-the-womens-march.html).

Smith-Spark, Laura. 2017. "Protesters Rally Worldwide in Solidarity With Washington March | CNN Politics." *CNN*. Retrieved August 22, 2022 (www.cnn.com/2017/01/21/politics/trump-women-march-on-washington/index.html).

Stacey, Judith. 1991. *Brave New Families: Stories of Domestic Upheaval in Late-Twentieth-Century America*. Berkeley, CA: University of California Press.

Stockman, Farah. 2017. "Women's March on Washington Opens Contentious Dialogues About Race." *The New York Times*. Retrieved August 22, 2022 (www.nytimes.com/2017/01/09/us/womens-march-on-washington-opens-contentious-dialogues-about-race.html).

Wallace, Kelly. 2017. "Women's March on Washington: Moms and Daughters Marching Together." *CNN*. Retrieved August 22, 2022 (www.cnn.com/2017/01/16/health/womens-march-washington-mothers-daughters/index.html).

Watson, Katarina. 2020. "Feminism's Popularity Reaches All Time Highs, Study Shows." *Ms. Magazine*. Retrieved August 22, 2022 (https://msmagazine.com/2020/08/10/feminism-popularity-reaches-all-time-highs-study-shows/).

Weber, Kirsten M., Tisha Dejmanee, and Flemming Rhode. 2018. "The 2017 Women's March on Washington: An Analysis of Protest Sign Messages." *International Journal of Communication* 12:2289–2313.

The Women's March. 2019. "Our Feminist Future." *Women's March*. Retrieved August 22, 2022 (www.womensmarch.com/).

Wortham, Jenna. 2017. "Who Didn't Go to the Women's March Matters More than Who Did." *The New York Times*. Retrieved August 22, 2022 (www.nytimes.com/2017/01/24/magazine/who-didnt-go-to-the-womens-march-matters-more-than-who-did.html).

Zito, Salena. 2017. "What the Women's March Was Missing." *CNN*. Retrieved August 22, 2022 (www.cnn.com/2017/01/23/opinions/women-why-march-zito-opinion/index.html).

PART 2

The Political

The Gender Revolution in
Electoral Politics

3

WOMEN'S POLITICAL POWER IN THE 2018 MIDTERM ELECTIONS

"Women Like Me Aren't Supposed to Run for Office": Women and Electoral Politics

In the 2018 midterm elections, Alexandria Ocasio-Cortez, a 28-year-old progressive political newcomer, defeated a ten-term Democratic representative, Joseph Crowley of New York (Harris 2018). In an ad she wrote herself, "AOC" declared,

> Women like me aren't supposed to run for office. I wasn't born to a wealthy or powerful family. Mother from Puerto Rico, dad from the South Bronx. I was born in a place where your ZIP code determines your destiny. It doesn't take 100 years to do this. It takes political courage. A New York for the many is possible. It's time for one of us (Ocasio-Cortez 2018).

This campaign revealed and expressed a collective identity that women and people of color—both politicians and voters—emphasized during the 2018 elections. Narratives of women's empowerment and their collective identity in 2018 were seen in this race for U.S. representative, as well as in state-level gubernatorial elections.

Focusing on how the 2018 elections crystalized the social changes that were already underway as part of the gender revolution, this chapter suggests that candidates' self-presentations and voters' perceptions reflect widespread cultural and social change. This election was exceptional for several reasons. First, women, especially Democrats, were elected to office in record numbers. Second, women politicians and voters played a significant role in flipping the U.S. House to a Democratic majority (Dittmar 2019). Women's intrusions into elected political office thus were lopsided in terms of political party and favored Democratic

DOI: 10.4324/9781003225331-6

women candidates. Third, women of color challenged electoral biases and were elected in districts with a majority of white voters (Dittmar 2019). Additionally, mothers of young children and young women challenged norms by running for office. Finally, in the words of political scientist Kelly Dittmar (2019), women "embraced gender as an electoral asset instead of a hurdle to overcome."

As a time with many representational "firsts," the election resulted in path-breaking diversity among the candidates elected to office (Lai et al. 2018). Women won more seats in Congress than ever before, with 25 women serving in the Senate and 101 women (with a record 43 women of color) serving in the House of Representatives (Center for American Women and Politics 2020). More openly lesbian, gay, bisexual, or transgender people were elected than in any prior election, including Colorado's Jared Polis (D-CO; the first openly gay governor to be elected in any state) and Kyrsten Sinema (D-AZ; the first woman U.S. senator from her state and first openly bisexual U.S. senator in the country) (Zraick 2018). Likewise, Ilhan Omar (D-MN) and Rashida Tlaib (D-MI) were the first Muslim women elected to Congress (Zraick 2018).

Women also made inroads into male political space in executive positions, which are often more difficult to obtain because candidates have to appeal to a wider constituency. To be elected in statewide elections, candidates need to appeal to rural, urban, and suburban voters, who typically represent varied ideological perspectives. Sixty-one women filed as candidates for governor in 2018, which was double the 2014 rate (Center for American Women and Politics 2018). In statewide elections for executive seats, nine women were elected as governors (including incumbents), seven as attorney generals, and 11 as state-level secretaries of state (Michigan made history by electing women for all three.) (Center for American Women and Politics 2020). The number of women serving as governor matched the previous records (in 2004 and 2007), and three states elected their first woman governor (Center for American Women and Politics 2018). There were eight open, nonincumbent seats for governor with women candidates (Georgia, Idaho, Kansas, Maine, Michigan, New Mexico, South Dakota, and Wyoming), five of whom were elected (Kansas, Maine, Michigan, New Mexico, and South Dakota; see Table 3.1) and three of whom became the first woman governors of their state (Maine, South Dakota, and Iowa) (Center for American Women and Politics 2018). A record number of women were also elected to state legislatures, increasing the nationwide total by 29 percent from just two years earlier (Dittmar 2019). By 2019, women comprised a historically unprecedented 28.9 percent of all state legislators, with women of color comprising 25.5 percent of these women (Dittmar 2019).

The election resulted in a shift in political power toward women and Democrats, but it also reflected important shifts in culture. Exit polls revealed that women, young adults, and those with at least some college education were the force behind the "pink wave" (CNN Politics 2018a). Reinforcing the importance

TABLE 3.1 Percent of Vote Received by Major Party Candidates

State:	Winning Candidate (Party): Percentage of Vote	Losing Candidate (Party): Percentage of Vote
Georgia[1]	Brian Kemp (R): 50.2%	Stacey Abrams (D): 48.8%
Idaho[2]	Brad Little (R): 59.8%	Paulette Jordan (D): 38.2%
Kansas[3]	Laura Kelly (D): 48.0%	Kris Kobach (R): 43.0%
Maine[4]	Janet Mills (D): 50.9%	Shawn Moody (R): 43.2%
Michigan[5]	Gretchen Whitmer (D): 53.3%	Bill Schuette (R): 43.7%
New Mexico[6]	Michelle Lujan Grisham (D): 57.2%	Steve Pearce (R): 42.8%
South Dakota[7]	Kristi Noem (R): 51.0%	Billie Sutton (D): 47.6%
Wyoming[8]	Mark Gordon (R): 67.1%	Mary Throne (D): 27.5%

of gender, the election was carried by voters who disapproved of Trump, agreed that more women should be elected, and thought that more attention should be paid to sexual harassment (CNN Politics 2018a). And as we will see, the election crystalized women's collective identity and the diffusion of women's and #MeToo movement frames into people's everyday lives.

In this chapter, we uncover the gendered messages that candidates presented to voters in the eight gubernatorial open seat races across the country that had women candidates. We focus on open seats rather than those with incumbents, as these candidates faced more difficult electoral challenges. Our data draw on the media and candidates' own gendered self-presentations, particularly advertisements and public appearances, as well as focus group interviews.

Our approach aims to capture how "elites" and institutional actors in politics "facilitate a movement's ability to produce cultural change" (Van Dyke and Taylor 2018: 490). We uncover how candidates' self-presentations are reflective of women's movement frames. Self-presentations have the potential to create broader change through cultural diffusion (Van Dyke and Taylor 2018). That is, candidates' self-presentations and political power emerged from the gender revolution while simultaneously helping to shape it by spreading ideology and movement frames to everyday lives. Social movements alter culture through shifts in movement frames, ideologies, identities, and even language (Van Dyke and Taylor 2018).

The extent to which a social movement can transform political parties and policy agendas can indicate its success (Amenta et al., 2018; Hutter et al. 2018). The political process approach focuses on "the political and institutional environment in which social movements operate" (della Porta and Diani 2015: 5). In particular, this approach sees social movements as developing within particular political opportunity structures, which may create favorable conditions for activism (Meyer and Staggenborg 1996) and transformations in worldviews. In this perspective, political parties represent an important aspect of this environment and help create arenas of "alliance and conflict" that can set agendas within political parties (Hutter et al. 2018: 325–326). For example, a social movement can draw politicians' attention to particular issues, especially if protest is picked up by the news media (Hutter et al. 2018). In the #MeToo era, this agenda-setting and party transformation occurred in both the Republican and Democratic parties, although often in opposing directions. Additionally, although political institutions exist outside of movements, they shape movements in important ways (Amenta et al. 2018). At the same time, the political process model narrowly focuses on activity that primarily targets the government and minimizes the importance of *culture* in social movement action, actors, goals, and strategies (Armstrong and Bernstein 2008); consequently, it typically misses the micro level and the link between the micro and macro levels.

Yet the Women's March itself propelled the election of women candidates in 2018. In contrast to previous social movements, which had protest as an end goal, the Women's March explicitly connected itself to electoral politics; protest was "redirected from 'the barricades to the ballots'" (Fisher 2019: 126). In doing so, the Women's March frame and collective identity opposed the Trump administration (Fisher 2019). Fisher (2019: 126) concluded, "There is no question that the Resistance [to Trump, triggered by the Women's March] contributed substantially to national politics around the 2018 election."

Here, we classify self-presentations according to an ideological spectrum that includes feminist, gender-nontraditional, gender-neutral, and gender-traditional approaches. As defined in Table 3.2, feminist self-presentations (on the most progressive side) focus on gendered social and political interests, gendered political issues, and an awareness of gender inequalities and patriarchy (see also Aronson et al. 2020). Breaking from previous research, our spectrum advances understandings of the complexity of campaigns' self-presentations and situates them within the broader women's movement in which they emerged.

Prior studies on women candidates typically emphasize a gender dichotomy, either drawing on or resisting gender stereotypes. "Feminine stereotypes" emphasize women's traits as "warm, nurturing, and sensitive" or "communal" (Bauer 2016; Bauer 2014; Lawrence et al. 2016; McGregor 2017; Meeks 2016).

TABLE 3.2 Summary of Spectrum of Gender Self-Presentations

Feminist	Gender Nontraditional	Gender Neutral	Gender Traditional
Focus on gendered social and political interests, gendered political issues, an awareness of gender inequalities and patriarchy	Stereotypical masculine gender roles, language or traits, such as swearing, toughness, and "fight"	Gender-blind perspectives, accomplishments, or policy positions	Stereotypical feminine gender roles, such as caretakers and family-oriented

In contrast, "masculine" traits are "aggressive" or "agentic" (Bauer 2014) or focus on "leadership" (Schneider 2014). This dichotomous way of understanding gender in electoral politics is simplistic. As sociologists West and Zimmerman (1987: 125) theorized in their classic essay, "doing gender" can be complex and involves a "routine accomplishment embedded in everyday interaction." Gender is "performed" and represents an "accomplishment" (West and Zimmerman 1987: 125). Here, we develop more complex frameworks to understand how women candidates present themselves.

As a result of the masculinity assumed in politics, candidates and their strategists carefully weigh whether to draw on, minimize, or challenge gender stereotypes in their campaigns (Dittmar 2015). They aim to strike a "balance" between "feminine and masculine traits and issues" when it comes to both self-presentation and policy stances (Dittmar 2015: 81). Women candidates running for executive offices (e.g., governor or president) typically adopt a "masculine" campaign style that emphasizes "toughness" and experience in male domains, while minimizing attention to women's issues (Carroll 2009). At the same time, to conform to norms surrounding femininity, many pay close attention to their tone (i.e., "to be tough but not mean") and appearance (i.e., dress professionally to "neutralize gender") (Dittmar 2015: 89, 105). In their analysis of women candidates' ads from 2018, Oliver and Conroy (2020) examined what they called "gender personality," which they defined as masculinity and femininity (as measured by the Personality Attributes Questionnaire). They found a "masculine advantage," regardless of the gender of the candidate. As Oliver and Conroy (2020: 6) put it, "Individuals with more masculine personalities, irrespective of their sex, will be more likely to perceive of themselves as qualified, be recruited, and eventually run for higher political office." As a result, women who are successful in running for office "are more masculine than the women who do not" (Oliver and Conroy 2020: 15).

The 2018 midterm elections were distinct in how women candidates were "doing gender" in their campaigns. Across the country and for a wide range of races, advertisements featured candidates pregnant or breastfeeding, highlighted their experiences with sexual assault or harassment, emphasized their military credentials, or showed images of them protesting Trump's inauguration (Axios 2018). Dittmar (2019) examined several notable examples of 2018 campaign messages that "draw upon distinctly gendered experiences." In this chapter, we analyze gendered self-presentations and voters' reactions to them in this pivotal election, focusing on innovations in electoral politics. All of the candidates strategically blended these approaches, and what follows is an analysis of how the 2018 women gubernatorial candidates fit into these self-presentations.

Through focus groups with voting-aged interviewees, we also uncover shifts in women's electoral power and culture on the ground. Women's demands for equality and the collective framework emphasized by women candidates and voters suggest profound transformations in the gender revolution. Candidates are altering how voters think about gender in the public sphere and how they respond to a larger context of social change. Through both the voters' eyes and the self-presentations of women candidates, women are increasingly challenging inequalities and claiming electoral power. This diffusion of women's movement ideologies to the broader culture suggests the dynamic relationship between social movements, electoral politics, and ordinary people's daily lives.

"We Need a Governor Who's Ready to Roll Up *Her* Sleeves and Get to Work!" Feminist Self-Presentations and Voter Reactions

Women candidates drew on feminist ideologies and women's movement frames in their self-presentations. Voters in our focus groups, especially women, responded favorably to rejections of gender inequalities. Embedded within feminist self-presentations were social movement frames that both candidates and voters drew on in 2018, including an emphasis on women's collective power, the recognition of the intersection between electoral politics and the #MeToo movement, and an awareness of intersectional feminism. Thus, women candidates and voters were innovators who created and appreciated new self-presentations and confronted gender inequalities and patriarchy.

Women's Collective Power

Most of the gubernatorial candidates pushed social change forward by emphasizing the collective rights of women during this election. In her victory speech after winning the Democratic primary nomination, Gretchen Whitmer, a white woman elected as governor of Michigan, emphasized the word "her," a nod to women's collective identity: "We need a governor who knows how to get things done, who's ready to roll up *her* sleeves and get to work!" (Whitmer 2018a). Whitmer also linked her campaign with women's movement frames. She drew on her experiences as a sexual assault survivor to connect with #MeToo and used images of herself at the Women's March on her campaign website and in her ads. Her emphasis on women's rights and self-determination appeared to be popular with women voters in Michigan, 60 percent of whom voted for her (CNN Politics 2018b). In contrast, in 2016, only 53 percent of women in Michigan voted for Hillary Clinton (CNN Politics 2016c). The 2018 election showed shifts in men's voting preferences as well: While 47 percent of men voted for Whitmer (CNN Politics 2018a), only 41 percent voted for Clinton two years earlier (CNN Politics 2016c).

This collective identity was repeated in Whitmer's response to the media after her 2019 State of the State gubernatorial address. Whitmer made national headlines when *Fox News* ran a story about social media posts that called her dress too "tight-fitting" and a "distraction" (The Real Daytime 2019). Whitmer pushed back against this criticism: "Boys have teased me about my curves since 5th grade.

My mom said 'hold your head high and don't let it bother you'" (Whitmer 2019). Emphasizing her own strength and her refusal to let these comments weaken her power, she said, "I'm *tough*, I can *take it*" (Whitmer 2019). Whitmer concluded by focusing on women's right to self-determination, free from harassment, "I've got a message for all of the women and girls like mine who have to deal with garbage like this every day: *I've got your back*" (Whitmer 2019). Her response effectively turned women's objectification on its head by refusing to accept it and confronting it collectively.

This signal to women to reject traditional stereotypes is intersectional in nature, as it cuts across gender and social class lines. Focus group innovators appreciated Whitmer's identification with women's movement frames of equality. Angel, a 54-year-old Black woman, saw Whitmer's strength as an inspiration for women to work collectively: "I do appreciate the principles that Whitmer's standing on because *it's not just about her*. She's looking at all aspects, women, men, low income, high class, how *we can all work together*." Angel also emphasized a collective identity with other "strong" women:

> *We* still have to overcome so many things *as women*. You really have to be a *strong, strong* woman to be able to stand *against men*. Because in this country, women are still considered second-class citizens in so many areas of life and politics has always been a male-dominated area.

Laura Kelly, a white woman who became the governor of Kansas, also linked the rise of women running for political office in 2018 to women's collective power. One interviewer observed that Kelly was "the only female candidate for the gubernatorial primary race" on either the Republican or Democratic side in Kansas. Kelly smiled and replied, "Yes, I noticed" (Kelly 2018). When asked if she was surprised or disappointed by this, she said,

> Given what's going on all over the rest of the country it is a little bit of a surprise that I'm the only one on the governor's ticket. But I think it's time. Bring women back to the table and put them in positions of leadership (Kelly 2018).

Kelly's victory was remarkable because Kansas voters helped to elect Trump in 2016, as only 36.3 percent voted for Clinton (CNN Politics 2018c; CNN Politics 2016b). In a way that reminded voters of women's history and advancement, Wyoming white Democrat Mary Throne displayed images of herself standing in front of a statue of the first woman justice of the peace in the United States in her ad announcing her campaign for governor (Throne 2017). These feminist self-presentations drew on the historical moment of women's activism to fuse connections with collective identity and empowerment; in doing so, they appealed to women voters.

Focus group innovators agreed that identification *as women* played an important role in the election. Taylor, an 18-year-old Black woman, declared, "There's a lot of injustice towards women, so I feel like women *stick together*, and that's why that happened. *Women stick together with other women.*" They were explicit in their belief that the election represented a shift in power. As Meghan, a 22-year-old white woman, stated, "Women have just had enough of always being told that they're not meant to have *control* of things." She highlighted the legacy of the women's movement: "Even the 1900s, or when they were fighting for women's rights back then, they weren't used to women wanting *power*." Although "making something of *ourselves*" and running for office was "a little scary for some people," Meghan considered equality important. Also drawing on collective language, she said, "*We're* just trying to make something of *ourselves*. Like, 'Hey, *we* can do just as much as men can do,' like more of a *feminist* thing." While making an explicit connection between women's electoral power and feminism, Meghan connected herself to the movement and women's right to self-determination.

Maram, a 21-year-old Middle Eastern woman, referenced Trump's presidency as an impetus for women (signaled collectively as "we" and "our") to seize power:

> After 2016, *we* were pushed to this point of discomfort to where *we* felt the need to say "enough is enough!" And now is *our* time to take back, or not even take back, he never really had it in the first place, but take things for *ourselves*.

Meghan agreed, "The way Trump talks about women, the way he degrades women, and then his followers view women, it's just a little bit too much to handle." She emphasized the "bigger picture" of social change, including changes in women in sports, education, and "becoming leaders" more generally.

Other women viewed the 2018 midterm elections in terms of larger social movement activism that fought against injustices during the Trump era. Nadine, a 20-year-old white woman, said, "The comments that Trump had made, some people wanted to just go against it and just show that the female *voice* in Congress should be *respected* more than how it was beforehand." Harper, a 23-year-old multiracial woman, said that Trump was trying to "inhibit women from making important decisions," such as on abortion. She saw the 2018 election year as a distinct break from the past, as women were brave in "*fighting back*" against Trump "to prove him wrong."

Angel also drew on the words "us" and "we" to emphasize that women are seizing power from men (contrasted with the word "they"):

> I will be voting for women. It's time for *change*. It's time for women to have a chance at this because men have been making *decisions for us* and *they* don't even know what *they're* making decisions for. At least let *us* get an opportunity to put some policies in place that benefit *us*. *We're* the ones that carry the

weight in the United States. *We women* do. *We* carry the weight. *We're* the ones that have the *strength* of this country. And so why not give *us* an opportunity to put some policies in place? Because it's time. It really is time. I want to see better for my granddaughters.

In Angel's account, women, collectively, deserve power and control over decision-making, a view that is common in the broader women's movement.

Links to the Women's Movement

Illustrating the diffusion of women's movement frames into electoral politics, innovator candidates and voters connected the influx of women in politics with the movement. Laila, a 43-year-old Black woman, said that the rise of women candidates running for office in 2018 was specifically due to "the women's movement. It was just time for it, you know?" Alyssa, a 29-year-old Black woman, explained the links as follows: "Just with the amount of women candidates that are running for this election, that does speak volumes of the *impact* of the #MeToo movement. It is already in the works and greatly making some *impact*."

Kiara, an 18-year-old Black woman, said that women in sports, "leadership positions," and "all the #MeToo stuff . . . influenced other women." She concluded, "There's a *change*, and you could be part of that *change*." Similarly, Nia, a 49-year-old Black woman, said, "When it came to this particular election, women were not going to say, 'Oh, Donald Trump, I'm going to do whatever you ask me to. Just push me, push me, push me.'" Instead, she thought that women were fearless and had the power of the #MeToo movement behind them:

Seriously, look, I'm *not* afraid of you and *we* are going in another direction with this. *We* are not doing this. There's the #MeToo movement. No, *we* are not going to be victims anymore. And women are going to *take over* and they're going to get him. Woo!

Likewise, Christina, a 36-year-old Black woman, said, "The #MeToo movement has had an impact on events like women coming into politics, because *we* want to be the *change* that *we* see." She thought that women in politics were "needed" to address women's concerns: "The issues and the policies that *we* feel are near and dear to *us*." Christina viewed the #MeToo movement as an attempt by women to try "to reclaim *our* voices." Drawing on the words "us" and "we" to highlight collective identity, she emphasized that voting for women promoted policies that protected other women within a transformed society: "The climate is *changing*. *We* want to *see change* and *we* want to see policies in effect that essentially protect women, and give *us* a little bit more freedom." Mia, a 20-year-old white woman, agreed, mentioning that voters are "switching parties" as a result of the 2016 election, "People have switched [political] party. They realized they need to be a part of the *change*."

Charlotte, a 23-year-old multiracial woman, thought that the rise of women in politics was linked with women "speaking" as part of the #MeToo movement. She said that "a lot of" the increased presence of women running "has to do with the #MeToo movement coming about. Women are *speaking up* generally of their pain." As a result, women began to find their voices more broadly, not just about sexual harassment and assault:

> You're not only taking a *stand for themselves* in terms of coming out about things that might have happened, but just overall. It's causing a trend for women to *speak out* in general, not just about that kind of issue.

She thought that women "may have been a little scared to come into places where a lot of men are" but that the #MeToo movement made them "more *confident*" and "more *comfortable*" in male-dominated spaces because they would be able to confront sexual harassment.

In one gender-similar focus group, three innovators discussed the role of the #MeToo movement in influencing women voters to support women candidates. When Pamela asked about their perceptions of the causes of women's success in 2018, Riley, an 18-year-old Black woman, referred to "Time's Up," a movement closely linked with #MeToo (Langone 2018). She said, "It might have to do with Time's Up. People are like, 'Oh, women actually can *do* things.'" When Pamela asked her to explain, she focused on the connection between social movements, courage, and politics:

> *Now* is the time for *women*. Where *we* can *do* more and like *say* more and *we'll* be taken more seriously. Men are scared. It has to do with the *courage*, because women are finally being taken seriously with the #MeToo and the Time's Up thing.

This perseverance in the face of male-dominated politics is linked to women's courage to speak out about the traumas of sexual assault. Jada, an 18-year-old Black woman, emphasized that women are more confident to speak out about harassment and assault and to advance in politics, partly because they identify with other women through the #MeToo movement: "You go out and you have a *confident* stand, people look at you, *confident*, and know what you're doing. Then they actually listen to you and put their votes toward you."

Interviewees saw themselves as supporting the #MeToo movement and the struggle for gender equality when they voted for women candidates. Zainab, a 32-year-old Middle Eastern woman, called the #MeToo movement a "jumping-off point" and a "major, major turning point" that caused an important "shift."

The movement "tipped everything over. Like OK, we're going to start taking women seriously. We're going to start *listening* to them." The movement led to an important "shift": "Because of everyone supporting these survivors, that led into, OK we're going to support women in all facets of life." Expressing a collective identity, Zainab went further: "If it was between a woman and a man in the Democratic Party, I would vote for the woman."

These discussions illustrate that innovator voters recognized, and were responding to, the gender revolution. The 2018 election coincided with the rise of the #MeToo movement and drew heavily on feminist perspectives. Their language stressed a collective identity, evidenced by the use of "us" and "we," and symbolized women's connection to other women and women's movement ideological frames. Their use of words like "change," "not afraid," "take over," "super-empowering," and "impact" illustrates transformations resulting from the gender revolution that are being diffused into the lives of ordinary people.

Intersectional Feminism

Additionally, several 2018 races highlighted another key focus of the women's movement: the intersections between race, ethnicity, and gender. In a particularly divisive and contested race in Georgia, white Republican Brian Kemp narrowly defeated Democrat Stacey Abrams. Abrams received national news coverage, as her candidacy was historic, potentially the first Black woman governor of any state. Abrams frequently exhibited feminist self-presentations, such as when she exclaimed that "a lot of the policies that have come out of the [Trump] administration have been so dangerous to women that there is no opportunity for silence" (The Circus on SHOWTIME 2018). Backlash followed from Kemp, who attempted to deflate Abrams's emphasis on collective identity. In one of Kemp's ads, a featured woman told voters that she was a survivor of sexual assault and claimed that "victims of sexual violence deserve better" than Abrams (Kemp for Governor 2018a). Similarly, linking Abrams with other women who were unpopular in conservative Georgia, another attack ad said that she was "being funded by Nancy Pelosi's California friends" and "loved by Hillary" (Republican Governors Association 2018). This backlash appropriated feminist issues and symbols to dismiss Abrams's historic candidacy.

Abrams and other Democrats spoke out against voter suppression, as an investigation found that the then attorney general Kemp improperly purged 340,000 voters from the voter registration lists (Durkin 2018); these voters were disproportionately Black. On the night of the election, Abrams insisted that these voices would not be silenced:

> There are votes that need to be counted. There are *voices* that are waiting to be *heard*. And I promise you tonight that *we* are going to make sure that *every*

vote is counted. Every single vote. Every vote is getting counted (The Guardian 2018).

Ultimately, the contest was quite divided by race: While 74 percent of whites voted for Kemp, 84 percent of people of color voted for Abrams (CNN Politics 2018d).

Other contests also revealed a clash between women of color and white men candidates. For example, Michelle Lujan Grisham of New Mexico became the first Democratic Latinx woman to be elected governor in the United States. She linked her Republican opponent Steve Pearce (a white man) to Trump while expressing her outrage about gender inequalities. One campaign ad displayed consecutive images of her male opponent and Trump with stern faces looking at the camera. The ad stated in disgust, "Like Trump, he believes a wife should 'submit' 'as a matter of obedience'" (Lujan Grisham 2018a).

Our focus group innovators remarked that the election highlighted the intersections between race and gender, an important dimension of the larger women's movement. For example, Christina drew on the collective language of "us" and "we" to highlight the intersectional aspect of women's power:

> The female presence that *we* brought to the elections, and actually winning the elections, really put *us* forward in a political stance, *as far as being women*. And not just white women. It was women of all colors and different races. That's what I liked about it.

Sasha, a 20-year-old Black woman, said that more women ran for office and were elected in 2018 than ever before because "there was a coalition." She emphasized the connection between the Women's March and electoral politics:

> They had created this *movement* of women voting, women running for office and they said that was going to be the *change*. One of the chants at the Women's March actually was "*power* to the polls," where all of the women were going to win the seats.

Using the words "our" and "us" to connect and identify with the racial and ethnic diversity of other interviewees, movement involvement, and the election, Sasha continued,

> That put in *our* heads, this is the movement that needs to happen. That's why it ended up being so many women in office because those messages were preached to *us* several times in different locations and then it made it to the media. *Power* to the polls.

Alexandra, a 38-year-old Black woman, responded to Sasha, emphasizing the historic intersections between race and gender,

> I actually would say it started before then [2018]. People now know that diversity is not a bad thing, seeing people of different colors and genders doing different things. I think that would go back as far as Barack Obama. It just chipped away. We are starting to see things chip away a little bit, this #MeToo movement. When you start chipping, chipping, this was a push that made it happen. This election, *we see all the women just storming the gates.*

Innovators thus saw this election as a power shift that they themselves identified with, and were participating in, as voters.

"We're Going to Impeach the Motherfucker": Gender-Nontraditional Self-Presentations and Voter Reactions

The 2018 gubernatorial candidates also displayed gender-nontraditional self-presentations. Innovator women candidates drew on women's movement frames in their demonstration of anger toward inequalities. They also assumed stereotypically masculine gender roles, by using aggressive language (sometimes even swearing) and by presenting themselves as "tough" and "fighters" (see Table 3.2). Swearing, and the anger behind it, deviates from gender stereotypes and is typically not accepted for women politicians. Research before the 2018 election assumed that women candidates faced a no-win situation: Many voters viewed them negatively if they violated gender stereotypes or if they were portrayed as too nurturing and sensitive (Bauer 2016; Bauer 2014; Burns et al. 2013; Dittmar 2015; Dwyer et al. 2009). Yet 2018 saw new ways for candidates to present themselves.

Women's Anger

Rashida Tlaib (D-MI), the first Palestinian American elected to Congress, created a national controversy at her swearing in ceremony when she called Trump a "motherfucker." The full context of her statement, particularly mentioning the lesson she conveyed to her son, was obscured by her critics and the media: "And when your son looks at you and says, 'Mama, look, you won, bullies don't win.' And I said, 'Baby, they don't because we're going to go in there and we're going to impeach the motherfucker'" (CNN Transcripts 2019). When Trump attacked "the squad," a group of outspoken congresswomen of color (including Tlaib, as well as Ocasio-Cortez, Omar, and Ayanna Pressley from Massachusetts), as foreigners on Twitter (He said, "Why don't they go back and help fix the totally broken and crime infested places from which they came?"), they held a press conference at which they stated, "We cannot, we will not, be silenced" (Killough 2019). Such displays of gender-nontraditional assertiveness and language were common in the 2018 election and many voters embraced this approach. This approach illustrates that women made their voices heard in 2018, emphasizing nontraditional self-presentations that drew on collective identities connected to women's movements.

Lujan Grisham also challenged traditional gender expectations in her self-presentations by displaying anger toward Trump. Commentators said that she "brands herself as someone who wants to *fight back* against Donald Trump" by refusing to let Trump keep National Guard troops patrolling the border in her state (The Young Turks 2019). In a postelection ad, dressed in safety goggles, heels, and a suit, Lujan Grisham ran full speed toward four walls and broke through them all, emerging covered in dust and debris. Before hitting the first wall, she said, "I'm Michelle Lujan Grisham. New Mexico is 49th for employment and 50th for schools. We've got to *bust through* some walls to make *changes*" (The Young Turks 2019). As she burst through another wall, men in hard hats and construction clothing behind her registered their shock. The last room in the ad featured an elementary school classroom with a photo of Trump pinned to the wall. Running directly toward his photo, she exclaimed, "And here's what I think of Trump's wall!" (The Young Turks 2019).

Interview participants called out the racism and sexism facing women of color in politics, linking it to gender-nontraditional self-presentations. Cam, an 18-year-old Asian American man, said that because Ocasio-Cortez "is so vocal and she's voicing her opinions, she's really bashed upon." Cam compared Ocasio-Cortez with Trump, as they both "come from no political background." Yet responses to them were very

FIGURE 3.1 New Mexico Governor Lujan Grisham Wearing Safety Goggles and Construction Dust in Her 2018 "Busts through Walls" Ad

Source: Retrieved from YouTube (The Young Turks, 2019, 1:32).

different: "As a woman of color, she's bashed down upon by conservatives. Those wouldn't be the same issues if it was a white male who was that vocal." Confronting racism and misogyny head on rather than more subtly illustrates the power that women in politics are demanding in the Trump era, as well as the ways that voters of all genders are supporting this transformation.

Several focus group participants specifically defended Tlaib's infamous comment and viewed negative reactions to her as an example of the gendered double standard in politics. Zainab said of Tlaib and other women in politics, "They're not allowed to state their strong opinions. They can't put out these polarizing statements. Men in power are allowed to say what they want to say and not get bashed for it." Joel, a 20-year-old white man, agreed. He said that when Trump "says things that could be considered rude, some people will see that as a sign of power, strength. Whereas if a woman were to say things like that, she might be seen as rude or politically incorrect."

Innovator interviewees pointed out that women who speak out are "labeled as aggressive," "argumentative," or "too emotional," whereas men are seen as "very passionate" about what they are saying. Kim, a 27-year-old white woman, said, "If a guy in leadership is really, really commanding and everything like that, people think, 'Oh, he's got his shit together.' But if a girl does it, she's a diva." Similarly, in a gender-similar focus group, three women dismissed stereotypes that women's hormones affect their ability to govern:

Jada: Women running for something in general, they're going to look at you differently just because you're a woman. "Oh, she's a female. She's going to be way more sensitive. She's going to cry about this or that." But if you look at President Trump, some of the things he does, well (pause), interesting.

Aria: [21-year-old woman] Like sending out tweets in the middle of the night?

Jada: [sarcastically] That's *not* PMS [premenstrual syndrome], right?

Zainab: If it was Hillary or any other woman, it would be like, "Oh look, she's PMSing. She's emotional. This is why women can't lead, because they're emotional." But Trump being emotional and throwing tantrums is looked on as OK.

Sarah, a 20-year-old white woman, remarked that women are stereotyped as not being able to "handle authority because they're too emotional or on their menstrual cycles." In contrast, she said, "I think it's important to crush those stigmas."

Similarly, in another focus group, Christina pointed out that men's anger is viewed as legitimate, "When men get mad about issues, people don't bring the emotional factor in. It's just like it's a fact." She pointed out that women are held to different standards than men; she said that if Clinton had spoken like Trump, people would have said, "Oh, she's a lady, she shouldn't be talking like that. She shouldn't do this, she should uphold herself this kind of way." Alex, a 21-year-old multiracial nonbinary interviewee, agreed, "Men are stereotypically seen as angry, and that's OK. When women are seen as angry, it's usually a bad thing. It's seen as something that's wrong." Christina responded, "Or we're PMSing," to which Alex replied, "Emotionally, chemically imbalanced." Women candidates in 2018 used innovative gender-nontraditional language, drawing on anger and even swear words; innovator voters responded positively to these self-presentations as part of the broader gender revolution.

Nontraditional Language and Roles

This election in general and gubernatorial races in particular were distinct because women candidates did not shy away from traditionally masculine language, images, emotions, or assertiveness. In doing so, they often captured, and propelled forward, the anger of voters, especially women and people of color. These candidates also blended gender-nontraditional self-presentations with traditional, gender-neutral, and feminist appeals.

For example, while driving on the freeway in her SUV in one campaign ad, Whitmer navigated deep potholes while lamenting about the unreasonable cost of auto repairs. Talking to the camera, she did not mince words:

> As governor, I want to actually focus on things that will make a difference in people's lives right now, like fixing the *damn* roads and doing it the right way with the right materials, so they stay fixed. It's time to get it done (Click On Detroit | Local 4 | WDIV 2018).

Her phrase "fix the damn roads" was repeated throughout her campaign, including during her Democratic nomination acceptance speech (WXYZ-TV Detroit | Channel 7 2018). News anchors said that her language appealed to many voters (WXYZ-TV Detroit | Channel 7 2018), yet mild swearing, even in such a folksy way, breaks out of gender stereotypes. Although many voters embraced Whitmer's language, some called for her to stay within traditional gender stereotypes. On social media, one woman said, "Just don't say *'damn'* anymore. It takes away from your ladyness." Another said, "Ladies shouldn't say *'damn'* in public" (Aronson and Oldham 2019).

The women in our focus groups viewed such language within a larger context of rejecting gender inequalities and supporting women in power. For example, in a gender-similar focus group, Alexandra said that Whitmer used such language to evoke anger, "Very truthfully, those *damn* roads, she did that for a reason, to spark an emotion, to spark *anger*." Alexandra continued, drawing on the words "us" and "we" to present a collective identity with the other women in the room,

> They gave *us* real living room conversations, the way *we* talk at home. You can understand "fix the *damn* roads." *We* can understand "impeach the *motherfucker*."

We can understand that. It's talking in a language that, regardless of your race, economic status, or gender, you can understand.

Swearing, which breaks taboos for women political leaders, is thus relatable and captures how people talk in their everyday lives. As Alexandra put it, "emotional language" serves "to get an emotional rise out of people. Women tend to use emotion to get the job done."

Nia directly linked Whitmer's language to a rise in women's power. Also drawing on collective language to express this point, she refused to accept inequalities:

We are totally out of the 1960s and '70s, when *we* had to be tamed and docile and did what the men said. *We* were coming out on *our* own. When Whitmer said "fix the *damn* roads," that's the emotion that she gave *us* that *I'm going to do something.*

Nia continued, linking Tlaib's statement with women's rejection of the status quo,

And the same thing with the young lady [Tlaib] who said "Donald Trump, impeach the *M. F.*" *We* are coming up. *We* are coming up. *We* are coming out and *we're not going to take it anymore. We're* done. *We're* done, *we're taking over.*

She concluded by rallying the group of women in the focus group, "Anybody else with *us*?"

The most frequently used gender-nontraditional words in the 2018 election were "fighter" or "fight" (Aronson, Oldham, and Lucas 2023). In a recent assessment of political candidates, Klein (2019) explained that while "men are assumed to be fighters . . . women have to overcome suspicions of weakness, which means they have to be much more explicit about their willingness to fight" (Klein 2019). In particular, Democratic candidates often positioned themselves in positions of strength in "fighting" powerful men, such as Trump or their opponents.

For example, Janet Mills, a white woman who became the governor of Maine, used the "fighter" language frequently in her campaign. A 30-second campaign ad, narrated by a man, used this word three times: "She spent her whole life *fighting* for us and she'll continue to *fight* for us as governor" (Janet Mills for Governor 2018). The ad went on to call Mills "straightforward and pragmatic." A young man featured in the ad emphasized the word "fight" when he said, "Janet will *fight* for hardworking folks" (Janet Mills for Governor 2018). In another ad, which Mills narrated herself, she emphasized her tough stance and victories:

When I became attorney general, I *faced down* the biggest bully the state has ever seen, Governor Paul Lapage. He wanted to take kids off of health care.

I said no. He sued in federal court. I *fought* back and I *won* (Janet Mills for Governor 2017).

Set to an image of Mills standing with her arms crossed and lips pursed, she said,

> I've *taken on* the Wall Street giants . . . and I've *won*. . . . I've *taken on* the major pharmaceutical companies when they cheated Maine citizens and I *won*. I've *taken on* Volkswagen of America for violating our clean air laws, and I *won*. I've *taken on* Paul Lapage time and time again and I've *won* (Janet Mills for Governor 2017).

The ad also showed a photo of Mills in a hard hat. In contrast to stereotypes that women have maternal instincts with children, Mills said of being a stepmother, "I had no idea how to bring up five daughters, but I did the best I could" (Janet Mills for Governor 2017).

Similarly, in a cheerful account of her biography, one of Whitmer's ads featured her walking through a lumber store, where she told viewers that it was the place of her first job (Whitmer 2018b). The ad shifted to a high school gym, where she caught a basketball that was forcefully thrown from the sidelines, as she told voters that she played sports and dreamed of becoming an *ESPN* anchor. The ad shifted to her home, where it emphasized gender-traditional roles. The ad continued with the Michigan legislative house behind her, as she said, "I was also the *first* woman as a *leader* in the Michigan Senate, where I *took on* the *tough fights* . . . *Fighting* to stop Governor Snyder's cuts to education and his corporate tax giveaways" (Whitmer 2018b). Emphasizing her resistance to another powerful man, she concluded,

> I've *had it* with Republicans like Donald Trump blowing up health care while your costs go up and up. . . . I want you to know that I'll work with everyone who wants to solve these problems and I'll *take on anyone* who stands in the way (Whitmer 2018b).

Dressed in a baseball shirt with the words "Michigan Strong," Whitmer's "Mean Tweets" ad sarcastically confronted gender stereotypes: "This one's from Gary. It's really clever. It says 'Get back in the kitchen'" (Whitmer 2018c). She responded bitingly, "I hope you didn't spend all night thinking up that one, Gary!" (Whitmer 2018c). She quickly dismissed other mean tweets with humor as well, saying adversarially, "Lame!" and "Buh Bye!" (Whitmer 2018c). She read, "What if Trump tweets about the race and calls her Gretchen Shitmer?" Whitmer's dismissive response was: "Oh that's clever. I haven't heard that since second grade" (Whitmer 2018c). Confronting stereotypes about appearance, she read a tweet that asked, "Why is your forehead always so reflective?" Looking annoyed, an assistant quickly came out and powdered her forehead. She responded, "Better?"

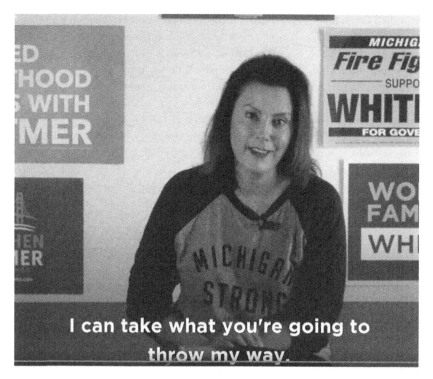

FIGURE 3.2   Michigan Governor Whitmer Wearing a "Michigan Strong" Shirt in Her
2018 "Mean Tweets" Ad

Source: Retrieved from YouTube (Gretchen Whitmer 2018c).

(Whitmer 2018c). Implying that women in politics face obstacles, Whitmer concluded by confronting gender stereotypes that attempted to make her submissive,

> We take a moment to laugh at this because I think it's important for people
> to see how *tough* this environment is. . . . I invite you to follow us on Twitter,
> even you, @MIGOP. I *can take what you're going to throw my way. I think we know*
> *where we stand* (Whitmer 2018c).

Paulette Jordan, a Native American Democratic candidate for governor of Idaho,
also stressed a tough image in an ad that called her a "Mother. *Leader. Defender* of
the West" (Jordan for Governor 2018). In these examples, we see that candidates
refused deferential self-presentations and opted instead for confrontational ones.

Women gubernatorial candidates in conservative, typically Republican, states
also drew on traditionally masculine interests and skills to present themselves as
in sync with voters. In an interview, when Abrams was asked about her "F" rating

from the National Rifle Association, she responded, "Let's be clear. I am not anti-gun. My *great-grandmother taught me how to shoot* when I was growing up in Missis-sippi. *I like trap shooting. I like target shooting*" (Swire 2018). In an effort to establish her gender-nontraditional credibility, she said, "I do not think that weapons of mass destruction like an AR-15 belong in civilian hands. *I've shot an AR-15* and you [the interviewer] probably have too. And while it's an amazing amount of *power*, it's also an amazing amount of destruction" (Swire 2018). In an ad called "Guys Like Me," testimonials from men of diverse racial backgrounds revealed that Abrams is a "tough" "fighter" who understood men's concerns (Abrams 2018a). A white man stated, "She gets it. She's *tough*. She's resilient. . . . She's *fighting* against tax hikes that are going to hurt guys like me." A Black man agreed, "Guys like me." Another man stated that men "that get up at the crack of dawn to go and work long hours. She *fights* every day for education, for better health care" (Abrams 2018a). This ad crossed gender and racial boundaries and suggested that Abrams could do so as well.

As the first woman elected as governor of South Dakota, Republican Kristi Noem, who is white, presented herself in one ad wearing a fraying baseball hat, jeans, and a flannel shirt. In the ad, Noem called herself a "*farmer, rancher,* and small business owner" (Noem 2018a). She explained, "I can still *ride a horse.* I can still *shoot a gun*" (Noem 2016). Noem's ads featured images of her herding cattle and driving a tractor. She said, "In my family, there were no girl chores or boy chores. . . . My mom said I was quite a tomboy when I was growing up. She had to tie me up to comb my hair" (Noem 2017). In an ad that showed her head-to-toe in military fatigues, Noem stated that she "started a *hunting lodge* from scratch" and discussed how her job as a farmer provided her with executive experience that qualified her to run the state (Noem 2017).

Reporters described Noem in gender-nontraditional terms: "Breaking the norm, hardly new for the conservative congresswoman, born, raised and still rancher on the 6,000-acre family plot" (Noem 2018b). One interview followed Noem to the gym, where she was lifting heavy free weights, a hobby she took up so that she could interact with members of Congress outside of "the smoky bar" (Noem 2018b). Noem stated,

> Well, for me, I'm married. It's not a good testimony for me to be having late-night drinks when my family is all the way across the country. I started think-ing out of the box. How can I get to have interaction with other members? For me it was the gym. We exercise together but we also talk about legislation (Noem 2018b).

Although Noem's statement that married women do not have "late-night drinks" with men emphasized traditional gender roles as a wife, she simultaneously rebuffed gender stereotypes by lifting free weights at the gym to interact with members of Congress.

FIGURE 3.3   South Dakota Governor Noem Wearing Her Characteristic Baseball Hat Talking with Military Personnel

Source: U.S. Department of Defense. The appearance of U.S. Department of Defense (DoD) visual information does not imply or constitute DoD endorsement.

Noem's approach presents a challenge to our analysis that nontraditional self-presentations are linked to progressive gender ideologies. Noem is not part of the women's movement but displays toughness in her self-presentations in ways that are similar to many of the progressive candidates. Although she assumes gender equality in her ability to govern and lead, her policy positions explicitly reject feminist ideologies (e.g., she is anti-abortion). Fusing nontraditional self-presentations with conservative views, Noem's approach signifies that self-presentations may be undertaken for many purposes, including appropriating aspects of feminist ideology and symbols of women's strength to appeal to voters. Noem was able to adopt nontraditional aspects of the women's movement in her campaign while simultaneously maintaining gender-traditional self-presentations and policy positions.

"My Mission Is to Talk about Issues": Gender-Neutral Self-Presentations and Voter Reactions

With the national news focused on her pathbreaking racial and gender identity, Abrams responded by strategically emphasizing gender-neutral and race-neutral policy positions and goals. On *The Daily Show*, Trevor Noah asked her, "Do you feel like sometimes people only focus on the fact that you would be making history, and not on the fact that you would be actually doing the job?" Abrams responded, downplaying race and gender,

> I think sometimes there is a Crayola version of policymaking that happens where they do focus on color. My mission is to talk about *issues*, to talk about education, and to talk about why it's so critical that we create jobs for everyone that pay a good wage. . . . But it's hard to get them to focus on that because I think they are so surprised by how far I've been able to come despite something they consider both a disqualifier and a really interesting fact that fits really nicely on a crayon. . . . *It doesn't really matter what race you are, you want a good governor who can lead* (The Daily Show with Trevor Noah 2018).

Abrams continued, reassuring voters that she did not favor issues that are a larger concern to Black voters, "I sound the same in north Georgia, which is predominantly white, in midtown Atlanta, in downtown Atlanta, and in Savannah. I sound the exact same. I never change who I am or what I talk about" (The Daily Show with Trevor Noah 2018). Deemphasizing gender, and here race as well, represented a strategy to appeal to the widest possible electorate, which is especially necessary in a gubernatorial election. By blending such gender-neutral approaches with those that both embrace and challenge traditional gender roles, women candidates target different types of voters. For Abrams, a gender- and race-neutral self-presentation sought to appeal to voters whose backgrounds differed from her own.

Another example of a gender-neutral self-presentation that sought to appeal to a wide range of voters comes from Mills's ad titled "One Maine." Fused with feminist, nontraditional, and traditional self-presentations, Mills also emphasized gender-neutral commonalities. Her voice is heard alongside the calming image of a lake in the wilderness: "We shouldn't be two Maines. We should be *one* Maine, working for the *same* goal, for the *same* people. We are *one* people" (Janet Mills for Governor 2017). Lujan Grisham projected a similar message in several ads, by focusing not on gender but instead on gender-neutral policy positions that appealed to a wide range of voters. Standing on an airport runway, she cataloged her experience by listing off her ability to successfully improve infrastructure, clean energy, and job training programs (Lujan Grisham 2018b). In these cases, candidates minimized attention to their gender and targeted a wide range of voters.

Whitmer also deemphasized gender at key times. After she won the election, many commentators noted that women were elected to not only the governor's office but also the Michigan secretary of state and attorney general offices. In response, Whitmer said that her campaign stayed "focused on the dinner table issues that really matter to families: health care and clean drinking water in my state, infrastructure" (CNN Politics 2018e). These gender-neutral self-presentations provide a space for the support of voters who might not embrace feminist and nontraditional self-presentations.

In fact, focus group men were more likely than women to emphasize the importance of the gender-neutral accomplishments of women candidates. Although focus group women emphasized the collective power of women candidates, the men more often emphasized that individual candidates brought forth a unique perspective. Although they supported women candidates, they deemphasized the role of gender and instead tied their support to individual merit. Derek, a 22-year-old white man, characteristic of other men's perspectives, described the individual preparation, qualities, and successes of women candidates: "Women that are running are the candidates that are more prepared than ever." He emphasized personal attributes such as intelligence:

> If you look at an *individual* that's in their mid-30s now, they were exposed to so much more and they were given so much more opportunity. And I think because you have this generation of really intelligent *individuals*, including women, that they see the opportunity now.

Although supportive of women candidates, men did not see themselves as part of the movement in the same way as focus group women.

Focus group men also viewed the 2018 election in terms of the successes of individual women candidates rather than broader social change connected to a movement. They frequently observed that individual women candidates were "encouraged" to run for office or that they were now "more accepted" and "more comfortable." Rather than seeing women as running in order to demand social change, they thought that particular candidates ran for office as a result of their unique qualifications. Ethan, a 28-year-old white man, said, "Women have just as much potential in office as men do." Caleb, a 21-year-old white man, explained that "a lot of female candidates" won in 2018 because "some people voted for them just because they're a woman." Thus, men supported the women candidates as a result of their individual contributions rather than the potential that the candidates had to contribute to the gender revolution.

Other men downplayed the salience and importance of gender in the 2018 election by focusing on the gender-blind *merit* of women candidates. Anthony, a 35-year-old Black man, said that he voted based on "what they *stand for*. A qualified person is what I think people should be looking for," not candidates' gender. Hunter, a 22-year-old white man, added, "Their *values*. And what they're *likely to do* when they get into the office." Hunter emphasized that he "would totally vote for a female candidate, *if I thought they would have the know-how on how to do the job*. If there was a *capable* woman candidate, I would totally vote for her." Similarly, in a gender-similar focus group, Matthew asked six men if a "candidate's gender impacts your vote at all," and they all answered negatively, underscoring instead "how *qualified*" an individual candidate is, as well as "the *content*" of the campaign. Adam, a 22-year-old Latinx man, used the word "but" to transition from valuing women as candidates to a gender-neutral approach: "I understand that we should give women more chances in the election, *but* I *don't* think gender should be an influence for who to vote for. I think it should be more about their *agenda.*"

Grayson, a 22-year-old Middle Eastern man, thought that voters need to move away from gender-based voting. He considered past

> political *background*, their political *standing*, *not* just focusing on the candidate from their gender perspective. I like to believe that we're a little *beyond that*, and we do put more value in who they are as a *person* and *not* what their gender is.

Leo, an 18-year-old Asian American man, concurred, "I have to agree with him. Gender, for me, it's *not* an issue at all. What I look for is their political aspect and what *contributions* they'll help us as people." Christopher, a 19-year-old Latinx man, pointed out that it is difficult to listen to women candidates who talk too much about gender. He said that candidates who "view gender as an ability" face "consequences." Drawing on fairy-tale analogies, Christopher said, "If you're too vocal, it's like the boy who cried wolf. Nobody's going to listen to you. You've got to find that Goldilocks factor." According to this view, women candidates should not be outspoken about gender.

Thus, women candidates drew on gender-neutral self-presentations to target voters who might not identify or align with the women's movement. When running for a gubernatorial seat, this type of strategic approach is effective, as it gives voters of different orientations a place of identification. While the men we interviewed were supportive of women candidates, they preferred more gender-neutral appeals.

"Mannnnnn . . . Gretchen Whitmer So Damn Fine She Makes Me Wanna Be a Democrat Again": Gender-Traditional Self-Presentations and Voter Reactions

The 2018 gubernatorial candidates also expressed a gender-traditional self-presentation at certain times during their campaign. Women candidates are subjected to judgment based on their appearance much more than men candidates, and they were aware of, and sometimes denounced, this double standard. At the same time, these candidates sometimes emphasized stereotypically feminine gender roles, such as their caretaking and family obligations. Women in politics face a "classic double bind," as stereotypical gender self-presentations can be risky and make a candidate appear "incompetent" (Meeks 2016; Lawrence et al. 2016; McGregor 2017). The 2018 candidates avoided this problem by blending their traditional self-presentations with feminist and nontraditional ones. Democratic women candidates also put gender-traditional issues at the forefront of their campaigns, including health care, education, and early childhood education (Aronson et al. 2020).

Women's Appearance

Reading a tweet from a voter in her "Mean Tweets" ad, Whitmer read, "Mannnnnn . . . Gretchen Whitmer so damn fine she makes me wanna be a Democrat again." Looking at the camera, she smiled in a flirty way and said approvingly, "We're going to win this election one vote at a time" (Whitmer 2018c). In addition to presenting herself as a tough, no-nonsense candidate, this example also suggests that Whitmer simultaneously used and played with traditional notions of femininity in her self-presentation.

When we asked whether men and women face different obstacles on the campaign trail, two focus group interviewees specifically discussed the sexualization of women candidates. Charlotte said, "Women in general are more *sexualized* than men." Anthony immediately recalled the case of Sarah Palin, the only woman to ever run on the Republican ticket for vice president: "Both parties *sexualized* Sarah Palin, saying how hot she is or how hot she isn't. I don't think they would have done that with a guy." In fact, in an analysis of news coverage, Trimble and her collaborators found that journalists and pundits emphasize women candidates' personal lives and bodies more often than those of men candidates (Trimble et al. 2013). The more powerful the position a woman candidate is seeking, the more likely media and social media will focus on her appearance and personal life (Wagner 2019).

Jeremiah, a 36-year-old multiracial man, said that for "female candidates, the media tends to make a lot of appearance, hairstyles, and clothing options. Male candidates don't tend to get that very often." William, an 18-year-old white man, echoed these points,

> A lot of the media coverage of women has nothing to do with their policies. It is: "What are they wearing? Who are they dating? How did that dress look on her at the debate?" Not, "What does she say at the debate?"

As reflected by Alyssa:

> When the news media is talking about a female candidate, they'll talk about the way that she dressed or her hair. What does that have to do with what she stands for? What does that have to do with what she's going to do for me as a citizen? They're not really focusing on what the candidate is standing for, what she actually wants to do. They're worried about physical appearance.

Thus, focus group participants were well aware of the gendered ways candidates' appearances are evaluated.

Women's Caretaking Role

Candidates in conservative states also emphasized gender-traditional caretaking roles. Although her campaign was a long shot, Jordan promulgated an ad in Idaho that said, "I hear you Idaho," in which she emphasized her faith, family connections, and caretaking. Featuring photos of her family on a shelf against a rustic wooden wall and images of Jordan riding a horse, talking to children, and attending church, the ad declared,

> Her family has been on this land for so many generations that Paulette and Idaho are frankly one in the same. In Idaho, the land can be unforgiving. We have to *care for each other, care for our families*, have faith in God (Jordan for Governor 2018).

"Personalization," or candidates' self-disclosure to voters, typically differs for men and women candidates (Lawrence et al. 2016; Meeks 2016). Men personalize more than women (McGregor et al. 2016) and benefit from a self-disclosure strategy more than women (Meeks 2016). However, when races are competitive, women tend to use personalization, especially highlighting their caregiving roles (McGregor et al. 2016). "Strategic stereotype theory" suggests that candidates draw on gender stereotypes that provide them benefits (Fridkin and Kenney 2015). For women, this could involve strategically drawing on stereotypes that they are caring (Fridkin and Kenney 2015). Women candidates may have an advantage when they conform to gender norms that emphasize "feminine" traits, such as honesty and authenticity, or highlight their "outsider" status (Dittmar 2015).

Many of the candidates studied here emphasized family connections and other nurturing self-presentations. For example, Kelly simultaneously connected motherhood to her own family of origin and state identity. Featuring images of her father, mother, and siblings followed by photos of her husband and children, she said, "I grew up in a military family. Lived all over. But Kansas was where we wanted to raise our daughters. Strong communities. Great public schools" (Laura Kelly for Kansas 2018). The ad concluded with an image of Kelly and her husband walking while holding hands. Mills took a similar approach, drawing on her caretaking roles to explain her stance on health care. With a backdrop of images of Mills with her husband, one ad stated,

> Twenty-nine years after we were married, my husband had a stroke and he spent a year in and out of hospitals and rehabs and nursing homes and the like and then passed away in September of 2014. I realized that what we were going through—high deductibles and copays and the cost of pharmaceutical drugs—was no different than what thousands of Maine families go through every year, every day across our state (Janet Mills for Governor 2017).

Noem also emphasized motherhood and family tragedy in an ad that stated, "When her father died in a tragic accident, she took over the family farm. She's also a businesswoman and a mom" (Conservative Reform Network 2012).

Like many women gubernatorial candidates, Whitmer seamlessly blended traditional femininity with gender-neutral, nontraditional, and feminist self-presentations (Aronson et al. 2020, 2023). In an ad quoted earlier, Whitmer walked through her kitchen, handed one child a lunch bag from the refrigerator and another a school textbook, adjusted her husband's tie, and then picked up a coat off the floor and hung it on a hook. She said, "I am *mom* of two, *stepmom* to three, *wife* of a small business owner, and the household quarterback for *everyone*" (Whitmer 2018b). The synthesis of these traditional self-presentations with other images creates complex messages that target voters with divergent backgrounds. This approach may reflect a "hybridized" strategy and "diverse strategic deployment of femininity" (Lawrence et al. 2016: 203, 197).

Abrams, who is not a parent herself, also fused gender-traditional self-presentations with other ways of depicting herself. While at Yale Law School, Abrams published the first of eight romance novels under the pseudonym Selena Montgomery with the goal of showing Black women that they were "as adventurous and attractive as any white woman" (Krug 2018). In 2018, Abrams's ads emphasized her family upbringing and caretaking abilities. Alongside photos of her parents, Abrams hugging a child, and Abrams handing a woman a home-cooked casserole, she said, "I come from a librarian mother and shipyard worker father who became United Methodist ministers. You know, they never let a lack of material possessions or the wrong zip

FIGURE 3.4   Georgian Gubernatorial Candidate Abrams Helping Someone Clean the Kitchen in her 2018 "Thrive" Ad

Source: Retrieved from YouTube (Stacey Abrams, 2017, 0:49).

code keep their children from dreaming" (Abrams 2018b). In another ad, Abrams was seen walking into someone's home, cooking spaghetti sauce in the family's kitchen, helping a child with math homework, eating at a dinner table with a name tag that said "Auntie Stacey," and driving a homemade casserole to another family's house. She stated, "Our parents had three rules: go to church, go to school, and *take care of each other.*" With the backdrop of two families holding hands and praying before dinner, she said, "We all found different ways to *care,* helping others to thrive, not just survive. Because it's always been about *caring for each other*" (Abrams 2017).

Abrams's emphasis on "caring" and "helping," along with cooking and creating family togetherness, provided a strategic contrast with her opponent, Brian Kemp, whose self-presentation was unapologetically white and hypermasculine. In one of his campaign ads, Kemp stood in front of an explosion in a large field as he said, "I'm so conservative, I blow up government spending" (Kemp for Governor 2018b). Wearing a flannel shirt while cocking the barrel of a shotgun, Kemp said, "I own guns that no one's taking away" (Kemp for Governor 2018b). The ad then followed Kemp to the driver's seat of a pickup truck, where he said, "I got a big truck, just in case I need to round up criminal illegals and take 'em home myself" (Kemp for Governor 2018b). With the camera up close in his face, Kemp doubled down on his brash statement: "Yep, I just said that" (Kemp for Governor 2018b). In another ad, Kemp cleaned the barrel of a gun in his living room and introduced someone sitting next to him as a "young man interested in one of my daughters." After Kemp quizzed him on policy positions and the young man answered correctly, referring to Kemp as "sir," Kemp pointed the gun at the young man and said, "We're going to get along just fine" (Kemp for Governor 2018c).

Traditional gender stereotypes that portray women candidates as cooperative or "communal" (Bauer 2016; Bauer 2014; Lawrence et al. 2016; McGregor 2017; Meeks 2016) were present in candidates' self-presentations. Lujan Grisham created an ad that featured a testimonial of a terminally ill man whom she had helped get insurance. Sitting in a chair with a walker and cane visible, he said, "When I was diagnosed with pancreatic cancer, I called Michelle for help. . . . She got me health coverage and she saved my family from bankruptcy" (Lujan Grisham 2018c). In conservative Wyoming, Throne stressed the importance of neighbors caring for each other:

> Neighbor was always a verb in my family because *neighbors work together.* Neighbors help build this fence. In Wyoming, *we have to work together.* It's how we survive. . . . Someday, this fence is going to need fixing and when it does, I want my *grandkids* to be here to fix it (Throne 2017).

Mills also emphasized protecting vulnerable people and working cooperatively with others. One of her ads stated,

> I guess it's in my nature to try to *protect* people who can't fend for themselves. I also can build coalitions across the state. And that's what I want to do as

governor. I want to *bring people together*. People I hear from are tired of partisan bickering. They are tired of the divisiveness, the polarization (Janet Mills for Governor 2017).

Featuring images of herself sitting and talking with a white senior citizen, talking to a smiling white child and her mother, and laughing with a woman of color, Mills highlighted her sensitivity and care for others:

> I want a state where every senior has heat in their home, every veteran has a place to go at night and a place to go during the day, every child has an equal opportunity for education and all new Mainers will be *welcome with an open and loving heart* (Janet Mills for Governor 2017).

These types of self-presentations symbolize candidates' credentials as caretakers and imply that they will also care for voters in traditional ways.

Focus group participants remarked that women candidates are judged closely on their attitude and demeanor, especially when it comes to caregiving and nurturing roles. Charlotte pointed out a paradox: Women candidates need to exhibit caregiving skills yet are simultaneously penalized for motherhood. She said that voters "really want to see a woman as more *nurturing*, as opposed to a male candidate." At the same time, she said that "the *mother* aspect of her might be more critiqued than if a male candidate is a father." That is, women candidates' use of language that emphasized their caretaking role is not typical of men in politics, and voters recognized this double standard.

Conclusion

The 2018 election illustrates the interplay between social movements, political power, and cultural change. Women candidates ran for office in the midst of the gender revolution, an "unsettled" time with the potential for "social transformation" and the "culture's influence on social action" (Swidler 1986: 278). As we have seen, it was an important year for women in politics, not only for their successes but also for innovative self-presentations, most notably gender-nontraditional and feminist ones. All of the gubernatorial Democratic candidates supported the women's movement frames and emphasized the collective rights of women. Not surprisingly, the only Republican candidate in our study did not emphasize feminist self-presentations. However, like the Democrats, Noem drew on the culture of the women's movement in notable ways, especially its language and images that defied gender stereotypes. In an effort to target a wide range of voters, including men and those who do not identify with the women's movement, the candidates simultaneously fused such self-presentations with gender-neutral and gender-traditional ones. Typical during times of rapid social change, we also witnessed "a contested cultural arena" (Swidler 1986: 279), characterized by the media's emphasis on women candidates' appearance and hypermasculine and racist attack ads.

Focus group interviews, uncovering how voting-aged people reacted to these transformations in politics, suggest women's movement cultural diffusion. The women we interviewed connected with candidates' use of women's movement frames that emphasized a feminist framework and defied gender stereotypes. Their language also expressed a diffusion of collective identity; they used words like "us," "we," and "them" to draw gender distinctions, as well as words like "change," "take over," "power," "control," "decisions," "fighting," and "storming the gates" to reflect recent transformations. In short, the women we interviewed saw themselves as part of a larger movement that seized power; they identified with the candidates who drew on such collective identities. Women supported women candidates as a result of gender and emphasized the importance of disruptions in gender and racial inequalities in political power. They viewed women's electoral successes not only as a reaction to Trump's election in 2016 but also as part of a larger movement that is challenging white hegemony and men's power. These women, from diverse racial and ethnic backgrounds, saw the Women's March protests and the #MeToo movement as integral to women's courage in the political sphere. That is, they thought that women are more "confident" and "empowered" in male-dominated spaces because of a new ability to speak out about their private experiences with sexual harassment and assault. They also emphasized an intersectional framework and recognized shifts in power toward women of color. They emphasized their collective identities as women in general, and often as women of color in particular.

The men we interviewed supported the notion of a "cultural lag." They did not "cling to cultural values" that reject women candidates altogether but were "reluctant to abandon familiar" approaches "for which they have the cultural equipment" (Swidler 1986: 281). They supported women candidates but did not see themselves as part of the movement. Without embracing the new cultural framework that the women had embraced, the men instead focused on a gender-neutral approach that supported women candidates because of their individual merit; they emphasized the importance of qualifications and particular individual characteristics. Given the large historical gender gap in men voting for women candidates (e.g., there was an 11-point gender gap in the 2016 presidential election [Center for American Women in Politics 2017]), this support for women candidates among the focus group men indicates a cultural shift. Yet men's approach illustrates a "cultural lag" because they did not embrace the larger social transformations that were underway. Despite limitations, voting for women candidates (even based on their individual merit) represents a step forward toward innovation, as it challenges the patriarchal basis of traditional electoral politics (e.g., the expectation that candidates are men).

As a distinctly American electoral winner-take-all process, gubernatorial races obviously take place within established political structures. Therefore, candidates must have widespread voter appeal. Successful candidates during these contests drew on a spectrum of self-presentations to strategically craft a complex and multifaceted image. This aspect of the election is certainly not pathbreaking. Additionally, the perspectives of the focus group men indicate that cultural transformations are uneven.

At the same time, the range of candidates' gender self-presentations was unprecedented and reflects a unique historical moment. Not only were women candidates outspoken and visible, but they also presented themselves in ways that drew on women's movement frames, including women's collective power and an emphasis on intersectional feminism. Although beyond the scope of our analysis in this chapter, it is useful to reflect on the 2016 presidential race. Dressed in her frequently remarked-on pantsuit, Clinton was berated for the tone of her voice and her "tough" self-presentation style (Aronson 2018). Although she attempted to "soften" her image, she was ultimately unable to overcome the misogyny that she faced on the campaign trail (Aronson 2018). In contrast, most of the 2018 gubernatorial candidates were innovators; they were unapologetically confrontational, assertive, and overtly feminist. Women voters embraced these self-presentations and reported that they facilitated their own identification with the #MeToo and broader women's movements.

Considered together, the gendered self-presentations of the candidates and the focus group women's emphasis on a collective identity reveal significant transformations in gender relations and a diffusion of women's movement culture. These findings point to the dynamic relationship between social movements, political power, and individual identities, as women candidates and voters refused to accept gender inequalities and challenged existing political structures in profound ways. In fact, feminist and nontraditional images and language contributed to a sense of women's power and agency. As innovator candidates and voters altered the political landscape, they reshaped views of women in politics and supported an intersectional critique of white male power. Thus, the 2018 election is an integral part of cultural transformations in the gender revolution.

Notes

1. CNN Politics 2018d
2. Ballotpedia 2018a
3. Ballotpedia 2018b
4. Ballotpedia 2018c
5. CNN Politics 2018g
6. Ballotpedia 2018d
7. Ballotpedia 2018e
8. Ballotpedia 2018f

References

Abrams, Stacey. 2018a. Guys Like Me. *YouTube*. Retrieved October 27, 2021 (www.youtube.com/watch?v=WMwwCNaI4z4).

Abrams, Stacey. 2018b. Foundation. *YouTube*. Retrieved November 1, 2021 (www.youtube. com/watch?v=6O8fMzlHMK8).

Abrams, Stacey. 2017. Thrive. *YouTube*. Retrieved November 1, 2021 (www.youtube.com/ watch?v=YI8hu2navrg).

Amenta, Edwin, Kenneth T. Andrews, and Neal Caren. 2018. "The Political Institutions, Processes, and Outcomes Movements Seek to Influence." pp. 449–465 in *The Wiley Blackwell Companion to Social Movements, Second Edition*, edited by David A. Snow, Sarah A. Soule, Hanspeter Kriesi, and Holly J. McCammon. Hoboken, NJ: John Wiley & Sons Ltd.

Armstrong, Elizabeth A. and Mary Bernstein. 2008. "Culture, Power, and Institutions: A Multi-Institutional Politics Approach to Social Movements." *Sociological Theory* 26(1):74–99.

Aronson, Pamela. 2018. "'I'm Not Voting for *Her*.' Internalized Misogyny, Feminism and Gender Consciousness in the 2016 Election." pp. 204–218 in *Nasty Women and Bad Hombres: Gender and Race in the 2016 Presidential Election*, edited by Christine Kray, Tamar Carroll and Hinda Mandell. Rochester, NY: University of Rochester Press.

Aronson, Pamela and Leah Oldham. 2019. "Representations of Gender in the 2018 Gubernatorial Elections." Presented at the Midwest Sociological Society Annual Conference. Chicago.

Aronson, Pamela, Leah Oldham, and Emily Lucas. 2020. "Gender Self-Presentations in the 2020 U.S. Elections." *Journal of Cultural Analysis and Social Change* 5(1):01. ISSN: 2589-1316.

Aronson, Pamela, Leah Oldham, and Emily Lucas. 2023. "Spectrum of Gender Self-Presentations among Women Candidates." *Journal of Cultural Analysis and Social Change* https://doi.org/10.20897/jcasc/13255.

Axios. 2018. "Women Campaigning for Office: Then vs. Now." *Axios* 1(2). www.hbo.com/ video/axios/seasons/season-1/episodes/episode-2/videos/women-campaigning-for-office-then-vs-now

Ballotpedia. 2018a. "Idaho Gubernatorial Ballotpedia Election, 2018." *Ballotpedia*. Retrieved November 1, 2021 (https://ballotpedia.org/Idaho_gubernatorial_election,_2018).

Ballotpedia. 2018b. "Governor of Kansas." *Ballotpedia*. Retrieved November 1, 2021 (https://ballotpedia.org/Governor_of_Kansas).

Ballotpedia. 2018c. "Maine Gubernatorial Election." *Ballotpedia*. Retrieved November 1, 2021 (https://ballotpedia.org/Maine_gubernatorial_election,_2018).

Ballotpedia. 2018d. "Governor of New Mexico." *Ballotpedia*. Retrieved November 1, 2021 (https://ballotpedia.org/Governor_of_New_Mexico).

Ballotpedia. 2018e. "South Dakota Gubernatorial and Lieutenant Gubernatorial Election, 2018." *Ballotpedia*. Retrieved November 1, 2021 (https://ballotpedia.org/ South_Dakota_gubernatorial_and_lieutenant_gubernatorial_election,_2018).

Ballotpedia. 2018f. "Wyoming Gubernatorial Election, 2018." *Ballotpedia*. Retrieved November 1, 2021 (https://ballotpedia.org/Wyoming_gubernatorial_election,_2018).

Bauer, Nichole M. 2016. "The Effects of Counterstereotypic Gender Strategies on Candidate Evaluations." *Political Psychology* 38(2):279–295.

Bauer, Nichole M. 2014. "Emotional, Sensitive, and Unfit for Office? Gender Stereotype Activation and Support Female Candidates." *Political Psychology* 36(6):691–708.

Burns, Sarah, Lindsay Eberhardt, and Jennifer L. Merolla. 2013. "What Is the Difference Between a Hockey Mom and a Pit Bull? Presentations of Palin and Gender Stereotypes in the 2008 Presidential Election." *Political Research Quarterly* 66(3):687–701.

Carroll, Susan J. 2009. "Reflections on Gender and Hillary Clinton's Presidential Campaign: The Good, the Bad, and the Misogynic." *Politics & Gender* 5(01):1–20.

Center for American Women and Politics. 2020. "Women in the U.S. Congress 2019—Archive." *Center for American Women and Politics.* Retrieved October 14, 2021 (https://cawp.rutgers.edu/women-us-congress-2019).

Center for American Women and Politics. 2018. "Results: Women Candidates in the 2018 Elections." *Center for American Women and Politics.* Retrieved October 14, 2021 (https://cawp.rutgers.edu/sites/default/files/resources/results_release_5bletterhead5d_1.pdf).

Center for American Women in Politics. 2017. "The Gender Gap—Voting Choices in Presidential Elections." *Center for American Women and Politics.* Retrieved November 1, 2021 (https://cawp.rutgers.edu/sites/default/files/resources/ggpresvote.pdf). https://cawp.rutgers.edu/sites/default/files/resources/results_release_5bletterhead5d_1.pdf

The Circus on SHOWTIME. 2018. Stacey Abrams on Women, #MeToo, The Mid-Terms, & More. *YouTube.* Retrieved October 26, 2021 (www.youtube.com/watch?v=RKWX_MRK9VE).

Click On Detroit | Local 4 | WDIV. 2018. Gretchen Whitmer Campaign Ad Michigan Governor 2018—Infrastructure. *YouTube.* Retrieved October 27, 2021 (www.youtube.com/watch?v=iQBSjB8N9Ns).

CNN Politics. 2018a. "2018 Midterms: Exit Polling." *CNN.* Retrieved October 14, 2021 (www.cnn.com/election/2018/exit-polls).

CNN Politics. 2018b. "2018 Midterms: Exit Polling." *CNN.* Retrieved October 14, 2021 (www.cnn.com/election/2018/exit-polls/michigan).

CNN Politics. 2018c. "Kansas Governor Election Results." *CNN.* Retrieved October 14, 2021 (www.cnn.com/election/2018/results/kansas/governor).

CNN Politics. 2018d. "2018 Midterms: Exit Polling." *CNN.* Retrieved October 26, 2021 (www.cnn.com/election/2018/exit-polls/georgia).

CNN Politics. 2018e. "@CNNPolitics." *Twitter.* Retrieved November 1, 2021 (https://twitter.com/CNNPolitics/status/1060167036167512065).

CNN Politics. 2018g. "Michigan Gubernatorial Election Results." *CNN.* Retrieved November 1, 2021 (www.cnn.com/election/2018/results/michigan/governor).

CNN Politics. 2016a. "Michigan Election Results 2016." *CNN.* Retrieved October 14, 2021 (www.cnn.com/election/2016/results/states/michigan).

CNN Politics. 2016b. "Kansas Election Results 2016." *CNN.* Retrieved October 14, 2021 (www.cnn.com/election/2016/results/states/kansas).

CNN Transcripts. 2019. "Smerconish Transcripts." *CNN.* Retrieved October 26, 2021 (http://transcripts.cnn.com/TRANSCRIPTS/1901/05/smer.01.html).

Conservative Reform Network. 2012. YG Network Ad: 'Fight for Us' Kristi Noem (SD-at Large. *YouTube.* Retrieved November 1, 2021 (www.youtube.com/watch?v=kIwocWr7guo).

The Daily Show with Trevor Noah. 2018. Stacey Abrams—"Minority Leader" and a Historic Race for Governor in Georgia. *YouTube.* Retrieved November 1, 2021 (www.youtube.com/watch?v=V-ub3f9WCnE).

della Porta, Donatella and Mario Diani. 2015. "Introduction." pp. 1–31 in *The Oxford Handbook of Social Movements,* edited by Donatella della Porta and Mario Diani. New York, NY: Oxford University Press.

Dittmar, Kelly. 2019. "Unfinished Business: Women Running in 2018 and Beyond." *CAWP—Center for American Woman and Politics.* Retrieved October 14, 2021 (https://cawp.rutgers.edu/sites/default/files/resources/press-release-unfinished-business.pdf).

Dittmar, Kelly. 2015. *Navigating Gendered Terrain: Stereotypes and Strategy in Political Campaigns*. Philadelphia, PA: Temple University Press.

Durkin, Erin. 2018. "GOP Candidate Improperly Purged 340,000 From Georgia Voter Rolls, Investigation Claims." *The Guardian*. Retrieved October 26, 2021 (www.theguardian.com/us-news/2018/oct/19/georgia-governor-race-voter-suppression-brian-kemp).

Dwyer, Caitlin E., Daniel Stevens, John L. Sullivan, and Barbara Allen. 2009. "Racism, Sexism, and Candidate Evaluations in the 2008 U.S. Presidential Election." *Analyses of Social Issues and Public Policy* 9(1):223–240.

Fisher, Dana R. 2019. *American Resistance: From the Women's March to the Blue Wave*. New York: Columbia University Press.

Fridkin, Kim and Patrick Kenney. 2015. *The Changing Face of Representation: The Gender of U.S. Senators and Constituent Communications*. Ann Arbor: University of Michigan Press.

The Guardian. 2018. Stacey Abrams v Brian Kemp: Inside the Bitter Battle for Georgia's Soul. *YouTube*. Retrieved October 26, 2021 (www.youtube.com/watch?v=i0cGOs7Jz_4).

Harris, Lee. 2018. "In Historic Upset, 28-Year-Old Alexandria Ocasio-Cortez Unseats 4th Ranking House Democrat Joe Crowley." *ABC News*. Retrieved October 14, 2021 (https://abcnews.go.com/Politics/historic-upset-28-year-alexandria-ocasio-cortez-unseats/story?id=56188380).

Hutter, Swen, Hanspeter Kriesi, and Jasmine Lorenzini. 2018. "Social Movements in Interaction with Political Parties." pp. 322–337 in *The Wiley Blackwell Companion to Social Movements, Second Edition*, edited by David A. Snow, Sarah A. Soule, Hanspeter Kriesi, and Holly J. McCammon. Hoboken, NJ: John Wiley & Sons Ltd.

Janet Mills for Governor. 2018. Need to Know. *YouTube*. Retrieved October 27, 2021 (www.youtube.com/watch?v=azwf642gZLw).

Janet Mills for Governor. 2017. One Maine. *YouTube*. Retrieved October 27, 2021 (www.youtube.com/watch?v=ptr6ZXsajVg).

Jordan for Governor. 2018. Pure Idaho. *YouTube*. Retrieved November 1, 2021 (www.youtube.com/watch?v=KJ3BX0ce8Ug).

Kelly, Laura. 2018. Ruckus. *KCPTOnline*. Retrieved October 14, 2021 (www.youtube.com/watch?v=sNIbHcb0c34).

Kemp for Governor. 2018a. Amy. *YouTube*. Retrieved October 26, 2021 (www.youtube.com/watch?v=T992JFfhWlc).

Kemp for Governor. 2018b. So Conservative. *YouTube*. Retrieved November 1, 2021 (www.youtube.com/watch?v=5Q1cfjh6VfE).

Kemp for Governor. 2018c. Jake. *YouTube*. Retrieved November 1, 2021 (www.youtube.com/watch?v=4ABRz_epvic).

Killough, Ashley and Clare Foran. 2019. "Congresswomen 'Squad' Respond to Trump's Attacks: The US 'Belongs to Everyone.'" *CNN*. Retrieved October 26, 2021 (www.cnn.com/2019/07/15/politics/squad-response-to-trump-racist-tweet/index.html).

Klein, Ezra. 2019. "Pete Buttigieg, Barack Obama, and the Psychology of Liberalism." *Vox*. Retrieved October 27, 2021 (www.vox.com/policy-and-politics/2019/4/16/18310769/pete-buttigieg-barack-obama-2020-presidential-announcement-hope-primary-democrats).

Krug, Nora. 2018. "How Stacey Abrams Turned Heartbreak Into a Career Plan—and Romance Novels." *The Washington Post*. Retrieved November 1, 2021 (www.washingtonpost.com/entertainment/books/how-stacey-abrams-turned-heartbreak-into-a-side-hustle-as-a-romance-novelist/2018/10/22/1bc44dfc-bb8a-11e8-bdc0-90f81cc58c5d_story.html).

Lai, K. K. Rebecca, Denise Lu, Lisa Lerer, and Troy Griggs. 2018. "The Faces of Change in the Midterm Elections." *The New York Times*. Retrieved October 14, 2021 (www.nytimes. com/interactive/2018/10/31/us/politics/midterm-election-candidates-diversity.html).

Langone, Alix. 2018. "#MeToo and Time's Up Founders Explain the Difference Between the 2 Movements—And How They're Alike." *Time*. Retrieved October 26, 2021 (https:// time.com/5189945/whats-the-difference-between-the-metoo-and-times-up-movements/).

Laura Kelly for Kansas. 2018. Restore. *YouTube*. Retrieved November 1, 2021 (www. youtube.com/watch?v=JtLE2HL-VyA).

Lawrence, Regina G., Shannon C. McGregor, Arielle Cardona, and Rachel R. Mourão. 2016. "Personalization and Gender: 2014 Gubernatorial Candidates on Social Media." pp 191–206 in *Communication and Midterm Elections: Media, Message, and Mobilization*, edited by John Allen Hendricks and Dan Schill. New York, NY: Palgrave Macmillan.

Lujan Grisham, Michelle. 2018a. Like Trump. *YouTube*. Retrieved October 26, 2021 (www. youtube.com/watch?v=jb1H-Cbx0Xg).

Lujan Grisham, Michelle. 2018b. Runway. *YouTube*. Retrieved November 1, 2021 (www. youtube.com/watch?v=wfdj7MZK8ro).

Lujan Grisham, Michelle. 2018c. Godsend. *YouTube*. Retrieved November 1, 2021 (www. youtube.com/watch?v=gzdalI0O0eU).

McGregor, Shannon C. 2017. "Personalization, Social Media, and Voting: Effects of Candidate Self-Personalization on Vote Intention." *New Media & Society* 20(3):1139–1160.

McGregor, Shannon C., Regina G. Lawrence, and Arielle Cardona. 2016. "Personalization, Gender, and Social Media: Gubernatorial Candidates' Social Media Strategies." *Information, Communication & Society* 20(2):264–283.

Meeks, Lindsey. 2016. "Getting Personal: Effects of Twitter Personalization on Candidate Evaluations." *Politics & Gender* 13(01):1–25.

Meyer, David S. and Suzanne Staggenborg. 1996. "Movements, Countermovements, and the Structure of Political Opportunity." *American Journal of Sociology* 101(6):1628–1660.

Noem, Kristi. 2018a. Tested. Proven. Conservative. *YouTube*. Retrieved October 27, 2021 (www.youtube.com/watch?v=0kDHkifsNVo).

Noem, Kristi. 2018b. CNN. *YouTube*. Retrieved October 27, 2021 (www.youtube.com/ watch?v=8G_PIS0JVFY).

Noem, Kristi. 2017. Experience | Kristi for South Dakota. *YouTube*. Retrieved October 27, 2021 (www.youtube.com/watch?v=Z1TCFSn0O7c&t=4s).

Noem, Kristi. 2016. I'm All in—Kristi for South Dakota Governor. *YouTube*. Retrieved October 27, 2021 (www.youtube.com/watch?v=Fa99bTrYTCM).

Ocasio-Cortez, Alexandria. 2018. The Courage to Change. *YouTube*. Retrieved October 14, 2021 (www.youtube.com/watch?v=rq3QXIVR0bs).

Oliver, Sarah and Meredith Conroy. 2020. *Who Runs? The Masculine Advantage in Candidate Emergence*. Ann Arbor: University of Michigan Press.

The Real Daytime. 2019. Governor Gretchen Whitmer's Controversial Dress. *YouTube*. Retrieved October 27, 2021 (www.youtube.com/watch?v=bYvKM5ao_vA).

Republican Governors Association. 2018. RGA Georgia TV Ad: "Stacey Abrams: Too Liberal For Georgia." *YouTube*. Retrieved October 26, 2021 (www.youtube.com/ watch?v=TETHJP6d2Os).

Schneider, Monica C. 2014. "Gender-Based Strategies on Candidate Websites." *Journal of Political Marketing* 13(4):264–290.

Swidler, Ann. 1986. "Culture in Action: Symbols and Strategies." *American Sociological Review* 51(2):273–286.

Swire, Brendan. 2018. GA Gubernatorial Candidate Stacey Abrams Smacks Down The View's Meghan McCain on Guns. *YouTube*. Retrieved October 27, 2021 (www.youtube.com/watch?v=N7szIjp5n0M).

Throne, Mary. 2017. Mary for Wyoming Announcement. *YouTube*. Retrieved October 14, 2021 (www.youtube.com/watch?v=39p4RFr3LA8).

Trimble, Linda, Angelia Wagner, Shannon Sampert, Daisy Raphael, and Bailey Gerrits. 2013. "Is It Personal? Gendered Mediation in Newspaper Coverage of Canadian National Party Leadership Contests, 1975–2012." *The International Journal of Press/Politics* 18(4):462–481.

Van Dyke, Nella and Verta Taylor. 2018. "The Cultural Outcomes of Social Movements." pp. 482–498 in *The Wiley Blackwell Companion to Social Movements, Second Edition*, edited by David A. Snow, Sarah A. Soule, Hanspeter Kriesi, and Holly J. McCammon. Hoboken, NJ: John Wiley & Sons Ltd.

Wagner, Angelia. 2019. "Media Sexism? Depends on Who You Are." *Policy Options Politiques*. Retrieved November 1, 2021 (https://policyoptions.irpp.org/magazines/march-2019/media-sexism-depends-on-who-you-are/).

West, Candace and Don H. Zimmerman. 1987. "Doing Gender." *Gender & Society* 1(2):125–151.

Whitmer, Gretchen. 2019. "@GovWhitmer." *Twitter*. Retrieved October 27, 2021 (https://twitter.com/govwhitmer/status/1096141313093914624).

Whitmer, Gretchen. 2018a. It's Time. *YouTube*. Retrieved October 14, 2021 (www.youtube.com/watch?v=070EJaCNd8Y).

Whitmer, Gretchen. 2018b. Gretchen Whitmer—In Your Corner. *YouTube*. Retrieved October 27, 2021 (www.youtube.com/watch?v=oVUCNGo77zY&t=1s).

Whitmer, Gretchen. 2018c. Gretchen Reads Mean Tweets. *YouTube*. Retrieved October 14, 2021 (www.youtube.com/watch?v=RRrcyPju_Kk&t=14s).

WXYZ-TV Detroit | Channel 7. 2018. Gretchen Whitmer Wins Democratic Nomination for Michigan Governor. *YouTube*. Retrieved October 27, 2021 (www.youtube.com/watch?v=C0uptqw2jGk).

The Young Turks. 2019. New Mexico Governor DOG WALKS Trump. *YouTube*. Retrieved October 27, 2021 (www.youtube.com/watch?v=tqr37uEIgiY).

Zraick, Karen. 2018. "Night of Firsts: Diverse Candidates Make History in Midterm Elections." *The New York Times*. Retrieved October 14, 2021 (www.nytimes.com/2018/11/07/us/politics/election-history-firsts-blackburn-pressley.html).

4

WOMEN'S POLITICAL POWER IN THE 2020 PRESIDENTIAL ELECTION

"That Little Girl Was Me": The 2020 Democratic Presidential Primary

During a Democratic presidential primary debate (Debate 1, June 2019), candidate and the then senator Kamala Harris (D-CA) upended traditional gender norms of women's niceness by aggressively confronting front-runner and the then former vice president Joe Biden. Harris, whose parents emigrated from India and Jamaica (The Biden-Harris Administration 2022), drew on her own experience with racial integration in school to stress the urgency of confronting racial inequalities. Interrupting the moderator, Harris challenged Biden's record on racial inequalities:

> I would like to speak on the issue of race. . . . There was a little girl in California who was part of the second class to integrate her public schools and she was bussed to school every day and that little girl was me. So, I will tell you that on this subject, it cannot be an intellectual debate among Democrats. We have to take it seriously. We have to act swiftly (TIME Staff 2019).

Voters responded favorably to Harris's assertiveness in polls and fundraising. Harris raised nearly $2.5 million in the days immediately following the debate (Goldmacher et al. 2019), with commentators attributing the jump to this encounter (Stevens 2019). Although Harris deviated from traditional gender self-presentations, she ultimately became Biden's running mate and made history when elected vice president.

The 2020 Democratic presidential primary was pathbreaking. Of the candidates who qualified for the debates, six women ran (Representative Tulsi Gabbard,

DOI: 10.4324/9781003225331-7

Senator Kristen Gillibrand, Senator Kamala Harris, Senator Amy Klobuchar, Senator Elizabeth Warren, and self-help author Marianne Williamson; see Table 4.1), the largest group to ever do so (Burns et al. 2020). Additionally, the first openly gay candidate for this office became a front-runner (a white man and former mayor of South Bend, Indiana, Pete Buttigieg). It was also the most racially diverse contest for this position, with seven people of color (Burns et al. 2020; Dittmar 2021a). There were two Black candidates in the first debate, including Senator Cory Booker and Senator Harris (see Table 4.1). The first debate included former Housing Secretary Julián Castro, who is Latinx, Asian American (the son of Taiwanese immigrants) tech executive Andrew Yang, and multiracial Representative Gabbard (see Table 4.1). Yet the race came down to Bernie Sanders and Biden, two straight white men in their 70s. Harris was the only candidate of color to qualify for the December debate (Debate 6), but she withdrew her candidacy before the debate; Warren and Klobuchar stayed in the race until March 2020 (Nelson 2021).

The field of candidates called into question the notion that women could not run for president. As Dittmar (2021b) put it: "They challenged any idea that there is a singular model for being a woman presidential candidate, pushing voters and media to accept the same diversity among women that they have long allowed—and even expected—from men." At the same time, concerns about "electability" against Donald Trump harmed the women candidates (Nelson 2021). As a result of the masculinity assumed in politics, particularly for high-level offices like president and vice president, women carefully weigh whether to draw on, minimize, or challenge gender stereotypes in their campaigns. Because no woman had ever been elected president, there is no model for women's success in running. In fact, Hillary Clinton's electoral defeat in 2016 may have increased concerns that Americans are not "ready for a female president."

Voters' views reflect social change and resistance. Since 1974, a declining number of people think that men are "better suited emotionally for politics than most women," yet in 2019, 13 percent still agreed with this statement (Carnevale et al. 2019). A Gallup poll showed more change when it asked, "Do you think the voters of this country are ready to elect a woman president, or don't you think so?" Only 78 percent agreed that they were ready to elect a woman as president in 2011 (Roper Center for Public Opinion Research 2016), but this had risen to 94 percent by 2019 (Gallup News Service 2019). In February 2020, another poll asked about barriers for women running for elected office and found that 39 percent of adults agreed that the "belief that the country isn't ready for a female president" was a "major barrier" and 28 percent thought it was a "minor barrier" (Morning Consult 2020). Only about one-third of adults thought that this belief was *not* a barrier for women candidates (Morning Consult 2020). Women voters were more likely to perceive this factor as a barrier than men voters (Morning Consult 2020). One explanation for these perceptions is women's family responsibilities, as only 43 percent labeled this factor as "not a barrier" (Morning Consult 2020). Streb

TABLE 4.1 2020 Democratic Primary Candidates in Late 2019 and Early 2020 (by Date Leaving Race)

Candidate's Name	Position and Location	Delegates Earned/When They Left the Race
Joe Biden	Former vice president; former senator from Delaware	2687 delegates/Nominated
Bernie Sanders	Senator from Vermont; former congressman	1073 delegates/April 8, 2020
Tulsi Gabbard	Congresswoman from Hawaii; Army National Guard veteran	2 delegates/March 19, 2020
Elizabeth Warren	Senator from Massachusetts; former Harvard professor	63 delegates/March 5, 2020
Michael Bloomberg	Former mayor of New York City; billionaire media executive	59 delegates/March 4, 2020
Amy Klobuchar	Senator from Minnesota; former attorney	7 delegates/March 2, 2020
Pete Buttigieg	Former mayor of South Bend, Indiana; military veteran	21 delegates/March 1, 2020
Tom Steyer	Billionaire former hedge fund executive; climate change and impeachment activist	0 delegates/February 29, 2020
Andrew Yang	Former tech executive who founded an economic development nonprofit	0 delegates/February 11, 2020
Cory Booker	Senator from New Jersey; former mayor of Newark	0 delegates/January 13, 2020
Julián Castro	Former Housing secretary; former mayor of San Antonio	0 delegates/January 2, 2020
Kamala Harris	Senator from California; former attorney general of California; former San Francisco district attorney	0 delegates/December 3, 2019
Beto O'Rourke	Former congressman from Texas; 2018 Senate candidate	0 delegates/November 1, 2019

Sources: Leatherby and Almukhtar (2020); Burns et al. (2020).

et al. (2008) asked about views toward a female president alongside other political issues (including "gasoline prices . . . going up" and "large corporations polluting the environment") and found that slightly more than a quarter of both men and women were "angry or upset" about the possibility of a woman president.

Examining the shape of the gender revolution through the 2020 Democratic presidential primary, this chapter considers the gender self-presentations of candidates of all genders. This group was the most historically diverse in terms of gender, race, age, and sexual orientation (Nelson 2021). This national stage expands on the more localized gubernatorial contests featured in Chapter 3. As in 2018, candidates were innovators; their self-presentations were unabashedly feminist, appealing to the power of women's collective identity. In particular, this chapter examines the gender self-presentations of 13 Democratic Party primary presidential candidates who were influential in late 2019 and early 2020: the eight men and four women who were in the primary debates in October 2019 (Debate 4), as well as billionaire Michael Bloomberg, a white man and former mayor of New York City, who qualified for subsequent debates in early 2020. Uncovering the gendered messages that candidates presented to voters, data draw on the media and candidates' own self-presentations, particularly in advertisements and public appearances. Focus group interviews, conducted prior to much of this election cycle, foretell how ordinary people of voting age view women candidates for president. We consider the outcome of the 2020 Democratic presidential primary and conclude with an analysis of the 2020 general presidential election.

"We Have So Many Women in Leadership Now": Feminist Self-Presentations and Voter Reactions

In a *CNN* town hall on May 21, 2019, a pharmacy student at Drake University who supported Warren questioned Democratic presidential candidate O'Rourke about reproductive rights: "Recently several states have introduced and passed bills that legally prohibit those with uteruses from exercising their reproductive rights. What specific actions will you take to allow us to gain back our right to our own bodies?" (O'Rourke 2019a). O'Rourke, a white man, formerly a U.S. representative (see Table 4.1), responded to this assertiveness by committing to take on what has historically been women's fight to control their own bodies: "For so long women have been leading this fight, shouldering the burden of making sure that their reproductive rights are protected. It's time that *all* of *us* join them in this fight" (O'Rourke 2019a). Like the other men who ran in the Democratic primary, O'Rourke positioned himself as embracing a framework of women's collective power, as evidenced by including himself in his phrase "*all* of *us.*"

Such explicit feminist self-presentations reflect the political power and agency of women in the election—as both serious candidates and voters. In Chapter 3, we argue that self-presentations are best represented by a spectrum, with feminist ones on the most progressive side. Feminist self-presentations focus on gendered political issues and an awareness of gender inequalities and patriarchy (see Table 4.2 and Aronson et al. 2020). This analysis revealed that men and women candidates were equally likely to include feminist labels in their Twitter bios, while men were more likely than women to use feminist self-presentations on their websites (Aronson et al. 2020). Feminist self-presentations in the Democratic Party primary espoused a rhetoric of women's collective power (especially concerns about feminist issues like reproductive rights), the #MeToo movement, and the intersection between

TABLE 4.2 Summary of Spectrum of Gender Self-Presentations

	Feminist	*Gender Nontraditional*	*Gender Neutral*	*Gender Traditional*
Women	Focus on gendered social and political interests, gendered political issues, an awareness of gender inequalities and patriarchy	Stereotypical masculine gender roles, language, or traits, such as swearing, toughness, and "fight"	Gender-blind perspectives, accomplishments, or policy positions	Stereotypical feminine gender roles, such as caretakers and family-oriented
Men	Focus on gendered social and political interests, gendered political issues, an awareness of gender inequalities and patriarchy	Stereotypical feminine gender roles, such as caretakers and family-oriented	Gender-blind perspectives, accomplishments, or policy positions	Stereotypical masculine gender roles, language, or traits, such as toughness and "fight"

Source: Aronson et al. (2020).

gender and racial justice. These issues are key components of women's movement frames and ideology. As a result of the presence of women candidates and a gender gap in voting (Dittmar 2021b), Democrats addressed racial and gender inequalities more explicitly than in previous elections.

Women's Collective Power

Women's collective power in the 2020 primary is illustrated by the prominence of gender issues, which were placed at the center of the Democrats' campaigns. These candidates connected to a women's movement frame by focusing on such issues as women's work, equal pay, sexual harassment, reproductive rights, and paid family leave. Yang, for example, was concerned about gendered work: "The average service retail worker is a 39-year-old woman making between 9 and 10 dollars an hour. . . . We need to start solving the problems of today" (Yang 2019). Yang also proposed "expand[ing] what we think of as work" by providing a monthly supplement to recognize the labor performed by women, including stay-at-home mothers: "This is a game changer for the waitress at the diner who's getting harassed by her boss. It's a game changer for the single mom who's stuck in an abusive relationship" (Yang 2019). Harris's (2019a) team posted a campaign video that touched on gender-neutral issues, such as Medicare and Medicaid, but then also espoused a feminist rhetoric when she called for fines on the profits of companies that do not pay gender-equal wages.

Candidates of all genders explicitly appealed to women voters, who are more likely to identify as Democrats and to endorse views that align with the Democratic Party (Center for American Women and Politics 2022a). In an ad titled "Women for Bernie," a racially and ethnically diverse group of young women on Sanders's campaign staff commented on their unlikely support for "an older white Jewish man" from Vermont (Sanders 2019a). A graphic designer said, "I know it doesn't make sense," but she and other women went on to explain that "his values" focus on concerns facing women, including child care, disproportionate student loan debt, paid family leave, health care, and climate change (Sanders 2019a). In a way that highlighted his feminist credentials, one woman stressed the impact that Sanders had on women of color in politics: "Senator Sanders has our back. He inspired Alexandria Ocasio-Cortez, Ilhan Omar, Rashida Tlaib, and he's going to support us to assume these leadership positions in a way that no one else will" (Sanders 2019a). The support of average women in leadership meant that Sanders stood "for women and people who have had experiences *like me* that encounter unexpected hurdles" (Sanders 2019a). The staffers went on to describe Sanders's support for women in power and gender equality by using the phrase "transform[ing] our country" (Sanders 2019a). Sanders's campaign focused on child poverty, childcare, and "end[ing] racism, sexism, homophobia, religious bigotry, and all forms of discrimination" (Sanders 2019b). In an interview with *Cosmopolitan* magazine, Sanders advocated for women's equal representation in government: "Half of elected officials in America should be women. Half of the Supreme Court should be women" (Pels 2019). Thus, Sanders's self-presentations emphasized a wide range of feminist issues, even controversial ones.

Other men candidates also emphasized the importance of women's collective power, particularly reproductive rights. Polls in 2020 found that women were more likely than men to support abortion rights and the rights of transgender people (Center for American Women and Politics 2022a). In a town hall, Buttigieg said,

> If we really care about women, if we really care about life, then we've got to make sure, from common-sense sex education to access to birth control, that we're preventing many of those unwanted pregnancies from happening in the first place (Fox News 2019a).

Buttigieg focused on women's right to self-determination: "The dialogue has got so caught up on where you draw the line that we've gotten away from the fundamental question of who gets to draw the line. And I trust *women* to draw the line" (Fox News 2019a). This view that the timing of legal abortion should be decided by women rather than politicians or the Supreme Court reinforces women's power and self-determination.

Klobuchar, a white woman and U.S. senator (see Table 4.1), discussed reproductive rights in her campaign and framed them in gender-divisive terms. When an interviewer asked her about abortion bans in Alabama, she responded by highlighting a gendered struggle, "What these *guys* are doing is unbelievable. I say *guys* because in Alabama, it was *all men* that voted for this." Klobuchar critiqued the "assault on women's health" more generally, including "taking away the right to choose, also taking away contraception" (The View 2019a). When asked if she supported "late-term abortions," Klobuchar talked about self-determination: "I am for *women* having the right to make a choice about *her own body*. These *guys* are *using women* as political pawns to set this up for a case to go to the Supreme Court" (The View 2019a). Here, Klobuchar's comments imply that women candidates more authentically understand the consequences of this gendered battle.

Candidates spoke explicitly about their own gendered experiences. In the January 2020 debate (Debate 7), Warren, a white woman and U.S. senator (see Table 4.1), drew on her experience as a working mother in an era when that was atypical to demonstrate her support of women's work:

> I've been there. . . . when I was a young mom, I had two little kids and I had my first real university teaching job. It was hard work. I was excited but it was childcare that nearly brought me down. . . . I was ready to quit my job. And I think of how many women my age just got knocked off the track and never got back on and how many of my daughter's generation get knocked off the track and don't get back on (First Five Years Fund 2020).

Similarly, Gillibrand, also a white woman and U.S. senator, ran an explicitly feminist campaign. Gillibrand, who was inspired to run after the 2017 Women's March and its "wave of women's political energy" (Lerer and Goldmacher 2019), centered her campaign on her experience as a working mother. A campaign speech said she would "fight for your children as hard as I would fight for my own," and her husband took time off work to care for their school-aged children while she was campaigning (Summers 2019). Here, motherhood becomes an asset rather than its typical perception as a liability (Summers 2019). Gillibrand's campaign featured what she called a "woman plus" platform: "The country would be so much stronger if women had greater voices" (Lerer and Goldmacher 2019). Lerer and Goldmacher (2019) pointed out, "There is no real precedent for Ms. Gillibrand's strategy," as she vigorously confronted powerful men in her own party over gender issues. Although she dropped out of the race prior to our data collection, this explicitly feminist approach likely pushed other candidates toward such innovation as well.

The "likability" of presidential candidates is gendered. When an interviewer asked Klobuchar about this issue directly, she responded positively, emphasizing the increased visibility of women in power,

> I'm actually just excited about what's happening right now. We doubled the number of women that had ever been on the stage for a primary debate in the presidential election. And the other fun little sidelight of all this is the husbands, [laughs] the [finger air quotes] "first men" [laughs] (NBC News 2019).

The possibility of having the first "First Gentleman" supporting the first woman president was noted frequently in the media. Klobuchar noted that Clinton running for president in 2016 "actually did break the glass ceiling, because of the fact that we have *so many women* that are in leadership now" (NBC News 2019).

Likewise, Warren drew on feminist issues and women's history in her campaign. In one interview, she mentioned that poor working conditions catalyzed women's activism and collective identity in the early 1900s. Warren referred to the 1911 Triangle Shirtwaist Factory Fire, which killed 146 workers in Manhattan, mainly immigrant teenage girls (The Late Show with Stephen Colbert 2019a). The fire was caused by corruption in the government, as the hazardous working conditions in the factory were previously known but no action was taken (The Late Show with Stephen Colbert 2019a). Emphasizing growth in women's collective power, Warren said that the fire was a "story about power": "After that fire, the *women* got organized, and they said, 'We're going to keep rallying. We're going to keep protesting'" (The Late Show with Stephen Colbert 2019a). She aligned with the legacy of Frances Perkins, who was influenced by the fire. Perkins became a force behind the New Deal, helping to rewrite labor laws, including the establishment of a minimum wage, unemployment insurance, and social security (The Late Show with Stephen Colbert 2019a). Warren connected these historical changes in women's agency to the possibility that her campaign could lead to the first woman president. Using the word "we" to include herself in social transformations in women's power, she said, "We can do the same" (The Late Show with Stephen Colbert 2019a). On the campaign trail, Warren was known to make "pinky promises" to young women and girls that "running for president is what girls do" (Iowa for Warren 2020). Thus, the 2020 Democratic primary candidates, both men and women, expressed the importance of women's collective power in their self-presentations.

Although commenting before this election, focus group innovators, especially women, connected having women candidates for president with the development of their own collective identities. In doing so, they illustrate that social movement frames can be diffused into everyday lives through political campaigns. Sofia, a 21-year-old Latinx woman, said that she thinks "having a female candidate is very influential" and is a form of "woman empowerment" that shows that "a woman can do the same things that a man can do." Sofia linked these changes to shifting norms, drawing on collective social movement language of "we" to refer to women:

> Compared to many years ago, *we*'re slowly stepping away from gender norms. *Women* can be engaged in higher powers, like president. *We*'re slowly going away from the norm and the stereotype that *we*, females, can't engage in the same thing that a man can. The standards have changed today compared to how it was before, when it wasn't even an option for females to be in power. So it's really good. It's really important to have diversity in our political system.

Sofia attributed her perspective to "being a female" and noted that her "views on a female president might be different from a male perspective." She saw this division adversarially. She said that men "might see it differently. *They* might have stereotypes put on women daily, like they are weaker. They can't perform the same tasks as men can. *They* might see that she's not fit for the job." Likewise, Alexandra, a 38-year-old Black woman, appreciated the diversity of the candidates: "We will never see a more colorful and gender diversified presidential election than the one that's coming up" in 2020. These examples suggest that campaigns help diffuse social movement frames and alignment with a collective identity to average people.

Several of the men also viewed the possibility of a woman president quite favorably. Jeremiah, a 36-year-old multiracial man, appreciated that women candidates focused on both gender issues (reproductive rights and "equal pay for equal work") and the concerns of "other social minorities by proxy." Women candidates addressed issues that are "closer to home" and "affect us as a society," whereas men candidates "don't think about those things after they leave the campaign trail."

A discussion between Dominic and Jonah, both 20-year-old white men, suggested that voters' perceptions are shifting as a result of the gender revolution's diffusion of new ideas. Dominic stated that he "heard from awful people that a woman shouldn't be president, that they don't have what it takes to get the job done." Jonah responded by saying that he was "surprised" that "people were expressing doubts" about Clinton in 2016. He asked incredulously, "What do you mean? She's an experienced politician. She's been in the game for 30 years." Jonah said hopefully, "Maybe now, come 2020, that sentiment will have gone away." Thus, focus group innovators, especially women, viewed women running for president as important for their collective identity as women, while some of the men saw the presence of women candidates positively and as advancing other social issues.

Links to the #MeToo Movement

Feminist self-presentations were also present in links that the candidates made to the #MeToo movement. The #MeToo movement frame of speaking out against powerful abusers can be seen in the increasingly acceptable norm for candidates to include accounts of sexual assault in their campaigns. Andrew Yang's wife, Evelyn Yang, used the words we will see in future chapters, including "platform," "talk," and "voice," to describe the positive aspects of survivors coming forward publicly with their experiences. Evelyn spoke out about her sexual assault by her doctor when she was pregnant:

> My experience with the sexual assault and then with all that happened afterwards is such a powerful and upsetting example of the truth that women are living with every day. And I just happen to be able to have a *platform* to *talk* about it. I need to use that *voice* (CNN 2020a).

As a result of multiple allegations against the doctor, a settlement resulted in the doctor losing his medical license and registering as a sex offender (CNN 2020a). However, he was not required to serve time and, despite being arrested, was later allowed to practice medicine again (CNN 2020a). Evelyn said that "it wasn't until after #MeToo and the Weinstein case came out that the victims in this case realized that we were betrayed. It's like getting slapped in the face and punched in the gut" (CNN 2020a).

Similarly, Chasten Buttigieg, Pete Buttigieg's husband, was also vocal about his experience with sexual assault at the age of 18:

> I remember somehow feeling like my parents would be so disappointed in me. And I don't know what it was about society that made me feel somehow that I had done something wrong, and to feel such shame and guilt for somebody else taking advantage of me. I'm so grateful for everyone who has *spoken up* because it made me feel *less alone* too, as somebody who held onto that for a really long time (ABC News 2020).

Like Evelyn's account, Chasten said the increased awareness as a result of #MeToo helped him feel connected with other survivors. Although these experiences were expressed by candidates' spouses rather than candidates themselves, they are vital parts of candidates' self-presentations in a society that inspects every aspect of their lives.

Consistent with the era's public revelations, candidates called out prior instances of sexual harassment and sexism. In the February 2020 debate (Debate 8), Warren attacked candidate Bloomberg for a history of sexist comments:

> I'd like to talk about who we're running against. A billionaire who calls women "fat broads" and "horse-faced lesbians." And no, I'm not talking about Donald Trump. I'm talking about Mayor Bloomberg. Democrats are not going to win if we have a nominee who has a history of hiding his tax returns, of harassing women, and of supporting racist policies (NBC News 2020).

By making Bloomberg's history on gender issues visible, Warren's alignment with #MeToo was outspoken.

Intersectional Feminism

Intersectional feminism, especially its connection to racial justice, was integral to the 2020 election. Democratic candidates appealed to the growing diversity of the electorate. As Dittmar (2021b) explained,

> Democratic presidential candidates also adopted language not commonly used in previous presidential elections, including "systemic racism," "implicit bias," "intersectionality," and "reproductive justice," among other examples of language that reflected candidates' recognition that their voter base expected them to be both better versed on and more vocal about axes of gender and racial inequity in 2020.

Candidates connected with the burgeoning racial justice movement, which itself challenged white male candidates' race and gender privilege by viewing them as possible weaknesses (Dittmar 2021a). Biden was confronted over his past positions on busing and his role in discrediting Anita Hill during the Supreme Court confirmation hearings for Justice Clarence Thomas (Dittmar 2021a). Former prosecutors Klobuchar and Harris faced criticism for cases involving racial bias in the criminal justice system (Dittmar 2021a). Another example comes from Gillibrand, who said that "institutional racism is real" and talked about racial disparities in the criminal justice system (Gillibrand 2019).

Candidates highlighted their understanding of intersecting systems of oppression, especially connections between gender, race, and sexuality. In a "*She* the People" presidential forum in 2019, Warren sharply criticized the myriad forms of discrimination that women of color face (Warren 2019a). A member of the audience asked Warren what she would do to address the "crisis" of racial inequalities in maternal mortality (Warren 2019a). Warren illustrated her knowledge and passion about the topic:

> Oh, great question. The best studies that I've seen put it down to just one thing: prejudice. That doctors and nurses don't hear African American women's medical issues the same way that they hear the same things from white women. We've got to change that and we've got to change it fast because people's lives are at stake (Warren 2019a).

Harris also touched on racial inequalities in maternal mortality in an interview:

> It's tragic because when you look at it, this is not an issue of the educational level of these women. It's not an issue of their socioeconomic situation. It is

literally about racial bias in the health-care delivery system. We need to train medical schools and doctors on how to take Black women seriously when they walk through that hospital door (Breakfast Club Power 105.1 FM 2019a).

Many of the candidates also emphasized their support for LGBTQ rights. Warren posted a campaign video addressed to participants in RuPaul's DragCon (Drag Race queens) event, emphasizing the importance of registering to vote:

> Hello DragCon! . . . I'm in this fight for full LGBTQ+ equality. We've got a lot of work to do to make sure that everyone is free to be who they are and to love who they love. A record number of trans Americans were killed last year—disproportionately trans women of color. We need to call it out and we need to fight back. . . . Equal means equal. Period (Warren 2019b).

As the first openly gay major party presidential candidate, Buttigieg both highlighted and minimized this pathbreaking status. An interviewer told Pete and Chasten Buttigieg, "You are doing something that is new in American politics," and then asked them if they felt they had to answer for this on the campaign trail (CBS Sunday Morning 2019). Chasten was the first to respond:

> I'd argue I don't have to answer for it. We passed marriage equality. I don't think I have to answer for my marriage anymore. But I do enjoy going out there with Pete and showing people that a gay marriage is just like a straight marriage. We have our same spousal quarrels over laundry and who takes the trash out and who forgot to pay the bill this week (CBS Sunday Morning 2019).

Pete added, "It's not designed to be political. It's just who we are. And being who we are has worked out really well for us so far" (CBS Sunday Morning 2019). As they emphasized the power of marriage equality, the Buttigieges engaged in a feminist self-presentation. Yet emphasizing their similarity to straight couples simultaneously minimized the novelty of having an openly gay candidate for president.

Given the diversity of candidates in this election, being a white straight man was sometimes considered a liability. In 2019, before O'Rourke announced his presidential run, an article noted that "O'Rourke is acutely aware . . . of perhaps his biggest vulnerability—being a white man in a Democratic Party yearning for a woman or a person of color, a Kamala Harris or a Cory Booker" (Hagan and Leibovitz 2019). To address this concern, O'Rourke stated that he would diversify his administration:

> The government at all levels is overly represented by white men. . . . That's part of the problem, and I'm a white man. So if I were to run, I think it's just so important that those who would comprise my team looked like this country. If

I were to run, if I were to win, that my administration looks like this country. It's the only way I know to meet that challenge (Hagan and Leibovitz 2019).

With such a diverse candidate field, O'Rourke's comments suggest that he recognized that his background and identity were a potential weakness.

"I Am Angry and I Own It": Gender-Nontraditional Self-Presentations and Voter Reactions

After a confrontation between Biden and Warren, during which he called her "angry," Warren refused to back down in a way that departed from her previous campaigns (Dittmar 2021a). The disagreement centered on both Biden and Buttigieg attacking Warren for "taking a 'my way or the highway' approach to her campaign," particularly her "Medicare for All" plan (Krieg and Bradner 2019). In response, Warren sent a fundraising email with the subject line "I *am angry* and I own it." In the email, she wrote, "Over and over, we are told that women are not allowed to be *angry*. It makes us unattractive to powerful men who want us to be quiet" (Krieg and Bradner 2019). When Biden was asked about the incident, he denied that his critique was rooted in gender stereotypes: "The strong women in my life are angry—they get angry about things. That has nothing to do with it" (Krieg and Bradner 2019). Yet Biden's dismissive comment did not address that the "likability" factor is more pronounced for women candidates than for men (Dittmar 2021a). That is, failing to conform to traditional gender stereotypes can have serious consequences for candidates, particularly women.

Nontraditional self-presentations for women include stereotypical masculine roles, language, or traits, such as swearing or toughness; for men, they include stereotypical feminine roles, such as caretakers and being family-oriented (see Table 4.2). An earlier analysis of these candidates' websites and Twitter bios revealed that women candidates were more likely to take a gender-nontraditional approach than were men (Aronson et al. 2020), which is consistent with masculine expectations of the office of the president.

Women's Nontraditional Self-Presentations

As in the 2018 gubernatorial races, women candidates used stereotypically masculine language, sometimes swear words or words like "fight" to describe their approach to politics. Nontraditional career experiences, such as work history in traditionally male occupations, were also highlighted. Previous studies find that women candidates running for executive offices typically adopt a "masculine" campaign style that emphasizes "toughness" and experience in male domains like defense, while minimizing attention to women's issues (Carroll 2009; Dittmar 2015). In an interview with Clinton's former communications director, Lerer and

Goldmacher (2019) reported that Clinton "struggled to talk about her gender, and essentially tried to copy the approach of the male presidential candidates who had preceded her." At the same time, to conform to norms surrounding femininity, research on previous elections found that women candidates paid close attention to their tone (i.e., "to be tough but not mean") and appearance (i.e., dress professionally to "neutralize gender") (Dittmar 2015: 89, 105). For offices other than president, Dittmar (2015) found that women candidates may even have an advantage when they conform to gender norms that emphasize "feminine" traits such as honesty and authenticity or appear to be political "outsiders" in a predominantly male field. Either way, women candidates carefully balance these gender self-presentations.

In 2020, candidates used gender-nontraditional language to disprove gender stereotypes about women's submissiveness. In a *CNN* interview, Harris was asked why she thought her approval ratings were so high; she emphasized her leadership experience and used the word "fight" twice:

> People want a leader who has a proven track record of knowing how to *fight* and be successful. I took on the *fight* of the big banks in the United States during the foreclosure crisis that robbed so many American families of their homes (CNN 2019a).

One campaign ad explained that Harris's mother "was a scientist and an activist" who taught her to "*fight* for justice" (Harris 2019b). She used the word "fight" three times and other nontraditional language like "taking on" and "defending" (Harris 2019b).

When Warren launched her exploratory committee for president, she described her gender-nontraditional career path, including her profession as a law professor and senator. She used gender-nontraditional language, like the words "fight," "beat," and "ran against." With a confrontational tone in her voice, Warren said,

> When Republican senators tried to sabotage the reforms and *run me out of town*, I went back to Massachusetts and *ran against* one of them—*and I beat him*. . . . Every person in America should be able to work hard, play by the same set of rules, and take care of themselves and the people they love. That's what I'm *fighting* for (Warren 2018).

Images in the ad featured Warren at rallies, including one in which she yelled into a bullhorn (Warren 2018).

These candidates struck a balance between gender-nontraditional self-presentations, which emphasize their ability to do the job of president, and gendered expectations of niceness and likability. When an interviewer asked her how she responded to Trump calling her "nasty," Harris smiled in a way that is expected for women candidates and stated that her concern was to "pursue justice" (CNN 2019a). Klobuchar's announcement that she was running for president was "overshadowed" by news of her treatment of staff members, in which unlikability was implied as a result of gender-nontraditional self-presentations (The Daily Show 2019a). Her staff told HuffPost that she was "habitually demeaning and prone to bursts of cruelty that make it difficult to work in her office for long" and that "her anger left staffers in tears. She threw papers and sometimes even hurled objects and one aide was accidentally hit with a flying binder" (The Daily Show 2019a). Klobuchar responded in a gender-nontraditional way that turned her "anger" into an asset of high standards: "I am *tough*. I *push* people, that is true. But my point is that I have high expectations for myself. I have high expectations for the people that work for me" (The Daily Show 2019a). When Klobuchar announced her campaign in the middle of a snowstorm, "Trump mocked her, tweeting it was bad timing since she's electing to fight global warming" (The View 2019b). His tweet read "By the end of her speech she looked like a Snowman(woman)!" The hosts of *The View* described Klobuchar's snappy response, directed toward Trump, "I wonder how your hair would fare in a blizzard." *The View* hosts said that she was "trying to *poke the bear*. When you *attack* him physically, you know that triggers him and if he attacks a woman for any physical appearance, that is when people cannot stand by that, it's just the times we're in" (The View 2019b). Another host speculated that Trump may "have *met his match*" (The View 2019b). Although these comments are not candidate self-presentations, they illustrate Klobuchar's refusal to allow Trump to criticize her.

Subsequently, Klobuchar fielded questions about her and other women candidates' likability. She was asked about a poll that found that Biden would win because the female candidates were "unlikable." Klobuchar responded, "Oh, that's not true, is it? So sad. I think we are really a quite likable lot" (NBC News 2019). She used gender-nontraditional language to call out sexism in the 2020 primary:

> We have all had *tough* jobs. We've had *tough* jobs that show that we know how to *lead* different ways before we got to the Senate. And I think when you have jobs like that, *not everyone likes you all the time*. In every job, you have to make *tough* decisions. . . . We wouldn't be on that debate stage and where we are running for president if we hadn't been *tough* enough to have those jobs (NBC News 2019).

Klobuchar returned to the concept of likability, pointing out that men candidates are spared: "So I am just like, 'seriously?' This is not a measure that we use with men. So I find all of us quite likable, myself" (NBC News 2019). Although she affirmed women candidates' likability in the end, her comments emphasizing "toughness" were important to her response.

In an interview with her husband that combined nontraditional and traditional self-presentations, Klobuchar further challenged the idea that a woman could not be president. Her husband, John Bessler, was asked his thoughts about becoming the first "first husband" and he responded, "Well, it would be historic" (CBS News 2019). In a way that played with the gendered roles of the First Lady, the interviewer asked if Bessler was starting to think about curtains for the Oval Office. His response was gender traditional: "No, I'm not doing that." Klobuchar reinforced traditional gender norms when she quickly added, "He's *not good* at that kind of thing. That is *not his thing*" (CBS News 2019). At the same time, they discussed his support of her candidacy, including continuing her campaign when she returned to the Senate. When the interviewer asked if they had ever envisioned her running for president, Bessler responded, "I never knew this would be happening, but this is exciting" (CBS News 2019). They also mentioned that she is 7.5 years older than him and that they met in a pool hall, both atypical. Emphasizing this nontraditionality while simultaneously normalizing it, Bessler said, "Yeah, I give my wife advice. She doesn't usually take it, like most spouses" (CBS News 2019). Such self-presentations of spouses are generally inspected as much as candidates' own self-presentations on the campaign trail.

Gabbard, who served in the army and completed two Middle East deployments, presented the most nontraditional self-presentation of the women candidates. She appeared on *The Joe Rogan Experience* (The Joe Rogan Experience 2019), which targets a millennial male audience, and *Fox News*, where she was praised for attacking Harris during the July debate (Debate 2; Fox News 2019b). Gabbard said, "I am a *two-time veteran of Middle East deployments*. I'm a *soldier*, currently still *serving* in the *army*" (Fox News 2019b). Similarly, in a video titled "Stand Up for the First Amendment," Gabbard drew on military language and images to respond to Google's shutting down one of her ads:

> We as a country cannot afford to only *fight* for our freedoms when we are the *targets*, but when someone else is the *target*, we turn our backs and walk away. This is a *danger* to all of us. . . . I can tell you that *as a soldier* that *I'm willing to lay my life* down to protect the rights and freedoms of every person in this country to speak their voice and make sure that voice is heard (Gabbard 2019a).

In a self-made video titled "Trump Offers to Pimp Out Our Military to His Saudi Masters," Gabbard drew on gendered imagery of military personnel as "prostitutes" as she objected to Trump's decision to send the military to Saudi Arabia. She said angrily that this decision was "a *betrayal of my brothers and sisters in uniform*, who are *ready to give our lives* for our country. . . . My *fellow service members* and I, we are not your *prostitutes*. You are not our *pimp*" (Gabbard 2019b). Gabbard also posted a video of herself working out on Twitter, in which she was doing push-ups, lifting weights, and sweating profusely (Gabbard 2019c). Gabbard's gender-nontraditional self-presentation established her ability to handle the masculine job requirements of president.

Turning to a consideration of focus group perceptions, some interviewees commented on the necessary gender nontraditionality of women candidates for president. Jasmine, a 40-year-old Black woman, emphasized that women candidates need to exhibit masculine self-presentations to be taken "seriously":

> It's almost as if the woman has to have some type of, I hate to say this, but *masculinity*. She can't be pretty, delicate, you know, they want her to be in a *pantsuit*. You have to be this. You have to be that. If she came out there all dolled up, they wouldn't take her seriously.

Jasmine pointed out that men voters think women candidates

> run off of emotions, instead of making a logical or analytical decision. Just by her being a woman, it's hard for a woman to even win over a man's vote, even if she's the right woman or the right person.

Jasmine emphasized a gendered power struggle and called men "they": "*They* [men] don't want a woman to have *control* over so many aspects of *their* lives." Alyssa, a 29-year-old Black woman, linked the expectation of masculinity with political power: "With politics in general, it's pretty much all about power. We know that power is pretty much considered a *masculine* trait." Alyssa pointed out that Clinton

> has the credentials, but people still couldn't get past the fact that she was a woman. It's common that people think, "will women be able to handle that type of job?" They look at women as, "Oh, we're just frail emotional creatures and we wouldn't be able to handle certain stuff like military action." For a woman to hold a position as president, the highest chair of the land, women do face different obstacles than men.

Derek, a 22-year-old white man, agreed, "Because it's traditionally been men, women have to prove more from an emotional standpoint." He said that voters "just assume that [presidential] candidates are *tough* individuals who are going to be *hard* on things."

Focus group women were concerned about such biases. Mia, a 20-year-old white woman, said that "there are still people who don't think that women should be president or be a leader." She went on to discuss stereotypes of the emotionality of women candidates:

> They analyze whether or not a woman will be suitable, like too *emotional* to be a leader or too *empathetic* to be a leader and make decisions with a more political mindset and the greater good mindset. They think a man is the only one who could do that, to decide what to do without having any kind of bias.

Alex, a 21-year-old nonbinary and multiracial interviewee, agreed, calling it "really stupid that people hold those thoughts." Michelle, a 19-year-old white woman, concurred,

> It's taken a while for us to get an African American president. It may take a while for us to get a female president. It just depends on how long and who's ready for it and when we will get out of the gender discrimination.

Some interviewees linked expectations of masculinity to gender differences in voting. Jin, a 21-year-old Asian American man, pointed out that women have to prove strength,

> A man just has to prove their policy or prove what they're running for. But women have to prove that they're *strong* enough, because it's a male-dominated field, and men just don't think women are *fit* to do it. Their thoughts are just *rock solid*. They just don't trust women. They don't think they're *capable* of running.

Jin thought that women's personal lives, dress, and manner of walking were judged more than men's; women candidates are "definitely in a deficit to start." Thus, for an executive position like president, the women candidates highlighted gender-nontraditional traits, yet some focus group participants questioned these expectations of candidates.

Men's Nontraditional Self-Presentations

Given norms for the office of the president, it is not surprising that men candidates placed less emphasis on nontraditional self-presentations than the women. They were also less likely than the women to use nontraditional labels in their Twitter bios and websites, and, when they did so, they focused primarily on their family roles (Aronson et al. 2020). Biden emphasized his family roles in his Twitter bio as "proud father and grandfather" and "husband to @DrBiden" (Aronson et al. 2020). In an interesting twist on the fatherhood role, an interviewer asked Sanders about a comment made by rapper Cardi B, who suggested that her fans should "vote for *Daddy* Bernie" (The Late Show with Stephen Colbert 2019b). Sanders said, "I thank her very much for her support" (The Late Show with Stephen Colbert 2019b). Yet he did not appeal to voters on the basis of fatherhood. O'Rourke, whose campaign ad highlighted the connection between fatherhood and the children who had been separated from their parents at the Mexican border, said,

> *Our daughter* Molly turned eleven this week. I'm on this stage for her, for children across this country, including some her same age who have been separated

from their parents and are sleeping on concrete floors under aluminum blankets tonight (O'Rourke 2019b).

In contrast to the other men candidates, Castro emphasized his role as son and grandson of women who immigrated, highlighting his mother and grandmother to identify with others who might not "feel like a front-runner" (Castro 2019).

In their focus on love, Booker and Buttigieg engaged in self-presentations that emphasized emotionality that is not typically displayed by men candidates. Booker used the word "love" to refer both to Black history and his relationship with his girlfriend. In an interview, he also commented on his girlfriend and domestic partner, Rosario Dawson. When asked about dating while running for the Democratic primary, Booker shifted the conversation from his presidential candidacy to Dawson:

> I just feel like she's gifted to me a better perspective on life and what's important and just more energy. I just feel like I'm the most blessed person on the planet to be dating her. She makes me more courageous *in my heart* and to speak on this campaign trail about issues that really matter to people at the *heart* level and not just the head level (The Real Daytime 2019).

This nontraditional self-presentation may challenge stereotypes about Black men as tough and lacking emotion.

Yet gender-nontraditional self-presentations for the men candidates were typically coupled with gender-traditional self-presentations in order to preserve their masculinity. In an ad called "Love," using both gender-traditional and gender-nontraditional language, Booker narrated, "I'm here today because of *love*. A heroic *love* that *pushed* people to *march*, knowing they could be *beaten*, and board buses, knowing they could be *bombed*. From Seneca Falls to Selma to Stonewall" (Booker 2019). Likewise, in an interview, Ellen DeGeneres (TheEllenShow 2019) challenged Booker's nontraditional self-presentations when she asked, "People want *toughness*. And you seem *really sweet and kind*, which is a great thing. But when people say you're *not tough enough*, what do you say about that?" He replied by asserting his traditional credentials while simultaneously challenging traditional notions of masculinity. Pointing to a documentary called *Street Fight* that featured Booker running against "one of the *toughest* political machines there are," he reasserted his masculinity: "We showed that you can *fight* the *toughest* of *fights* and *win*" (TheEllenShow 2019). He explained that traditional and nontraditional self-presentations can coexist, "But people make this mistake where they confuse being *strong* with being mean, or being *tough* with being cruel" (TheEllenShow 2019). Rather than "*fighting* darkness with darkness," he wanted to "bring light, decency, and grace back to our politics. You judge a leader not by how much they *push people down* but by how much they *lift people up*" (TheEllenShow 2019). This imagery seeks to combine Booker's "sweet and kind" side with stereotypical masculine credentials of strength.

Similarly, DeGeneres asked Buttigieg about a tweet by conservative commentator Rush Limbaugh that asked "How is this going to look? A 37-year-old gay guy kissing his husband on stage next to Mr. Man, Donald Trump?" (TheEllenShow 2020). After rolling his eyes and laughing, Buttigieg responded by reasserting his masculinity through his military experience and simultaneously challenging traditional conceptions. He said that Limbaugh "just has a different idea of *what makes a man* than I do" (TheEllenShow 2020). He wondered aloud to the audience,

> When I was *packing my bags for Afghanistan*, Donald Trump was working on Season 7 of *Celebrity Apprentice*. . . . And since when is *strength* about the *chest pounding* or the *loud-mouth guy* at the end of the bar? The *strongest* people I know are not the loudest people. They are the ones who have the *deepest sense of who they are*, what they value, and *what they care about* (TheEllenShow 2020).

Turning to the crowd where his husband was sitting, he said, "And one of those people, by the way, one of the *strongest* people I know, is my husband" (TheEllenShow 2020). Buttigieg's rhetoric openly rejected the traditional idea that a gay man is not as "manly" as a straight man, and he challenged these traditional norms throughout his presidential campaign. At the same time, Buttigieg was careful to remind voters that he had the masculine credentials of having served in the military during the war in Afghanistan.

These concurrent self-presentations established the men candidates as both tough and capable of expressing feelings. As a result of the stereotypical masculinity assumed necessary for the role of president, it is not surprising that the women candidates more frequently exhibited gender-nontraditional self-presentations.

"I Don't Expect People to Vote for Me Because I'm a Woman": Gender-Neutral Self-Presentations and Voter Reactions

Gender-neutral perspectives downplay gender, display a gender-blind approach, and/or focus on gender-neutral accomplishments or policy positions (see Table 4.2). This form of self-presentation was the most common in both the Twitter bios and the website bios for these candidates (Aronson et al. 2020), as well as the ads and media representations. These gender-neutral approaches are thought to have the most widespread voter appeal.

Examples of gender-neutral self-presentations are accomplishments or policy positions related to issues like the economy, the environment, or health care. Tom Steyer, a white businessman (see Table 4.1), centered much of his campaign on the economy. In an interview, he described his reason for running,

> No one was talking about what I think are the two most important things. One is that we aren't going to get any of those progressive policies until we break the

corporate stranglehold that they have on the economy. This government works for corporations. . . . Can we break this corporate stranglehold and are we going to solve climate change? (The Late Show with Stephen Colbert 2020)

We will not detail neutral self-presentations in depth here, given our thorough consideration in Chapter 3. Rather, we focus on particular moments when the candidates sought to reassert gender neutrality by deemphasizing the historic nature of their candidacy and focusing on gender-neutral merit. For example, in an interview, Harris downplayed her gender and race:

I don't expect people to vote for me because I'm a woman. I don't expect people to vote for me because I'm a person of color. I believe that people are going to elect me because they believe I am the *best* one for the job at this point in time (Dovere 2019).

When asked why she was not more explicit about the historic nature of her candidacy, Harris replied that she "doesn't have to be" (Dovere 2019), thus minimizing race and gender in her self-presentation. Buttigieg also stressed that despite demographic differences, politicians can communicate with one another across boundaries: "We can say, 'I've got this experience, you've got that experience. What can we talk about that brings us together?'" (Breakfast Club Power 105.1 FM 2019b).

Like the 2018 midterm elections, focus group men were more likely than women to emphasize the importance of the gender-neutral accomplishments of women candidates. Unlike the women focus group participants, who emphasized that they would support a woman candidate for president *because she is a woman*, the men were focused on the gender-blind *merit* of women candidates. Joel, a 20-year-old white man, said,

There exists more people who would be willing to vote for a female candidate just to finally get a female candidate and to get rid of this voting for someone who's a man just because he is a man. I *disagree* with voting for someone specifically because they're a man or because they're a woman.

He continued, explaining that he does not "like it" when people try "to balance that out" by voting "only because they're a woman." Instead, Joel preferred a gender-blind approach in which voters "are deciding based on if they're a *legitimate* candidate or not, to actually have their *view* be represented." Likewise, Carter, a 21-year-old Middle Eastern man, said, "I don't think that people really care as much about *gender*. They care more about the *policies*." Carter went on to say that voters might "subconsciously" dismiss a woman candidate as "not as good because she's a woman" or view women in terms of their "female roles" (like being a mother), while men are viewed in terms of their credentials ("he does this, he has this degree"). Despite these subconscious factors, Carter concluded by emphasizing gender neutrality, "If you have *good policies*, people can make decisions logically." Similarly, Anthony, a 35-year-old Black man, argued that Clinton's defeat in 2016 was not a result of her gender but because she prioritized gender issues over bread-and-butter economic concerns: "People were saying, 'OK, what bathroom do you want me to go to? What does that have to do with me feeding my family and jobs?'" Mitchell, a 20-year-old white man, pointed out that resistance to social change plays a role in voters rejecting women as candidates: "People don't like change. For the last 44 presidents, we've had a male president."

In one gender-similar focus group, interviewees objected to voting for Harris for president solely because of her gender. Caleb, a 21-year-old white man, argued that her career did not meet progressive criteria despite being a woman:

> Kamala Harris recently announced her campaign. But I think if you actually look at her career, you look at the things that she stands for, especially during her time as a prosecutor, a lot of the things that she stands for are actually very regressive. And I don't think that if she was a male she'd be seen as a quote-unquote trailblazer, or some progressive icon. Due to the uniqueness of female candidates, I think that there can be greater praise heaped on those who do fit a mold, and the desire to see women in government, even if their ideas might not be all that authentic, new, or progressive.

Dominic agreed with Caleb's assessment that "Kamala Harris has regressive policies. She's been able to really use identity politics very well."

Several of the men went further, resisting gender-conscious voting altogether. When asked about the number of women in politics, Gabriel and Isiah, both Asian American men in their early 20s, responded indifferently, reinforcing the view that merit takes priority. Gabriel asked first, "What are we at right now?" Isiah said, "I don't know. I don't care." Gabriel responded by describing three groups of voters in 2016, "'No, because Hillary's a woman'; 'Yes, because she's a woman.' And a third group would be, 'Just pick one who's *more qualified, regardless of gender*.'" Luke, a 22-year-old white man, said that he heard "a lot more of, 'I want to vote for Hillary *because* she's a woman,' instead of who's *qualified*, whose viewpoints they agree with."

Adnan, a 21-year-old Middle Eastern man, first appeared to recognize the obstacles that women running for president face but concluded in a gender-neutral way. He pointed to "a very big obstacle between men and women. People would see a woman rising to power and almost feel a little bit uncomfortable about it." Adnan emphasized the gender-traditional expectations that women face: "When there's a woman in power, or a woman candidate, it's very easy for jokes to become sexual, to become degrading, to become discriminatory." Although aware of these obstacles, Adnan concluded in a gender-neutral way, "It depends *not* on whether you're a man or a woman. It depends if you're *qualified* for the job."

Two women espoused a gender-neutral position on women running for president. Sofia, who was quoted earlier as endorsing a woman for president based on gender alone, said, "Gender *shouldn't* matter if a person's going to be our next president or whatever, because at the end of the day, *we're all human.*" Kiara, a Black 18-year-old woman, agreed, "It doesn't make sense to me to put gender over what you *believe in.*" In summary, men focus group participants more often than women took a gender-neutral perspective that voting for president should be based predominantly on merit.

"You Better Learn How to Cook": Gender-Traditional Self-Presentations and Voter Reactions

In an Indian food cooking show with Mindy Kaling, Harris emphasized her Indian heritage and yet admitted, "Can I tell you something? I've never made Dosas" (Harris 2019c). Harris was surprised to see that Kaling, like Harris's mother, stored spices in reused instant coffee glass jars (Harris 2019c). She talked about her grandparents while cutting onions and warmly greeted Kaling's father, who joined them in the kitchen for a few minutes (Harris 2019c). When Kaling rated the dish a B-minus and said "I was nervous cooking in front of you," Harris reassured her maternally, "But you shouldn't be. You're such a good cook. This is very good" (Harris 2019c).

For women, traditional self-presentations emphasize feminine gender roles, such as household work or family care, highlighting their status as wives and mothers (see Table 4.2). For men, traditional masculine identity is presented in terms of strength, independence, leadership, courage, and success in traditional masculine workplace roles, such as the military (see Table 4.2). In these candidates' Twitter bios, half of the women and one-quarter of the men used gender-traditional self-presentations (Aronson et al. 2020). Considering website bios, just 3.2 percent of women's and 7.2 percent of men's self-presentations were traditional, suggesting that these candidates sought to deemphasize traditional gender roles (Aronson et al. 2020). Our expanded analysis here illustrates that candidates drew on traditional self-presentations strategically to appeal to particular groups of voters. Suggesting the gendered divide between resisters and innovators, many of the focus group men took traditional stances toward women candidates for president, while focus group women opposed gender stereotypes.

Women's Traditional Self-Presentations

Because of the masculinity assumed in the office of president, very few of the women candidates' self-presentations were gender traditional. In fact, women candidates in 2020 drew on gender-traditional self-presentations less than the 2018 gubernatorial candidates. Harris was one notable exception and strategically presented herself

FIGURE 4.1 Democratic Primary Presidential Candidate Harris in a Kitchen Cooking Bacon-Fried Apples (with Campaign Staffer)

Source: Retrieved from YouTube (Kamala Harris, 2019e, 0:34)

as likable. In a video that introduced her campaign, she spoke straight to the camera, often with a smile and an image that looked airbrushed. Perhaps to shore up her maternal credentials, as she does not have biological children of her own, she said, "Let's claim our future. For ourselves. *For our children.* And for our country" (Harris 2019d). Like the cooking show mentioned earlier, Harris posted a video on her campaign website, in which she cooked her mother's recipe (pancakes with apples and bacon) at her Iowa chair's house (Figure 4.1) (Harris 2019e). Making references to her mother with upbeat music playing in the background, Harris's campaign staffer said, "So you've always loved cooking." Harris replied, "Yes, well my mother said to me, 'Honey, you like to eat good food. You better learn how to cook'" (Harris 2019e). Voters sometimes support feminine characteristics: A study before the election that manipulated images of Harris's face to look more "masculine" or "feminine" found that more feminine representations of Harris's face were associated with more positive evaluations of her (Cassidy and Liebenow 2021).

Although most of the women candidates shied away from traditional self-presentations, gender and racial bias in media coverage persisted in the 2020 Democratic primary in ways that attempted to push women into traditional roles. For example, a *Saturday Night Live* (2019) parody featured Kate McKinnon as Warren, who said in a breathy voice,

> I am in my natural habitat, a *public school on a weekend.* . . . . When Bernie was talking "Medicare for All," everybody was like, "Oh, cool." And then they

turned to me and said, "*Fix it Mom.*" And I'll do it, I'll do it, *because that's what moms do.* You know, with Dad you eat birthday cake for breakfast and then go to Six Flags and then *I hold your hand while you throw up in my purse.* . . . It ain't fun, *but I will do it.*

Although a parody of Warren, such representations reinforce traditional gender expectations. Likewise, Tucker Carlson's show on *Fox News* (2019c) sarcastically attacked positive media coverage of Harris that compared her to Barack Obama: "She's like Obama 2.0. But even more woke with even more diversity points." Carlson mocked Harris's debate confrontation of Biden over busing: "The *Washington Post* rushed to her rescue, 'Kamala Harris's Takedown of Joe Biden Was More Brutal Than It Seems,' read the headline." In gender-traditional terms, Carlson mocked Harris: "Yeah, *brutal.* She just *dominated* the guy. So ludicrous. She *didn't* actually *dominate* anybody and she's *not dominating* anybody" (Fox News 2019c). As the media presents candidates in traditional gender ways, it raises questions about whether or not women are capable of achieving the masculine requirements of president. It is likely for this reason that the women candidates largely rejected traditional self-presentations.

Men's Traditional Self-Presentations

In an ad titled "That's a President," a narrator extolled Biden's qualifications while aggressive music played loudly in the background (Biden 2020). Photos featured Biden in a variety of military situations—walking by a line of saluting cadets, talking to President Obama in a cabinet meeting, talking to a group of soldiers, and staring at the camera with his characteristic Ray-Ban aviator sunglasses with a military helicopter behind him (Figure 4.2) (Biden 2020). The deep-voiced narrator stated, "This job is about *protecting* Americans. . . . It takes *strength, courage*, compassion, resilience. That's a president" (Biden 2020). Although the ad also showed Biden hugging two women when the word "compassion" flashed across the screen, the self-presentation was unambiguously hypermasculine and was clearly intended to emphasize toughness and strength (Biden 2020). Dittmar (2021b) argued that Biden's campaign and his emotionality were deployed in ways that are consistent with masculinity: When "Biden shared experiences of overcoming personal grief and called for greater empathy and compassion, he elevated these traits as more indicative of presidential strength than aggression, force, or a lack of emotion."

Likewise, Bloomberg released an ad targeting women, yet rather than appearing overtly feminist, the ad featured gender-traditional language and images. On a stage with women holding pink and blue campaign signs (which traditionally emphasize gender divisions and a gender binary) that said "women for Mike," several women gave testimonials of support (Bloomberg 2020). Although the ad

FIGURE 4.2 Biden Standing in Front of Military Plane Wearing Aviator Sunglasses and a Tough Expression in His "That's a President" Ad

Source: Retrieved from YouTube (Joe Biden, 2020, 0:13) U.S. Department of Defense. The appearance of U.S. Department of Defense (DoD) visual information does not imply or constitute DoD endorsement.

featured a Bloomberg speech stressing his "belief in opportunity for all," it also subtly portrayed stereotypes. In a supposed "woman-to-woman" moment, a featured speaker talked in a language of individuals rather than collective identity: "*I*, like all of *you*, am a *woman* for Mike" (Bloomberg 2020). The ad drew on women's stereotypical housework roles: "If you are ready to *clean out* the Oval Office and get things done, then welcome to Bloomberg 2020" (Bloomberg 2020). Conjuring a 1952 ad for Dwight D. Eisenhower, the ad ended with women repeatedly chanting a potentially romantic phrase: "We *like* Mike! We *like* Mike!" (Bloomberg 2020). Instead of emphasizing a feminist agenda by discussing policy issues, Bloomberg's ad subtly reinforced traditional gender norms.

Other gender-traditional self-presentations on the part of men candidates included masculine presentation styles. For example, Castro confronted Biden in the September debate (Debate 3) and was asked by a news anchor if he regretted "attacking" Biden (CNN 2019b). He responded that he did not. In an ad that recounted Trump's failures as a businessman, Steyer (2019) aggressively wagged his finger at the camera while emphasizing his own successful experiences in business: "Unlike the other candidates, I can *go head to head* with Donald Trump on the economy and expose him for what he is: a fraud and a failure." In two interviews, Steyer repeatedly interrupted his hosts. On one show, titled "Tom Steyer *Gets Blunt* about Trump's Racism," Steyer stated aggressively, "Mr. Trump has a problem with non-white people. . . . He's a liar" (NowThis News 2020).

Similarly, he drew on gender-traditional language to emphasize toughness when he told *The View* (2019c),

> Whoever is going to be the Democratic candidate is going to have *to go toe to toe* [with Trump] and is going *to be able to take him down*. . . . Whoever is going to be the Democratic candidate is going to have to be credible and *go after* Trump and his *supposed strength*.

Another gender-traditional self-presentation was to feature their wives in ads. After Sanders's heart attack in 2019, he appeared with his arm around his smiling wife in a video that was shot on a cell phone: "I'm feeling so much better. Thank you for all of the love and warm wishes that you sent me. See you soon on the campaign trail." His wife, Jane, spoke next: "Thank you all so much. It really made a difference" (Sanders 2019c). Other candidates also used their wives as traditional props in campaign appearances. To make the announcement that he was running for president, O'Rourke, looking directly at the camera, was featured sitting next to his silent wife, who held his arm while facing him and smiling admiringly (O'Rourke 2019c). O'Rourke found himself at the center of a controversy after joking about his wife raising their three kids "*sometimes* with my *help*" (North 2019). After he realized that this gender-traditional comment was a misstep in the current climate, O'Rourke quickly apologized for the appearance of inequality in his childcare responsibilities (North 2019). Yet at times, he seemed unaware of the implications of his gender-traditional self-presentations. In an article that drew on gender and racial privilege, O'Rourke said, "I want to be in it. *Man*, I'm *just born* to be in it, and want to do everything I humanly can for this country at this moment" (Hagan and Leibovitz 2019).

In the 2020 primary, sexual misconduct allegations against Biden and Bloomberg highlighted gender-traditional behavior. An article in *GQ* questioned Bloomberg's popularity when almost 40 sexual harassment and discrimination lawsuits had been filed against him (Bassett 2020). Bloomberg was reported to have said, "I would do you in a second" and "I'd like to do that piece of meat" (The Late Show with Stephen Colbert 2019c). Similarly, *The Daily Show* (2019b) pieced together a number of newsclips to tell the story of Biden's inappropriate behavior toward women, centering on a former Nevada state lawmaker who labeled his behavior as inappropriate but not sexual. *The Daily Show* (2019b) host mockingly labeled the scandal "sniffkissgate" because it involved Biden "smelling" her hair and kissing her on the top of her head. The host commented, "That sounded super creepy. . . . How come you've never seen him doing it with men?" (The Daily Show 2019b). These incidents, and notably, Tara Reed's accusations against Biden, which received media attention in the general election, resulted in responses from the candidates.

Although the candidates' behaviors from previous time periods were gender traditional, the candidates defended themselves to reassure voters. These responses recognized the gendered dynamics of the primary and the power of women candidates and voters alike. *The Daily Show* (2019b) featured Biden's responses:

> In my many years on the campaign trail and in public life, I have offered countless handshakes, hugs, expressions of affection, support, and comfort. And not once—never—did I believe I acted inappropriately. If it is suggested I did so, I will *listen respectfully*. But it was never my intention.

Likewise, when Reed accused Biden of sexually assaulting her nearly three decades earlier, he responded by denying her claims while simultaneously using language deployed in the #MeToo era: "*Believing women* means *taking the woman's claim seriously. But* in the end, in every case, the truth is what matters. And in this case, the truth is, the claims are false" (Glueck et al. 2020). Biden's response, rooted in believing, listening, and respecting women, differed significantly from Trump's self-presentation during the *Access Hollywood* scandal. Trump not only dismissed his previous comments as irrelevant but even justified them in gender-traditional terms as "locker-room talk." Traditional self-presentations in this primary, when present, were combined with other types of self-presentations, as candidates responded to a gender revolution that contributed to a diverse candidate field and changed electorate.

"The Standards Are Different": The Primary Outcome and Electability

Despite the pathbreaking diversity and the wide range of self-presentations of the candidates, the last two remaining candidates were white men in their 70s. For some, Biden's nomination solidified traditional views about the role of gender and race in presidential elections. In fact, studies have found that gender played a negative role in how the women candidates were evaluated. Dittmar (2021b) explained that "Biden benefited and Warren suffered the most from voters' risk-aversion," in terms of which candidate could best defeat Trump. According to Terkel (2020), Warren could not escape the disadvantage of being a woman, particularly regarding questions of electability. In a March 2019 poll, voters were asked which candidate would be able to beat Trump and the top three rated candidates were white men, followed by Harris and then Warren (Terkel 2020).

Primary contests differ from general elections. One experiment using hypothetical candidates found that primary voters had a preference for women candidates (Khanna 2019). However, other studies focusing on this particular election have found disadvantages for women and people of color. Nelson (2021) found that Democratic primary and caucus voters relied on race and gender in evaluating candidates. Women candidates had to overcome questions about their candidacy; they had to both prove that they could win *and* explain why they were the best candidate to compete against Trump (Dittmar 2021a).

In our focus groups, Christina, a 36-year-old Black woman, reflected on how women candidates for president are judged differently than men. Christina pointed out that they are criticized for not being "feminine enough," their clothing is scrutinized, and they have more difficulty "financially with raising money." She concluded, "The standards are different. Men can get away with a lot more." This "concurrent campaign of belief" suggests that women candidates faced greater barriers to demonstrating their qualifications and experience (Dittmar 2021a). Research has suggested that women candidates need to demonstrate that they are *more* qualified than men candidates; it is not enough to be "as qualified" as their male counterparts (Fulton and Dhima 2021).

Concerns about electability were especially pronounced in how Democratic primary and caucus voters evaluated women candidates. Yet electability may actually serve as a "smokescreen" for not wanting to support a woman candidate (Nelson 2021). That is, fears of *other* people's sexism may be driving the concern about electability (Nelson 2021). One study found that while 74 percent of voters said they would vote for a female for president, only 33 percent thought their neighbors would do so (Terkel 2020). Nelson (2021) also found that racial resentment and sexism worked to Biden's benefit and Harris's disadvantage among white Democrats. Those who voted for Biden had a higher mean level of "hostile sexism" than those who voted for Warren; Biden also benefited more than Warren from racial resentment (Nelson 2021).

Focus group participants, mainly men, pointed out that gender stereotypes prevent voters from supporting a woman running for president. Aran, a 20-year-old Asian American man, referred to Clinton in 2016 when he said, "There's a lot of people still out there with the stigma [of women candidates] that [think], 'Oh, she's a female, I don't want her in office.' That idea itself probably kept them from voting for her." Deven, who has a similar background, agreed, although he thought that voters would be "silent" about their perspectives,

A lot of people would have probably not voted for her because she's a woman but probably weren't outspoken about it. They probably would've kept that to themselves. There's a lot of people, even a lot of minorities and Democrats, who separate the gender roles. They don't believe in a woman being in power.

Li, an 18-year-old Asian American man, emphasized that gender-traditional expectations are an obstacle for women running for president: "If you look back from the beginning of the presidents before, there's never been a woman who is a president. People are skeptical of change and of accepting change." Li recognized this resistance to women's power as backlash: "I think that's some backlash or obstacles that they may face." Thus, the outcome of the primary suggests that the gender revolution remains incomplete.

"She Is Ready to Do This Job on Day One": The 2020 General Presidential Election

The 2020 election illustrates progress in women's collective power, the political power of women of color in particular, as well as vigorous challenges. Considering congressional and state legislative seats, women ran and were elected in record numbers in 2020, yet the gains were smaller than in 2018 (Dittmar 2021a). Dittmar (2021b) said that the election represented a "major milestone in Black women's political leadership" and a record number of women of color served in Congress and state legislatures in 2021 (Dittmar 2021a). Over two-thirds of Black women voted in 2020, more than 90 percent of whom voted for Biden-Harris (Dittmar 2021b). Taken together, Black women played "pivotal roles in voter mobilization and voter turnout" (Dittmar 2021b). While in 2018 it was disproportionately Democratic women who were elected, in 2020, Republican women accounted for the majority of the increases in wins by women candidates (Dittmar 2021a). Yet Republican women continue to account for a minority of women in office; at least twice as many Democratic women serve in Congress and state legislatures (Dittmar 2021a).

The Collective Power of Women and People of Color

Walking onstage in twin navy blue suits and white shirts, Biden and Harris together made their first announcement that she would be running for vice president. This announcement foretold an important historic moment. Biden introduced Harris in gender-nontraditional language as "*tough, experienced*" and a "*proven fighter* for the backbone of this country" (C-Span 2020). He emphasized that Harris "knows how to *govern*. She knows how to make the *hard calls*. She is ready to do this job on day one" (C-Span 2020). When Harris took the microphone, she began by echoing her readiness for this role when she said, "I am ready to get to work" (C-Span 2020). Recognizing the historical legacy of women before her, Harris said, "I am so proud to stand with you. And I am so mindful of all of the heroic and ambitious women before me whose sacrifice, determination, and resilience makes my presence here today even possible."

Harris's speech covered many self-presentations. In a traditional self-presentation, Harris, who her stepchildren call "Mamala," emphasized her role as stepmother: "*Family* means everything to me too. . . . And I've had a lot of titles over my career, and certainly vice president will be great, but *Mamala* will always be the one that means the most" (C-Span 2020). Harris drew on a historical reference to her family history to highlight the emergent Black Lives Matter movement, saying that what brought her parents together "was the civil rights movement of the 1960s" (C-Span 2020). She described attending marches and protests as a young child "strapped tightly in my stroller." She credited her parents for her devotion to justice and told racial justice activists to keep "up the *fight*" (C-Span 2020).

While a full analysis of innovation and resistance in the 2020 general election is beyond the scope of this chapter, we examine the implications of this election for how we think about gender and politics. In particular, we consider whether Harris's election as vice president is largely symbolic or has real, tangible implications. While Harris recognized her historic role and praised Biden for choosing "the first Black woman as his running mate" (C-Span 2020), she concluded by emphasizing her role as a supporter of Biden, "Electing Joe Biden is just the start of the work ahead of us and I couldn't be prouder to be *by his side*" (C-Span 2020). While the phrase "by his side" might be uttered by any vice president about a president, it is notable that a Black woman, defeated in her run for the presidency, said it about a white man. The phrase ironically points out that while Harris shattered a glass ceiling through being elected, she still is in a *supportive* role to the president rather than being the president herself.

Voting patterns in 2020 were also both gendered and racialized, exposing deep divisions that will carry into the future. Since 1980, women have voted and registered to vote at higher rates than men (Center for American Women and Politics 2022b). In 2020, 74.1 percent of women and 71.2 percent of men reported that they were registered to vote; of eligible voters, 68.4 percent of women and 65 percent of men reported voting in 2020 (Center for American Women and Politics 2022b). This pattern held for all racial groups and levels of educational attainment (Center for American Women and Politics 2022b).

In the general election, despite the narrowing gender gap in voting compared to 2016, women voters were still disproportionately responsible for electing the Democratic ticket (Igielnik et al. 2021). Considered historically, there has been a gender gap of between 4 and 12 percentage points in every presidential election since 1980 with women more likely to vote for the Democrat in each year since 1996 (Center for American Women and Politics 2022c). In 2020, the majority of women voted for Biden, while the majority of men voted for Trump. However, the majority of white women voted Republican in every presidential election since 2000, while the majority of women of color have voted for the Democratic candidate (Center for American Women and Politics 2022c; Junn and Masuoka 2020). The same is true for the divide by marital status: Married women were more likely to support Trump (51 percent), while unmarried women voted for Biden (63 percent) (Center for American Women and Politics 2022c). As Gothreau (2021) reminded us, although the idea of the "gender gap" is useful,

Women are neither a monolith in their political beliefs, nor a unified voting bloc. Not all women are moved by the same issues and concerns, and cross-cutting identities of race, ethnicity, religion and sexual orientation often pull women voters in different directions, particularly in the hyper-partisan context of American politics. Instead of trying to characterize women voters uniformly, we would be better served to recognize the diversity among and within groups of women.

Thus, the voting patterns of Black women were especially vital to the election of the Biden-Harris ticket.

The Democratic National Convention emphasized women's role in path-breaking ways in the 2020 presidential election. A variety of speakers and videos focused on women and fundamentally important key Democratic issues, including education, childcare, and domestic violence, and highlighted women's roles in social movements, including gun control and climate change (MSNBC 2020). It featured Warren expressing concerns about the pandemic and childcare with a (gender-traditional) public school classroom as a backdrop. It contained a clip from a child talking about deportation. Additionally, Clinton, dressed symbolically in white, a color worn during the women's suffrage movement, mentioned that

> a hundred years ago yesterday, the 19th Amendment to the Constitution was ratified. It took seven decades of suffragists marching, picketing, and going to jail to push us closer to a more perfect union. . . . Tonight, I'm thinking of the boys and girls who see themselves in America's future because of Kamala Harris (MSNBC 2020).

The convention also gave a tribute to Nancy Pelosi, the first woman Speaker of the House of Representatives. Pelosi spoke about her shift from a focus on her husband and five children to her first run for Congress and her election as Speaker, which she referred to as "breaking the marble ceiling" in a speech at the time (Democratic National Convention 2020). Shifting to more aggressive music, the tribute moved to Pelosi's toughness as she asserted her "power" against Trump's "temper tantrum" when she repeated twice, "The power of the Speaker is awesome" (Democratic National Convention 2020). It featured her on the *Late Show*, in which she said, "If you go into the arena, you have to be prepared to *take a punch*. You also have to be prepared to *throw a punch*." Yet Pelosi pulled back from nontraditional self-presentations and supported traditional ones when she added, "*for the children*" (Democratic National Convention 2020).

The convention also featured an acceptance speech from Harris that emphasized her historic role, recognizing Black women activists who fought "for a seat at the table" (McCarthy 2020). Harris's speech was historically new in many respects, as she expressed concerns about "structural racism" and highlighted her mother's legacy in raising "proud, strong Black women" (McCarthy 2020). Harris also made links to the #MeToo movement, as she said she "*fought* for children and survivors of sexual assault" (MSNBC 2020).

The 2020 general election pushed social change forward and represents a key to the gender revolution: From innovator candidates with feminist and nontraditional self-presentations to the gender gap in voting. The election represents a turning point in women's collective power and candidates' realization of this political agency. And yet resisters remain strong, suggesting an incomplete revolution.

Resisting Women's Collective Power

At a campaign rally in Florida, Trump diminished the historic nature of Harris's presidential candidacy by inciting anger at the possibility that a woman could be president: "By the way, Kamala will *not* be your *first female president*" (Bloomberg Quicktake: Now 2020). The crowd at the rally booed when they heard Harris's name mentioned, to which Trump slammed his hand down on the podium and repeated, "She will *not* be your *first female president*." He resisted her candidacy for gendered reasons: "It's *not* the way *it's supposed to be.* We're *not* supposed to have a socialist president, *especially any female* socialist president. *We're not going to have it. We're not going to put up with it*" (Bloomberg Quicktake: Now 2020). These comments sow seeds of discord and object to women who dare to run for high-level positions. Trump and his Republican allies also repeatedly mispronounced Harris's first name on the campaign trail, often emphasizing the mispronunciation: "If you pronounce her name wrong she goes *crazy*" (CNN 2020b). Trump repeatedly used gendered and racialized dehumanizing language to disparage Harris and drew attention to her defiance of electoral norms, such as calling her "mean," "aggressive," "disrespectful," "phony," "totally unlikable," a "communist," and a "monster" (Astor 2020).

Trump explicitly drew on stereotypes to emphasize his own "masculine credentials" and to "emasculate his opponents" (Dittmar 2021b). Although previous research has argued that Trump's appeal is linked to individual voters (particularly rural and white voters, who see themselves as victims of globalization and demographic change), men are at the center of this narrative (Ferree 2020). Ferree (2020: 900) stated, "Gender glues together many of the anxieties generated by social change, both in fostering engagement with collective expressions of conventional political masculinity and encouraging a powerful, intersectional resistance to the narrative of 'restoring greatness.'" Although gender is rarely explicitly a reason for voter preferences, voters draw on gender in unconscious ways (Ferree 2020). As Ferree (2020: 905) put it, "Voters themselves rarely articulate gender as a reason for party or candidate preference, but the frames on which they draw are gendered."

Masculinity is tied to the Republican Party more generally. There are large gender gaps and gaps between Democrats and Republicans on whether or not it is a "good thing" that "society looks up to masculine men" (Parker et al. 2020). While 78 percent of Republicans agreed that it was a "good thing" that society values masculinity, only 49 percent of Democrats agreed (Parker et al. 2020). While two-thirds of men (68 percent) thought that it was a "good thing," only 56 percent of women agreed (Parker et al. 2020).

In the 2020 general election, Republicans emphasized the performance of masculinity and whiteness in their claims to power (Ferree 2020). Ferree (2020: 900) said that Trump operated within a framework of "racialized hegemonic masculinity." The intersections between race and gender can be seen in the makeup of Congress: While only 38 percent of Democratic U.S. congressional representatives are white men, 90 percent of Republican congressional representatives fit this description (Ferree 2020). Republican imagery is less ambivalent than Democratic imagery, which is associated with more feminine characteristics (Ferree 2020). Analyzing U.S. political parties, Brownstein (2012) said that "a gender binary has been written symbolically into partisan identification." That is, Democrats are viewed as the "party of transformation" and Republicans as the "party of restoration" in terms of race, family, and social change (Brownstein 2012). Thus, resistance to women's collective power in the presidential election was forceful.

While the election's outcome was tied to the gender revolution, obviously other factors were also at play. In particular, the election took place amid the COVID-19 pandemic and was affected by this context. In the beginning of the pandemic, people of color were more likely to contract and die from COVID-19; women and people of color disproportionately suffered economic hardships resulting from the pandemic. The pandemic influenced the election in monumental ways.

Conclusion

The 2020 Democratic presidential primary highlighted many changes resulting from the gender revolution. It brought feminism and the #MeToo movement into electoral politics in a major way. The primary illustrated women's power and agency; the diversity of the candidates was unprecedented and the range of candidates' self-presentations were markedly feminist and nontraditional. Yet while there is much evidence to suggest that candidates were innovators, there was also traditionality and resistance to innovation.

All of the Democratic candidates supported women's movement frames and emphasized the collective rights of women. Intersectionality was an important campaign theme, especially addressing racial justice and support for LGBTQ rights. Evidencing the ties between the #MeToo movement and institutionalized politics, candidates and their spouses shared revelations of personal experiences with sexual assault and harassment on the campaign trail. These experiences are important indicators of social change for several reasons. First, they illustrate that the #MeToo movement has influenced the political sphere. Instead of hiding experiences of sexual assault, candidates and their spouses spoke out about them. This shift is notable, as it has become increasingly acceptable for personal accounts of sexual assault to reach large audiences. Thus, identifying with the #MeToo movement was considered an asset in politics, reflecting feminist self-presentations and a shift in the broader culture.

Likewise, although they blended self-presentations, the women candidates were notably nontraditional, as they sought to establish themselves as *tough enough* to be president. Men candidates less often embraced nontraditional self-presentations and, when they did, were careful to simultaneously preserve their masculinity through traditional self-presentations. Yet in contrast to Trump's emphasis on traditional masculinity, the men candidates responded to a changed electorate and diverse candidate field by fusing gender-traditional self-presentations with feminist and nontraditional ones. Focus group participants of all genders were generally supportive of women running for president. Yet suggesting resistance to voting decisions based on gender, the men were more likely than the women to focus on the importance of gender-neutral merit.

A skeptic might argue that feminist and gender-nontraditional self-presentations are not genuine but instead seek to capture the attention and allegiance of voters—that all self-presentations represent a type of political pandering. That is, some critics argue that progressive self-presentations are only surface-level changes rather than resulting in deep political changes. While there is some truth in that argument as politicians "read the room" and alter how they present themselves to voters in order to get elected, the presence of feminist issues and gender-nontraditional self-presentations push the public agenda and voters' expectations in new directions. Candidates are increasingly becoming aware that feminist issues are important to voters and that they must address progressive and feminist causes if they want to be successful.

What meaning should be attributed to Harris's election as vice president? Is she one step away from becoming president or does her position affirm gender inequalities and women's subservience to men? We believe that the 2020 election is consistent with the uneven pattern of social and cultural changes of the gender revolution; it is simultaneously revolutionary and innovative yet contains moments of reversal of progress and resistance. The 2020 Democratic primary took place in a highly "unsettled" time (Swidler 1986). It took place in the midst of the pandemic, at a peak of Black Lives Matter activism, and at a time of vigorous challenges to Trump's presidency. As a time of social, cultural, and economic upheaval, the primary contained the potential for "social transformation" and "culture's influence on social action" (Swidler 1986: 278).

As women and people of color secure high-profile positions, some progressives and feminists worry about the "famous first" dilemma. For example, now that we have had a woman of color as vice president and, subsequently, a Black woman appointed to the Supreme Court, will voters shy away from supporting women and people of color in power, assuming that the glass ceiling has been shattered? Will politicians and voters view equality as complete and stop pushing for further social change and more equal representation? We argue instead that the movement of women and people of color opens the door for new ideas of what political leadership looks like.

In fact, the 2020 primary election represents a gender revolution for several reasons. The diversity of the candidates called into question the notion that women could not run for president or vice president. Additionally, the candidates of all genders were innovators. Due to the influx of women and people of color running, the rhetoric shifted in a feminist direction and emphasized the power of women voters. In contrast to the 2018 gubernatorial contests, 2020 women candidates were less likely to utilize traditional self-presentations to strategically craft a complex and multifaceted image. The men, in contrast, did so to preserve traditional masculinity. The women candidates' self-presentations diverged sharply from Clinton in the 2016 election. Clinton was frequently berated for her "tough" self-presentation style and attempted to "soften" her image (Aronson 2018), while these women candidates were unapologetically confrontational, assertive, and overtly feminist.

At the same time, the revolution is incomplete and partial, as ultimately, the women candidates were not successful. Many Democratic voters struggled with the idea of nominating a woman to run against Trump, and gendered ideas about who is "electable" harmed women's campaigns. In the general election, Trump and others attacked Harris in gendered and racialized ways. Democrats, although progressive on gender and feminist issues, ultimately resisted nominating a woman for this office. Thus, the 2020 election advanced women's power in electoral politics yet simultaneously illustrated that there are limits to such rapid social change.

Yet on the whole, the diversity and gendered self-presentations of the candidates reveal an expansion of women's political power. As candidates continue to alter the political landscape, they reshape views of women's electability and offer an important critique of white male power. Although symbolic, norms around the clothing choices of women candidates illustrate one aspect of this cultural change. In contrast to just three years earlier, when Clinton generated headlines, and was sometimes berated and sometimes loved, for her characteristic "pantsuits," wearing pants instead of skirts had become normative for the women candidates for president in 2020. This seemingly trivial cultural shift in norms and expectations illustrates how quickly society forgets that the old norms existed. That is, like the nearly undetectable, unconscious shift in our ideas about what a woman candidate for president *should* look like, the 2020 Democratic primary altered our ideas about *who* can run for president or vice president.

We have seen that political ideas about women's collective power have become diffused into everyday understandings. Innovators, who push social change forward, have embraced women's political power. As we will see in the next section of this book, this diffusion of the gender revolution has also occurred in the everyday lives of people on a more personal level.

References

ABC News. 2020. "ABC News Presents 'Running Mates' With Chasten Buttigieg." *YouTube*. Retrieved May 9, 2022 (www.youtube.com/watch?v=BYBQXzXCkj4).

Aronson, Pamela. 2018. "'I'm Not Voting for *Her*.' Internalized Misogyny, Feminism and Gender Consciousness in the 2016 Election." pp. 204–218 in *Nasty Women and Bad Hombres: Gender and Race in the 2016 Presidential Election*, edited by Christine Kray, Tamar Carroll, and Hinda Mandell. Rochester, NY: University of Rochester Press.

Aronson, Pamela, Leah Oldham, and Emily Lucas. 2020. "Gender Self-Presentations in the 2020 U.S. Elections." *Journal of Cultural Analysis and Social Change* 5(1):01. ISSN: 2589-1316.

Astor, Maggie. 2020. "Kamala Harris and the 'Double Bind' of Racism and Sexism." *The New York Times*. Retrieved May 12, 2022 (www.nytimes.com/2020/10/09/us/politics/kamala-harris-racism-sexism.html?referringSource=articleShare).

Bassett, Laura. 2020. "Why Is Bloomberg's Long History of Egregious Sexism Getting a Pass?" *GQ*. Retrieved May 12, 2022 (www.gq.com/story/bloomberg-sexism).

Biden, Joe. 2020. That's A President | Joe Biden For President. *YouTube*. Retrieved May 12, 2022 (www.youtube.com/watch?v=vlP3yfRZ5gg).

The Biden-Harris Administration. 2022. "Kamala Harris: The Vice President." *The White House*. Retrieved May 9, 2022 (www.whitehouse.gov/administration/vice-president-harris/).

Bloomberg Quicktake: Now. 2020. Trump on Harris: 'Kamala Will Not Be Your First Female President'. *YouTube*. Retrieved May 12, 2022 (www.youtube.com/watch?v=70HcVHUfDtQ).

Bloomberg, Mike. 2020. Women for Mike. *YouTube*. Retrieved May 12, 2022 (www.youtube.com/watch?v=fYGdR0sUMUM).

Booker, Cory. 2019. Love. *YouTube*. Retrieved May 10, 2022 (www.youtube.com/watch?v=3f6g-tWhKoc).

Breakfast Club Power 105.1 FM. 2019a. Kamala Harris Talks 2020 Presidential Run, Legalizing Marijuana, Criminal Justice Reform + More. *YouTube*. Retrieved May 10, 2022 (www.youtube.com/watch?v=Kh_wQUjeaTk).

Breakfast Club Power 105.1 FM. 2019b. Pete Buttigieg on Political Honesty, His Black Agenda, Open Homosexuality + More. *YouTube*. Retrieved May 10, 2022 (www.youtube.com/watch?v=zunsfxjyOAE&t=1516s).

Brownstein, Ronald. 2012. "The Coalition of Transformation vs. The Coalition of Restoration." *The Atlantic*. Retrieved May 12, 2022 (www.theatlantic.com/politics/archive/2012/11/the-coalition-of-transformation-vs-the-coalition-of-restoration/265512/).

Burns, Alexander, Matt Flegenheimer, Jasmine C. Lee, Lisa Lerer, and Jonathan Martin. 2020. "Who's Running for President in 2020?" *The New York Times*. Retrieved May 9, 2022 (www.nytimes.com/interactive/2019/us/politics/2020-presidential-candidates.html).

C-Span. 2020. "Campaign 2020 | Joe Biden Introduction of Senator Kamala Harris as Running Mate." *C-Span*. Retrieved May 12, 2022 (www.c-span.org/video/?474731-1%2Fjoe-biden-introduces-senator-kamala-harris-running-mate).

Carnevale, Anthony P., Nicole Smith, and Kathryn Peltier Campbell. 2019. "May The Best Woman Win? Education and Bias Against Women in American Politics." *GIWPS*. Retrieved May 12, 2022 (https://giwps.georgetown.edu/resource/may-the-best-woman-win/).

Carroll, Susan J. 2009. "Reflections on Gender and Hillary Clinton's Presidential Campaign: The Good, the Bad, and the Misogynic." *Politics & Gender* 5(01):1–20.

Cassidy, Brittany S. and Hayley A. Liebenow. 2021. "Feminine Perceptions of Kamala Harris Positively Relate to Evaluations of Her Candidacy." *Analyses of Social Issues and Public Policy* 21(1):29–50.

Castro, Julian. 2019. Julian Castro for President 2020. *YouTube*. Retrieved July 2019 (www. youtube.com/watch?v=LtY0SZPMIT0).

CBS News. 2019. First on CBSN: Amy Klobuchar and Husband Talk Life and the 2020 Campaign. *YouTube*. Retrieved May 10, 2022 (www.youtube.com/watch?v= c38aTEQxodU).

CBS Sunday Morning. 2019. Extended Interview: Presidential Candidate Pete Buttigieg and Husband Chasten. *YouTube*. Retrieved May 10, 2022 (www.youtube.com/ watch?v=BukHlw2oXZQ&t=155s).

Center for American Women and Politics. 2022a. "Gender Gap Public Opinion." *Center for American Women and Politics*. Retrieved May 9, 2022 (https://cawp.rutgers.edu/ gender-gap-public-opinion).

Center for American Women and Politics. 2022b. "Gender Differences in Voter Turnout." *Center for American Women and Politics*. Retrieved May 12, 2022 (https://cawp.rutgers. edu/facts/voters/gender-differences-voter-turnout).

Center for American Women and Politics. 2022c. "Gender Gap: Voting Choices in Presidential Elections." *Center for American Women and Politics*. Retrieved May 12, 2022 (https://cawp.rutgers.edu/gender-gap-voting-choices-presidential-elections).

CNN. 2020a. "Evelyn Yang Reveals She Was Sexually Assaulted While Pregnant." *YouTube*. Retrieved May 9, 2022 (www.youtube.com/watch?v=wMbIQgCRtjw).

CNN. 2020b. "President Trump Repeatedly Mocks Sen. Kamala Harris." *YouTube*. Retrieved May 12, 2022 (www.youtube.com/watch?v=lbGrvhHK9FU).

CNN. 2019a. "Kamala Harris Responds to Trump Calling Her 'Nasty'." *YouTube*. Retrieved May 10, 2022 (*www.youtube.com/watch?v=ju0y7ZTgmA0*).

CNN. 2019b. "Cuomo to Julian Castro: Do You Regret Attack on Joe Biden?" *YouTube*. Retrieved May 12, 2022 (www.youtube.com/watch?v=6IscAVZzOqoCuomo to Julian Castro: Do you regret attack on Joe Biden?).

The Daily Show. 2019a. Kamala Harris Wants to Legalize Weed & Amy Klobuchar's Temper Is Questioned. *YouTube*. Retrieved May 10, 2022 (www.youtube.com/watch?v= j-LxrPrXJO8).

The Daily Show. 2019b. Joe Biden Faces Backlash for His "Hands-On" Approach to Politics. *YouTube*. Retrieved May 12, 2022 (www.youtube.com/watch?v=KkREGzfSCAY).

Democratic National Convention. 2020. Tribute to Speaker Nancy Pelosi. *YouTube*. Retrieved (www.youtube.com/watch?v=Cm1uIk30QL0).

Dittmar, Kelly. 2021a. "Tracking Gender in the 2020 Presidential Election." *2020 Presidential—CAWP Reports*. Retrieved May 9, 2022 (https://womenrun.rutgers.edu/ 2020-presidential/).

Dittmar, Kelly. 2021b. "Reaching Higher: Black Women in American Politics 2021." *Center for American Women and Politics*. Retrieved May 12, 2022 (https://cawp.rutgers.edu/ node/4675).

Dittmar, Kelly. 2015. *Navigating Gendered Terrain: Stereotypes and Strategy in Political Campaigns*. Philadelphia, PA: Temple University Press.

Dovere, Edward-Isaac. 2019. "Kamala Harris Is the Jan Brady of the 2020 Race." *The Atlantic*. Retrieved May 10, 2022 (www.theatlantic.com/politics/archive/2019/05/ kamala-harris-tries-break-through-2020-race/589546/).

Ferree, Myra Marx. 2020. "The Crisis of Masculinity for Gendered Democracies: Before, During, and After Trump." *Sociological Forum* 35(S1):898–917.

First Five Years Fund. 2020. Child Care in the CNN/Des Moines Register Presidential Debate. *YouTube*. Retrieved May 9, 2022 (www.youtube.com/watch?v=YxHlp5Ooki8).

Fox News. 2019a. Town Hall with Pete Buttigieg | Part 1. *YouTube*. Retrieved May 9, 2022 (www.youtube.com/watch?v=p97xg-keEKg&t=6s).

Fox News. 2019b. Tulsi Gabbard Sounds off after Ripping Kamala Harris at Debate. *YouTube*. Retrieved May 10, 2022 (www.youtube.com/watch?v=OUsU-oFyFUw).

Fox News. 2019c. Tucker: What Do You Know About Kamala Harris? *YouTube*. Retrieved May 11, 2022 (https://youtu.be/BN4fHXCPpnM).

Fulton, Sarah A. and Kostanca Dhima. 2021. "The Gendered Politics of Congressional Elections." *Political Behavior* 43(4):1611–1637.

Gabbard, Tulsi. 2019a. Stand Up for The First Amendment. *YouTube*. Retrieved May 10, 2022 (www.youtube.com/watch?v=XDZvXF5G0rw).

Gabbard, Tulsi. 2019b. Trump Offers to Pimp out Our Military to His Saudi Masters. *YouTube*. Retrieved May 10, 2022 (www.youtube.com/watch?v=9Jo8QU2s_5I).

Gabbard, Tulsi. 2019c. "Those Days When You Don't Feel like Exercising and Tell Yourself You'Re Too Tired or Don't Have Time—Just Do It. You'Ll Be Glad You Did. #Motivationmonday #Fitness #Health #tulsi2020." *Twitter*. Retrieved May 10, 2022 (https://twitter.com/TulsiGabbard/status/1191466692754518021).

Gallup News Service. 2019. "Residential Candidates—Gallup News Service April Wave 2." *Gallup News | Nonpartisan Analysis of Critical Global Issues*. Retrieved May 12, 2022 (https://news.gallup.com/file/poll/257495/190509PresidentialCandidates.pdf).

Gillibrand, Kirsten. 2019. "Today in Youngstown, OH, a Woman Asked: 'This Is an Area That, Across All Demographics, Has Been Depressed Because of the Loss of Industry and the Opioid Crisis. What Do You Have to Say to People in This Area About So-Called White Privilege?'." *Twitter*. Retrieved May 10, 2022 (https://twitter.com/SenGillibrand/status/1149498925339910146?ref_src=twsrc%5Etfw%7Ctwcamp%5Etweetembed%7Ctwterm%5E1149498925339910146%7Ctwgr%5E%7Ctwcon%5Es1_c10&ref_url=https%3A%2F%2Fpublish.twitter.com%2F%3Fquery%3Dhttps3A2F2Ftwitter.com2FSenGillibrand2Fstatus2F1149498925339910146widget%3DTweet).

Glueck, Katie, Lisa Lerer, and Sydney Ember. 2020. "Biden Denies Tara Reade's Assault Allegation: 'It Never Happened'." *The New York Times*. Retrieved May 12, 2022 (www.nytimes.com/2020/05/01/us/politics/joe-biden-tara-reade-morning-joe.html).

Goldmacher, Shane, K. K. Rebecca Lai, and Rachel Shorey. 2019. "The 5 Days That Defined the 2020 Primary." *The New York Times*. Retrieved May 9, 2022 (www.nytimes.com/interactive/2019/08/17/us/politics/2020-democratic-fundraising.html?searchResultPosition=14).

Gothreau, Claire. 2021. "Everything You Need to Know About the Gender Gap." *Center for American Women and Politics*. Retrieved February 23, 2023 (https://cawp.rutgers.edu/blog/everything-you-need-know-about-gender-gap).

Hagan, Joe and Annie Leibovitz. 2019. "Beto O'Rourke: 'I'm Just Born to Be in It': Riding around with Beto O'Rourke as He Comes to Grips with a Presidential Run." *Vanity Fair*. Retrieved May 10, 2022 (www.vanityfair.com/news/2019/03/beto-orourke-cover-story).

Harris, Kamala. 2019a. Me, Maya, and Mom. *YouTube*. Retrieved May 9, 2022 (www.youtube.com/watch?v=5MXlmmER3-g).

Harris, Kamala. 2019b. America's Promise. *YouTube*. Retrieved May 10, 2022 (www.youtube.com/watch?v=stkkh8RyGno).

Harris, Kamala. 2019c. Kamala Harris & Mindy Kaling Cook Masala Dosa. *YouTube*. Retrieved May 11, 2022 (www.youtube.com/watch?v=xz7rNOAFkgE).

Harris, Kamala. 2019d. Kamala Harris: For the People. *YouTube*. Retrieved May 11, 2022 (www.youtube.com/watch?v=Ls7OSwHMoBc).

Harris, Kamala. 2019e. Kamala Harris Cooks Bacon-Fried Apples. *YouTube*. Retrieved May 11, 2022 (www.youtube.com/watch?v=ql7YHR4Dwg0).

Igielnik, Ruth, Scott Keeter, and Hannah Hartig. 2021. "Behind Biden's 2020 Victory." *Pew Research Center—U.S. Politics & Policy*. Retrieved May 12, 2022 (www.pewresearch.org/politics/2021/06/30/behind-bidens-2020-victory/).

Iowa for Warren. 2020. Pinky Promises in Iowa. *Facebook*. Retrieved May 9, 2022 (www.facebook.com/watch/?v=172874700693172).

Joe Rogan Experience #1391. 2019. Tulsi Gabbard & Jocko Willink. *Youtube*. Retrieved February 23, 2023 (https://www.youtube.com/watch?v=PdYud9re7-Q).

Junn, Jane and Natalie Masuoka. 2020. "The Gender Gap Is a Race Gap: Women Voters in US Presidential Elections." *Perspectives on Politics* 18(4):1135–1145.

Khanna, Kabir. 2019. "What Traits Are Democrats Prioritizing in 2020 Candidates?" *CBS News*. Retrieved May 12, 2022 (www.cbsnews.com/news/democratic-voters-hungry-for-women-and-people-of-color-in-2020-nomination/).

Krieg, Gregory and Eric Bradner. 2019. "Elizabeth Warren Responds to 'Angry' Charge: 'I Am Angry and I Own It'." *CNN*. Retrieved May 10, 2022 (https://edition.cnn.com/2019/11/08/politics/elizabeth-warren-joe-biden-sexism-charges/index.html).

The Late Show with Stephen Colbert. 2020. Tom Steyer: Corporations Are Not People. *YouTube*. Retrieved May 10, 2022 (www.youtube.com/watch?v=Fci40DfoxN4).

The Late Show with Stephen Colbert. 2019a. Elizabeth Warren: A Country That Elects Donald Trump Is Already In Trouble. *YouTube*. Retrieved May 9, 2022 (www.youtube.com/watch?v=9Yiga2dDysQ).

The Late Show with Stephen Colbert. 2019b. Cardi B Wants Her Fans To 'Vote for Daddy Bernie'. *YouTube*. Retrieved May 10, 2022 (www.youtube.com/watch?v=wpkO9yVei1U).

The Late Show with Stephen Colbert. 2019c. Accusations of Sexist Comments Haunt Michael Bloomberg's Presidential Bid. *YouTube*. Retrieved May 12, 2022 (www.youtube.com/watch?v=Uve_Cl-Kcvk).

Leatherby, Lauren and Sarah Almukhtar. 2020. "Democratic Delegate Count and Primary Election Results 2020." *The New York Times*. Retrieved February 23, 2023 (https://www.nytimes.com/interactive/2020/us/elections/delegate-count-primary-results.html).

Lerer, Lisa and Shane Goldmacher. 2019. "'This Is My Space': Kirsten Gillibrand's Unabashedly Feminist Campaign." *The New York Times*. Retrieved May 9, 2022 (www.nytimes.com/2019/02/12/us/politics/kirsten-gillibrand-president-feminist.html).

McCarthy, Tom. 2020. "Kamala Harris's DNC Speech Claimed a New Moment for Progressive Democrats." *The Guardian*. Retrieved May 12, 2022 (www.theguardian.com/us-news/2020/aug/20/kamala-harris-dnc-speech-democrats-progressives).

Morning Consult. 2020. "National Tracking Poll #200205 | Morning Consult Gender Crosstabs." *NBC Universal*. Retrieved May 12, 2022 (https://ots.nbcwpshield.com/wp-content/uploads/2019/09/LX-Morning-Consult-Gender-Crosstabs.pdf).

MSNBC. 2020. DNC Spotlights Women's Struggles, Achievements on Night of Harris' Historic VP Nomination. *MSNBC YouTube*. Retrieved May 12, 2022 (www.youtube.com/watch?v=MZb8M-cECcI).

NBC News. 2020. Elizabeth Warren Attacks 'Arrogant Billionaire' Michael Bloomberg over Treatment of Women. *NBC News. YouTube*. Retrieved May 9, 2022 (www.youtube.com/watch?v=QD4csGWPo6o).

NBC News. 2019. Klobuchar Shuts Down Question On Women Candidates Being 'Unlikable.' *NBC News YouTube*. YouTube. Retrieved May 9, 2022 (www.youtube.com/watch?v=lZNUECC8Sr8).

Nelson, Kjersten. 2021. "You Seem like a Great Candidate, but . . .: Race and Gender Attitudes and the 2020 Democratic Primary." *The Journal of Race, Ethnicity, and Politics* 6(3):642–666.

North, Anna. 2019. "We Asked the Dads Running for President What They Do for Child Care." *Vox*. Retrieved May 12, 2022 (www.vox.com/policy-and-politics/2019/5/22/18633044/2020-election-democrats-child-care-kids-men?fbclid=IwAR0M53uwDL7ScSdzm1HLunBr_MrAOfwzJnBAIPoMtqnSn-0bUaHYWLNZohE).

NowThis News. 2020. Tom Steyer Gets Blunt About Trump's Racism. *NowThis YouTube*. Retrieved May 12, 2022 (www.youtube.com/watch?v=hKHljHXvkcA).

O'Rourke, Beto. 2019a. Protect Reproductive Rights. *CNN Town Hall YouTube*. Retrieved May 9, 2022 (www.youtube.com/watch?v=-lFjXj1JvN4).

O'Rourke, Beto. 2019b. A New Kind of Politics. *YouTube*. Retrieved May 10, 2022 (www.youtube.com/watch?v=hhUvg2gD2G4).

O'Rourke, Beto. 2019c. Running for President. *YouTube*. Retrieved May 12, 2022 (www.youtube.com/watch?v=mVeYxBpphw8).

Parker, Kim, Juliana Menasce Horowitz, and Renee Stepler. 2020. "3. Americans See Society Placing More of a Premium on Masculinity than on Femininity." *Pew Research Center's Social & Demographic Trends Project*. Retrieved May 12, 2022 (www.pewresearch.org/social-trends/2017/12/05/americans-see-society-placing-more-of-a-premium-on-masculinity-than-on-femininity).

Pels, Jessica. 2019. "Cosmo Asks Bernie Sanders the Questions Young Women Want Answered." *Cosmopolitan*. Retrieved May 9, 2022 (www.cosmopolitan.com/politics/a29255694/bernie-sanders-cosmopolitan-interview-election-immigration-gun-control-healthcare-young-women/).

The Real Daytime. 2019. Does Senator Cory Booker Think That Rosario Dawson Is Ready To Be His First Lady? *YouTube*. Retrieved May 10, 2022 (www.youtube.com/watch?v=Ghk0DqcPVU0).

Roper Center for Public Opinion Research. 2016. "Madame President: Changing Attitudes about a Woman President." *Cornell University*. Retrieved May 12, 2022 (https://ropercenter.cornell.edu/blog/madame-president-changing-attitudes-about-woman-president).

Sanders, Bernie. 2019a. Women for Bernie. *YouTube*. Retrieved May 9, 2022 (www.youtube.com/watch?v=0iUTnCRl_JI).

Sanders, Bernie. 2019b. I'm Running for President. *YouTube*. Retrieved May 9, 2022 (www.youtube.com/watch?v=s7DRwz0cAt0).

Sanders, Bernie. 2019c. Thank You From Bernie and Jane. *YouTube*. Retrieved May 12, 2022 (www.youtube.com/watch?v=8UBtDJ9Hkqk).

Saturday Night Live. 2019. Elizabeth Warren Town Hall Cold Open. *SNL YouTube*. Retrieved May 11, 2022 (https://youtube/CPDr9wGNEfg).

Stevens, Matt. 2019. "Kamala Harris Surges in 3 Polls After Strong Debate Performance." *The New York Times*. Retrieved May 9, 2022 (www.nytimes.com/2019/07/02/us/politics/kamala-harris-polls.html).

Steyer, Tom. 2019. Trump Is a Fraud. *YouTube*. Retrieved May 12, 2022 (www.youtube.com/watch?v=ZKIPR4LROMA).

Streb, Matthew J., Barbara Burrell, Brian Frederick, and Michael A. Genovese. 2008. "Social Desirability Effects and Support for a Female American President." *Public Opinion Quarterly* 72(1):76–89.

Summers, Juana. 2019. "'Carer-Feeder': Gillibrand Plays up Motherhood in 2020 Race." *AP NEWS*. Retrieved May 9, 2022 (https://apnews.com/article/north-america-ap-top-news-politics-lifestyle-ny-state-wire-dc67b4f47c8941bfbb0287ced06dc731).

Swidler, Ann. 1986. "Culture in Action: Symbols and Strategies." *American Sociological Review* 51(2):273–286.

Terkel, Amanda. 2020. "Elizabeth Warren Could Never Escape the Baggage of Being a 'Female Candidate'." *HuffPost*. Retrieved May 12, 2022 (www.huffpost.com/entry/elizabeth-warren-female-candidate_n_5e606661c5b62d548c9d00dd).

TheEllenShow. 2019. Full Interview: Senator Cory Booker on Rosario Dawson, Trump's Tweets, and a Female Vice President. *YouTube*. Retrieved May 10, 2022 (www.youtube.com/watch?v=a2y7w4Oq9_0).

TheEllenShow. 2020. Pete Buttigieg Responds to Controversial Rush Limbaugh Comments. *YouTube*. Retrieved May 10, 2022 (www.youtube.com/watch?v=Etr-5SEDlP0).

TIME Staff. 2019. "2020 Democratic Debate Night 2: Read the Full Transcript." *Time*. Retrieved May 9, 2022 (https://time.com/5616518/2020-democratic-debate-night-2-transcript/).

The View. 2019a. Sen. Amy Klobuchar 'Extremely Concerned' Abortion Bans Will Overthrow Roe v. Wade. *The View*. *YouTube*. Retrieved May 9, 2022 (www.youtube.com/watch?v=P-_IOULlCzc).

The View. 2019b. Klobuchar Announces Presidential Run. *The View YouTube*. Retrieved May 10, 2022 (www.youtube.com/watch?v=EHW9MGn6jCI).

The View. 2019c. Tom Steyer Discusses His 2020 Campaign. *The View YouTube*. Retrieved May 12, 2022 (www.youtube.com/watch?v=vdzI21snMb8).

Warren, Elizabeth. 2019a. Elizabeth Warren at the 2019 She the People Presidential Forum. *YouTube*. Retrieved May 10, 2022 (www.youtube.com/watch?v=ZRLdH4NCXqg).

Warren, Elizabeth. 2019b. Elizabeth's Message to RuPaul's DragCon. *YouTube*. Retrieved May 10, 2022 (www.youtube.com/watch?v=r2Sn5XbJEfA).

Warren, Elizabeth. 2018. Elizabeth Warren Launches Exploratory Committee for President. *YouTube*. Retrieved May 10, 2022 (https://youtu.be/rbH0RU4GcVo).

Yang, Andrew. 2019. Andrew Yang on the View (Full Interview). *YouTube*. Retrieved May 9, 2022 (www.youtube.com/watch?v=y6NdhXGXpp0).

PART 3

The Personal

Diffusion of the Gender Revolution into Everyday Lives

5

CHANGING AND CONTESTED DEFINITIONS OF SEXUAL CONSENT

"The Norm That's Been Set for Years": Understanding Traditional and Innovative Norms about Consent

In a focus group with five younger men, Don, a 58-year-old white man, emphasized the most gender-traditional perspective that we heard. He began by counseling the other men about how they could "get a lot further" with women through flattery. In a poignant statement, Don instructed the younger men:

> I've never seen a female that doesn't like to be talked to nicely. They all get on me, no matter what age. They love to be talked to nicely, sweetly. You go along while you can. They're different from males. Males have to treat a female that way. Just for their own good. That talking thing with a female goes a long way. Women love to talk.

Don briefly paused, laughed, and then continued, "Men are going to get a lot further and avoid a lot of confrontation and make it easy on themselves." Although it is not clear what happens when a man can no longer "go along while you can," some type of coercive behavior is implied. In this quote, "talking" serves the function of "getting a lot further" without having to resort to "confrontation."

Although Don, the oldest focus group participant, had more conventional views than the other men, about half of the younger men (50 percent of the men; n = 20; see Table 5.1) also expressed views that objectified women and viewed gender relations in highly traditional ways. Some interviewees questioned sexual harassment and assault accounts because they challenge women's subservience to men. Hunter, a 22-year-old white man, said that such accounts were "violating the

DOI: 10.4324/9781003225331-9

TABLE 5.1 Distribution of Men's Perspectives by Racial and Ethnic Background

	Types of perspective			
	Resister	Innovator	Fused	Total
White	4	3	6	13
Middle Eastern or North African	4	1	2	7
Hispanic/Latinx	3	0	0	3
Black	1	0	2	3
Asian American	4	1	5	10
Multiracial	2	0	0	2
Unknown	2	0	0	2
Percent (n)	50% (20)	12.5% (5)	37.5% (15)	100% (40)

norm that's been set for years. Tradition." Jin, a 21-year-old Asian American man, agreed, "A lot of women are raised to be silent. Men are raised differently; a lot of men can get away with a lot of things that they do wrong."

The clash between traditional and innovative views of gender relations has contributed to contestation over definitions of consent. While some men continued to rely on traditional perspectives, the #MeToo movement has increasingly called these norms into question. In this context, understandings of consent differ between genders. While many of the men saw women as sexual objects who they win over or convince to engage in sexual activity, the women defined these behaviors as coercive and were outspoken about situations that make them uncomfortable.

Previous research has emphasized the complexity of consent, which is exacerbated by power dynamics and traditional gender roles. As Murray and Brotto (2021: 419) described it, "sexual scripts for heterosexual relationships in the Western world stipulate that men should be the ones to initiate sexual activity, push to the next level of physical intimacy, and to desire women." In fact, one-third to two-thirds of women (depending on the study) reported "consenting" as a result of verbal sexual coercion, such as pressure or manipulation tactics (Pugh and Becker 2018). Researchers have argued that verbal coercion should be considered non-consent, as power dynamics may result in women "giving in" to men who do not take "no for an answer" (Pugh and Becker 2018: 2, 7; Muehlenhard et al. 2016). In fact, studies have revealed that some men perceive "the word 'no' . . . as something to be overcome" (Muehlenhard et al. 2016: 471). In their review of the research, Muehlenhard and her collaborators (2016: 471) concluded that some men "may claim ignorance about understanding non-consent cues" while simultaneously recognizing that "miscommunication is likely." These seemingly incongruent ideas are rooted in traditional gender scripts in which women's responsibility is to resist men's advances and communicate their non-consent clearly enough (Pugh and Becker 2018). Burkett and Hamilton (2012) found that women embraced traditional ideas before the #MeToo era: They saw women as having personal sexual agency at the same time as they accepted the coercive aspects of heterosexual sex.

Pugh and Becker (2018) developed a model to distinguish between freely given consent, non-consent (including verbal coercion), and compromise or compliance "problem sex." In their formulation, "problem sex" is consensual but unwanted; it might be undertaken to maintain a relationship or as a result of societal pressure. Other researchers agreed that "wanting to have sex" and "consenting to have sex" are typically treated as interchangeable, yet ambivalence and uncertainty are often based on cultural pressures (Muehlenhard et al. 2016; Fenner 2017; Conroy et al. 2014). Although these carefully developed ideas uncover a range of types of unwanted sex, they do not capture the more clear-cut affirmative consent understandings of our innovators, nor do they take into account change in these definitions over time.

In a context in which public redefinitions of the boundaries between consent and sexual assault are rapidly shifting, innovators in this study defined everything *outside of* "freely given consent" (Pugh and Becker 2018: 4) as nonconsensual. In contrast to the views of the majority of the focus group men, affirmative consent was viewed as the standard. Innovators viewed unwanted sex as sexual assault, including when it resulted from compliance or societal pressure. This approach differs from Pugh and Becker's (2018) model, in which some unwanted sex is classified as consensual, even though it is not desired.

Focus group interviews reveal how the #MeToo movement has become diffused into people's everyday lives. In this chapter, we consider how different genders think about sexual consent. On the ground, people's everyday concerns reveal both cultural transformations and challenges to these widespread shifts. As innovators challenge traditional scripts through the endorsement of affirmative consent and move the gender revolution forward, resisters pull back on the social change created by the #MeToo movement. This push and pull suggests that the gender revolution in ideas about consent has progressed but is still incomplete.

"A Looser Definition of Consent": "Tradition" and Resistance to Social Change

Using data collected before the #MeToo era, Hirsch and Khan (2020) found that both men and women students at an elite college (Columbia University) articulated a commonly understood ideal of affirmative consent. In their study, only about one-third of sexual assaults involved physical force. Most assaults started as "sexual situations that are consensual, until they are not" (Hirsch and Khan 2020: xxxiii). In their study, although both men and women held affirmative consent as the ideal, it was rarely actually practiced. Instead, both men and women relied on indirect language or interpretation of body language as indicators of consent. Although Hirsch and Khan did not find gender differences in *definitions* of consent, they interviewed several men who did not initially label their actions as nonconsensual but, upon reflection, realized that they had committed sexual assault. Other older studies have extensively documented that college students often rely on subtle cues to indicate consent; in fact, young adults view verbal communication as "unnecessary because consent was 'obvious'" (Muehlenhard et al. 2016: 471). Although research in prior eras has found minimal gender differences in definitions of consent, there were gender differences in the use of verbal cues. Verbal cues were commonly expected by women, while men reported relying more on nonverbal cues (Jozkowski et al. 2014; Jozkowski and Humphreys 2014). Overall, explicit verbal consent is used less often than nonverbal cues, and both are shaped and undermined by intoxication (Jozkowski et al. 2014; Jozkowski and Humphreys 2014; Jozkowski and Wiersma 2014).

Our study, conducted after the #MeToo movement took hold, examines the diffusion of movement frames into people's everyday lives. In fact, innovative ideas about consent have spread throughout culture and society. Interviewees reported reading about these topics in the news, having conversations with their friends and family, and reflecting on issues of consent. In contrast to older studies, our interviews suggest that the gender revolution is changing how ordinary people think about consent. Yet these innovations are met with resistance, as some people hold onto traditional conceptions, ideas, and identities.

Interviewees diverged quite sharply by gender in their very definitions of consent. Most of the men's definitions were more "loose" or "laissez-faire," while the women's definitions were perceived by the men to be more "strict" or "textbook." While the women and nonbinary interviewees embraced an affirmative consent standard, most of the men operated with a traditional "no means no" standard that drew on stereotypical rape scripts. The men also pointed to "gray areas," such as the influence of alcohol, that they found to be disconcerting. In this context, men used personal strategies to lessen their perceived vulnerability to "false" accusations. These discourses are based on two underlying assumptions: Men and women are adversaries and, relatedly, men are the initiators and aggressors while women are gatekeepers and passive recipients of heterosexual sexual interactions.

Our findings capture perspectives that have eluded other studies. In addition to taking place after #MeToo became widespread, our sample and methodology diverges from previous studies. Our sample is more diverse in age and racial and class backgrounds than prior studies that have examined consent and sexual assault. In a comprehensive review of previous research on sexual consent, Muehlenhard et al. (2016: 481) pointed out that existing research has "consisted largely of White students," who may have divergent experiences than people of color. About a quarter of our participants were white, about a quarter were Black, about 1 in 6 were Middle Eastern or North African, 1 in 6 were Asian American, and the remainder were Hispanic/Latinx or multiracial (see Introduction and Appendix 1). This diversity is important, as people from different racial and ethnic backgrounds have different rates of sexual victimization, with white women experiencing higher rates than Latinx, Black, or Asian American women (Breiding et al. 2014; Robinson 2022). While Hirsch and Khan's (2020) sample was diverse in racial background, it was primarily upper-middle-class college students who espoused, at least verbally, a "politically correct" version of affirmative consent. In contrast, our sample is not drawn from an elite group of students and is diverse in social class background: About one-third were first-generation college students and about half came from low-income backgrounds (see Introduction and Appendix 1).

Additionally, our methodology was highly effective at eliciting a wide range of perspectives rather than those that are socially desirable. The focus group format allowed us to tap into not only individual attitudes but also participants' reactions to others' viewpoints. Our deliberate and careful strategy of conducting both gender-similar and mixed-gender focus groups, with facilitator composition reflecting the gender makeup of the groups, yielded data that other researchers have not yet been able to capture. Although we cannot make generalizations about how people of particular backgrounds view consent, we are able to provide a picture of how average people on the ground think about these issues.

Turning to an in-depth analysis of the focus groups, participants often stated that a simple yes or no in response to the initiation of sexual activity were easily understood terms. However, resister men typically then went on to explain that consent is actually quite a bit more complicated. When we asked a mixed-gender focus group if they thought that there was confusion about how to define sexual consent, Jeremiah, a 36-year-old multiracial man, illustrated a paradox: "It seems murky, but I think that a yes or a no is pretty simple." He went on to agree that these concepts are confusing due to flux in their definitions in the #MeToo era: "I don't think the definitions are set." Jeremiah referred to lawmakers and societal leaders as "they": "I don't think they can create enough clarity for everybody to understand. I just don't think that people share the same ideas when it comes to assault, harassment, abuse, any of those things. I think it's confusing for some." Thus, what at first seemed "pretty simple," Jeremiah labeled confusing upon further reflection. In the same focus group, Kiara, an 18-year-old Black woman, sharply challenged Jeremiah's view that definitions of consent were "murky," adversarially calling men "you": "*You* know what yes and no is. Everyone knows what that is."

Damien, an 18-year-old Black man, jumped into the conversation, initially responding with clarity in a way that supported Kiara's position: "Universally, yes and no. That's obvious. You're not going to misinterpret yes." Yet Damien then implied that, in a context of traditional gender roles, obtaining consent from a woman is actually more complicated today: "Some people probably look for body language, and they may misinterpret that. Or they may think that, 'She's just teasing me or something.'" This clash between women's and men's views was common.

Damien also stated that men should explicitly ask for consent when there is confusion: "That's when you should actually use yes and no. You should actually directly ask. You don't want any amount of confusion to lead to something that would be negative, like assault or harassment." In this formulation, women are assumed to be passive recipients of the sexual encounter (since men need to "directly ask") and, as we have seen, are also frequently perceived to be "teasing" men. The last comment is reminiscent of traditional victim-blaming narratives, as women's behavior is viewed as the source of men's confusion. This perspective also assumes a double standard surrounding the enjoyment of sex: Damien presumes that women are ambivalent or unclear about their desires, as their consent is not obvious. This double standard also reflects traditional gender norms.

The majority of focus group men perceived a sharp contrast between women's and men's definitions of consent. Implying that nonconsensual behavior exists on a continuum, they used such phrases as "extreme variants," "black and white," "textbook definition," and "hardline yes and no" to describe clear-cut cases of rape. In these situations, which draw on stereotypical rape scripts, they thought that men and women agreed that sexual assault had occurred. Conversely, these resisters used phrases like "lower-level situations," "lower-level things," "gray areas," "stepping stones," and "smaller things" to describe what they considered to be "lesser" offenses. As we will see, the women and nonbinary interviewees defined these "smaller" situations as sexual assault. In claiming that "lower-level things" represent confusing situations, these men actively contested women's empowerment and self-determination and minimized the seriousness of these incidents. Yet research has suggested that these distinctions are not important when it comes to the mental health of the victims. Even "lower-level situations" that do not meet the "severe or pervasive" legal standard can lead to mental health problems among survivors, such as self-doubt, lack of confidence, and depression and anxiety (Cipriano et al. 2021: 343; Willness et al. 2007).

Resister men did not recognize that there are laws and policies to guide definitions of sexual coercion; rather, coercion was defined moment to moment by individual actors. Bryson, a 31-year-old white man, emphasized an adversarial relationship that hinges on communication between individual women and men. He linked different levels of assault with "male" and "female sides":

A lot of it depends on communicational situations. I think for the *more extreme variants*, like rape, most people would see that as definite. But I think in the *lower-level situations*, if the communication wasn't there, it might *not* be seen as something that would implicitly be a sexual harassment or assault, whereas on the female side it may be.

Here, perceived gender differences in communication result in a situation in which women define the interaction as sexual harassment or assault, while men do not. The standard of affirmative consent is rejected in favor of the indefinite and flexible nature of these definitions. In this context, Bryson dismissed women's perceptions as invalid.

In a context in which definitions of consent are shifting, some men realized that their own past behavior may now be considered problematic or even sexual assault. Prompted by a discussion among focus group participants, Pamela asked whether people "are thinking back to their past behavior and thinking, 'Wait, I did such and such?'" Jeremiah replied, laughing, "Oh, yeah. Heck yeah. I mean I can't speak for everybody else." This response suggests that as new norms develop, people look at their past actions and see them anew, as reprehensible. And yet Jeremiah's laughter made light of this situation rather than recognizing his potentially deleterious actions.

This troubling perspective was repeated by many others. Caleb, a 21-year-old white man, said,

> The more serious cases of sexual harassment and sexual assault are a lot more clear. Obviously, no one's going to debate what rape is. No one's going to debate what domestic abuse is. But I think that when it comes to the *stepping stones* to these things, the *smaller things* that on a scale lead to the more serious offenses, I think that it can be difficult to define exactly what these things were.

Claiming that legal definitions are unclear, Caleb continued,

> When you get to these *lower-level things* that aren't full-on violence and aren't full-on rape, I do think that it's a little bit harder, especially legally, to define where these things end, where these things begin, where you have explicit consent, where you don't have explicit consent.

Caleb suggested that legal definitions of consent involve looking at a situation "clinically," which does not take into account the complexity of real relationships:

> If you look at things in a legal sense, you have to look at things clinically. You have to look at things in a simple calculus. But when you're actually dealing with human relationships, and you're actually dealing with human sexual relationships, whether speaking from experience or speaking from the truth of knowing how humans operate with each other, there often, in genuine relationships isn't a moment where people stop and say, "Oh, are you OK with this? Do I have your explicit consent?" There's no exact form that you sign to say, "Yes, I consented to having sex with you."

Caleb concluded by saying that the actual way that sexual encounters often occur "isn't clinical or black and white at all." Thus, on the one hand, Caleb assumed that rigid gender roles continue to structure heterosexual sexual relationships: Men are the clear initiators and aggressors of sexual contact and women's role is to respond to these advances by affirming or denying consent to men's actions. Yet he stressed that this approach is ultimately unachievable, resulting in an unresolved situation, because men do not ask for explicit consent. In this perspective, there is simply no resolution. Caleb ultimately rejected an effort to engage in actions that support an affirmative consent standard. Furthermore, by referencing a formal signed consent "form," Caleb seemed to mock and dismiss the importance of having all parties agree to sexual activity.

In example after example, resister men argued that men define sexual harassment, assault, and consent differently than women. These traditional gender practices and interactions have set the stage for conflict today. When asked how women and men view consent, Deven, a 20-year-old Asian American man, responded as follows:

> Men are traditionally used to coming onto women, and that implies them doing things or touching them in ways that a lot of women aren't comfortable with. And women are usually very outspoken about that. But I feel like men just have a *looser* definition of consent.

Although the men drew on a wide range of terms to describe this gender divide, men's "loose" or "laissez-faire" definitions of consent were contrasted with women's "strict" or "very textbook" definitions. Dominic, a 20-year-old white man, not only contrasted men's and women's definitions of consent but also described "gray areas":

> There is a *gray area* when you're looking at sexual harassment, where you always have to be on your guard because you never know when something could escalate and become really serious. So a lot of women will be *very textbook* if something meets the definition of sexual harassment, whereas a lot of men are more *laissez-faire*.

That is, men "won't immediately call it sexual harassment just because they're not always on their guard and they don't have to worry about that as much." Here, gender differences in definitions of harassment and assault were attributed to the argument that women are more alert to these problems. In contrast, men did not see a need to define assault in such "textbook" ways because they do not directly experience it themselves. This type of dismissal of women's perspectives relinquishes men from responsibility for sexual assault.

Other men also cited examples of conflicting views of women's and men's definitions. Cam, an 18-year-old Asian American man, stated, "If a male just excessively pats or touches a female in the workplace or something, because of his prior notions, he might consider that less offensive than the female might if she would prefer not to be touched." Cam admitted that he did not always agree with how women define violations of consent: "Maybe what a female might consider overly excessive touching, I wouldn't view as wrong." Leo, an 18-year-old Asian American man, agreed, explaining that differing perceptions of consent stem from differences in "how people interpret things. Overall, it's just how we perceive things, because there's no absolute answer to everything."

In one focus group, two Middle Eastern men discussed how a statement might appear to be a joke to one person but harassment or even assault to another. Malik, 19 years old, said,

> I think it's just in the context of the situation. What would define sexual harassment, especially verbal sexual harassment? Sometimes you could be in a completely joking manner. Things were said that would otherwise, to a complete stranger, be considered assault, for instance.

Ahmad, 21 years old, agreed, "Yeah." Malik then finished his thought, "A lot of it is very context-defined." This discussion suggests that context varies by individuals, which implies that definitions of harassment and assault are arbitrary. Furthermore, conflating sexual harassment and assault with "joking" minimizes the seriousness of the former.

Likewise, Jeremiah stressed that differences in cultural norms result in verbal street harassment being perceived positively in one environment but negatively in another:

> It's a lot about how you view the world, how you're raised, what's culturally OK. If a person is walking down the street and the first person catcalls them and they respond positively, maybe that's just the norm in that environment. But it gets taken outside and they get a negative response. They wouldn't understand why that negative response came. So I can see how it can be confusing.

Jeremiah viewed this context-dependent situation as confusing in terms of whether or not verbal street harassment is acceptable to women, who he labeled generically as "a person." By seeing street harassment as context-dependent, Jeremiah reduced systemic power differentials into individual interactions that can be written off as culturally dependent and gender neutral.

In a mixed-gender focus group, two men and one woman discussed their perception of context-dependent definitions at some length. Anthony, a 35-year-old Black man, started off the conversation: "People have these de facto bubbles that they live in. So it depends on where you are." He explained one context where sexual assault was often acceptable: "The college campus will be different than spring break somewhere, which definitely has signs of rape culture" (where sexual violence is normalized and excused). Referring to the abuse that children have suffered at the hands of clergy as leaders look the other way, Anthony mentioned sexual abuse that occurs in "the church community: It's different factions and different groups that are going to have different levels of awareness." In fact, decades after a church scandal, 1,700 priests and clergy members considered by the Roman Catholic Church to have been "credibly accused of child sexual abuse" have "little to no oversight from religious authorities or law enforcement" (Lauer and Hoyer 2019).

Amelia, a 20-year-old multiracial woman, promptly added that men "get away" with sexual assault or harassment in certain contexts but not others:

> Because we're on a college campus and we're receiving so much information all the time, this is the hub where you find the new information that will make us the most informed. But when you feel like you can get away with it, it doesn't matter. And then in terms of the church where we're trying to protect certain people, where we turn a blind eye.

Anthony replied, "Well, I was talking about spring break," which was followed by laughter from other participants. Amelia reiterated her point, "Yeah, when you turn that blind eye, you're going to get away with it."

At this point, Pamela asked the group, "What do you mean by spring break?" Anthony answered, "Rape culture stuff goes on. Where you smack a girl on her butt and it's like, 'Ha, ha, ha, ha.' But if you do that somewhere else, it won't be acceptable, you know?" Pamela clarified this point, "So there's different definitions in different places?" Anthony responded affirmatively, "Yeah." In this exchange, rape culture, in which sexual assault is normalized, is viewed as acceptable behavior in some contexts, namely, on spring break and in the church. Although Anthony appeared to express concern about rape culture by using language from the women's and #MeToo movements in his use of the phrase, he turned the topic of sexual assault into a joke about spring break. Yet Amelia did not find the joke to be funny, emphasizing instead that men get "away with it" in contexts where people "turn a blind eye."

In other focus groups, the issue of alcohol consumption sparked discussions of context-dependent definitions of consent. For example, Jeremiah said, "There are other factors, like blackout drunk, asleep, or angry, that can be blurry for some people. If somebody can't say yes or no, then it's probably a good idea not to mess with that person." Anthony expressed his concern about a new law: "I've heard of a law in California where they're defining consent as you can't be intoxicated. When you keep changing the lines of consent, you keep changing the lines of what is rape." Anthony then went on to describe what he called "extreme" situations, accusing others, presumably women, of saying that "just complimenting" or "looking too long in seductive ways" is assault. By equating rape and sexual assault with discomforting glances or compliments, the effect of sexual assault on survivors is minimized and trivialized.

In summary, most of the focus group men were resisters who expressed traditional gender norms and were aware that their definitions of consent are at odds with recent social and cultural changes. In seeing their own definitions as diverging from women's, most of the men were aware that their views are out of sync with emerging norms. Therefore, these men resisted the profound social and cultural changes that are underway. By attributing differences in consent to "misunderstandings" and gender differences in perception and communication, most of the men emphasized individual-level interactions as the basis for sexual assault. That is, rather than viewing sexual assault within a collective framework in which we are all responsible, individualized solutions become the focus. One of the ways that men contested a collective framework in favor of an individualized one was to argue that consent is context-specific, where definitions of consent that apply in one situation do not apply in others.

"If You Feel Violated, the Story Ends There": Men's Innovative Perspectives

Not all of the men endorsed traditional views of gender norms; half expressed progressive perspectives that deviated from this approach. In contrast to those quoted earlier, a handful of men (n = 5, 12.5 percent of the men interviewees) entirely rejected traditional views of sexual consent, assault, and harassment (see Table 5.1). An additional 37.5 percent (n = 15) fused progressive and traditional discourses together to create a discourse that simultaneously rejects and embraces the social and cultural changes that are underway in the #MeToo era (see Table 5.1). Although we cannot draw any conclusions based on such small numbers of men in each racial or ethnic category, Table 5.1 illustrates that men who were innovators or held fused perspectives were more likely to be white or Asian American, while resisters came from a wide range of racial or ethnic backgrounds.

This patchwork of old and new ideologies and perspectives reflects our current era of rapid social change and suggests the uneven progress made by the gender revolution. In such contexts, it takes time for new perspectives to fully take hold and shift completely to create more widespread cultural change. In some ways, then, the men who embraced transformations in gender relations, even only partially, are innovators who propel social change forward.

In particular, five men wholeheartedly supported women's definitions of sexual consent and assault. Adnan, a 21-year-old Middle Eastern man, pointed out that even "in the eyes of the law . . . you can never be 100 percent objective" in determining whether or not someone consented. As a result, he argued that the subjective interpretation of those who are vulnerable needs to be taken into account:

A part of it is still subjective. It's how you feel. If you are uncomfortable, if you feel violated, the story ends there. It should stop. It should be understood that this is not what's going to happen. This should not happen.

Adnan admitted that shifting definitions of consent in the #MeToo era are not necessarily easy to understand, although he implied that "people's mindsets" need to change: "That's a very hard thing to change. You're talking about changing people's mindsets."

In contrast to the resisters quoted earlier, Isiah, a 24-year-old Asian American man, thought that concerns about confusion over sexual consent were overstated. He mentioned mandatory workplace trainings on consent and assault that have become commonplace in the #MeToo era as a factor that contributes to clearer understandings around consent:

> I don't think there would be any confusion because nowadays, every other place you go, there's always some organization and it's mandatory for people to take [training]. So it does define what sexual assault means and how to report it and all. So I don't think there should be any confusion.

Implying that men who commit sexual assault know what they are doing, Isiah continued, "And even for people, even for men, I don't think it should be confusion on both sides. Not for them, not for the one who does it."

Most of the men who fused traditional and new perspectives accepted women's right to self-determination when it came to public cases, such as Supreme Court Justice Brett Kavanaugh, and/or recognized positive gains from the #MeToo movement. Two of these men, Jonah and Caleb, combined innovative and resistant ideas about sexual consent into their discourses about gender relations. In a gender-similar focus group with six other men, Jonah's and Caleb's comments stood out as atypical. Both white men in their early 20s, they concurrently expressed traditional and innovative views. Earlier we heard Caleb distinguish between serious offenses of sexual assault and "smaller things," "*stepping stones,*" and "*lower-level things*" that are "*difficult to define* exactly what these things were."

At the same time, these men dismissed men's fear and perceived vulnerability to changing definitions of sexual consent. Caleb said,

> There's a lot of men who try to point to these things and say, "Oh look, anybody can be accused." There's a lot of men who really exaggerate these things and say, "Oh, I can't talk to any woman now because I'm afraid that I'm going to be accused of this, this, and this."

Caleb explained that the men who were most concerned about being accused of sexual assault need to consider their treatment of women and their own behavior:

> But I think that maybe those are the men that should be the most concerned anyways because if you have that attitude, that your normal actions can be construed as sexual harassment, and that you can be accused while innocent

or something, I think that you might want to examine the way that you treat the opposite sex. You might want to examine the way that you yourself behave.

Jonah agreed immediately, explaining that men who took advantage of women were the ones who were the most frightened by the #MeToo movement:

> I'd agree. I think a lot of those guys got so used to some of the things they were doing, they're like, "It's not bad." And they saw this blow up [as a result of the movement], and they're like, "Oh, my God." I completely agree that if you do have to take a step back and say, "I guess we can't talk to women now." All people want is respect and obviously you weren't giving it to them.

In these examples, we see men embodying the contradictions of the current era by combining multiple perspectives. They expressed some confusion about how to precisely define sexual assault today. At the same time, they drew a line that separated their own confusion with the perspective of other men who they thought should be afraid of accusations of sexual assault. Both Caleb and Jonah entirely dismissed the idea that men's fears are justified. These quotes reveal that some men are joining with women to be cultural innovators, as they create new definitions of sexual consent. And yet other men are fusing traditional and innovative ideas together. These men, expressing views that at least partially critiqued traditional ideas espoused by resisters, help to move the gender revolution forward, even if only partially.

"Yes Means Yes and Everything Else Means No": Women's Views about Affirmative Consent

On a snowy February afternoon, Pamela asked a focus group of six women if they thought that "men and women are defining sexual consent differently." Jada, an 18-year-old Black woman, was the first to respond, describing a chasm between women's and men's perceptions of consent: "With dudes, it's like, 'Yes is yes, but then yes equals no.' And 'She's playing hard to get. She just wants me to try harder.' And then you try harder, and it just escalates really quickly." Here, Jada captured an "escalation" in men's behaviors toward women that involves both a misunderstanding (men perceiving women as playing "hard to get") and a fundamental difference in how men and women view the words "yes" and "no."

Previous research, conducted before the #MeToo era, was somewhat divided on the topic of gender differences in consent. Many studies documented similarities between men and women, especially concerning the lack of clarity in definitions around consent (Hirsch and Khan 2020). In addition, some prior research has suggested that affirmative consent may be *rejected* by women, who have been traditionally stigmatized when they provide an "enthusiastic yes" (Jozkowski et al. 2017: 237). In a context in which women are taught that they will be viewed negatively if they are promiscuous, women have traditionally been socialized to be demure and hesitant about seeing themselves as sexual agents (Jozkowski et al. 2014). In contrast, other studies have argued that gender differences in consent were present prior to the #MeToo era; women often view consent as a process that unfolds via cues over time, while men perceive consent or lack thereof as a specific, definitive event (Jozkowski et al. 2018). Research has found that women prefer explicit verbal consent more than men do (Humphreys and Herold 2007; Jozkowski et al. 2013).

Yet significant cultural change has occurred since earlier studies were conducted. Focus group women clearly articulated a model of affirmative consent that deviates from what is traditionally expected. In previous eras, the legal and policy standard on most college campuses focused on women's refusal to engage in sexual activity, often framed in terms of the word "no" (e.g., "no means no"). Affirmative consent, although not new, has become a more widespread standard.

Affirmative consent was pioneered by Ohio's Antioch College in 1991 and first adopted in statewide legislation in California in 2014. The law states:

> "Affirmative consent" means affirmative, conscious, and voluntary agreement to engage in sexual activity. It is the responsibility of each person involved in the sexual activity to ensure that he or she has the affirmative consent of the other or others to engage in the sexual activity. Lack of protest or resistance does not mean consent, nor does silence mean consent. Affirmative consent must be ongoing throughout a sexual activity and can be revoked at any time (California Legislative Information 2014).

In response to concerns about widespread sexual assault on college campuses (Hirsch and Khan 2020), many universities and some states have revised their policies and laws to reflect this standard. These changes reflect transformations in public definitions in the #MeToo era. The University of Michigan, for example, adopted a new policy on sexual misconduct in 2019. The policy defines consent as "a clear and unambiguous agreement, expressed outwardly through mutually understandable words or actions, to engage in Sexual Activity." The policy continues:

> Consent is not to be inferred from silence, passivity, or a lack of resistance, and relying on non-verbal communication alone may not be sufficient to determine Consent. Consent is not to be inferred from an existing or previous dating or sexual relationship (University of Michigan 2019).

Additionally, it allows for the option to change one's mind: "Consent can be withdrawn by any party at any point." Furthermore, it specifies that someone who is incapacitated, including through the use of drugs or alcohol, is "unable to give Consent" (University of Michigan 2019). The innovators endorsed similar definitions of consent.

Changes in views of consent have resulted in conflict with men's resistance to shift their views. Interviewees of all genders perceived gender relations in terms of contestation. Some women argued that although they have clarity about their *own* desires, men feign confusion. Zainab, a 32-year-old Middle Eastern woman, said, "There's just that misunderstanding of consent because we're taught that there's a stereotypical way of saying 'that means no.' But *yes means yes*, and we have to learn that *everything else means no*, if it's not *explicitly yes*." Zainab adversarially used the word "you" to refer to men: "Yes means yes and everything else *you* are supposed to take as meaning *no*." She emphatically stressed that everything outside of affirmative consent was sexual assault: "Like, *no*. There's *no* consent here."

These and other quotes suggest that the #MeToo movement has influenced innovators' everyday definitions, insisting on the need for an explicit and affirmative yes in response to advances. Kiara emphasized the simplicity of this idea: "I don't see any confusion in yes and no." Kiara implied that, because consent is obvious, perpetrators *know* when they are committing sexual assault: "People *know* what they're doing when they're about to do something." By calling into question men's assertions that they are confused about consent, Kiara challenged the male dominance upon which these views are based. Her rejection of male dominance fits within the #MeToo social movement frame.

Focus groups revealed a direct clash: While innovators of all genders are creating new definitions of consent, most men are resisters pushing for traditional definitions. For example, when we asked one focus group, consisting of five men and three women, whether there is confusion about how to define sexual assault, Ahmad agreed, "Yes, how to define sexual assault and how to prove that consent actually did happen." Harper, a 23-year-old multiracial woman, immediately and directly challenged his concern about "false" accusations: "Between consent and no consent, or what? Because how is that obscured?" Implying that alcohol use nullifies consent, Harper stated that consent can *only* take place when men and women are "both in that right mind. Or are you physically impaired where you cannot make a decision? Then you do *not* proceed with anything."

In the same focus group, Angel, a 54-year-old Black woman, echoed Harper's points and pointed out racial differences in definitions of sexual consent: "In the African American culture, consent is *clearly* defined. We *know* what rape is. We *know* what sexual assault is, and we *know* what it looks like. That right there. [pointing with her finger for emphasis] That's consent." Angel went on to explain that Black women respond to sexual assault differently from women of other backgrounds: "Black women will slap you and hit you back. We fight back. But in other cultures, the women don't do that because they've been trained to be docile." By using the word "we," Angel expressed a social movement frame rooted in a collective identity, with Black women viewing their interests as connected to those of other Black women.

In a context in which men are assumed to initiate heterosexual sexual activity, the women and nonbinary interviewees uniformly emphasized that men need to acquire a verbal "yes" from their partners. Nadine, a 20-year-old white woman, suggested that men should "ask" in confusing sexual situations. She described this process as awkward but necessary: "If you don't know 100 percent, then just ask. Sometimes men are embarrassed to ask, because it gets different reactions." One of Nadine's classmates laughed when another student said that her boyfriend "asked... the first time he kissed her." In response to "everyone's" laughter, Nadine stated: "Honestly, what if *I* [referring to her classmate] didn't want it? *You* need to *ask*." Nadine continued, stressing that verbal consent clears up misunderstandings, "If men are more aware of this consent and they *ask* about it," then women will realize of men, "Oh, do *you* not know the answer?" Although this example emphasizes that women and men have an equal responsibility to affirmatively communicate with each other, Nadine divided women and men through the linguistic contrast of "you" to refer to men and "I" to refer to women. This linguistic contrast positions different genders on opposing cultural sides. This chasm is characterized by opposition and contestation and reflects the #MeToo movement's frame and its diffusion into everyday lives.

Consent in the #MeToo era means that traditionally nondominant genders are becoming full sexual agents, who can withhold or change their preferences for sexual activity at any time. Alex, a 21-year-old multiracial nonbinary interviewee, commented on what the men said were confusing "gray areas." They explained, "It's not just because you say yes, all yes to everything. You have the *right to say no in between* and *say no to certain things* or be unsure about it." However, Alex thought that this view of affirmative consent was atypical among men: "Most people don't take that into consideration." The terminology of "rights" that Alex drew on indicates a legal framework that gives priority to affirmative consent. Rima, a 20-year-old Middle Eastern woman, commented that prior consent does not necessarily lead to future consent when she stated that sexual assault can happen within marriage: "It doesn't have to be in the workplace or with strangers, it could literally be with your husband."

Innovators argued that traditional rape scripts are outdated in the current era. In this context, affirmative consent was important to these interviewees because men's actions that deviate from traditional "rape scripts" (i.e., those that involve screaming and physical resistance to stranger attacks) were viewed as nonconsensual. Kayla, a 21-year-old Black woman, said that, contrary to stereotypes, "whispering no" represents non-consent. She said that people believe that "there's one singular definition of sexual assault: If she's *screaming* no and things like that." Kayla went on to counter the idea that there is "only one way that you can react. And if you don't react that way, that means you were OK with it and now you're just upset that it happened." Kayla stated that men (adversarially called "they") incorrectly assume that a whisper is not enough: "So if she's *not screaming no*, then *they're* [men] like, 'Oh well, I don't think it was rape, because I think she *whispered* it maybe.'" Jada agreed with Kayla about the pitch of women's voices: "Just because she's not *screaming* and *hollering*, saying, 'No, don't do this,' it doesn't mean that she *wanted* to do that, or she *wanted* to go along with it." In this adversarial context, men disregard women's wishes. It is interesting to note that words indicating different volumes in speaking are used here, as we will see them again in reference to women coming forward with accounts of sexual assault.

Women also defined verbal manipulation as sexual assault. Aria, a 21-year-old woman, described her own experiences with her ex-boyfriend as coercive and pointed out that women are sometimes pressured or manipulated into saying yes. In Aria's case, her ex-boyfriend pressured her into agreeing to have sex with him in ways and at times that she did not wish to do:

> I remember one of my exes. If I didn't do X, Y, and Z, he'd be like, "You don't love me? You don't want to be with me?" And I'd be like, "What? No, no, no, I love you. I'm just, I'm not feeling good." And try to like, give explanations to other things. And then, he would constantly try and coerce me into doing what *he* wanted me to do. And then as soon as I'd push him away, he's like, "Oh you just don't love me. Oh, you just don't want to be with me."

Aria described diverting him by saying that she wanted to watch TV: "'I just want to watch TV, OK? *The Bachelor* is coming on. This is *my* show. I want to watch it, OK?' Like, this is *my* time." Comments like these illustrate that innovators in the #MeToo era are increasingly viewing verbal coercion as unacceptable and instead embrace the idea of affirmative consent.

Some women went even further to argue that body language that conveys fear or lack of interest is sexual assault. Nadine said that women's body language and verbal cues are ignored by men, who use the "excuse" of confusion as a justification for sexual assault. Calling men "you" adversarially, she said,

> Yes is yes. No is no. And there's phrases in between that may not mean exactly what *you* are hoping for, *but it means no*. People use that as an excuse like, "Oh, I thought she wanted it." Like, no. Don't think. Listen. People will give you all the information you need.

She continued to say that any ambiguous behaviors outside of an enthusiastic yes represent assault: "Everyone knows what sexual consent is. But then whenever *they're* accused of something, *they're* going to be like, 'Oh, I don't know.' No, *you* know very well what happened."

When we asked a focus group with only one woman if men and women thought about sexual consent, assault, and harassment differently, a man, Jin, responded first, but tentatively: "That's a hard one to say." Jasmine, a 40-year-old Black woman, however, decisively contradicted him. Symbolizing an adversarial relationship by the linguistic contrast of the aggressive roles of men ("you" and "they") and gatekeeper roles of women ("I" and "we"), Jasmine said, "Definitely, because if *we* don't vocalize it, *they* feel *they* have the consent. So if a woman doesn't say no, *they* feel like *they* have the consent. But a man will say, 'Well, she never said no.' And if she's unconscious or if she's constantly pushing *you* or whatever, it might be giving *you* signals, then *you know* that's no.'" According to Jasmine, men are *able* to read a variety of nonconsensual situations, including vocalization, incapacitation, or body language, but they *claim* that they need to hear the word "no." This focus on body language contradicts markedly from the resisters quoted earlier.

In her gender-similar focus group, Alexandra, a 38-year-old Black woman, thought that some men lack an ability to read nonverbal cues. Yet their ignorance does not excuse men (called "they" here) when they commit sexual assault:

> *They* [men] don't necessarily know how to read verbal cues or body language. And I think that's where the confusion is, that if a woman doesn't explicitly say, "No, don't touch me. No, I don't want to have sex," *they* don't understand.

Unlike Jasmine, Alexandra did not assume that men were feigning ignorance. However, she still emphasized affirmative consent and labeled men's violation of it as assault: "I don't even think *they* know that *they* are committing sexual assault." In this perspective, sexual assault occurs when a woman does not wish to have sex, even if the only expression of her displeasure is body language.

In a focus group with three other women and three men, Amelia agreed that body language, instead of only verbalization, conveys non-consent. When we asked, "Are there certain definitions of sexual consent that are agreed upon?" Amelia answered, "yes and no." Charlotte, a 23-year-old multiracial woman, stated that these definitions are "blurry." Amelia went on to explain, "We like to use body language instead of just talking. And we don't want things to be awkward so we'll just get it over with." Amelia pointed out that as a result of the traditional socialization of women to be submissive to men, women go along with "things" that they did not realize until later that they "didn't have to do." Amelia said,

> For us on a college campus when we're just learning how to do things or it's our first time experiencing things, maybe you didn't learn to communicate very well with other people and you just go with the flow sometimes. And later, you find out, "I didn't have to do that."

She said that she had "internalized" situations that were "not right" and she and her friends had previously "laughed off" coercive experiences. Although research has suggested that women are more likely to redefine harassment as inappropriate as they get older (Blackstone et al. 2014), recent historical transformations in our very definitions have encouraged these redefinitions, especially for women.

Compliance to requests for sex in a context of fear is sexual assault, even when women do not explicitly say no. Jada explained that women "go along with" sex out of fear of male violence:

> In some cases, it'll be a dude and a girl and they might be kissing, but the girl might not want to go that far, but the dude keeps going. She doesn't want to have to make it awkward in saying no and just stop, so she does it to be polite.

In addition to not expressing feelings out of awkwardness, women also comply because of fear of male violence. As Jada pointed out, a woman might

> not say no or make it aggressive or whatever so she just goes along with it. Some women just feel like, "If I don't go along with this, there's no telling what could happen." They think in their head, "If I don't go along with this, he might get aggressive with me. He might hit me. He might push me," anything like that. So they just do it to do it.

Similarly, Aria, whose ex-boyfriend was coercive, pointed out that some women do not conform to the popular cultural myth of "screaming" because they fear further violence from men: "A lot of people are confused. People aren't super educated on consent." Aria said that there is a stereotype that

> the girl has to be screaming, "No, leave me alone," actively fighting. In reality, some women don't want to fight that much because they don't want to get knocked out and then not know what's happened to them, and not be able to have some control.

In this assessment, women comply to requests for sex because they are afraid of male violence and lack of control over their circumstances. In an era of rapid social change, innovators thus define these situations as sexual assault.

Innovators wanted men, assumed to be the initiators, to be aware that some women verbally consent but may not actually want to have sex. Mia, a 20-year-old white woman, suggested that, due to the changing nature of sexual desire, men need to exercise care when assuming consent: "There's a lot more to it than yes and no because people say yes and then they change their mind or people say yes but their *body language does not say yes*." Mia pointed out that sexual assault can occur "by a friend or someone they don't know that well. It's also relationships too, where that could be a problem." Kayla also described a situation when a woman's body language should convey to a man, who she designates through the word "you," that she is not consenting: "She's actively turning away from *you*, getting her body in a defensive position. Or *you* scared her in some way, or *you* coerced her after harassing her for X amount of time." This approach goes a step further than verbal affirmative consent and emphasizes the importance of reading body language. These definitions include as nonconsensual both verbal sexual coercion and "problem sex" (Pugh and Becker 2018). These innovators thus developed definitions of consent that focus on sex that is both "freely given" *and* desired. This approach centers on women's agency and suggests that #MeToo era social movement frames have become diffused into everyday understandings.

Since studies before the #MeToo era found similarities in women's and men's definitions of consent (Muehlenhard et al. 2016; Fenner 2017; Conroy et al. 2014), the sharp divergence found here is striking. As mentioned, in a study conducted just before the 2017 visibility of the movement, Hirsch and Khan (2020) found that *both* men and women at Columbia University articulated affirmative consent as an ideal. However, on that campus, this ideal sharply diverged from the way that consent actually worked in the moment. In their interactions, which usually involved alcohol, both men and women reported relying on body language or circumstances (such as being alone in a room together) as indicators of consent (Hirsch and Khan 2020). Although men and women who attend elite colleges may articulate the affirmative consent model in theory, their behavior does not reflect this approach (Hirsch and Khan 2020). Our interviewees, who were far more diverse in terms of age, social class, and racial and ethnic background, instead indicate a deep gender divide in the #MeToo era: While the women held affirmative consent as the standard, most of the focus group men rejected it. This divergence suggests that the movement has influenced ideas about consent more profoundly for innovators than resisters. Innovators also viewed the problem of sexual assault collectively and systemically rather than as an isolated case of a few "bad" men who violated their wishes.

"If You Want to Do Something, You Say You Want to Do It": Toward Equality and Mutuality

Although a gender revolution is clearly in the works, it will not be complete until the existing paradigm is disrupted and replaced with one that is based on full equality and mutuality. In theory, an affirmative consent model assumes two equals who freely choose to engage in sexual behavior and communicate their agreement verbally. In reality, however, gender norms and persisting inequalities interfere with the creation of an equal and mutual paradigm of consent. Torenz (2021: 721 and 724) argued that gender roles are "structurally embedded" within affirmative consent, as it is based on "heteronormative concepts of male sexuality as active-initiating and female sexuality as reactive-receptive." Additionally, this standard assumes that "miscommunication is a cause of sexual violence" and, in doing so, dismisses research on sexual compliance and unwanted sex (Torenz 2021: 721). In these situations, gender inequalities result in women feeling "obliged to consent" as a result of "external power relations" and "internalized heteronormative discourses" (Torenz 2021: 721). For example, women have internalized the feeling of a need to be "nice"; the affirmative consent standard does not recognize that some people are more vulnerable to these pressures than others (Torenz 2021).

Although innovators endorsed affirmative consent, most did *not* challenge basic gender roles and norms inherent in heterosexual sexual interactions. That is, the quotes above assume rigid gender differentiation in roles, in which men initiate and women accept or reject their advances. In particular, the language of "yes" and "no" assumes that men are asking for sex and women are making a decision. Although an endorsement of affirmative consent represents a step forward in recognizing women as agents of their own sexuality, most of the quotes above do not articulate a completely new gender paradigm.

Quotes from a handful of interviewees provide hints about what a more complete gender revolution would look like. Jada stated her view of verbal consent when she said, "As a woman, you know what consent is. If you *want* to do something, you *say* you want to do it." In Jada's formulation, initiation of sexual activity stems from women's sexual desire, not men's. Harper echoed this emphasis on verbal consent but used the word "we" to describe a mutual decision to have sex: "You either say, 'Hey, are *we* going to do this?' or 'Hey, *we're* not.'" To Harper, this process should be easy for both parties to understand: "Consent should be cut and dried." These quotes illustrate a perception of women as agents of their own sexuality. Not only do they affirmatively state what they want, but they also break traditional heterosexual scripts by rejecting a system of male initiation and female gatekeeping. In doing so, this view breaks with traditional views of women's objectification and passivity. Although it is certainly plausible that the interviewees engaged in sexual activity that was woman-initiated in the ways suggested by Jada and Harper, their discourses and language reflect more traditional gender frameworks.

Likewise, some men question a gender system in which they are responsible for pursuing women and convincing them to engage in sex (Torenz 2021). Murray and Brotto (2021) provided evidence that the sexual scripts around desire may be evolving for heterosexual men. The men in their study wanted their female partners to take a more dominant role during sex, including initiating and communicating her desire (Murray and Brotto 2021). While social pressures may make it difficult for men to admit this perspective in a focus group with other men, quotes by Caleb and Jonah earlier begin to question rigid gender norms around men's aggression. As explored earlier, both men rejected the idea that the #MeToo movement should make men afraid of their interactions. Caleb went further, challenging men's aggression, especially men who wield power over women through sexual assault and harassment:

> These things aren't normal. It's people who harass, people who intimidate, people who use their power to get things without consent. And I think that if you express worry for yourself over these things, that's an indicator that you should probably have some introspection.

Although he did not explicitly reject men's initiation and resisted other social changes, Caleb challenged the idea that manhood is necessarily and always associated with harassing, intimidating, and using power. A rejection of male initiation and aggression points to a way forward, yet it simultaneously reveals the limits of the current gender revolution.

Conclusion

This chapter documents how everyday understandings of consent are changing and reflect a diffusion of #MeToo movement ideology. In contrast to the clear affirmative consent definitions of the women and nonbinary interviewees, the majority of focus group men resisted change and emphasized what they called "gray areas." Underlying men's perspectives is an assumption of traditional gender roles regarding heterosexual sex: They are initiators and even aggressors, while women are the gatekeepers whose role is to embrace or reject men's advances. While half of the men resisted changes underway as a result of the gender revolution, a handful fully rejected traditional views of sexual consent. In addition to these innovators, over one-third fused progressive and traditional discourses to create a patchwork of old and new ideologies that contains both traditional and innovative ideas about gender norms.

In contrast to the resisters, who by and large emphasized that sexual assault is defined as men violating women's verbal statements of "no," innovators emphasized the importance of affirmative consent, or "yes means yes." In doing so, women and nonbinary interviewees asserted their own definitions and narratives in ways that run counter to traditional definitions of consent. This approach demonstrates women's rising agency and empowerment in the #MeToo era, as they defined consent according to their own perspectives in ways that validated their own sexuality and agency. These important changes illustrate the diffusion of social movement ideology, as they are taking place not only among public figures in the media but also in the everyday lives of ordinary people.

The #MeToo movement has affected how people think about consent by challenging its very definition. Although some men presented themselves as confused about the definition of consent, on the whole they actively contested women's perspectives. For their part, the women and nonbinary interviewees wanted to feel respected in a deliberate and rational way. As the majority of men asserted their own opposition to women's definitions of consent, they attempted to reinforce traditional gender scripts under terms of inequality, such as accepting men's aggression without challenge. It is not surprising that these changes are uneven, as it takes time for new perspectives to take root and to shift norms and discourse.

Ultimately, innovators have pushed cultural change forward, as new standards of consent increasingly become enshrined in laws, policies, and (perhaps more slowly) gendered norms. It is appropriate to use the term "revolution" because

women and nonbinary interviewees are insisting on affirmativ
everyday lives in ways that are historically new. At the same '
its to the gender revolution. Although interviewees rejecte'
self-determination, most did not challenge an integral par
ity: the initiator-gatekeeper framework of heterosexual relationsh...
women approached relationships with men in an adversarial way, and their discussions of consent reflected gender contestation and division, the deepest, and
most personal, gender revolution will not be complete until the entire gender-
differentiated system is dismantled. Until we move into a framework that is based
on mutual respect and collective responsibility for sexuality, the ideal of affirmative
consent will continue to rest on heteronormative discourses, the objectification
of women, and patriarchal arrangements. Within this context, then, the gender
revolution has moved in important directions so far and has great potential for
future transformations.

References

Blackstone, Amy, Jason Houle, and Christopher Uggen. 2014. "'I Didn't Recognize It as a
Bad Experience Until I Was Much Older': Age, Experience, and Workers' Perceptions
of Sexual Harassment." *Sociological Spectrum* 34(4):314–337.

Breiding, Matthew J. and Sharon G. Smith, Kathleen C. Basile, Mikel L. Walters, Jieru
Chen and Melissa T. Merrick. 2014. "Prevalence and Characteristics of Sexual Violence,
Stalking, and Intimate Partner Violence Victimization—National Intimate Partner and
Sexual Violence Survey, United States, 2011." *MMWR* 63:8. Retrieved January 21, 2022
(www.cdc.gov/mmwr/pdf/ss/ss6308.pdf).

Burkett, Melissa and Karine Hamilton. 2012. "Postfeminist Sexual Agency: Young Women's
Negotiations of Sexual Consent." *Sexualities* 15(7):815–833.

California Legislative Information. 2014. "SB-967 Student Safety: Sexual Assault." *Bill
Text—SB-967 Student Safety: Sexual Assault.* Retrieved January 21, 2022 (https://
leginfo.legislature.ca.gov/faces/billTextClient.xhtml?bill_id=201320140SB967).

Cipriano, Allison E., Kathryn J. Holland, Nicole Bedera, Sarah R. Eagan, and Alex S. Diede.
2021. "Severe and Pervasive? Consequences of Sexual Harassment for Graduate Students and Their Title IX Report Outcomes." *Feminist Criminology* 17(6):343–367.

Conroy, Nicole E., Ambika Krishnakumar, and Janel M. Leone. 2014. "Reexamin-
ing Issues of Conceptualization and Willing Consent." *Journal of Interpersonal Violence*
30(11):1828–1846.

Fenner, Lydia. 2017. "Sexual Consent as a Scientific Subject: A Literature Review." *American Journal of Sexuality Education* 12(4):451–471.

Hirsch, Jennifer S. and Shamus Khan. 2020. *Sexual Citizens: Sex, Power, and Assault on Campus.* New York, NY: W. W. Norton.

Humphreys, Terry and Ed Herold. 2007. "Sexual Consent in Heterosexual Relationships:
Development of a New Measure." *Sex Roles* 57(3–4):305–315.

Jozkowski, Kristen N. and Terry Humphreys. 2014. "Sexual Consent on College Campuses: Implications for Sexual Assault Prevention Education." *Health Education Mono-
graph* 31(2):30–35.

.kowski, Kristen N., Jimmie Manning, and Mary Hunt. 2018. "Sexual Consent In and Out of the Bedroom: Disjunctive Views of Heterosexual College Students." *Women's Studies in Communication* 41(2):117–139.

Jozkowski, Kristen N., Tiffany L. Marcantonio, and Mary E. Hunt. 2017. "College Students' Sexual Consent Communication and Perceptions of Sexual Double Standards: A Qualitative Investigation." *Perspectives on Sexual and Reproductive Health* 49(4):237–244.

Jozkowski, Kristen N., Stephanie Sanders, Zoë D. Peterson, Barbara Dennis, and Michael Reece. 2014. "Consenting to Sexual Activity: The Development and Psychometric Assessment of Dual Measures of Consent." *Archives of Sexual Behavior* 43(3):437–450.

Jozkowski, Kristen N., Zoë D. Peterson, Stephanie A. Sanders, Barbara Dennis, and Michael Reece. 2013. "Gender Differences in Heterosexual College Students' Conceptualizations and Indicators of Sexual Consent: Implications for Contemporary Sexual Assault Prevention Education." *The Journal of Sex Research* 51(8):904–916.

Jozkowski, Kristen N. and Jacquelyn D. Wiersma. 2014. "Does Drinking Alcohol Prior to Sexual Activity Influence College Students' Consent?" *International Journal of Sexual Health* 27(2):156–174.

Lauer, Claudia and Meghan Hoyer. 2019. "Almost 1,700 Priests and Clergy Accused of Sex Abuse Are Unsupervised." *NBC News*. Retrieved September 1, 2022 (www.nbcnews.com/news/religion/nearly-1-700-priests-clergy-accused-sex-abuse-are-unsupervised-n1062396).

Muehlenhard, Charlene L., Terry P. Humphreys, Kristen N. Jozkowski, and Zoë D. Peterson. 2016. "The Complexities of Sexual Consent Among College Students: A Conceptual and Empirical Review." *The Journal of Sex Research* 53(4–5):457–487.

Murray, Sarah Hunter and Lori Brotto. 2021. "I Want You to Want Me: A Qualitative Analysis of Heterosexual Men's Desire to Feel Desired in Intimate Relationships." *Journal of Sex & Marital Therapy* 47(5):419–434.

Pugh, Brandie and Patricia Becker. 2018. "Exploring Definitions and Prevalence of Verbal Sexual Coercion and Its Relationship to Consent to Unwanted Sex: Implications for Affirmative Consent Standards on College Campuses." *Behavioral Sciences* 8(8):69.

Robinson, Devonae. 2022. "Ethnic Differences in the Experiences of Sexual Assault Victims." *Applied Psychology Opus*. Retrieved September 1, 2022. (https://wp.nyu.edu/steinhardt-appsych_opus/ethnic-differences-in-the-experiences-of-sexual-assault-victims/).

Torenz, Rona. 2021. "The Politics of Affirmative Consent: Considerations from a Gender and Sexuality Studies Perspective." *German Law Journal* 22(5):718–733.

University of Michigan. 2019. "Umbrella Policy." Retrieved January 21, 2022 (https://sexualmisconduct.umich.edu/wp-content/uploads/2019/10/Policy_10.3.19_clean.pdf)

Willness, Chelsea R., Piers Steel, and Kibeom Lee. 2007. "A Meta-Analysis of the Antecedents and Consequences of Workplace Sexual Harassment." *Personnel Psychology* 60(1):127–162.

6

RESISTERS RESPOND TO SOCIAL CHANGE CREATED BY #METOO

"It's Like Airplane Crashes, Right?" Individualized Perceptions of Sexual Assault

In a mixed-gender focus group, Pamela, asked, "How big of a problem do you think sexual assault and harassment are today?" Jasmine, a 40-year-old Black woman, was the first to respond, stating that it was "huge." Jasmine went on to define sexual assault as an unwanted "slap on the butt" or "rubbing your shoulder" and explained that women are "programmed to just accept" it.

Revealing fundamental differences in definitions of sexual consent and assault, Carter, a 21-year-old Middle Eastern man, sharply disagreed with Jasmine. Carter emphasized that he did not have *direct* evidence of sexual assault, which nullified its existence: "I don't really *see* sexual assault, like the rubbing the shoulders thing. I don't *see* anyone ever doing that." Carter acknowledged that his definition might be due to gender differences. He spoke to Jasmine, "Maybe I'm not exposed to it as much as you are. Maybe because I'm a guy." He continued by excusing and dismissing the actions that Jasmine defined as sexual assault when they occur in contexts when people know each other, "And if they do that ['slap on the butt' or 'rubbing your shoulder'], then it's people who are close." Carter emphasized that public cases drew attention to sexual assault in ways that exaggerate its prevalence:

> Most of the stuff that I'm seeing is on the news, sexual assault on the news. The guy from Michigan State [convicted rapist Larry Nassar] or [Supreme Court Justice] Brett Kavanaugh. I don't really see it personally, but I just see all news.

Turning to a metaphor of airplane crashes, which Carter equated with sexual assault, he minimized it and dismissed its prevalence as minor:

DOI: 10.4324/9781003225331-10

It's like airplane crashes, right? You think that airplanes were really dangerous because you see all these airplanes crash in the news. But really, an airplane is safer than a car. So when you're exposed to something over and over again on the news, you think it's a *bigger* problem than it really is. Maybe that's what all these people are talking about.

Thus, because he is a "guy" who did not experience or "see" sexual assault directly, Carter assumed that its actual prevalence is low. In quickly dismissing Jasmine's argument that sexual assault includes unwanted touching, Carter viewed his own definitions of sexual consent and assault as more valid.

Positioning their own definitions above women's definitions reasserts male dominance in an era that has called it into question. As we have seen, the vast majority of the men we interviewed (87.5 percent, n = 35) espoused traditional views about gender relations (see Table 6.1). Among these men half (50 percent, n = 20) wholeheartedly expressed gender traditional views; an additional 37.5 percent (n = 15) fused progressive and traditional discourses to simultaneously reject and embrace the social and cultural changes underway as a result of the #MeToo movement (see Table 6.1). Table 6.1 illustrates how these perspectives were distributed by racial and ethnic background. Although the number with each perspective is too small to make generalizations, we see that resister men come from all racial and ethnic backgrounds. Those with innovator and fused perspectives were more often from white or Asian American backgrounds (see Table 6.1).

In contrast to the innovators, resisters thought that public awareness of sexual assault in the #MeToo era overstates its actual prevalence, which they viewed as rare and isolated to a small number of perpetrators. Concerns about the perceived widening definition of sexual assault, especially the standard of affirmative consent, has made some men feel vulnerable to what they view as "false" accusations. To avoid such perceived vulnerability, strategies included avoiding sexual contact when a woman had been drinking and occasionally avoiding romantic relationships with women altogether.

While the #MeToo movement has altered women's definitions of sexual assault, men minimized sexual assault. In particular, they contested and trivialized new definitions by making them equivalent to more serious infractions. Terrell, a 25-year-old Black man, responded to Jasmine's and Carter's points by supporting Carter. Terrell said that someone could be accused of sexual assault for kissing someone on the cheek: "If you just walk up to somebody and kissed him on the cheek, you can either take it as sexual assault or they can take it as just being a friendly gesture." Here, incidents are defined arbitrarily; one interpretation is that the kiss is sexual assault while an equal interpretation is that it is "a friendly gesture." These comments assert men's definitions of sexual assault and harassment. Interestingly, by using a male pronoun, Terrell implied that men are as likely as women to receive unwanted kisses. In another focus group, Leo,

TABLE 6.1 Distribution of Men's Perspectives by Racial and Ethnic Background

	Types of perspective			
	Resister	Innovator	Fused	Total
White	4	3	6	13
Middle Eastern or North African	4	1	2	7
Hispanic/Latinx	3	0	0	3
Black	1	0	2	3
Asian American	4	1	5	10
Multiracial	2	0	0	2
Unknown	2	0	0	2
Percent (n)	50% (20)	12.5% (5)	37.5% (15)	100% (40)

an 18-year-old Asian American man, was concerned that "tapping" someone on the shoulder would be called harassment: "People can interpret them differently, 'Oh, touching them, that's sexual harassment,' or just tapping them on the shoulder." Although such comments at first appear to take sexual assault seriously by defining small violations under its heading, they ultimately dilute and minimize its meaning by making all claims equal to "a kiss on the cheek" or "a tap on the shoulder."

Thus, as we will see, most of the resisters did not acknowledge the prevalence of sexual assault in the same way as innovators, who emphasized its ubiquity and normalization in everyday life. This individualized way of viewing sexual assault diverges from the innovators' views that its significant prevalence reflects a widespread social problem. As a result, the majority of men interviewees asserted male dominance through viewing their own definitions of sexual assault as more justifiable and rational than women's. As they did so, these resisters challenged the social and cultural changes in definitions that are being diffused throughout the general population as part of the gender revolution.

"Not That I'm Condoning Rape, But . . .": Traditional Rape Scripts

Before the #MeToo era, victim-blaming discourses commonly minimized the existence of sexual assault (Gravelin et al. 2019). Previous research found that men were more likely than women to engage in victim blaming (Pinciotti and Orcutt 2017). In our interviews, traditional forms of victim blaming were much less common than widespread concerns about "false" accusations. Yet a minority of focus group men did occasionally draw on traditional victim-blaming tropes to dismiss cases of sexual assault, often using the word "but" as a justification for their perceptions. Don, a 58-year-old white man, drew on traditional victim-blaming discourses in his gender-similar focus group. As the oldest man, Don positioned himself as an expert compared to the younger men. While laughing, he stated, "Last night on TV, not that I'm condoning it, *but* a lot of times women are dressing awfully provocative, showing almost all their tits." Continuing to laugh, he went on, "*They're asking for it*, you know what I mean?" Careful to distinguish himself from endorsing rape, he laughed again and stated, "I mean, not that I condone it or anything. *But* I can say they're like the fuel to the fire. Dressing like hookers, it's like, 'Yeah, we didn't dress like that before.'" Although Don qualified his last statement ("Well, I don't know if that's completely true"), he concluded with a traditional victim-blaming narrative that women are "asking for" rape: "It's not right no matter what, *but* sometimes there are added factors that need to be taken into consideration." Although several of the men in Don's focus group reacted nonverbally with surprised facial expressions, no one directly challenged his comment.

Other victim-blaming perspectives among the men were less blatant but present nonetheless. Jonah, a 20-year-old white man, pointed out that the behavior of Hollywood producer and convicted rapist Harvey Weinstein used to be defined as a career deal rather than sexual assault. Although he admitted that Weinstein "is a terrible person," Jonah also implied that he helped actresses obtain parts in films in exchange for sex. Jonah argued that the definition of this behavior shifted as a result of the #MeToo movement:

> It started to be labeled as rape when the #MeToo movement really started to blow up. That was really fascinating for me to see *how this shady definition has been changing, not* that I agree with anything that he did.

Although Jonah distanced himself from Weinstein's behavior at the end of his statement, he then used the word "but" to explain his confusion over consent: "*But* I do think it's getting hard to define in some ways." Aran, a 20-year-old Asian American man, also emphasized women's supposed choice to exchange sex with Weinstein for movie parts: "The #MeToo movement definitely did open my eyes to see what actually happens in Hollywood and *how women got their way into movies.*" Here, Aran did not recognize the associated power dynamics of the interaction, which the #MeToo movement is increasingly labeling as coercive.

Thus, although blatant victim blaming was rare, many men minimized sexual assault through their lack of awareness of power differentials and coercive environments. This approach does not see sexual assault as a widespread societal problem rooted in gender inequalities but one of unclear individual interactions, in which women are partially at fault. Their comments are an interesting juxtaposition with Weinstein's conviction, which was heralded as a "watershed moment" in the #MeToo era, as he was convicted despite no physical or forensic evidence against him. Furthermore, some survivors admitted that they had relationships with him after being sexually assaulted. The media has rightly said that Weinstein's conviction represents "a new era of empowerment for women," in which their accounts are believed and are less linked to victim blaming (Ransom 2020). Yet as we have seen from our interviewees, this legal victory was not reflected in the everyday consciousness of many men. In fact, these interviewees often resisted social, cultural, and even legal changes that resulted from the movement.

"She Just Didn't Like Working with Me": False Accusations

Widespread concern about "false" accusations has become pronounced in the #MeToo era and reflects rapidly shifting norms and expectations. Noah, a 33-year-old multiracial man, described an incident that preceded a sexual harassment complaint against him at work:

> I'm on the computer. I'm logged into my account. I'm doing something. A female coworker comes up and she starts doing something that she's not supposed to be doing. She's trying to help. But she starts doing something she's not supposed to be doing. And so I verbally and physically moved her hand away. Didn't slap it away, just gently moved it away and said, "No." I corrected her verbally and physically moved her away.

While Noah asserted that he had done nothing wrong, what followed later surprised and angered him: "Months later, she made a complaint that I touched her inappropriately." Noah insisted that "she just didn't like working with me." His supervisor responded to her complaint by relocating him. Noah stated angrily, "Fortunately, there were video cameras and they showed that it was nonsense. But I had to be moved out of that location because that complaint was made." At the same time, he rationalized the move as his own preference rather than a reprimand, saying that he wasn't moved "*because* of that, but because I *wanted* to be moved."

Obviously, we did not witness this event and do not have firsthand knowledge about what actually transpired. Yet Noah reframed the incident so that he could present it in a positive light, as his own choice to be relocated. It is interesting to note that rather than acknowledge that his actions were perceived negatively by his coworker and supervisor, Noah deflected responsibility and fully denied the accusation against him.

Unlike the women we interviewed, the men did not view either sexual assault or "false" accusations as a *social* problem. Rather, they largely saw these issues in a personalized, individualized framework in which individual actors are responsible for harming other individual actors. Although the men occasionally used language that drew a boundary between women and men (e.g., "us," "you," "them," and "they"), they were far less likely to do so than the women participants. Despite their concerns about the impact of potential "false" accusations, resisters did not express a collective identity *as men*, nor did they demand a *social* response. As a result, one significant gender difference that emerged in our interviews is that women embraced a collective identity *as women*, demanding social change, whereas men were instead *reactive* to these demands.

Although research on false allegations indicates that their prevalence is very low, the men interviewed here expressed significant concerns about them. One review of research found that false allegations constituted somewhere between 2 and 10 percent of *reported* sexual assault or rape cases (Lisak et al. 2010). Since a minority of cases are reported to the police (around 10 percent), the proportion of false reports to police in comparison to the total number of rapes and sexual assaults is even lower, around .002 to .008 percent, according to one researcher (Fielding 2018). That is, it is estimated that far less than 1 percent of reports are indeed false.

Recent longitudinal research has suggested that men vary in their concerns about false accusations. In particular, men's "gender-identification" matters (Szekeres et al. 2020: 1). After the emergence of #MeToo, the men who were less gender traditional became more progressive over time, while the men who were more gender traditional continued to endorse traditional and sexist gender roles (Szekeres et al. 2020).

As focus group facilitators who draw on feminist research methods that center on and respect participants' experiences, we take men's fears and concerns seriously. In fact, Matthew has frequently heard his friends and classmates express concerns about false accusations. Although we do not doubt that some allegations are indeed false, our writing about this topic includes quotation marks around the word "false." Nevertheless, we use these quotation marks to draw attention to the difference between subjective concerns, which are high, and their actual likelihood, which are very low.

Resisters were so concerned about "false" accusations that they saw their prevalence and damage as equal to sexual assault. The perception that these two traumas were equally problematic was demonstrated by their linguistic juxtaposition and inclusion of the word "but" in their accounts. In a gender-similar focus group with eight men, Matthew asked, "How big of a problem are harassment and assault?" Cam, an 18-year-old Asian American man, responded that the #MeToo movement "creates an environment where men aren't getting away with things like they might in more sexist eras." While this statement at first appears to support the movement, Cam continued, using the word "but" to equalize the negative impacts of sexual assault and "false" accusations, "*But* things like false accusations or politically motivated accusations put an impact on someone's career." Cam's perspective on traditional gender relations, where men can "get away with things," has been called into question by the #MeToo movement. Rather than celebrate this historical change, his response was skepticism.

The commonly held perception that "false" accusations are equivalent to sexual assault trivializes the severity of sexual harassment and assault. Gabriel, a 23-year-old Asian American man, said that harassment and assault are not "as high as the media puts it out to be." Suggesting that the problem is not harassment and assault but reports of it, Gabriel explained that although incidence may *not* be higher, reporting is. Aran agreed and said that women are more "outspoken" about sexual assault. Deven, a 20-year-old Asian American man, extended these points, using the word "but": Sexual assault "is really prevalent. *But* then there's also the side where being falsely accused of sexual assault is also a *big* problem." He continued by saying that both sexual assault and "false" accusations are a "hot topic" in the media. Equating the two minimizes the impact of sexual assault on survivors and reasserts male dominance.

The concept of false accusations has a racialized history. Blacks make up 49 percent of those who were wrongly convicted since 1989 (Carrega 2020). As Banner (2019) pointed out, social media posts about high-profile cases, such as Bill Cosby, often express concern about Black men being falsely accused of raping white women. A long history of lynching, racism, and imprisonment supports these concerns. For example, 60 years after Emmett Till was murdered and his accused murderers were acquitted, Carolyn Bryant, who testified in 1955 that Till "grabbed" and "threatened" her, recanted her testimony (see Banner 2019). A recent study of race and wrongful convictions found that "a black prisoner serving time for sexual assault is three-and-a-half times more likely to be innocent than a white sexual assault convict" (Gross et al. 2017: iii). Although the issue of "false" accusations is legitimately clouded by racism in the criminal justice system, it is also linked to gender and power.

Our focus groups reveal that many men have, in fact, subjectively absorbed this "false" accusation narrative and have applied it to their own lives. Men perceived women as having significant power, while they viewed themselves as powerless and defenseless to any career-ruining accusation that a woman might throw their way. The "false" accusation narrative is based on an assumed adversarial relationship between women and men, in which women accuse men for seemingly frivolous reasons. As a result, the resisters in our study cast doubt on sexual assault and harassment claims in general, suggesting the uneven progress of the gender revolution during the #MeToo era.

"It's Such an Easy Lie": Fear and Vulnerability

Men's reactions to the #MeToo movement, and specifically to "false" accusations, consist of both legitimate fear and vulnerability and resistance to women's rising power. As people come forward publicly with stories of sexual assault, resisters respond to this new visibility with uncertainty. The "false" accusation narrative also represents contestation of women's assertions of self-determination. While innovators are creating new definitions of sexual consent and assault, resisters reassert their power to define interactions in traditional ways. By questioning the legitimacy of the accusations, men defend themselves against women's challenges to male privilege. This approach reinforces hegemonic masculinity, because it seeks to maintain patriarchal power structures (Connell and Messerschmidt 2005). In a context in which many women are affirming their right to self-determination through speaking out, concerns about "false" accusations are an attempt to reassert dominance.

Although concerns about "false" accusations are not new, the explosion of public cases of sexual assault during the #MeToo era has resulted in a wide-spread "false" accusation narrative. In 2019, over 80 percent of surveyed men were "very concerned" or "somewhat concerned" about workplace "false" accusations (Elsesser 2019). Concerns that women "falsely" claim sexual assault or harassment are common: 31 percent of those surveyed in 2020 viewed it as a "major problem," 45 percent viewed it as a "minor problem," and only 22 percent said it was "not a problem" (Graf 2020). Men, especially Republican men, were more concerned than women about "false" accusations and less likely to express concern about sexual harassment going unpunished.

The large number of men who spoke openly in the focus groups about their fears and vulnerability to "false" accusations vividly illustrates that the #MeToo era has influenced men's everyday experiences. They expressed a pervasive, deep-felt fear of the power of the #MeToo movement, which has rapidly transformed understandings of sexual consent and assault for survivors, the majority of whom are women. In contrast, most of the focus group men perceived these transformations to be detrimental to their interests *as men*.

Resisters were troubled by the likelihood of "false" accusations and viewed themselves as subjected to the arbitrary whims and dislikes of women. William, an 18-year-old white man, pointed out that public accusations have an impact without the supposed neutral evaluation of a trial: "There's an accusation and there's immediate consequences, and that's it. There's no trial, there's no evaluation." Carter agreed and expressed concern about his own vulnerability,

> There's no trial, there's nothing, right? If my ex-girlfriend just went to court right now and said, "He sexually assaulted me," everyone would believe her. Why would she lie? But there will be nothing I could do, nothing I could say to disprove her.

In such a "he-said, she-said" situation, William thought that people would automatically side with the woman, even if she was lying in order to "hurt" a man: "Such an easy thing to do, such an easy lie. If you want to hurt somebody, you can definitely hurt someone with that lie, because no one's going to believe you."

Christopher, a 19-year-old Latinx man, described what he viewed as trivial sexual assault allegations as "potentially a dangerous case of the boy who cried wolf, where you just accuse somebody if you don't like him." Christopher said that when women "cry wolf" because they "don't like" a man, it is unclear what the "truth" is. As a result, "false" accusations were perceived as "a dangerous thing" because they have the potential to destroy a man's "reputation." Christopher continued, "I don't know which accusations are true and which ones are not. If you send a false allegation against somebody with sexual assault, their reputation is ruined with actual evidence." It is revealing to note that Christopher called the hypothetical allegation "false" in spite of the existence of "actual evidence" of assault.

Although these statements reflect a legitimate fear in some respects, they also suggest contestation. These resisters perceived women to hold a new kind of power over them and they were disturbed by it. Aran said, "Even if you didn't do anything, women still have *a lot of power* when it comes to this situation." In fact, the burden of proof was perceived to be on the accused rather than the accuser: "If they accuse you of sexual assault, there's a whole trial and everything. There's a lot of shit that men have to go through, to get off their backs." As he angrily pointed out, "In the end, their name is ruined. I didn't do it, but still, because of one false accusation, my life is going down. A lot of men are aware of that kind of situation." Thus, the perceived struggle for power in this example pits men and women against each other and ultimately favors women.

In focus group after focus group, resisters voiced their concerns about the negative consequences of frivolous "false" accusations. Luke, a 22-year-old white man, said, "If I'm just doing something and someone disagrees with my viewpoints, they shouldn't be able to destroy my reputation by saying that I did something." Gabriel labeled it "false allegations." Luke continued, "Yeah. That's the whole point of innocent until proven guilty." Anthony, a 35-year-old Black man, said: "It's dangerous when you don't have proof. That's a dangerous landscape to be in where someone can accuse you of something." Li, an 18-year-old Asian American man called accusations a "slippery slope." Li explained his skepticism, "Sometimes I hear about it and it's like, 'Come on, you think that's really true?'" Thus, these men resisted the increased visibility of accusations and viewed them as not only unfounded but also dangerous.

Others pointed out that women benefit from "false" accusations, although the perceived advantages to women were not stated explicitly. Deven said that women have "the opportunity to gain something from falsely accusing someone of rape" but didn't specify what women gained. Cam went a step further and implied that "false" allegations may serve to "help" women's careers while hurting men's: "Any type of false accusation can either help someone's career or ruin someone's career." Here, seeing women and men as engaged in a battle for status and career advancement, "false" reporting harms men while bolstering women's advancement.

The primary focus of concern about "false" accusations was that they ruin men's careers. Typically, there was little discussion of the effect on the rest of men's lives, including their mental health and relationships. Terrell said that accusations result in "arresting the person or things like that, or at least causing that person to lose their job or prestige." Although he did not specify the implications, Gabriel said that a "false" accusation "just defames his name, just slander." Anthony said that while he "supported the #MeToo movement," he was also concerned about the way that accused men "lose their jobs immediately. It's like, 'We believe this statement. No matter what, you lose your job.'" Instead, Anthony thought that people should pause and consider the situation: "Wait a minute. We don't even know. Just because someone says something doesn't necessarily mean it's true." He thought that people should weigh the evidence of the accusation before they believe it: "Everything needs to be put under fire. If someone says something, it should be put to the test and let the chips fall where they may." Thus, despite a politically correct statement showing his support of the #MeToo movement, Anthony also wanted to subject accusers to evaluation prior to believing them.

The Republican Party strategically deployed the language of "false" accusations during the 2018 U.S. Senate confirmation hearings for Supreme Court Justice Brett Kavanaugh. Kavanaugh was accused of sexually assaulting Christine Blasey Ford when they were teenagers and her testimony heightened awareness of #MeToo. Specialists in digital research tracked the Republican messaging that was pushed out to the public through Twitter during the hearings. Republicans first emphasized "the core American value of the 'presumption of innocence': that a person is innocent until proven guilty" (Rosenblatt and Lake 2018). The criminal justice system uses this standard, although the confirmation hearings had no links to a criminal proceeding. This narrative "mobilized men" to support Kavanaugh (Rosenblatt and Lake 2018). When retweets of these messages slowed down, Republicans shifted to a different narrative that personalized the problem by claiming that all men are vulnerable to "false" accusations (Rosenblatt and Lake 2018). To reinforce a "coherent and deliberate" Republican social media campaign (Rosenblatt and Lake 2018), Donald Trump declared in an interview that it is "a very scary time for young men in America" (Diamond 2018). Thus, through a media and social media blast aimed at supporting Kavanaugh's confirmation, Republicans effectively advanced a "false" accusation narrative that appealed to many men.

Focus group resisters viewed accusations as "politically motivated" when they reflected on the Kavanaugh hearings. Thiago, a 25-year-old Latinx man, said that the Kavanaugh hearings "opened up the potentiality of some of those accusations being politically motivated, and it's very scary." Thiago directly linked his own fears about "false" accusations to the Kavanaugh hearings:

I truly believe that it is kind of scary that people can come over and accuse me of doing something like that when there's no evidence, and it changes the public view of that person for the rest of their career.

Thiago argued that high-profile cases like Weinstein and Cosby make average men afraid of the consequences of committing sexual assault. Yet his statement accepted that sexual assault had occurred:

> It's demonstrating the fact that no matter how high profile these people are, you can still *get knocked down* if you *do something wrong* in accordance with sexual assault. And so that trickles down to lower echelons of society to say, "OK, well this is not right. And no one's *safe*, you're going to get *caught*, period."

These comments are revealing on several levels. First, they suggest the extent to which high-profile cases influence resisters' everyday sense of vulnerability. Second, Thiago did not question whether or not Weinstein or Cosby had actually committed sexual assault. Rather, his fear was focused on men's "safety" and getting "knocked down" or "caught." What is especially striking is that Thiago was concerned with the accountability of perpetrators who had done "something wrong" regarding sexual assault. This disturbing perspective reinforces the idea that men should not be held accountable for their own criminal actions.

Similar to the perception that women have power in the court of public opinion and the legal system itself, resisters expressed concerns about women's power in reporting to the police. Luke described his concern that women's police reports were public: "Report to the cops and then everyone around you knows that this is happening. And knows this about you. And that's something that I know a lot of people are much more concerned about." Aran agreed with Luke and expressed confidence that when women report sexual assault to the police, it is adequately investigated:

> You're reporting it to the cops. They're going to do their job. Maybe there could be an argument made that, 'Oh, they're just going to ignore you,' but most of the time, if you report it, they'll look into it.

Thus, resisters assumed that reports of sexual assault were adequately investigated by the police, that they resulted in immediate and public consequences for the men, and that the burden of proof rests with the accused, not the accusers. Crime statistics do not bear out these men's fears. Only 230 out of 1,000 cases of sexual assault are reported to the police and only 4.6 out of 1,000 sexual assaults lead to incarceration (Rainn.org 2020a). In fact 13 percent of survivors have said that they did not report the sexual assault because they believed that the police would do nothing to help them (Rainn.org 2020a). Many of the women we interviewed were highly skeptical that the police would adequately investigate reports of sexual assault.

Why do men express such deep concerns about "false" accusations if, in fact, their incidence is extremely low? One explanation is that men's perceptions of gender differences in definitions of sexual consent leave them feeling vulnerable to accusations of sexual assault.[1] That is, they are aware that ideas about consent have changed. These shifting norms and expectations leave men feeling unsettled and unsure about what constitutes consent in the #MeToo era. Times of rapid social and cultural change are characterized by a "crisis" (Kuhn 1962; Rochon 1998) and result in "unsettled cultural periods" (Swidler 1986: 277). During such times, existing paradigms are transformed and replaced by new ones through challenges to existing paradigms (Kuhn 1962). It takes time for new cultural values to take hold, and transition periods can be difficult for those who subscribe to old paradigms, as we see with many of the focus group men during this gender revolution. As new worldviews, symbols, ideologies, and rituals emerge, it takes time for previous ones to lose legitimacy (Swidler 1986).

However, as we have seen, resisters are also directly contesting the rise of women's power. As they do so, they are reasserting traditional gender roles in which their dominance is secure. As women erode these inequalities, they rethink traditional roles and insist that men treat them as equal and mutual sex partners. This shifting ground has left many resisters challenging women's power through expressions of "false" accusations. Some even went so far as to suggest that perpetrators should not be accountable for criminal actions. Thus, resisters cling to traditional frameworks and fight to maintain the status quo through the "false" accusation narrative.

"Men Are Just Avoiding Women": Strategies to Avoid Accusations

As a result of rapidly changing definitions of consent, many of the men have undertaken particular strategies to lessen their perceived vulnerability of being accused of sexual assault. When asked about the impact of the #MeToo movement, Deven stated, "I think men are definitely more careful, more mindful about it." He continued, referring directly to himself, "I think I'm more careful." Cam agreed, "Men are more conscientious of following the definition. And I feel like that can be considered one of the benefits of the #MeToo movement, the fear of not being on the other side of the movement." These comments suggest that the diffusion of #MeToo movement frames has influenced men's daily lives and behaviors.

Some focus group men engaged in specific strategies to lessen their chances of "false" accusations. Hunter, a 22-year-old white man, observed changes in other men's behaviors, which he saw as motivated by avoiding negative consequences:

> Maybe some of the men might respect women's distance. They respect women's space on their wishes and stuff, mainly because they don't want to offend the women. But also, now they have a *reason, to avoid repercussions* and stuff like that because it is a big, big deal.

Gabriel discussed a recent news story about men who are avoiding relationships with women altogether. He called women "them" adversarially and framed relationships as a "confrontation": "Men are just avoiding them to avoid this *confrontation*, because if I do something a little bit out of line, well, guess what? I got HR [Human Resources] on my back." William confirmed this idea: "That's something that I see in my peers a lot, is fear to even enter into a relationship for fear of that happening at one point. Because of how public the #MeToo movement is." These resisters suggested that an adversarial relationship between genders, rather than mutuality and understanding, was common as norms rapidly shift due to the movement.

As a result, resisters recognized the implications of accusations and were concerned about women's rising power. Anthony, who earlier expressed his concern about California's affirmative consent law, drew on the law's discussion of intoxication to help him develop a strategy to avoid a potential "false" accusation. He decided that he would avoid having sex with new partners who were intoxicated. Anthony described a specific situation during which he chose to terminate an interaction with a woman who had been drinking: "I've been in situations where I met somebody off Tinder and they were intoxicated. And I don't want to [have sex]. 'No. I don't know you like that.'" Yet even once his relationships progressed, Anthony thought that alcohol complicated the issue of consent: "It is kind of confusing because what if you date somebody a few times, and you plan on getting drunk. It's hard to say, you know? So it can be confusing." Thus, in response to the fear that they could be "falsely" accused, the men sought to lessen their perceived vulnerability. In the #MeToo context, previous assumptions of male dominance have been called into question.

"Not All Boys": Shifting Responsibility to Other Men

Although these conversations reveal deep changes in men's behaviors and worries as a result of #MeToo, they simultaneously shifted responsibility to a generic "other" man or group of men. That is, resisters personally claimed to be knowledgeable about consent but vocally doubted other men's awareness. Jack gave the men in his focus group a pass on responsibility: "I'm pretty sure *everyone in this room clearly knows* what the definition of sexual assault is, but I don't think I can extend that to *everyone outside this room*." As Grayson, a 22-year-old Middle Eastern man, put it, "I think there are formal definitions of what sexual harassment is, but *not everybody is aware* of what they are, so that needs to be made more public, and *people* need to be more aware of those things." Hunter agreed, "There are concrete definitions, but I feel *many people are ignorant* of the definitions. So when it happens to them, *they* might not know the exact definition unless someone enforces the definition on them." On one level, these perspectives may indicate that these men are supportive of women's definitions of sexual consent and assault. On another level, however, the claim that they themselves understood the definitions while "others" were ignorant deflects responsibility for the issue. It also reduces sexual assault and harassment to an individual, rather than a social, problem. This deflection denies that they themselves could take steps to reduce violence in society.

Many of the men thought that the required university sexual assault prevention training taught them what they needed to know about consent and assault. Research has suggested that sexual assault prevention trainings are most effective when they involve participant discussion and active learning techniques (Borges et al. 2008). In contrast, this particular training was merely a 15-minute online module, during which students could multitask or engage in other types of distracted behaviors. These types of trainings have been developed and marketed to universities.

Thus, although a step in the right direction, the training's online nature may limit a full understanding of complex definitions that would be better understood through discussion. The content of the training also reinforced traditional initiator-gatekeeper expectations. Looking carefully at this particular training (created by a de-identified company), students were told the following:

> Communicating what you want and don't want is a normal, natural, and expected part of healthy communication. When it comes to sexual activity, asking for consent is a powerful way to connect meaningfully with another person and demonstrate that you care and respect them.

The training continued by stating that "nonverbal cues . . . don't provide enough information for a person to *really* know what someone intends to communicate." Reflecting affirmative definitions of consent, the training defined it as "an ongoing process because people's needs or interests can change during a single experience, as well as over the course of a relationship."

Although this training put forward an affirmative consent standard, it did not challenge the gender inequalities that underlie the initiator-gatekeeper framework assumed in heterosexual relationships. In an example of "what a conversation about consent could look like," the training praised a man, Nick, for "being careful to ask for Ella's consent to different activities throughout the night." The example stated that Ella consented to kissing Nick but that she "froze" when he touched her shirt, which led Nick to "check in with Ella." This vague description implied verbalization but did not state it outright. The example concluded by praising Nick for respecting "her choice." When the training talked about "coercion," it included "verbal or nonverbal, physical and/or emotional actions." Although the training was clear that sexual coercion is used to manipulate or pressure someone, it also blurred the line between coercion, sexual assault, and miscommunication through vague and imprecise meanings of these terms: "Sexual assault does not happen as a result of miscommunication, and coercion is *not* consent." Leaving the difference between sexual assault and miscommunication unarticulated could potentially leave aggressors to claim the latter.

As imperfect as the training is, focus group resisters asserted that as a result of completing it, it was "not them" who misunderstood the boundaries of consent. Thiago believed that the training immunized him from confusion and therefore trouble with sexual harassment and assault:

> I feel like their definition was very concise, very strong, and the definition itself is not currently a problem. I think that it's quite clear to me. The very basis of sexual assault. I personally understand what that line is.

Li concurred that the training made the definitions clear. He contrasted his knowledge with older generations of men:

> For *our generation*, doing the training and stuff, it's becoming more of an open and accepted knowledge that everyone should know, and so people are being educated about it. While *other people* that are *older than us*, and the cases that you hear about, people aren't so educated about what the line is between each.

In Li's statement, older generations of men were perpetrators, while the younger generation, who had the benefit of the training, were not.

Other resisters mentioned their own high morals and upbringing as further proof that it was "not them" who were confused about consent. Jeremiah, a 36-year-old multiracial man, claimed that "other" men were often confused by the boundaries of consent:

> *Other people.* I'm not saying that I'm above confusion, but it is confusing for *some people* because some of us have not been raised with the hardline yes and no understanding. And I think that *people* find it confusing. *People* are selfish and think that what *they* want is more important than what somebody else may want.

Using such phrases as "they," "other people," and "not me" allowed the men to divert responsibility of harassment and assault to others. Interestingly, these phrases are gender neutral, implying that men are not the only perpetrators.

Another way that participants shifted responsibility through a "not me" framework was to emphasize the small number of perpetrators of sexual assault. Carter said that only a "small amount" of "deviant" people were perpetrators of violence against women:

> A small amount of people get this idea to sexually assault somebody. There's a bell curve of people, right? These people are all at the end. They have this deviant behavior. I think it's a very small part of the population.

Carter also stated that the small number of people who commit sexual assault do so because of their upbringing.

Dominic, a 20-year-old white man, also adopted a "not me" framework when describing who he believed was responsible for sexual harassment and assault:

> Say there is 2 percent of men who are sexually harassing people, but they could each do it 50 times. So the rest of the 98 percent of the men, obviously, they don't really see it. They don't notice it. But as women, it seems very clear that it happens a lot.

Here, Dominic shifted the blame to a vaguely defined 2 percent of "other" men. He also minimized sexual assault by making it seem that there are only a small proportion of men that should be held accountable. This approach frames the problem as individualized and rare rather than a broad-scale societal issue.

The focus group dynamic resulted in resisters collectively using a "not me" framework. As a group, they emphasized that they themselves were immune to confusion around consent, while "others" outside of the group were the problem. Matthew asked a focus group with six men, "How did the #MeToo movement change how you view sexual assault, harassment, and consent?" Aran answered, "Me as a person, overall, most of the time I just have a general respect for women." Gabriel agreed, "It's always the same for me. . . . Nothing changed for me, yeah, same thing. Decent human respect, decency." Aran replied, "We don't have to go around worrying about getting caught for sexual assault, because *we're* just not like that. *We* haven't grown up in that kind of situation or atmosphere." In this interaction, the two men together shifted responsibility for sexual harassment and assault to men who were raised in a different environment. This perspective reflects an individualized understanding that assumes that a few "bad" men are perpetrators. This stance contrasts sharply with the one taken by the innovators, who view rape culture in terms of its widespread reach over people's lives.

In a mixed-gender focus group, Pamela asked, "Do you think that men and women think about sexual consent, assault, and harassment differently?" Harper, a 23-year-old multiracial woman, ignited the men's use of the "not me" framework when she answered, "Whenever alcohol is involved. A girl's drinking alcohol. A guy's drinking alcohol, sometimes flirting with someone. And maybe a guy takes it too far. It's always the guy." Harper said that even a minor compliment from a woman leads men to assume that she is interested in sex:

> You could be nice. Alcohol doesn't even have to be involved. You could be like, "Oh, my God, that shirt looks really great on you." And he could be like, "Oh, my God, she wants me." *Boys are like that.*

In fact, Muehlenhard et al. (2016) found that men perceive women as exhibiting more sexual interest than the women perceive of the same interaction.

After Harper's generalization about men that called out "the guy" and "boys," three of the men in the group quickly chimed in to shift accountability away from themselves and toward "other" men. Khalid, a 21-year-old Middle Eastern man, said, "*Not all boys.*" Ahmad, another 21-year-old Middle Eastern man, jumped in and added, "Yeah, just to add on to what you're saying. *Not all boys.*" Finally, Noah echoed, "*Not all boys.*" At this point, laughter erupted among the focus group members. Despite the humor in this situation, it revealed the extent to which men want to distinguish themselves from other men who do not respect women's wishes.

In this approach, sexual assault became an individualized problem requiring *individuals* to have higher levels of decency or morality. This rhetoric used by the men shifted responsibility for the prevention of sexual assault away from themselves and toward some nameless and faceless "others." Although we are not implying that these men were perpetrators, their use of a "not me" or "not us" framework emphasized that sexual assault was not *their* problem but someone else's. This stance does not call for a social response or framework. These men resisted viewing widespread societal rape culture as needing to be viewed collectively. Furthermore, gender inequalities or power differences between men and women become invisible when the problem is framed in individualized terms. Research on social media responses to the #HowIWillChange posts on Twitter found a similar "not all men" pattern, indicating men's resistance to taking action to change societal rape culture (PettyJohn et al. 2019). As Chandra and Erlingsdóttir (2020: 7) argued:

> The common response of "NotAllMen" to any individual account of sexual harassment indicates the need to see each victim in isolation, each perpetrator as a unique aberration, rather than face the acknowledgment of a systemic malaise that impacts "all men." The sustaining of a patriarchal control over women's bodies is precisely what is under attack in this movement.

As it does so, this rhetoric challenges the #MeToo movement and social and cultural changes in the gender revolution. Although subtle, these perspectives reassert male domination over women and resist the #MeToo movement frame that exposes sexual assault as systemic rather than a problem of a few isolated individuals.

"It Just Doesn't Get as Much Coverage": Shifting Responsibility to Women Perpetrators

While 1 in 6 American women have experienced attempted or completed rape, only 1 in 33 men (3 percent) have had this experience in their lifetime (Rainn. org 2020b). Specifically, 82 percent of childhood victims and 90 percent of adult victims are women (Rainn.org 2020b). Despite these gender disparities in the prevalence of sexual assault, focus group resisters were concerned that the #MeToo movement's focus on women obscures male sexual assault survivors. By implying that men and women experience sexual assault at similar rates, focus group men minimized widespread violence against women in our society. Their critiques of the #MeToo movement for ignoring sexual assault against men ultimately delegitimizes women's power in publicly naming their experiences as assault.

In a way that criticized the goals of the #MeToo movement, Li took issue with the lack of media coverage on sexual assault against men:

> When there's a case of sexual harassment or anything against females, it's obviously brought up more right away and it's more in the popular eye. It doesn't happen as much with men coming out, saying, "This happened to me." I guess it just doesn't get as much coverage and obviously it's not viewed at all by people.

This framing—that it is a lack of media coverage of sexual assault against men rather than a disproportionate number of cases by gender—minimizes widespread violence against women and girls by equalizing its incidence among men and boys.

Similarly, Cam argued that sexual assault against men is "devalued" as a direct result of #MeToo:

> While the #MeToo movement . . . applies to both males and females, assault against males is *devalued* both by males and females. For example, if a person comes out and says that a woman raped him, the more stereotypical response is, "You should feel good about it," something like that. So across both genders, assault against females is strongly viewed as incorrect and wrong, but even males view assault against males as less of an issue currently.

Interestingly, Cam assumed a female perpetrator in cases of male sexual assault rather than a male perpetrator. He emphasized that this different treatment is unequal: "Hopefully it changes and becomes more *equalized* for *us*." Cam said that, according to societal expectations, a man being raped by a woman is supposed to be a man's "pride moment": "If a female rapes a male, it's viewed as a good thing even though you felt fully uncomfortable, fully nonconsensual and probably felt terrible afterwards." Cam also stated that men alleging rape or sexual assault are viewed negatively by society. He described his perception of a typical reaction to such a revelation: "Why are you coming out with this? You're a male, you got to have sex, enjoy it." Although Cam critiqued traditional gendered assumptions that men are never assaulted and that men are supposed to embrace sex even when it is coercive, his statements represent a type of mental gymnastics that distorts the reality of gender and power. In his formulation, sexual assault against men is perpetrated by women rather than other men. Additionally, his critique of the #MeToo movement for "devaluing" sexual assault against men obscures and minimizes the gendered power dynamics that the movement challenges.

Undoubtedly, male victims of sexual assault, regardless of the gender of the perpetrator, experience many negative emotions, including shame as a result of not being able to conform to gendered expectations. However, research has suggested that men, not women, are far more likely to be perpetrators in cases of male rape and sexual assault. When acting without male co-perpetrators, women are perpetrators in only about one-quarter of rape or sexual assault incidents that have male victims (Friedersdorf 2021). Thus, the sole emphasis on women as perpetrators on the part of the focus group participants is misplaced.

While concern about male survivors is justified, this approach shifts responsibility for sexual assault away from men as perpetrators. Sang, a 19-year-old Asian American man, continued this line of thinking, "I've heard about stories where men don't even realize they're being raped, maybe it's by a partner or someone else. They don't want to do it, but the female forces themselves on them and they don't realize it." Sang echoed Cam's sentiment that male survivors experience difficulty, "And they feel bad about it, they have emotional problems. Men being raped is not thought about, and sexual assault against males is not thought about in the same way as females being sexually assaulted." Cam agreed with Sang, and added that men believe that they cannot be raped: "Yeah, I agree with him, and then they start to have psychological problems about it because of the belief that, 'It wasn't rape because I'm a male.'" Terrell also expressed concerns about female perpetrators:

> Because a woman is initiating, if they were to admit that that happened to them, that they didn't like it, then people would probably laugh at that male, so that person would end up basically having to accept those types of actions toward him.

Although focus group men expressed legitimate concerns about the stigmas facing men survivors, this demand for equal recognition assumes that men are assaulted at rates that are comparable to women. This discourse minimizes assault against women and underestimates the prevalence of male perpetrators.

The men also discussed a double standard around sexual discourses in which men are unfairly stereotyped as sexually driven and powerful aggressors. They believed that these stereotypes can lead to "false" accusations against men. Christopher talked about the "macho guy perspective" and its unfair painting of a stereotypical image of men: "Those are a huge danger, those stereotypes, overgeneralizations." Christopher said that stereotyping men as "macho" results in men being unfairly and preemptively targeted as harassers or assaulters. Ethan, a 28-year-old white man, mentioned that public conversations around Trump's "locker-room talk" ("Grab 'em by the pussy") was viewed negatively when coming from men but not when coming from women:

> You heard about Trump having that kind of talk and it makes him look like a complete A-hole, a woman hater. He's sexist. He's a bigot. And then if a woman said something similar about a man, I don't think society in general would look at it as negatively.

In this formulation, men are chastised for behavior that women can get away with because of societal gendered expectations. In this context, Ethan explained that "we try to boost women up in society" and that "we're not going to try to push them back down." In an ironic twist, Ethan implied that women can get away with things that men cannot because they are traditionally disadvantaged. That is, due to inequality, people will not challenge women's bad behavior in the same way as they will men's. In summary, resisters critiqued the #MeToo movement for failing to recognize men survivors, an approach that inaccurately assumes equal incidence of sexual assault across genders.

"I'm on the Fence about the #MeToo Movement": Women's Fused Perspectives

About one-quarter (n = 8) of the focus group women expressed fused perspectives that deviated from the progressive views of gender relations espoused by the other three-quarters of women interviewees (see Table 6.2). Four women provided some critiques of the #MeToo movement. Unlike the resister men, however, they blended progressive and traditional discourses to create a perspective that simultaneously rejected and embraced recent social and cultural changes. Four interviewees echoed the comments from the men featured earlier that were concerned about the lack of focus on men survivors. Although these women in part resisted social change, they combined these perspectives with innovative ones. Table 6.2 illustrates how these perspectives were distributed by racial and ethnic background. Although the number with each perspective is too small to make generalizations, we see that innovators come from all racial and ethnic backgrounds, while those with fused perspectives were more often from Black, Asian American, or multiracial backgrounds (see Table 6.2).

As we will see in Chapter 7, Alexandra, a 38-year-old Black woman, was concerned that boys are not socialized to understand consent. Like other innovators, she endorsed an affirmative consent definition. At the same time as she appreciated the "voice" that the movement allowed, she was concerned with

TABLE 6.2 Women and Nonbinary Interviewees' Perspectives by Racial and Ethnic Background

	Types of perspective			
	Resister	*Innovator*	*Fused*	*Total*
White	0	7	0	7
Middle Eastern or North African	0	3	0	3
Hispanic/Latinx	0	2	0	2
Black	0	11	4	15
Asian American	0	1	1	2
Multiracial	0	1	3	4
Unknown	0	1	0	1
Percent (n)	0	76.5 (26)	23.5 (8)	100 (34)

"false" accusations and the danger to men. Linguistically similar to the men in this chapter, Alexandra used the word "but" to transition from her support to her doubts:

> I'm going to have an unpopular opinion here, *but* I'm *on the fence* about the #MeToo movement. The concept of it, giving women a *voice*, is very important because sexual assault does happen. *But* we are also seeing it being used as a *weapon* on us. Just because I say it happened doesn't make it so. We are charging people in the media without [evidence]. You're basically guilty till proven innocent and I'm having a problem with this because of the #MeToo movement.

She explained the negative career consequences for men:

> All I have to say is, "Oh well, doctor so and so did this to me," and he's crucified. I don't like the fact that all I have to do is say someone did something and there is no trial. There's no jury. There's no exchange of any information.

Alexandra juxtaposed "voice" and "weaponize": "It's becoming to me a little *dangerous* because just like it's giving women a *voice*, it's also women using it to *weaponize* it." Although she was quick to clarify that there's no "justification" for sexual assault and that there are "real people who are victims," some women are not "victims." Alexandra thought that reports sometimes sought "to get this outcome." When Isabella, a 21-year-old Latinx woman, disagreed, Alexandra responded by saying that some women in the #MeToo movement are taking "accountability off ourselves" by presenting themselves as victims instead of someone who "got played" by a man.

Several women expressed similar critical remarks about the #MeToo movement and often paired them with positive perspectives. Christina, a 36-year-old Black woman who emphasized women's collective responses to gender inequalities in ways typical of innovators (see Chapter 7), was concerned about men getting called out for complimenting women:

> Men don't really know what is crossing the line and what is meant as a compliment. Some women are like, "Oh no, don't talk to me like that." But you might just be like, "Hey, you look nice today." It doesn't mean I'm going to sexually assault you later. But with #MeToo, a lot of women, not a lot, but some women, are pushing that to be the thing, and it really shouldn't be.

The misunderstanding between men and women in this example suggested that compliments were being misconstrued by the movement.

Amy, a 19-year-old Asian American woman, agreed that there are problems with #MeToo. She said that while "the idea" of the movement is "really good," she also used the word "but" to transition to a negative view: "*But* I think nowadays it's become more of like revenge." Amy described a situation in which one student accused another of sexual assault:

> I've heard of cases where this one student blamed another student for sexual assault, and it never happened. *But* she disliked him because he broke up with her. And so she decided to create this whole tale of how he assaulted her, and she put on the #MeToo thing, and then they went through the whole process and found out that nothing happened. His whole reputation was torn down because of that lie.

She pointed out that occasionally "victims themselves, because it happened so long ago, misremembered things." She used the word "but" to transition from her perceptions of positive to negative aspects of the movement: "That idea of created awareness for sexual assault is a good idea, *but* people have taken it to become revenge on people who they don't like."

After Nadine, a 20-year-old white woman, disagreed with these comments, Christina jumped back into the conversation by arguing that there should be "reverse action," "punishment," and "repercussions" for "the person that makes those false accusations" because "if you are found to be lying, you ruin the reputation" of the accused. When Mia, a 20-year-old white woman, sharply disagreed that false reporting is common, Christina stuck to her point of view:

> There's two sides to each coin, that's what I'm trying to say. In order to maybe protect more victims of sexual assault, there does need to be some type of prosecution or some type of penalty or punishment for the person that's lying.

She pointed out that false accusations "hinder what you're trying to do when you have a whole group of people or a movement trying to change things in society." She suggested that society is fragile: "It really just takes one little thread to unravel one piece of an entire woven knit." In this metaphor, Christina suggested that the existence of any false accusations served to undermine the #MeToo movement and its accompanying social change.

Several other women supported the movement yet expressed concerns that male survivors do not receive as much attention as female survivors. Nia, a 49-year-old Black woman, used the trope of women as perpetrators to highlight the gender-neutral aspects of #MeToo when she stated that a "battle" was occurring: "It's going to be anybody that's doing anything wrong because men are not the only ones that are doing wrong to women. There are women that are doing wrong to young boys." Harper said that men are not visible in the movement because of cultural expectations around masculinity and heterosexuality: "The men that have been assaulted, they're probably not a part of this group, this #MeToo movement. It's probably strictly women. Men think it will make them look less masculine or like they're gay or something because they're men."

Amelia, a 20-year-old multiracial woman, also pointed out that cultural expectations hindered men's reporting:

It's not just women. Men can be raped and sexually assaulted too. It takes a lot for them, because they want to be this strong, tough guy, a stereotype. But I think it can be thought of in a different way because if you're a guy that's maybe smaller and maybe more prone to attacks and fear, that can be you. Men can carry around the pepper spray too, you never know. Women can overcome some men depending on who they are.

Angel, a 54-year-old Black survivor who we will hear from in Chapter 7, agreed that women are more likely to report assault or rape than men. She said that the movement was important to her understanding her own experience, yet since it "focuses on the women's issue," it does "not make it less of an issue for men."

Although these comments support men survivors, which is an important position, they also have the larger effect of diminishing women's accounts of sexual assault in the #MeToo era. Like the men we heard from earlier, these types of comments minimize the highly disproportionate prevalence of sexual assault. In calling for a more gender-neutral approach, these comments reflect at least some level of skepticism about #MeToo on the part of these women, who otherwise fell into the innovator category. This blending of approaches is not surprising as the #MeToo movement frame has taken hold but is not fully embraced, even by some people who generally support it.

Conclusion

On the whole, this chapter reveals that most of the men were resisters who contested changes brought about by the #MeToo era, including many of the social movement frames that innovators pushed forward. Discourses around sexual harassment and assault centered on concerns about "false" accusations. Resisters were worried about being "falsely" accused and several recounted instances of "false" accusations toward themselves or people they knew. This fear of "false" accusations among these men, two-thirds of whom were men of color (n = 27, 67.5 percent) is likely rooted in deep-standing historical realities of racism in the United States. And yet this narrative assumed an adversarial relationship between women and men in which women were "out to get" men arbitrarily. There was almost a sense that any man is vulnerable to accusations at any time for no apparent reason. Additionally, these resisters took a "not me" approach, whereby they sought to distance themselves from "other" men who were seen as the perpetrators. And many minimized the negative impact of sexual assault by seeing it as equal in harm to being "falsely" accused. Thus, men viewed sexual assault as an individual problem affecting only a small number of people, which greatly contrasts with the social problem perspective and collective identity we will see in Chapter 7.

Although traditional victim blaming was not a central narrative, the concern about "false" accusations is widespread and suggests that resisters view women as adversaries who are seeking to usurp male power. This approach suggests that men are challenging and contesting the rise of women's voices and demands for sexual self-determination. That is, rather than blaming women for provoking assault due to their behavior or dress, more of the men are questioning whether or not the sexual interaction occurred in the first place. This approach distances men from responsibility. In this scenario, men are not even in the room, as they deny in advance that any sexual interaction even occurred. In this case, the woman must be constructing the "false" accusation to "get back at" him. The #MeToo era is thus characterized by the perspective that women are adversaries, albeit adversaries that men, in a traditional gender role framework, must persuade to have sex with them. Their accounts are riddled with fear of "false" accusations that could destroy a man's career.

Additionally, nearly a quarter of the focus group women expressed some concerns about "false" accusations or some skepticism about the #MeToo movement, although they fused these ideas with more progressive perspectives that mirrored those of the other innovators. This finding illustrates that the gender revolution is still underway. As social change occurs, even those who support the #MeToo movement frame also maintain some traditional perspectives. This blending of ideologies indicates that there is a "cultural lag" (Swidler 1986: 281) in discourses as change unfolds.

When considering these findings from the standpoint of the #MeToo movement, one might wonder if this story is a pessimistic or optimistic one. There are certainly points in both columns, but we think that it is ultimately an optimistic story. On the pessimistic side, men's definitions of consent, harassment, and assault are very troubling. The finding that they view men's definitions as different and "looser" than women's reveals that they may not be fully seeking to understand how women view this important issue. Many men are operating with traditional notions of gender differences in the responsibility for sexual relationships, especially initiation and gatekeeping roles. Although gendered views are converging, this chapter also reveals the profound ways these men are contesting women's power. As they do so, they are resisting the social transformations that are pulling back toward more traditional arrangements.

Thus, social change during the gender revolution is uneven. One can expect that significant changes in culture and identity will be accompanied by contestations. Resisters may be lagging behind the changes that innovators have made to culture and yet they are still evolving. For example, the near absence in the focus groups of traditional forms of victim blaming for sexual assault is an important and notable theme. Additionally, it is not entirely negative that men are concerned about being accused of sexual assault. The power of the #MeToo movement has started the process of upending traditional power differences in people's daily lives. As a space that has publicly challenged men's behavior in new ways, the movement has brought to light a new discourse on sexual consent, assault, and harassment that has been diffused into the general population. In this context, the power of the #MeToo movement legitimately frightens men. Although its transformations are still far from complete, #MeToo is altering how ordinary people think about sexual consent and assault. Resisters are engaged in a process of self-reflection and fear that may motivate more careful responses in interpersonal relationships. Thus, although many of the findings in this chapter reveal that a deep gender divide has opened up, transformations from the gender revolution are profound.

Note

1. Thank you to Shamus Khan for discussing this idea with us, February 5, 2020.

References

Banner, Francine. 2019. *Crowdsourcing the Law: Trying Sexual Assault on Social Media*. Lanham, MD: Lexington Books.

Borges, Angela M., Victoria L. Banyard, and Mary M. Moynihan. 2008. "Clarifying Consent: Primary Prevention of Sexual Assault on a College Campus." *Journal of Prevention & Intervention in the Community* 36(1–2):75–88.

Carrega, Christina. 2020. "'Because They Can Get Away With It': Why African Americans Are Blamed for Crimes They Didn't Commit: Experts." *ABC News*. Retrieved February 4, 2022 (https://abcnews.go.com/US/african-americans-blamed-crimes-commit-experts/story?id=70906828).

Chandra, Giti and Irma Erlingsdóttir. 2020. "Introduction." pp. 1–23 in *The Routledge Handbook of the Politics of the #MeToo Movement*, edited by Giti Chandra and Irma Erlingsdóttir. New York, NY: Routledge.

Connell, R. W. and James W. Messerschmidt. 2005. "Hegemonic Masculinity: Rethinking the Concept." *Gender & Society* 19(6):829–859.

Diamond, Jeremy. 2018. "Trump Says It's 'a Very Scary Time for Young Men in America'." *CNN*. Retrieved February 15, 2022 (www.cnn.com/2018/10/02/politics/trump-scary-time-for-young-men-metoo/index.html).

Elsesser, Kim. 2019. "Of All The Gender Issues At Work, Men Are Most Concerned About False Harassment Claims From Women." *Forbes*. Retrieved February 4, 2022 (www.forbes.com/sites/kimelsesser/2019/01/10/of-all-the-gender-issues-at-work-men-are-most-concerned-about-false-harassment-claims-from-women/#2104a2d1866a).

Fielding, Jackie. 2018. "Men Fear False Allegations. Women Fear Sexual Misconduct, Assault, and Rape." *Minnesota Law Review*. Retrieved February 4, 2022 (https://minnesotalawreview.org/2018/11/25/men-fear-false-allegations-women-fear-sexual-misconduct-assault-and-rape/).

Friedersdorf, Conor. 2021. "The Understudied Female Sexual Predator." *The Atlantic*. Retrieved February 15, 2022 (www.theatlantic.com/science/archive/2016/11/the-understudied-female-sexual-predator/503492).

Graf, Nikki. 2020. "Sexual Harassment at Work in the Era of #MeToo." *Pew Research Center's Social & Demographic Trends Project*. Retrieved February 4, 2022 (www.pewsocialtrends.org/2018/04/04/sexual-harassment-at-work-in-the-era-of-metoo/).

Gravelin, Claire R., Monica Biernat, and Caroline E. Bucher. 2019. "Blaming the Victim of Acquaintance Rape: Individual, Situational, and Sociocultural Factors." *Frontiers in Psychology* 9(2242):1–22.

Gross, Samuel R., Maurice Possley and Klara Stephens. 2017. "Race and Wrongful Convictions in the United States." The National Registry of Exonerations, *Newkirk Center for Science and Society*, Retrieved September 1, 2022 (https://repository.law.umich.edu/cgi/viewcontent.cgi?article=1121&context=other).

Kuhn, Thomas S. 1962. *The Structure of Scientific Revolutions*. Chicago, IL: University of Chicago Press.

Lisak, David, Lori Gardinier, Sarah C. Nicksa, and Ashley M. Cote. 2010. "False Allegations of Sexual Assault: An Analysis of Ten Years of Reported Cases." *Violence Against Women* 16(12):1318–1334.

Muehlenhard, Charlene L., Terry P. Humphreys, Kristen N. Jozkowski, and Zoë D. Peterson. 2016. "The Complexities of Sexual Consent Among College Students: A Conceptual and Empirical Review." *The Journal of Sex Research* 53(4–5):457–487.

PettyJohn, Morgan E., Finneran K. Muzzey, Megan K. Maas, and Heather L. McCauley. 2019. "#HowIWillChange: Engaging Men and Boys in the #MeToo Movement." *Psychology of Men & Masculinities* 20(4):612–622.

Pinciotti, Caitlin M. and Holly K. Orcutt. 2017. "Understanding Gender Differences in Rape Victim Blaming: The Power of Social Influence and Just World Beliefs." *Journal of Interpersonal Violence* 36(1–2):255–275.

Rainn.org. 2020a. "The Vast Majority of Perpetrators Will Not Go to Jail or Prison." *RAINN*. Retrieved February 15, 2022 (www.rainn.org/statistics/criminal-justice-system).

Rainn.org. 2020b. "Victims of Sexual Violence: Statistics." *RAINN*. Retrieved February 15, 2022 (www.rainn.org/statistics/victims-sexual-violence).

Ransom, Jan. 2020. "Harvey Weinstein Is Found Guilty of Sex Crimes in #MeToo Watershed." *The New York Times*, February 24. Retrieved February 4, 2022 (www.nytimes.com/2020/02/24/nyregion/harvey-weinstein-trial-rape-verdict.html).

Rochon, Thomas R. 1998. *Culture Moves: Ideas, Activism, and Changing Values*. Princeton, NJ: Princeton University Press.

Rosenblatt, Alan and Celinda Lake. 2018. "Social Media Reveal the Story Arc Republicans Used to Defend Kavanaugh." *The Nation*. Retrieved February 4, 2022 (www.thenation.com/article/archive/social-media-kavanaugh-gop-message/).

Swidler, Ann. 1986. "Culture in Action: Symbols and Strategies." *American Sociological Review* 51(2):273–286.

Szekeres, Hanna, Eric Shuman, Tamar Saguy. 2020. "Views of Sexual Assault Following #MeToo: The Role of Gender and Individual Differences." *Personality and Individual Differences*. 166(110203):1–6.

7

INNOVATORS SPEAK OUT ABOUT SEXUAL ASSAULT IN THE #METOO ERA

"I've Learned to Just Stop Taking Shit": Speaking Out

Maram, a 21-year-old Middle Eastern woman, described how she at first accepted and then began to confront the men who harassed her at her job as a coffee shop barista. She shared how "a little group of old men" who were "creeps" would call her "sexy" and "beautiful" every day: "They would harass me straight to my face. And in the beginning, they took advantage of my customer service smile and attitude. I just accepted it and moved on." Although Maram did not report this behavior to her supervisor, she came to realize that she did not have to accept harassment. She "started being mean" by calling them "gross" and "grandpa" or "uncle" in Arabic to "emasculate them" and to "disarm them with my attitude." She concluded, "I've learned to just stop taking shit." Like Maram, women have changed how they respond to sexual harassment and sexual assault as a result of the rapidly changing culture of the #MeToo era. Some have posted their experiences on social media or spoken about them publicly for the first time, while others have responded in private ways. These responses suggest that the #MeToo movement's frame has moved into everyday life as the gender revolution becomes diffused among the general population.

Although sexual harassment is still ubiquitous, it is increasingly challenged in the #MeToo era. Despite variation in estimates, one study found that 59 percent of women experienced sexual harassment or unwanted sexual advances (Graf 2018). Another national study found even higher prevalence: 81 percent of women reported experiencing some form of sexual harassment or assault in their lifetime and 51 percent reported experiencing unwelcome sexual touching (Stop Street Harassment 2018). The federal Equal Employment Opportunity

DOI: 10.4324/9781003225331-11

Commission, which is charged with enforcing civil rights laws, including those related to gender discrimination, received more complaints as #MeToo gained steam. There was a 13.6 percent increase in sexual harassment complaints between 2017 and 2018, and this increase held steady in 2019 (U.S. Equal Employment Opportunity Commission 2019). Due to changes in the nature of work as a result of the COVID-19 pandemic in 2020, including increased remote work, complaints after this time may need to be considered separately.

Although public revelations of sexual assault and harassment continue to explode in the news media, we did not anticipate that interviewees in our focus groups would come forward with their deeply personal stories in a group of strangers. Moreover, we did not ask any interview questions about these experiences, but participants were quick to share them voluntarily. Rather than shame, silence, and hiding their stories, the courage of these public revelations shows that #MeToo has influenced people's everyday lives. The visibility of these experiences suggests that the movement has influenced not only leaders and celebrities but also ordinary people, on the ground, in their everyday lives. This alignment with the #MeToo movement's frame suggests the power of social movement diffusion.

That is, experiences are becoming public in unprecedented ways. Angel, a 54-year-old Black woman, described how her own trauma with rape as a teenager was ignored during the 1980s. The police investigated her report, but "it was dropped": "When I was a teenager, I was raped. I never talked about it. There was nothing else said about it to this day. So I get the assault, but nobody cares." Angel went on to describe the lifelong impact in terms of lasting flashbacks: "These memories are still taking precedence in our lives. We listen to music or we see something visually, and it takes us back to that memory of being assaulted or raped." For her, these traumatic memories have a new outlet in the #MeToo movement, and Angel drew on metaphors of speaking ("platform" and "discuss") to explain its impact. Survivors "need a *platform* in order to be able *to discuss* these things that happened to them with other women who understand—and men, too, who understand and have empathy and compassion for what they've been through."

A new conceptual framework is growing among innovators in our study that recognizes sexual harassment and assault as a systemic, rather than individual, problem. Unlike many of the resisters, innovators are increasingly viewing male violence as a widespread *social* problem. Even their language draws a clear gendered line, as they emphasize that women ("us" and "we") do *not* accept the definitions or perspectives advanced by men ("you," "they," and "them"). This framework differs from previous eras, especially among the women who came of age in the 1990s and early 2000s, the so-called postfeminist era. Those years have been characterized as individualistic and depoliticized in perceptions of gender inequalities (Aronson 2017; Aronson 2003).

Innovators are using a new framework and language to understand sexual consent; in doing so, they create social and cultural change. Women's views, which in the past were quite similar to men's, now diverge sharply from men's, many of whom resist these changes. Innovators are also now more willing to expose the ubiquity of sexual assault and harassment and to openly question the gender inequalities upon which they are based. The power of defining consent on their own terms, as well as speaking openly about their experiences, is an indicator of women's growing agency in the #MeToo era. In their daily lives and in the larger cultural context, innovators are emphasizing women's empowerment and rejecting the idea that men should be excused for inappropriate, or even criminal, actions. As a result of the #MeToo movement, innovators are articulating a collective identity, pushing cultural and social change forward and calling into question male domination. These elements of the #MeToo movement frame are all part of the gender revolution. In addition, men's innovative perspectives overlap with those of women's in three primary areas: viewing sexual assault as a widespread social problem, supporting the women who come forward in public cases, and embracing positive views of #MeToo more generally.

"We Have Normalized Rape": Sexual Assault as a Social Problem

The #MeToo movement focuses on widespread violence against women. The rates are disturbing: One-quarter to one-third of undergraduate women had "non-consensual" experiences while on campus (Koss et al. 1987; Elger 2019; Hirsch and Khan 2020). Young adulthood, between the ages of 18 and 24, is the highest risk period for sexual assault. Although it occurs at alarming rates on college campuses, the rates are similar for those who do not attend college (Sinozich and Langton 2014). Innovators were aware of this high prevalence. In fact, the most commonly used words to describe the problem were "huge" and "big"; many used the word "still" to indicate that this social problem has not gone away despite its increased visibility because of the movement. Olivia, a 27-year-old white woman, said, "I seem to hear about it often, so I feel like it's *still* a *big, big* deal." Sofia, a 21-year-old Latinx woman, used similar words: "It's a *really big* problem. It's *still* going on, and always will be, until we put an end to it." Sexual assault is hidden for many reasons, including fear and shame. For many women, telling their story is very difficult. Rima, a 20-year-old Middle Eastern woman, explained that it takes courage: "Some people take years to work up the *courage* to come out with that."

Yet the #MeToo movement is changing the way that women talk about and report sexual assault. Reports from the Bureau of Labor Statistics Criminal Victimization have suggested that it has influenced reporting. In 2016, it was estimated that 23.2 percent of rape and sexual assaults were reported to police. By 2017, the percentage reported nearly doubled to 40.4 percent (Morgan and Truman 2018: Table 6). Although reporting rates dropped back down to 24.9 percent in 2018, they rose again in 2019, to 33.9 percent (Morgan and Truman 2020: Table 6).

Our interviews suggest that women's everyday concerns about sexual assault are very much at the front of their minds. In a gender-mixed focus group, all three women participants engaged in a detailed discussion when we asked about the prevalence of sexual assault and harassment. Maram started the discussion by saying the problem is "gigantic and super underrepresented." She recalled a campus Take Back the Night event that she attended two years earlier, during which many of her friends shared their experiences during the "speak out." (Take Back the Night, which began in the 1970s, is an annual march to protest violence against women and recognize women whose lives have been touched by violence.) That evening made Maram realize the commonality of sexual assault:

So many people that I walk by every day have been victims and survivors. It just puts everything into perspective. It's a lot. It's not talked about as much as it needs to be. Things are just so normal to us.

She credited a new focus on survivors coming forward with their accounts for encouraging their voices to be heard: "I'm very thankful for the #MeToo movement because now we see how often it occurs." Amelia, a 20-year-old multiracial woman, agreed, stating that the #MeToo movement "showcases a lot of sexual assaults that aren't being reported." Charlotte, a 23-year-old multiracial woman, agreed, "It hasn't really changed the number of cases. It's just as prevalent as it ever was. We didn't realize it because it was concealed so much." Amelia hoped that increased visibility would lead to "better resources," like expanded rape kits, so that "people could get the consequences they deserve."

For innovators, sexual assault was not just an individual experience of a small number of women. Rather, they viewed the normalization of rape culture as a broad-scale social problem. They pointed to how the #MeToo movement has redefined this social problem through public visibility. Alyssa, a 29-year-old Black woman, said, "It's rape culture. We have *normalized* rape. We've *normalized* sexual assault." She expressed concern about the large number of cases that she read in the newspaper every day: "Women have been degraded or have been assaulted or raped or whatnot. The way that has been *normalized* in American culture is really sickening to me. And it's a *very huge, huge* problem." Alyssa emphasized that most people are "numb" to this issue and praised the #MeToo movement for revealing its prevalence: "I'm really glad that the #MeToo movement is around to bring these things to light because it needs to be shown. It needs to be brought to life."

The women in the focus groups emphasized their collective identity as *women*. They saw sexual assault not as an isolated experience of a few women but in terms of a broader rape culture that reflects gender inequalities. Christina, a 36-year-old Black woman, thought that society should reverse the way that children are socialized: "Instead of just teaching our daughters about not getting raped, let's teach our sons about not committing rape." She went on to emphasize awareness of women's collective interests, calling men "they" and contrasting them with women's issues (labeled "our"):

> Men just don't see *our* issues as *their* issues. A lot of young men don't have children. And even men with children still can't see that these are issues that their daughters are going to face, issues that their wives are going through, if *they* are not a part of the *change*, or don't become a part of the *change*.

Christina made a link with the #MeToo movement's divisions between genders, as she suggested that men should start to "see *our* issues as *their* issues" in order to "become part of the *change*." This perspective focuses not on individual responses to women's vulnerability to sexual assault (in which women take steps as individuals to minimize its likelihood) but on a *collective* response. The collective response involves men recognizing women's issues as their own and taking steps to "become a part of the change." These innovators viewed sexual assault and harassment as a significant *social* problem. Thus, the gender revolution has helped to develop a collective identity among women that emphasizes the ubiquity of sexual assault and increasingly calls into question male violence against women.

"Protecting Yourself": Fear and Vulnerability

Innovators fused traditional fears of stranger attacks with an awareness that most sexual assault occurs between people who know each other. In an era when public revelations are common, women felt vulnerable and always at risk. Yet traditional "rape scripts" focusing on stranger attacks teach women to fear strangers instead of people they know (Stanko 1995). In contrast, the National Institute of Justice (2010) reported that 90 percent of college women who experience sexual assault know their perpetrators.

Innovators expressed concern about such assaults. Brianna, a 21-year-old Black woman, described her fear of being alone in a car with a man she knew: "Someone could just come up and grab my boob. That makes me feel like maybe I don't want to ever be the last two people in the car, especially if it's just me and you." Brianna mentioned the need for constant vigilance: "You are aware of your space more when it comes to that person because they think it's acceptable for someone to do that." Kayla, also a 21-year-old Black woman, described her discomfort about being the only woman in a room: "When you walk into a room, I'm sure all of you have felt it, you're very acutely aware of, 'I'm the only woman in here.' Or, 'I'm the only Black woman.' You don't want to be that girl." These comments suggest that recent efforts to "believe" survivors are uneven. In a context in which women of color are less likely to be believed than white women, Kayla's intersectional framing makes sense.

Many of the women also mentioned traditional rape scripts and the ways they had internalized a fear of stranger assaults. Alyssa tried to prevent sexual assault through her daily actions, including not "walking at night" and not wearing clothing that draws "attention" to herself. She said there are "certain things that, as a woman, I have to really be concerned about" that men don't have to consider:

> Even how I dress when I do go out somewhere. What I have on may be fine. But then I will find myself looking at it. Is this too low? Is this too short? I do whatever I can do to not draw attention to myself.

Amelia also questioned what she wore and whether she should talk with someone "alone": "I should dress a certain way, so people don't think of me *this* way. Or, 'Should I speak with you alone?' Or I want to look cute, but I don't want to wear a skirt because I'm scared." These constant internal dialogues represent a type of risk analysis in which women weigh their actions and vulnerability to sexual assault, typically by strangers. Kayla said that women who come forward receive the message that they are to blame when they are asked, "Well, why did you wait so long?" and "Well, what were you wearing?" She rejected these victim-blaming narratives, reporting that the "plethora of different questions that are asked" serve to "beat you down" and diminish reporting.

Several innovators recounted a specific exercise that they saw on social media that revealed gender differences in daily concerns. Charlotte described gender differences "in terms of protecting yourself":

> That post going around about what men may do to protect themselves: Men had maybe one thing on the list and women had this whole list, like pepper spray or keeping a key out for whatever I might face, in terms of always being aware. Women have to do that more than men. We actually had to make a list like that in one of my classes. And all the guys in my class were so shocked by all the things.

When it came time to raise their hands to indicate that they had engaged in each type of rape or assault prevention method, "Every single girl in the class" did so, in contrast to "maybe a couple of guys." Rima said, "Each girl had raised their hand at least five times. It's just so different in terms of protecting ourselves and what *we* do *every single day.*" Thus, the daily experience of being a woman still involves a pervasive fear of sexual assault from strangers and responsibility for prevention.

Mia, a 20-year-old white woman, also discussed gender differences in perceptions of vulnerability: "I don't think men experience it nearly as much. There's so many things that men don't think about when they're in public that women do." She gave a list of women's restrictions and strategies for rape prevention:

> Women don't walk outside unprepared at night. They have that thought in the back of their mind. They unlock their door and lock it quickly. They make

sure no one's in the back seat. They make sure they have some kind of weapon, even their keys.

In one of Mia's classes, there was a discussion about such strategies and she reported that the men in her class had "never once thought about all of these things. Women are way more aware of it because it's a looming threat in everyday life." Alex, a 21-year-old multiracial nonbinary interviewee, agreed with Mia,

> Women are desensitized to the little, everyday things. You go to your car and you make sure your keys are in your hand. That's just normal. It becomes normal. Protecting yourself becomes the norm. And men usually don't have that as their norm, thinking that they have to protect themselves.

Nadine, a 20-year-old white woman, described a discussion in one of her classes in which one woman took out her bike chain and said, "This is what I use." The men in class were "astonished" that women "have to think about this." Nadine pointed to gender "differences in perception" and said that "maybe if a man had a daughter, he would think about it." These comments suggest that although discourse and perceptions of stranger attacks have shifted as a result of #MeToo, some old cultural narratives hold firm. These traditional rape scripts blame women for sexual assault, emphasizing that they must individually protect themselves from attacks.

"In My Situation, It Wasn't Really Like That": Sexual Assault in the #MeToo Era

Coinciding with their idea that affirmative consent should be the standard, the focus group women described experiences that violated this definition. Alyssa contrasted her experiences with the way that sexual assault is displayed in movies and books:

> I thought of sexual assault and harassment or rape as something that was forcibly done, where someone's actually pinning you down and forcing themselves on you. That's what I thought it was. In my situation, it wasn't really like that.

Alyssa's description of her own sexual assault involved the absence of affirmative consent: "They just kind of did it, but I didn't say no. I didn't say stop. But I knew at that point that I felt very uncomfortable and that I didn't want it to happen."

Compared to previous eras, when survivors often did not define their nonconsensual experiences as rape or sexual assault (Donde et al. 2018), innovators in the #MeToo era see anything outside of affirmative consent as assault. While

Alyssa stated that although there is not a "clear definition of sexual assault, rape, or whatnot," she argued that definitions should be based on *women's* perceptions:

> It can be defined as *however you may feel*. If you feel that you were violated, if you feel uncomfortable, if you feel some sort of uneasiness about it, then it is what it is. I think you can absolutely *define it how you want to define it*.

This definition validates survivors' perspectives and places their definitions at the center of the interaction.

Many interviewees directly linked their support for the #MeToo movement with their own experiences with sexual trauma. Jasmine, a 40-year-old Black woman, discussed flashbacks and post-traumatic stress disorder (PTSD) in a deeply personal way:

> Women or people who go through a traumatic experience, they bury it. They forget it until something else comes about that triggers it. A scent, a smell, someone else's story, a setting. That's when all those memories come back. And most of the time you don't remember. You can't remember—check it from my experience. You can't remember your settings. Who was there, who was at this party, who was there. But you could remember the exact details of what that man did to you and that lets me know that most of the time the story is true. What do they call it? PTSD. That's how you bury it. And then something else comes back and it brings it back.

This description of PTSD suggests that #MeToo has been so personal for many survivors because it reactivates old memories to hear others' similar experiences. Jasmine pointed out that women telling their stories is a method of healing: "That's what's happening with a lot of these women. It's great for women to voice what happened to them. It's a way for them to move forward in life."

Instead of hiding in shame, a culture around visibility and speaking out has emerged. As more survivors speak out, cultural ideas about survivors and sexual assault are transformed. This increased visibility lets survivors see that their previously private traumatic experiences are actually shared and common. In the digital age, the use of #MeToo hashtags on social media has led to the rapid dissemination of innovative ideas to others.

Definitions of sexual assault have changed over time; new definitions are based on an affirmative consent standard. Jasmine's account illustrates the assertion by innovators that some women did not realize that they had been assaulted until the #MeToo movement became visible. Despite being the only woman in her five-person focus group, Jasmine assertively challenged the way that the men in the room defined sexual assault: "I think women are sexually assaulted on a daily basis, and half of them don't even know they're sexually assaulted." She described its pervasiveness and the way women are both "desensitized" and "programmed to just accept" it. In her definition, sexual assault included an unwanted "slap on the butt" or "rubbing your shoulder." This broad definition was based on a lack of affirmative consent and, as we saw in Chapter 6, was vigorously challenged by the resisters in her focus group.

Likewise, Rima said, "Someone could be raped and not even know it." She emphasized that not defining rape as rape differs from silence: "Someone could be raped and not even have said anything." Isabella, a 21-year-old Latinx woman, agreed, "Some people don't even know that they're going through sexual assault, like when you're married in a toxic relationship. You don't see the red signs. You don't see what's going on." Drawing on metaphors of "speaking" and "voice" and contrasting them with darkness, Isabella credited the #MeToo movement for changing how women define their own experiences by "allowing people that have been *shut down* and not given a *voice to speak up.*" Suggesting that further change is needed, she continued, "But still, there's millions that are *still in the shadows* and still don't have the ability to *speak up.*" Although being in the "shadows" implies shame and hiding one's experiences, Isabella's previous quote indicates that some women are too enmeshed in gender-dominant ("toxic") relationships to see their own subordination.

As a result of the movement, many women disclosed experiences that they did not define as sexual assault at the time they occurred. Kayla thought that women might not initially define a sexual encounter as sexual assault but may later wonder whether they explicitly said no. She explained, "That also leads into why certain people don't report what happened to them, because they're like, 'Well, if I sit and think about it, I don't necessarily remember explicitly saying, "I don't want to do this."'" In a familiar pattern, Kayla also discussed the "normalization" of sexual assault and the way she came to define her own experiences differently later in life: "It's pretty sad, because I realized once I got older that stuff that happened when I was younger was not right." After mentioning that she used to view coercive heterosexual romantic relationships as acceptable, such as the relationships presented in the *Twilight* series, she later realized that this approach "wasn't OK. When I got older, I was like, 'What the hell is this?' What was I reading? Why was this OK? I was sort of pushed to believe that these things were OK."

Kayla's redefinition of her own experiences coincided with both getting older and the rise of the #MeToo movement. She began to see that she had internalized an acceptance of sexual assault:

I didn't realize that I was a part of that. You would be sitting around with your friends, and you'd be like, "Oh, this guy came up and I think he tried to touch my butt." And you and your friends are all laughing about it. I think you get taught at a young age that certain things come with the territory of being a woman. It shouldn't have been something that I laughed off or that anybody else around me should've laughed off. But it gets internalized.

Charlotte agreed, "So many people are coming out with that. People who didn't realize they might have been raped or whatever in the first place are understanding that's what happened. So they have something to say now."

These quotes suggest that the diffusion of the #MeToo movement has led to a context in which innovators are redefining unwanted sexual encounters as sexual assault. They are also speaking out about their own experiences and challenging both inequalities in socialization and the normalization of sexual assault in women's everyday lives. In this context, innovators are clearly breaking away from past traditions of silence, shame, and hiding. They are also rejecting patriarchal conditions that tie such experiences to "the territory of being a woman."

At the same time, these accounts hint at self-blame, as women question their own previous views in light of changing definitions. Although these innovators may look back on their previous views critically, these reevaluations should be understood as a result of the dramatic changes that have resulted in new expectations. In fact, as culture shifts, it takes time for new norms and ideas to take hold.

"Boys Hit Them on Their Butt at Seven": Socialization and Sexual Assault

Innovators opposed gendered socialization that leads women to accept sexual assault as simply part of their daily lives. Jasmine stated,

> Little girls don't even know the definition of sexual assault. There are certain things that women don't pick up on because they've been desensitized. And their parents have always said, "Boys will be boys, they're just playing," or, "If he does that, it means he likes you." Or, "If you're dressed like that, you deserved it." No big deal.

Brianna echoed these points, "Boys are socialized differently from girls at a very young age. Boys are taught to be aggressive and girls are not taught that typically." As a result, Brianna argued, girls often experience "inappropriate touches" at a young age. She said that sexual assault

> happens to people as young as three and four. Girls come home saying boys hit them on their butt at seven. That's still an act. To them, that can still be considered sexual assault because it's an inappropriate touch that they didn't consent to.

She attributed this problem to socialization, as "parents aren't having that conversation" with their boys. As a result, "there is confusion around consent" on the part of adult men. Brianna said that most parents dismiss the problem in terms of, "Oh well, they're just playing and they're just kids." However, she attributed adult male violence to developing "bad habits" that are not "nipped in the bud" as children. Brianna explained that men do not see "grabbing" or "touching" as sexual assault, while women do. Men do not consider these actions "as big of a deal compared to someone who was raped." However, Brianna saw gender differences in perceptions as only "a difference in the severity." Jasmine agreed, "It is a big deal. I think we've been programmed to just accept."

Innovators often mentioned traditional rape scripts while simultaneously rejecting them. Alexandra, a 38-year-old Black woman, said that girls are socialized to play "hide, go get it" while boys "chase the girl around the playground." This "rite of passage" results in boys thinking, "Oh, I won." This unequal situation breeds men, adversarially called "they," who do not understand affirmative consent: "I talk to guys and they think, 'Oh, she didn't actually say no.' *They* didn't *hear* the word no." In contrast to Alexandra's belief in affirmative consent, it is only when women say no that "*they* [men] know they did something wrong." Alex linked these gender differences in socialization to street harassment: "It also starts very young, especially for women that develop early. Just walking down the street. You get comments. You get leers. You get the second glance, even the touches." They saw the ubiquity of harassment as incongruent with an individualized solution to this social problem: "You're just supposed to do stuff to prevent rape for yourself." Jada, an 18-year-old Black woman, agreed, "At a young age, *we're* taught that if something happens, not necessarily to brush it off, but *we* just don't know what to do after that." This socialization of women to passively accept men's sexual advances is consistent with traditional rape scripts and heteronormative initiator-gatekeeper assumptions. As a result, men are not being "actually educated" about a "true definition" of consent.

Innovators' affirmative consent standard differed greatly from the standards of many men because gendered socialization carries over to adulthood. Kayla said, "I don't hear anybody sitting their sons down and saying, 'OK, I'm going to teach you about consent right now.'" In Kayla's focus group, other innovators joined in a dialogue about how boys' lack of socialization about consent negatively affects men's behaviors as adults. Zainab, a 32-year-old Middle Eastern woman, stated that the problem is that men "don't know the definition of consent." Kayla continued, "I think it's not taught to *them*." Zainab agreed, "Right, exactly." This adversarial language, drawing on words like "they" and "them," clearly distinguishes men's views from their own.

Jasmine described a past encounter between her boyfriend and his teenage son that disturbed her: "The boy came home and my boyfriend said, 'Oh, you got some, cool.'" Jasmine was outraged: "Would you say that to your daughter? You know what I mean? You're teaching your son that it's 'get as many as you can. Score as many as you can. Take this girl home. Do this.'" She viewed this dangerous socialization as widespread: "We will say, 'Well, is that your girlfriend?' Or, 'How many girlfriends?' Or, 'How many kisses did you get?'" Jasmine thought this emphasis on "wanting" and "getting more" was unacceptable: "I think it's a matter of time and educating the younger people and the generations behind us." Alyssa agreed, using the word "you" to refer to men,

> When we're teaching about sexual assault or whatnot, I think we need to also teach, "OK, *you* don't do this." Like if someone says no, no. That's it. Or ask about consent instead of putting all the responsibility on women.

These innovators thus challenged gendered socialization that contributed to the ubiquity of sexual assault and fought against the chasm on definitions of consent between genders.

Innovators called out the TV, film, and music industries for normalizing sexual assault. Kayla discussed the popularity of accepted sexual assault scenes in movies:

> When you think of your favorite romance scene where he grabs her arm, which in real life would be super aggressive, grabs her arm, spins her around, and just kisses her. And she's supposed to think, "Oh wow, this means he loves me." And things like that are normalized. A lot of time we normalize behavior that if in real life this happened, you wouldn't be saying that.

Conveying romance in aggressive ways negatively socializes girls. Zainab had to stop watching the television show *Scandal* because it led to "flashbacks": "It's set up to be romantic, but no. It's basically, you're getting raped." Harper, a 23-year-old multiracial woman, mentioned that rap music promotes the exploitation of women: "'I just threw 20 dollars to a stripper and she did everything I wanted.' Women aren't portrayed the same way in music as men. It's terrible." According to these innovators, such media contributes to violence against women.

"I Don't Know How to Deal with This Situation": Changing Norms around Sexual Harassment

The new norms being created were evident in innovators' conversations. Part of the transition in redefining previously acceptable experiences as unacceptable has led to confusion about how to interact, especially where to draw the line between "flirting" and harassment. Ling, a 29-year-old international student, described receiving inappropriate texts from a male friend and not knowing how to respond: "He sent me some emojis with a private part of the man." Alexandra laughed under her breath, and asked, "Was it an eggplant? Was it the purple emoji?" Ling said, "The emoji is very cute and also very, very bad." She laughed nervously and said, "I don't know how to deal with this situation." As an international student, she thought that this type of communication might be common between men and women in the United States: "I don't know where he got this emoji, but I believe that maybe when men and women chat, they probably use that a lot. But I don't know." She was unsure how to respond but settled on "changing the topic" to prevent him from sending more of those texts. Ling was unsure whether he was trying to "make a joke or didn't think that it was a big deal" when he sent another emoji and "after that he just stopped." Alexandra pointed out that the interaction was confusing:

> We could easily say that was inappropriate for him to say that, but she doesn't even know how to say, "That was inappropriate." And so he's probably thinking, "Oh, I'm sending this as a nice way to flirt, without actually sending her a picture of my cock." So you see how those messages get blurred?

As the #MeToo era ushers in new norms, confusion results when someone operates with old patriarchal definitions.

Likewise, Jasmine was unsure whether to report her coworkers for sexual harassment: "Every day at work, I see something. And every day a coworker does something. And I'm always, like, 'Should I go to Human Resources?' I'm always questioning it." Jasmine was reluctant to report one man because at 45 years old, he came of age before the #MeToo movement. She implied that he was operating with obsolete definitions and understandings of what constitutes sexual harassment when she concluded, "I don't think he means any harm. But I think a certain generation of men think that certain things are OK." Thus, although Jasmine herself classified her coworker's behavior as sexual harassment, she wrote it off because he came of age before new norms had taken hold.

Generational differences in what men view as acceptable behavior left innovators feeling vulnerable to older men's advances. Riley, an 18-year-old Black woman, recounted a "gross" interaction with an older man when she was 13:

> I was at the dentist with my mom. I was in the lobby. This old man was like, "What's your [phone] number?" And I was like, "No." And he was like, "Are you sure?" And I was like, "Uh-huh" [affirmative]. Then he left, but I was clearly little, so it was gross.

Similarly, Alex received unwanted attention from one of their father's friends:

> My dad has this friend that he's known forever and he's a good guy. He's active in his community. And we were at an event and he was looking me up and down. And at the time I was like 17, 18, and this was a man in his 50s that was staring me up and down. He definitely had that look, just that look you recognize. If he didn't know who my father was, he would've done something. Not necessarily in an abusive way, but he probably would have flirted a bit more.

Alex's parents observed the situation and intervened. Alex reported that their mother "never felt comfortable around him" and their father maintained his distance from the man because "he always does that to women." The other innovators supported Alex, pointing out that one reason why men "get away with" sexual assault is that they are viewed as leaders. Christina said, "He was held in esteem within his community, so everybody was just like, 'Oh, that's him, that's just how he is.'" Christina disagreed with this notion, "That's how a lot of men get away with it, because they are seen to be community involved, and they're leaders, and they take care of the household." In some of these stressful situations, the interviewees were teens when they confronted older, more powerful men.

Innovators also challenged the traditional and stereotypical idea that survivors who are perceived as attractive should "expect" harassment. This type of victim-blaming narrative occurred in their own educational institution, which they thought was supposed to protect them. Zainab described a friend's experiences with sexual harassment by another student and the lack of institutional support that her friend received when she reported it. She said that the staff member essentially blamed her friend for the harassment. Zainab's friend was asked, "Are you just trying to get back at him?" And she was told, "Look at you. You are very beautiful. Of course he's going to be flirting with you." Zainab's friend reported being told that no intervention could take place "until he physically touches you" and that "very, very inappropriate comments and questions" would not prompt intervention.

In Zainab's eyes, the institution turned "it's back on her" through victim blaming and inaction, as the report "didn't go anywhere." She angrily questioned institutional policy, "What if he's shoving you into the back of his car?" Kim, a 27-year-old white woman agreed, "Then it's too late. The university, where I pay to learn, I should be safe, right? Not really." Victim blaming angered interviewees, who viewed them as expressions of structural gender inequality. In rejecting these traditional tropes, they created and insisted on an alternative narrative, one that respected women's right to pursue their education free from harassment.

Kayla dismissed another stereotype: that a victim's attractiveness is "automatically a huge factor in whether or not she gets believed." Kayla said that if a victim "is not conventionally attractive," then her story is doubted. She said that people dismiss the account: "I don't see why he would even want to touch you. I don't see why he would want to do X, Y, and Z to you, because you aren't pretty, because you aren't beautiful." Alternatively, attractive women are believed but harassment is minimized: "Well, you're beautiful, so that's going to happen. You should expect that." Yet these innovators challenged the stereotypical lose-lose situation that survivors often experience. In doing so, they powerfully rejected stereotypes and traditional scripts and were outraged that the harassment was not taken more seriously by the institution.

"People in Power Usually Get Away with That":
Visibility and Power

Due to the public nature of revelations in the #MeToo era, innovators thought that public cases have changed how men and women interact and communicate with each other. Meghan, a 22-year-old white woman, said, "If you have power, you think sexual assault was an OK thing to do, because people in power usually get away with that." She explained her reasoning in terms of lack of accountability, speaking in the first person to represent someone with power:

> I know this is wrong. I'm still going to do it. Because I know at the end of the day nothing is going to happen to me. I'm not going to get punished for it. So I might as well just do it, but I know it's wrong.

Nia, a 49-year-old Black woman, argued likewise that powerful men get away with sexual harassment and assault:

> It started with Trump. So it's not going to stop there, until they make the head guy in charge accountable for his actions. So once you stop the top guy from doing it or getting away with it, the domino effect is going to be there.

Nia labeled the way that "politicians get away with so much" as "horrible, ridiculous and disgraceful."

Innovators thought that popular male entertainers and athletes are often not held accountable. According to Alyssa,

> There's a comedian who was accused of sexual harassment. I think he was masturbating in front of some of his people that he worked with. He admitted it's wrong and that he was going to take time off to himself. And recently he came back to do a comedy show and he was welcomed with applause at his show and just went and did a skit like normal.

Alyssa connected this incident and others that involve politicians: Although "they'll say, 'Oh, this is wrong,' there's some that don't say anything at all. Their silence is a hell of a lot more than what their words can say."

In a similar vein, Kiara, an 18-year-old Black woman, discussed another public case, when Charles H. Ellis III, the bishop who officiated Aretha Franklin's funeral, placed his arm around pop star Ariana Grande and touched her breast. Kiara made it clear that this incident constituted sexual assault:

> First of all, you shouldn't go under her arm, you go around her arm. And then my second thing about it was, breasts are more fatty. You could tell the difference

where you're touching. You know what you're touching. And I thought it was inappropriate. And I think he knew what he was doing.

Christina mentioned that public cases show that women are often regarded as sexual objects by men in power. She pointed to R. Kelly, the singer found guilty in 2021 after decades of sexually exploiting a child, bribery, racketeering, and sex trafficking: "It's a good example of what's really going on, and how women are regarded as objects, as sexual objects, as being less than human. I think people get blinded by celebrity status." Aria, a 21-year-old woman, expressed her anger at how the police investigate accusations against well-known male athletes: "They say, 'Oh yeah, we'll try and get him.' It's been three months. 'Oh, I can't find him.'" Aria questioned the efforts made by the police when she stated, "He's playing a [sports] game and you can't find him? He's right here. Ten thousand people know where he's at." This lack of accountability sends a strong negative message to survivors.

Public cases were a lightning rod for gender divisions and innovators thought that they affected everyday relationships. Kim pointed out that some men posted social media memes that mocked the sexual assault convictions against Bill Cosby. She said of one of these posts, "That's not funny. You're pretty much saying you would rape someone. It's taken so lightly. These guys are reaffirmed that it's OK, over and over again. And then the comments reaffirm it." Lakin, a 22-year-old Black woman, argued that men do not take public cases seriously, mentioning men's posts as evidence: "When I go on social media, I can't tell if some people are being genuine about changing or if they're just cracking jokes." She described one type of post that she viewed many times, in which men said, "Hey, if I did something to you a few years ago, and you think that was sexual assault, I apologize." Lakin was outraged by this lighthearted way that men confronted the #MeToo movement: "Are you actually serious about that or are you just joking around because you think the whole thing is funny?"

Accusations of sexual assault against high-profile men have resulted in an environment in which women perceive men as adversarial toward them. In this context, innovators argued that men protect and support each other. Kim said, "It's polarizing too because men, even if they're *not* rapists and they've *never* done anything wrong sexually to women, they're going to side with men or feel like they're being attacked." She understood this approach as one of vulnerability to accusations: "Somehow they feel like, 'Anyone could do this to me.' They align themselves with, 'He's a guy and I'm a guy and I believe him.' Maybe because they're scared." Despite her sympathy for men's fears of being accused of sexual assault or harassment, she said that men "are not scared for the right reasons." Instead, men feel that "everyone is out to get them now. Everything is a witch hunt." Kim did not agree with this line of thinking and linked gender antagonisms to her own work experience. She described a differential level of mentoring that she received in her internship compared to a male intern because her male supervisor was afraid of being in a room alone with her: "Honestly, I would rather them be scared and leave the door open."

Kayla also used the phrase "witch hunt" to highlight her concern that men do not adequately support women:

> A lot of men think it was some kind of witch hunt rather than women being encouraged to step forward and say, "This happened to me and I want anyone else that this happened to know that they're not alone." I think men feel some camaraderie with other men just based off the fact that they're men.

Kim agreed,

> I feel like men use it as a joke. I've heard guys, when they're acting stupid or whatever, like the other day I heard a guy in one of my classes say, "I don't want to hold the door open for anyone. I don't want to get #MeToo'd." And it's like, what does that even mean? I think I understand what he meant, but it was weird. I feel like people take the #MeToo movement as just another social justice warrior thing. And guys use it as a way to be annoyed with sensitivity or emotional intelligence.

As these innovators were concerned about resisters' trivialization of sexual assault, they disputed concerns about the purpose of the #MeToo movement. Rather than the movement undermining men's rights, innovators asserted that its purpose was supporting women, which they saw as a distinct and necessary approach.

In drawing attention to public cases of sexual assault, these innovators exhibited a sharp critique of gender inequalities. They rejected arrangements that subordinated women's self-determination. They illustrated that public cases and the discussion around them have pushed public consciousness, at least among women, toward greater recognition of new ways of understanding sexual assault and harassment. By reinforcing #MeToo movement frames, these innovators move the gender revolution further into people's everyday understandings of larger cultural events.

"It's Given a Voice to the Voiceless": Support for #MeToo

About three-quarters (n = 26, 76.5%) of the women and nonbinary interviewees (from all backgrounds) expressed wholehearted support for the #MeToo movement (see Table 7.1). In doing so, they emphasized a sense of collective identity and embraced an expansion of women's power. In particular, they thought that #MeToo provides an unprecedented space for survivors to tell their stories. In this approach, many drew on metaphors to vividly contrast what it means to come forward rather than to stay silent. When we asked about how they saw the #MeToo

TABLE 7.1 Women and Nonbinary Interviewees' Perspectives by Racial and Ethnic Background

	Types of perspective			
	Resister	Innovator	Fused	Total
White	0	7	0	7
Middle Eastern or North African	0	3	0	3
Hispanic/Latinx	0	2	0	2
Black	0	11	4	15
Asian American	0	1	1	2
Multiracial	0	1	3	4
Unknown	0	1	0	1
Percent (n)	0	76.5 (26)	23.5 (8)	100 (34)

movement, they drew on words like "light," "speak," "platform," "courage," and "voice" and contrasted them with the time before the movement, when survivors stayed "silent" and in the "shadows." The linguistic juxtaposition of light and dark, as well as voice and silence, represents an awareness of a shift from private, hidden sexual assault to its visibility and recognition. This process connects women together, builds collective identity, and represents social movement ideology diffusion.

Maram said that she is "thankful" for the movement because it "encourages more women to *speak out*." The movement emboldened her to share her own experiences of sexual assault with other women: "I definitely felt more comfortable talking to my friends about it." Likewise, Alyssa said that #MeToo is "great." She contrasted the metaphors of telling, talking, "voice," and "platform" with those who did not "talk" and were "voiceless" in previous eras:

> It's great that it's given a *voice* to the *voiceless*. I've had friends that, ever since the #MeToo movement has gained popularity, have come in and confided in me about their experiences with sexual harassment or assault and they've never even *talked* about it. Now we've just given people a *platform* to *say* what's on their mind and in their heart and to also be able to *tell* their story and to *tell* their truth.

Sharing these experiences with other women creates a sense of collective identity through speaking about one's experiences. Here, the #MeToo movement reignites the practice of sharing experiences as part of consciousness-raising and collective identity building that was important during the second-wave women's movement. At the same time, the movement departs from the past in its public, rather than private, nature (Chandra and Erlingsdóttir 2020), as digital communications are spread over vast social networks.

In fact, the courage to speak out publicly is built into the movement's ideological frame. In this way, the diffusion of #MeToo movement ideology can be seen as non-activists tell their stories and redefine their experiences and identities in relation to the movement. As women share their experiences, other women develop the capacity to come forward. Jasmine emphasized that women's "courage" is contagious:

> I think the #MeToo movement is great. I think it's great that so many women are *coming forward with their stories*. A lot of them were too scared, ashamed. *One person comes forward, that brings the courage of all the other women*. For a woman to come forward and *tell her story* takes a lot of *strength*.

This diffusion process happens as digital and social media transmits social movement ideologies from person to person and is supported by other women.

Innovators pointed out that as social change occurs in one arena, it expands into other areas of women's everyday lives. Although social movement scholarship theorizes about diffusion to non-activists, this spillover to other domains suggests a process that is more broadly transformative. More and more, the diffusion of movement frames leads non-activist women to refuse to accept gender inequalities in other life spheres. Jasmine illustrated this transformation process when she said, "The #MeToo movement *empowered* a lot of women to come forward, not just to come forward with their stories, but *empowered* them to just go *further in life*, to *not* be so *overshadowed* by a male." As we saw in Chapter 3, interviewees thought that #MeToo and the rise of women in politics expanded equality in other male-dominated spheres and led to the development of women's self-confidence and embracing a collective identity.

Nadine emphasized the connection between the movement and the goal of pushing social change forward when she said, "Now, with the #MeToo movement, *we're* definitely trying, *we're* starting a change that should have happened a long time ago." Mia responded, focusing on "courage" and shifts in how women are perceived, "I think that it has to do with the *courage*, because women are finally being *taken seriously* with #MeToo and Time's Up." In a way that highlighted their collective identity as women and the impact of the gender revolution, these innovators thus emphasized the connection between #MeToo, politics, and social change. As they saw it, the movement has broadly transformed many arenas.

Innovators recognized that these social and cultural changes have led to gendered conflict. In particular, women's rejection of male dominance as a result of #MeToo has resulted in a battle between women and men. Nia used the phrase "bitter battle" to describe women's refusal to accept inequalities in the Trump era:

> The president of the United States is given a green card to everybody but the women. The women have also given the green card to say, "We are *not going*

to take it anymore. We're not doing this." So now it's a *bitter battle, the #MeToo movement versus anybody.*

Nia's adversarial framing implies that as women stand up for themselves, the movement can attack "anybody." As a result, Charlotte reported that men and women had different reactions to the movement: "For women, it's more like a way to be more *courageous*, and for men, it's more of a reason to be scared now." She emphasized that women need to continue to be "conscious in their environment, protecting themselves," while men need to be "careful not to make a wrong move" or an action that is "perceived" to be wrong. Taylor, an 18-year-old Black woman, was annoyed that "there's a large population of men that feel that they're being hated on because of the movement" because #MeToo is "really just about change and how we should fix society." Taylor continued, saying that the movement "is happening for a good reason. We do need the change, but men are holding us back." These quotes suggest that #MeToo has led to a perceived battle between women and men, in which women's courage is leading to men's fear, while most men are resisters who are holding back more complete social transformations.

"This Could Have Been My Daughter or My Sister": Men's Innovative Perspectives

While this chapter centers on the experiences and perspectives of innovator women, some of the men also expressed innovative ideas. This approach represents more than just a politically correct response and appears to be a genuine concern for reducing gender inequalities and supporting the #MeToo movement. Half of the men (20 out of 40) embraced either exclusively progressive views on gender (n = 5, 12.5 percent) or, more commonly, fused discourses containing both progressive and gender-traditional views (n = 15, 37.5 percent; see Table 7.2). Men's innovative perspectives overlapped with those of women's in three primary areas: viewing sexual assault as a widespread social problem, supporting the women who come forward in public cases, and embracing positive views of the #MeToo movement more generally. Although those with fused perspectives did not fully support transformations from the gender revolution, even only partial innovation can move social change forward.

Many of these men diverged from the men who were resisters to emphasize the high prevalence of sexual harassment and assault. Like the innovators quoted earlier, this perspective recognizes these issues as social problems rather than seeing them within a more individualized framework. Leo, an 18-year-old Asian American man, called them "big problems since they are still occurring." Two men referred to specific statistics to demonstrate the common nature of sexual assault. Malik, a 19-year-old Middle Eastern man, stated, "One in five or one in four college students are sexually assaulted. That's crazy. There's a definite

TABLE 7.2 Distribution of Men's Perspectives by Racial and Ethnic Background

	Types of perspective			
	Resister	Innovator	Fused	Total
White	4	3	6	13
Middle Eastern or North African	4	1	2	7
Hispanic/Latinx	3	0	0	3
Black	1	0	2	3
Asian American	4	1	5	10
Multiracial	2	0	0	2
Unknown	2	0	0	2
Percent (n)	50% (20)	12.5% (5)	37.5% (15)	100% (40)

problem there." Similarly, William, an 18-year-old white man said, "1 in 6 . . . It's a very big problem." Derek, a 22-year-old white man, said that women have to deal with this issue on a "grand scale." Aran, a 20-year-old Asian American man, called the problem "huge." He was concerned that comedians "joke" about sexual assault, which he saw as a "serious matter." Jin, a 21-year-old Asian American man, defined "locker-room talk" as common in its prevalence rather than as discussions that are a function of private, male-only spaces: "It's called 'locker-room talk' for a reason, because it happens pretty much everywhere." Adnan, a 21-year-old Middle Eastern man, called sexual assault a "huge problem." He said that people "hear about" sexual assault "on a daily" basis and referred to its "normalization" as "a really big problem." He concluded that "we have a long way to go."

Several men mentioned underreporting, including Luke, a 22-year-old white man, who used "but" to transition away from a resister's discussion of "false" accusations: "There are some false accusations, *but* there's a lot that aren't reported." Deven, a 20-year-old Asian American man, agreed, "Even today, it's not that easy for women to come out and say that they've been sexually assaulted. So a lot of it is unreported to the police." Although this perspective was rare among focus group men, their recognition of the widespread prevalence of sexual assault is necessary for it to begin to be defined as a social problem.

Two of the men reported seeing sexual harassment among their friends and coworkers, and these realizations helped them develop an understanding of how widespread it is. Caleb, a 21-year-old white man, described seeing his coworkers in the restaurant industry regularly sexually harassed on the job:

There was a lot that went on. Although there was never any sexual violence, there was never any full-on assault, there was a lot of harassment. There was a lot. It wasn't vague harassment either. It was unwanted touching, unwanted comments, unwanted advances, and it would happen frequently.

Although Caleb did not define regular "unwanted touching" as a form of sexual violence, he approached the women who were harassed and asked, "Are you alright?" and "Why did you tolerate that?" He reported what they told him:

> 50/50. Half of it was about, "OK, well, I don't want to jeopardize my job. I don't want to jeopardize my position here." The other half almost minimized it themselves. Like, "Oh, it wasn't that bad. I've just gotten used to it. Like that's what [this person] does." I found that kind of scary. It's the *normalization* from the victims themselves, and I just thought that that was the strangest response that I ever got.

Witnessing sexual harassment firsthand led Caleb to recognize that it is underreported. However, Caleb minimized minor instances of harassment by calling them "lower-level things" when he said, "They're definitely underreported. I'm not saying that violent rapes go unreported, although they do, but I think that a lot of the lower-level things go unreported."

Dominic, a 20-year-old white man in the same focus group, went further, drawing on an "iceberg" analogy to describe systemic underreporting of all types of experiences:

> I know all the way from the least to the most serious. From my friends I know stuff goes unreported, no matter what it is, all the time. There's not a single doubt in my mind that the amount that gets reported is just the tip of the iceberg compared to what there actually is.

In summary, these men expressed innovative ideas that recognized the widespread nature of sexual assault and harassment and its impact on survivors. One factor in the development of this perspective appears to be knowing someone with these experiences or witnessing it firsthand.

Additionally, although a minority, some men voiced their support for women survivors who had spoken out in high-profile cases with well-known male perpetrators and a few even linked these cases to gendered power dynamics. Much of the discussion around this topic was in the context of the confirmation hearings of Supreme Court Justice Brett Kavanaugh. While these men stated that they initially believed Kavanaugh's side of the story, they shared in their focus groups their eventual belief that Kavanaugh's accuser, Christine Blasey Ford, was telling the truth and voiced support for her as a survivor.

For example, Joel, a 20-year-old white man, criticized Kavanaugh's past behaviors and actions while discussing this case:

> I would disagree that Kavanaugh had such a squeaky-clean record. From what I understand, he had a pretty big drinking problem when he was around

college age. And when he would drink, he was not the nicest of people. And there have been several stories that can back that up.

Joel explained how at the beginning, he viewed each side of the story equally, but learning about Kavanaugh's past behavior helped him to eventually believe Ford over Kavanaugh: "I tried to go in 50/50, give each person an equal chance. But that really pushed me over to the side where I wouldn't be surprised if someone like him were guilty of that." Although Joel tried to stay neutral, accounts of Kavanaugh's potentially predatory behavior in the past moved his views. Caleb also believed Ford over Kavanaugh: "I thought that her testimony was very effective. I shifted away from giving him the benefit of the doubt and shifted more to a position of, 'Wow, he could have actually done this.'" Although both of these men ultimately were against Kavanaugh's confirmation and voiced their support for his accuser, they admitted that at the outset, they believed Kavanaugh's account, suggesting that their automatic response was to reinforce a gender divide. Yet these men displayed innovation that went beyond simple partisan categories, as they doubted Kavanaugh's fitness for the position exclusively because of his past predatory actions toward women.

Some went further, suggesting that the sheer seriousness of the allegations against Kavanaugh should have prevented him from ever assuming office. Adnan shared an innovative view:

> Personally, if someone can bring credible allegations against someone who's going to be a Supreme Court justice, you shouldn't be a Supreme Court justice in the first place. That person is going to be in charge of some of the biggest decisions in our country. And for that to be even partially questioned at any critical level, I don't think that should be the person in charge of those decisions.

Carter, a 21-year-old Middle Eastern man, agreed, "I believe her. And in society's eyes, they look at that and think that's an unforgivable crime. And we especially can't have someone who did that go to office." After first commenting on the seriousness of sexual assault and harassment, Deven agreed that Kavanaugh "shouldn't have been appointed. So there's innocent until proven guilty, but for a crime like that, you should really be able to prove yourself innocent before you're given that position of power." These comments suggest that these men operated within a nonlegal framework when it comes to those in power: If someone is accused, they should have to prove their innocence convincingly before taking office.

Yet such high-profile cases have "desensitized" people to the issue of sexual assault and harassment. Jin said,

> He's a Supreme Court justice and he's there in office right now. I think this stuff is happening because we're really trying to figure out where the morals of our country are and why people are allowing certain people in office to make these crazy decisions and just get away with it.

Jin included himself in this process:

> A lot of times now I'm personally desensitized. I think I'm just used to it. I'm just expecting every politician to act like that. I think that's the problem. I wish that there was a little bit more backlash toward these people.

This kind of reflection illustrates how resilient inequality and patriarchy can be.

Caleb recalled a family discussion about former Hollywood producer Harvey Weinstein, who at the time had been accused of numerous instances of sexual assault and has since been convicted. Caleb said that his family members

> weren't defending Weinstein. They weren't saying he was a good guy, an upstanding citizen or anything like that. But they objected to the labeling of him as a rapist because under their view, even if he coerced women to have sex with him, even if he sexually harassed women, he shouldn't be labeled any terms associated with that, because at the end of the day, the women still chose to remain in the room when he was naked, to engage in sexual relations with him. I disagree with this, and I think that it ignores the role of coercion and power in these dynamics.

This acknowledgment that men in positions of power often use their status as a tactic of coercion to pressure women into having sexual relations with them was atypical of the men. Here, some members of younger generations are starting to question gendered power dynamics.

In fact, four of the focus group men viewed the #MeToo movement quite positively. Hunter, a 22-year-old white man, said, "I agree with the #MeToo movement. Women are basically showing a greater sense of self-efficacy. They are capable and competent for that position or job and very confident to do something. That's a good thing." Although Derek was "positive," he added a "caveat": "It's positive. That's the only way. I mean, it's positive with a caveat. Positive because you've given people a greater platform to express the troubles and the things they've gone through. *But* you know, it has room to grow." Although Derek did not explain what he meant, he recognized that people have had a chance to express their previously private troubles through the movement.

Two men, Caleb and Jonah, suggested that visualizing their own family members as survivors helped them to see the importance of #MeToo. Caleb began by describing how (genderless) "people" use power and stature, but then he quickly shifted to clarify that he understood these "people" to be "men":

> The #MeToo movement has shown the way that some *people* will use power, some *people* will use their stature, and some, *not people, men* will use their power, will use their stature, and will use means to, maybe, to sexually assault women or sexually harass or sexually intimidate women. It might not be full-on violent

rape that you see in TV, but it's still a problem nonetheless. And it still shows that even if it's under the surface and less obvious, that we still do have issues to deal with despite the progress that we've made.

Caleb called #MeToo "really necessary" to address the way that people without "enough power" have been "victimized, treated, and mistreated." Although "one actress in Hollywood's not going to have enough power to take down an executive in the film industry," he believed that the movement would lead to more dramatic social and cultural change: "It really shows how when people band together, when people who have been victimized come together, you can have *light* brought to these issues, that it's not impossible." Jonah, a 20-year-old white man, agreed, pointing out that someone in his family could have these experiences,

> I'm happy #MeToo happened because all the air time that it got. I do think it changed a decent amount of minds who heard the testimonies of these women. And they could have been my daughter, kind of thing. We all knew obviously sexual harassment and things like this are happening, but I was amazed at the scale, in which the people that I watch on TV, how much it happens. I was just really amazed by that. So I'm really glad that it happened, it came out.

Caleb responded to Jonah, also focusing on the potential personal relevance of the movement, "I also heard that a lot. This could have been my daughter, this could have been my sister." As these men recognized the potential relevance of #MeToo for the women in their lives, they embraced the changes brought about by the movement.

In summary, although only a small number of men wholeheartedly embraced innovative perspectives, a larger number blended innovation and traditional perspectives that supported aspects of the #MeToo movement. Some of the focus group men viewed sexual harassment and assault within a broad framework that led them to recognize gendered power dynamics in interactions, in both high-profile cases and everyday ones.

Conclusion

The public discussion of personal experiences with sexual assault and sexual harassment among strangers in focus groups, particularly when we did not ask them, illustrates the profound effect of the #MeToo movement in everyday lives. Instead of hiding in shame, participants shared their stories publicly. Many women redefined past experiences as sexual assault, as the #MeToo movement has allowed them to challenge the remnants of traditional gender ideologies. Metaphors of "voice" were common. Instead of viewing sexual assault and harassment as an *individual* problem caused by a few "bad apples," these innovators saw harassment and sexual assault as a *collective* and *social* issue. Innovators' emphasis on the normalization of male violence and gender inequalities illustrates the diffusion of #MeToo movement frames into everyday lives as they increasingly reject patriarchal arrangements. As we have seen, a minority of the focus group men were also innovators who diverged from resister men and saw sexual assault as a widespread social problem. Even though some men blended innovation and traditional views, they began to acknowledge and reject imbalances in power. Their innovative perspectives reflect, and help to create, social change that challenges gendered power dynamics.

As innovators approached gender relationships in an adversarial way, many also renounced men's power over their self-determination. In doing so, they embraced movement frames and asserted their own definitions in ways that ran counter to the majority of men's narratives. This reflects women's rising agency and empowerment and suggests the diffusion of #MeToo era movement frames into everyday life. These innovators are thus creating definitions that validate women's sexuality and agency.

With the ubiquity of sexual assault, gender differences in definitions, and the widespread recognition that women are socialized to accept men's demeaning and criminal actions, readers might come away from our interviews pessimistic that the gender revolution has not gone further. While there is much to be concerned about, there are also signs of progress in these discourses. These voices reveal deep and pronounced social changes, as the gender revolution is taking place in the daily life of ordinary people. It is appropriate to use the term "revolution" because innovators of all genders are rejecting gender inequalities and transforming unequal relationships. Challenges to patriarchal arrangements are taking place not only among public figures in the media but also in people's everyday lives.

References

Aronson, Pamela. 2017. "The Dynamics and Causes of Gender and Feminist Consciousness and Feminist Identities." pp. 335–353 in *The Oxford Handbook of U.S. Women's Social Movement Activism*, edited by Holly J. McCammon, Verta Taylor, Jo Reger, and Rachel L. Einwohner. New York, NY: Oxford University Press.

Aronson, Pamela. 2003. "Feminists or 'Postfeminists?': Young Women's Attitudes Toward Feminism and Gender Relations." *Gender & Society* 17(6):903–922.

Chandra, Giti and Irma Erlingsdóttir. 2020. "Introduction." pp. 1–23 in *The Routledge Handbook of the Politics of the #MeToo Movement*, edited by Giti Chandra and Irma Erlingsdóttir. New York, NY: Routledge.

Donde, Sapana D., Sally K. Ragsdale, Mary P. Koss, and Alyssa N. Zucker. 2018. "If It Wasn't Rape, Was It Sexual Assault? Comparing Rape and Sexual Assault Acknowledgment in College Women Who Have Experienced Rape." *Violence Against Women* 24(14):1718–1738.

Elger, Dana. 2019. "Student Survey on Sexual Misconduct Provides New Knowledge: Campus Climate Survey Sponsored by AAU Shows Changes From 2015." *The University Record*. Retrieved February 1, 2022 (https://record.umich.edu/articles/student-survey-on-sexual-misconduct-provides-new-knowledge).

Graf, Nikki. 2018. "Sexual Harassment at Work in the Era of #Metoo." *Pew Research Center's Social & Demographic Trends Project*. Retrieved February 1, 2022 (www.pewsocialtrends. org/2018/04/04/sexual-harassment-at-work-in-the-era-of-metoo/).

Hirsch, Jennifer S. and Shamus Khan. 2020. *Sexual Citizens: Sex, Power, and Assault on Campus*. New York, NY: W.W. Norton & Company.

Koss, Mary P., Christine A. Gidycz, and Nadine Wisniewski. 1987. "The Scope of Rape: Incidence and Prevalence of Sexual Aggression and Victimization in a National Sample of Higher Education Students." *Journal of Consulting and Clinical Psychology* 55(2):162–170.

Morgan, Rachel E. and Jennifer L. Truman. 2018. "Criminal Victimization, 2017." Bureau of Justice Statistics. Retrieved February 4, 2022 (https://bjs.ojp.gov/content/pub/pdf/cv17.pdf).

Morgan, Rachel E. and Jennifer L. Truman. 2020. "Criminal Victimization, 2019." Bureau of Justice Statistics. Retrieved February 4, 2022 (https://bjs.ojp.gov/content/pub/pdf/cv19.pdf).

National Institute of Justice. 2010. "Victims and Perpetrators." Nij.ojp.gov. Retrieved February 4, 2022 (https://nij.ojp.gov/topics/articles/victims-and-perpetrators).

Sinozich, Sofi and Lynn Langton. 2014. "Rape and Sexual Assault Victimization Among College-Age Females, 1995–2013." Bureau of Justice Statistics. Retrieved February 1, 2022 (https://bjs.ojp.gov/content/pub/pdf/rsavcaf9513.pdf).

Stanko, Elizabeth A. 1995. "Women, Crime, and Fear." *The ANNALS of the American Academy of Political and Social Science* 539(1):46–58.

Stop Street Harassment. 2018. "The Facts Behind the #MeToo Movement: A National Study on Sexual Harassment and Assault." Retrieved February 1, 2022 (www.stopstreetharassment.org/wp-content/uploads/2018/01/Full-Report-2018-National-Study-on-Sexual-Harassment-and-Assault.pdf).

U.S. Equal Employment Opportunity Commission. 2019. "Charges Alleging Sex-Based Harassment (Charges Filed with EEOC) FY 2010—FY 2020." Retrieved February 1, 2022 (www.eeoc.gov/statistics/charges-alleging-sex-based-harassment-charges-filed-eeoc-fy-2010-fy-2020).

CONCLUSION

Social Change and the Future of the Gender Revolution

On November 7, 2020, newly elected Vice President Kamala Harris took the stage to claim victory in a bitterly divided, pandemic-ravaged nation. Wearing white to honor suffragists, Harris emphasized the collective power of women:

> Generations of women—Black women, Asian, White, Latina, Native American women . . . who worked to secure and protect the right to vote for over a century: 100 years ago with the 19th Amendment, 55 years ago with the Voting Rights Act and now, in 2020, with a new generation of women in our country who cast their ballots and continued the fight for their fundamental right to vote and be heard. . . . But while I may be the first woman in this office, I will not be the last, because every little girl watching tonight sees that this is a country of possibilities (The Washington Post 2020).

Harris's election as vice president and this speech in particular express the time of simultaneous progress and resistance that we have named the "gender revolution." Indeed, the gender revolution has continued, as subsequent elections have shown. For example, the 2022 midterm elections pushed the gender revolution forward, as concerns about a loss of women's autonomy (after the loss of a federal right to abortion) and attacks on democracy created "an earthquake" (Bruni et al. 2022) that drove voters to support Democrats, women candidates, and reproductive freedom ballot initiatives in unpredicted numbers and places.

Changes resulting from the gender revolution are also experienced on the personal level, in the everyday lives of ordinary people. Riley, an 18-year-old Black woman, described how average women apply the progress of women in electoral politics to their own lives. As a result of seeing women get elected,

DOI: 10.4324/9781003225331-12

changes spill over to other domains: "Women might feel like they would be *taken seriously* in a more male-dominated area." Jada, an 18-year-old Black woman, expanded, "Recently, there's been a lot of women's *empowerment*. And *you've got all this empowerment behind you.* These women are more *confident* going out and trying to pursue things." Using the word "we" to signify a collective identity, Jada continued, "This is an *empowering* generation in a way. *We* always *support each other* or *have each other's backs.*" Empowerment is contagious; support from other women, including those in electoral politics, affects ordinary women's confidence and ability to speak out:

> It can make you feel *more confident* going out, to *do* what you want to do or *say* what you want to say, to *get your point across.* And then people *listen.* It's a lot of *support.* And you can go really far with *support* behind you.

Interconnections like these illustrate the power of the gender revolution in ordinary people's daily lives.

Expressions of culture, interwoven with the experiences of ordinary people, paint a picture of how electoral politics and #MeToo have been reshaping everyday life in more egalitarian ways. Transformations in gender relations have become diffused throughout society, influencing and connecting the *political* and the *personal* realms. In analyzing an extensive volume of data, from a content analysis of national news media and campaign materials to local focus group interviews with a highly diverse sample, we teased out this complexity of transformations in women's power. By triangulating these different types of data, we see that the people we call "innovators" (who push social and cultural change forward through new ideas and practices) are demanding greater gender equality in electoral politics, the public sphere, and interpersonal relationships. By focusing not only on leaders, activists, and agents of the movement but also on ordinary people's experiences, this book has shown how the gender revolution is created by innovators and challenged by those we label "resisters" (who stick to traditional conceptions and challenge innovations).

Although reception to such changes is uneven and occurs within a context of resistance and contestation, the gender revolution represents something deeper than simply the pendulum swinging between progressive and regressive gender politics; it represents deeper cultural changes. For example, while innovators are demanding gender equality in politics and intimate relationships, resisters are increasingly aware of rising accountability. In fact, innovative ideas are already widespread and have influenced our society and culture in profound and irreversible ways. That is, women's movement ideology has become diffused and incorporated into people's daily lives. These cultural and social transformations in electoral politics and people's lives have created, reinforced, and caused resistance to, the gender revolution and will carry forward into the future.

Gender Revolution: Progress and Backlash

The gender revolution has been propelled by three factors. First, reactions to Donald Trump's unprecedented presidency ignited a social movement in which innovators, especially women, gained political power. The 2017 Women's March, the largest single-day demonstration in U.S. history, pushed for gender equality using confrontational tactics that rejected traditional gender norms. This movement has influenced elections. Women have been running for office in record numbers, winning seats at unprecedented rates, and achieving offices that they have never occupied before. They are also creating new gender self-presentations and, in turn, shifting norms for future women candidates. The gender revolution ushered in a new era of candidate self-presentations that are strikingly gender nontraditional and feminist, compared to previous eras of more pronounced gender-traditional and gender-neutral self-presentations. Candidates draw on women's movement ideology, emphasize feminist issues, and embrace new language and approaches. Innovator voters, especially women, propel these changes in electoral politics as they reject inequalities and espouse collective gender identities, a "we."

Second, the gender revolution was sparked by the #MeToo movement as it emerged and quickly spread across politics, popular culture, electronic media, social media, the workplace, and the courts. Ideas from the movement spread from celebrities to people from historically marginalized groups, including disabled women, people of color, and nonbinary people (Chandra and Erlingsdóttir 2020). The affirmative consent standard embraced by the innovators, and increasingly institutionalized in laws and policies, asserts the power of self-determination. High-profile cases, such as those of convicted perpetrators Larry Nassar and Harvey Weinstein, have altered public discourse and expectations for criminal prosecution.

Third, electronic media and social media supercharged the dissemination of innovative ideas. The #MeToo movement helped usher in an era of social movement "contagion" and diffusion that moved from leaders and activists to average people. In this digital age, expressions of "personalized politics," such as bodily references on protest signs, have become commonplace (Weber et al. 2018). The number of women who spoke out publicly in our focus groups about their painful stories of sexual assault illustrates the extent to which the #MeToo movement frame has shaped everyday lives. This platform gives voice to previously hidden traumatic experiences through its striking visibility.

Innovators and Resisters

The emerging picture reveals the push and pull of innovation and resistance. Innovators viewed the political and the personal realms within a broader framework of gender inequalities and women's agency, while resisters maintained an individualized framework on behalf of traditional arrangements. Perspectives tend to be fluid and volatile; they fluctuate over time, although they never return exactly to the previous paradigm. These diverging and contested perspectives reveal a disruption and reassertion of gender inequalities. Rather than being able to say that the #MeToo movement has "succeeded," progress and reversal unfolds over time. Change is not "complete" or "incomplete" but dialectical, with ideological pulls and pushes influencing each other, and ripe with contestation, hence the word "revolution."

Innovation occurs at both the political and personal levels. In politics, the election of innovator women candidates, such as Harris and Governor Gretchen Whitmer, points to a widespread acceptance of gendered social and cultural change among a significant group of people. Although a woman did not become president in 2020, the vice presidential glass ceiling was shattered and created new norms. The social movement that sparked a reaction to Trump's presidency contributed to an electoral penalty of five percentage points for his preferred candidates in 2022 (Cohn 2022a). The 2022 midterm elections also resulted in a historic number of women elected to the U.S. House (over a quarter), as governors (nearly a quarter, including two openly lesbian governors), and to statewide executive offices and state legislatures (both slightly below one-third) (Center for American Women and Politics 2022). The five women governors first elected in 2018 and featured in Chapter 3 were all reelected (Michelle Lujan Grisham [D-NM], Laura Kelly [D-KS], Janet Mills [D-ME], Kristi Noem [R-SD], and Whitmer [D-MI]); the majority of new women in Congress in 2018 were also reelected (Astor 2022); and five gubernatorial contests had all-women matchups (Fitzgerald 2022). Young voters, especially women, turned out in high rates and voted for progressive candidates (De Vise 2022). As President Joe Biden summarized the 2022 election, "Women in America made their voices heard, man. Y'all showed up and beat the hell out of them" (De Vise 2022).

Additionally, focus group innovators embraced a collective identity in ways that powerfully rejected patriarchal arrangements. In doing so, they applied a women's movement frame to their everyday lives. The innovators pressed for *social* (not *individual*) solutions, including more women in power and greater gender equality. They also recognized the systemic and ubiquitous nature of sexual misconduct. They insisted that consent can change, be withdrawn at any time, and is communicated both verbally and through body language. The power of supporting women candidates, defining consent on their own terms, and speaking openly about their experiences indicates women's growing agency in the #MeToo era.

The focus group men who embraced innovator perspectives also illustrate social change. A handful of men explicitly rejected traditional views of sexual consent, assault, and harassment; they emphasized gender equality in both their support for women candidates and definitions of consent. Likewise, about one-third of the men fused progressive and traditional discourses. Although the patchwork approach does not wholly embrace women's self-determination, it illustrates that social change is underway. Despite being only partial, these innovations help to push change forward. The merging of these perspectives suggests a "cultural lag" (Swidler 1986: 281), in which new and traditional paradigms exist simultaneously.

Despite the dramatic changes brought forward by the innovators, traditional roles were reaffirmed by resisters and a gendered gulf in experiences continues. On the political level, many election outcomes affirm traditional roles, including Trump's 2024 presidential candidacy. The racism, sexism, and homophobia still present in electoral politics show the continued influence of resisters.

As most of the focus group men fell into this group, they viewed gender inequalities in politics and interpersonal relationships not as *social* problems but as discrete, individual-level circumstances. They often judged women candidates in stereotypical ways and viewed sexism in the media as isolated rather than systemic events. They distanced themselves from #MeToo, the women's movement, and feminism. On the personal level, our time of rapid social change is leading to confusion around the norms that govern interactions between genders. Rejecting affirmative consent standards, most resisters emphasized "gray areas" and argued that men's definitions of consent were more "flexible" than women's. Their resistance was evident in their concern about "false" accusations. They viewed sexual assault and harassment within an individualized framework in which some men are "bad apples" and saw "misunderstandings" about consent as isolated incidents.

Even so, although innovators reject men's power on many levels, most did not challenge a key component of gender inequality: the initiator-gatekeeper assumption of heterosexual relationships. Although the affirmative consent standard theoretically moves away from the traditional gender roles embraced by resisters, even the innovators did not challenge gender norms inherent in heterosexual scripts. The gender revolution will not be complete until the very basis of the gender-differentiated heterosexual framework is dismantled. That is, until we move into a system based entirely on mutual respect and collective responsibility for sexuality, affirmative consent will continue to emphasize heteronormative relationships, the objectification of women, and patriarchal arrangements—even though the gender revolution points toward further mutuality, understanding, and collective respect.

Implications of the Gender Revolution

Looking ahead, one implication of the gender revolution is that over time, more men may become innovators and resistance may become less widespread and vigorous. Innovators, including the women who ran for political office, the focus group women, and some of the focus group men, push change forward through the creation of new paradigms, ideas, ideology, language, and collective identities. In our "unsettled cultural period," ideological competition challenges traditional perspectives (Swidler 1986: 277), and these perspectives may become increasingly "delegitimized" (Jasper and Polletta 2018: 66). Although resisters often reject approaches for which they do not "have the cultural equipment" (Swidler 1986: 281), this cultural lag may eventually fade away. As there is less resistance to new ideas, culture progresses and new perspectives become "normal" rather than "highly controversial" (Rochon 1998: 17).

As new ideologies of equality diffuse throughout society and culture, they become embedded in laws and practices, which leads them to become normative, expected, and even enforced. For example, Title IX, which reached its 50th anniversary in 2022, continues to influence educational equality. Although some specific protections are contested, expectations of gender educational equality have become socially normative and widely endorsed. Likewise, while reproductive rights have been unduly restricted and LGBTQ rights hang in the balance, outrage over regression to previous eras is vigorous; people are refusing to allow hardwon personal freedoms to be taken away.

As people accept new ideas and practices in their everyday lives, these often become taken for granted. When social movement frames diffuse and become increasingly accepted by the general public in response to demands and pressures, new ideas become normative within culture and society. When this happens, a critical mass of ordinary people become innovators. Like previous eras, when feminist ideologies become diffused into our cultural norms, feminism can be paradoxically "everywhere and nowhere" (Reger 2012) at the same time. Ideologies of equality can profoundly influence people's lives and identities while simultaneously appearing to be invisible (Aronson 2017; Aronson 2008).

Social change is not a linear, smooth progression; it is always messy and incomplete. The gender revolution is taking place on multiple terrains, which further challenges its momentum. While there is progress on issues like sexual consent or women in politics, for example, more regressive elements predominate in other arenas, like reproductive and LGBTQ rights. In this sense, countermovement frames can be as powerful as social movement frames, producing deep divisions. The gender revolution is a long, continuous struggle with many fronts. (Indeed, in social movement parlance, it is "one struggle, many fronts.")

By seeing social and cultural transformation in this manner, we conclude with optimism, even if it is tempered optimism. On the pessimistic side, the COVID-19 pandemic dramatically and abruptly shifted our normal way of life. It resulted in deepening gender inequalities in women's work and the household division of labor, as women were disproportionately burdened with housework and childcare (Zamarro and Prados 2021). Pandemic lockdowns contributed to rising violence against women, especially domestic violence (UN Women 2022). The media has turned a blind eye to the gendered nature of mass shootings and the way that guns and violence are tied to American masculinity (Katz 2022). Resisters have attacked democracy, voting rights, women in politics, LGBTQ and reproductive rights, and the racial justice movement. For example, Florida's 2022 "Don't Say Gay" law limits discussions of LGBTQ identities and issues in the classroom (Lavietes 2022).

The 2022 reelection of Republican Ron DeSantis as governor of Florida by 19 percentage points shows resisters' persistence in, as DeSantis put it, "fight[ing] the woke" ideology in our institutions (ABC Action News 2022). Likewise, the Amber Heard-Johnny Depp trial (in which the jury sided with Depp against Heard's accusations of domestic violence and Heard was subjected to widespread condemnation on social media) exposed "anti-feminist backlash" (Taub 2022). Some commentators declared that this "orgy of misogyny" was directed at all women (Donegan 2022) and signaled the "death of #MeToo" (Goldberg 2022a).

Most notably, the Supreme Court's 2022 decision in *Dobbs v. Jackson Women's Health Organization* overturned *Roe v. Wade*, which had guaranteed women's right to abortion for nearly a half century. One in three women lost access to abortion within two months following the decision and a bitter battle for reproductive rights will continue (Shepherd et al. 2022). The decision deeply affects women's agency, challenges women's health, and calls into question the basis of their citizenship (Cottom 2022). Mourning the loss of feminism's momentum and power, Goldberg (2022b) described our time as "fearful, hopeless and even nihilistic" because backlash thwarted optimism and confidence that social change was moving toward equality. These setbacks are very real, as are the divisions that the gender revolution has produced.

And yet the gender revolution must be considered a long, continuous struggle. Although many of these setbacks are pulling us back toward a framework of traditional gender relations, they are also being vigorously contested. Although the Heard-Depp trial has been called a "retrograde force" that illustrates that "#MeToo hasn't really made much progress" in terms of accountability (Fossett 2022), the case itself should not be considered a "referendum on #MeToo" or ushering in the "death" of feminism (Shure 2022; Taub 2022). In fact, the #MeToo movement has been credited with recent high-profile case decisions (including the 30-year sentence received by R. Kelly after decades of sex trafficking and sexual assault of teenage girls, the verdict against Bill Cosby after decades of sexual misconduct, and the largest settlement ever reached by an American university to compensate survivors of sexual assault, in which the University of Michigan will pay $490 million to 1,050 claimants alleging abuse by the late Dr. Robert Anderson [Blinder 2022; Bowley et al. 2022; Closson 2022]).

Furthermore, an Associated Press (2021) survey found progressive change over time in people's attitudes toward #MeToo: In 2021, 54 percent said that recent attention to these issues made people more likely to speak out, while 61 percent agreed that this attention has been good for women (This was up from 45 percent in January 2020.). Thus, as Bokat-Lindell (2022) pointed out, "#MeToo still looms large in the cultural imagination." And as we have seen here, new expectations and norms are emerging in people's everyday lives surrounding the very definition of consent. The significance of this deep cultural change must be appreciated. #MeToo is one moment in a larger struggle for self-determination and equality.

Likewise, despite devastating blows to feminism and women's rights as a result of the *Dobbs* decision, the gender revolution is evident in social movement activism and the elections that immediately followed it. Many progressives expected that overturning *Roe* would result in an Armageddon of sorts, with women essentially stripped of the power of self-determination. Not only is that fear not coming to pass, but elections since this decision also represent a historic rejection of efforts to limit women's autonomy and power. Innovators are working within the legal system in places where abortion is illegal; people on the ground are making donations for pregnant people to travel to other legal states; employers—from Walt Disney to Walmart (the country's largest employer)—have been expanding coverage of abortions and related travel expenses; and new medical fronts (especially medical abortion via oral medication) will likely continue to expand access. Kazin (2022) likened the *Dobbs* decision to prohibition and predicted that the 60 percent of Americans who disapprove of the decision will "rebel against authorities who decree what they can do with their own bodies."

In contrast to commentators who lamented feminism's failures or even death, Solnit (2022) challenged us to examine the *Dobbs* decision within the long arc of history. She argued that eliminating the right to abortion will not eradicate "the belief in that right." Citing historical changes in women's equality, including new federal and state laws resulting from the #MeToo movement, she concluded, "The last decade has been a rollercoaster of gains and losses, and there is no neat way to add them up. The gains have been profound, but many of them have been subtle." Indeed, innovators have created new identities and people are not willing to give those up. The reality on the ground is that efforts to reverse personal rights are ultimately unenforceable. Despite the Supreme Court decision and the overeager restrictions imposed by many states, the legal and legislative path is being laid for massive challenges to these reversals of personal freedom.

The results of elections following *Dobbs* provide compelling support for our argument that the gender revolution is still underway, and by the time this book is in your hands, even more changes are inevitable. The *Dobbs* decision led to a surge in people, especially women, registering to vote. Within a week of the decision, in otherwise conservative Kansas, which had the nation's first ballot referendum on abortion rights, over 70 percent of newly registered voters were women (Paris and Cohn 2022). Kansas saw high turnout and record numbers supporting abortion rights by a very wide margin (Cohn 2022b). This initial support for reproductive freedom continued in the 2022 midterm elections. About one-third to three-quarters of voters in Michigan, Vermont, and California voted to amend their state constitutions to protect reproductive freedom, while over half of voters rejected ballot initiatives in Kentucky and Montana that would have eroded abortion rights (New York Times 2022). In fact, despite the predicted Republican "red wave," support for reproductive rights was "one of the big reasons Democrats defied history and staved off deep midterm losses" (Lerer 2022).

Exit polls and interviews suggested that voters from all parties were motivated by their support for abortion rights, even in places that did not have a ballot referendum (like Pennsylvania, Virginia, Minnesota, and New Mexico) (Knoll and Smith 2022). Nationally, 27 percent of voters in exit polls said that abortion was their top issue (Kamarck and Galston 2022). Democrats successfully linked abortion to health care and voters' fears about extremism among Republicans (Lerer and Dias 2022). Representative Diana DeGette (D-CO) said, "It was all tied together. . . . People were thinking, 'I'm worried about the economy. I'm worried about freedoms being taken away,' and they were worried about democracy, too" (Lerer and Dias 2022). Thus, conservative candidates faced voters' opposition (Weisman and Glueck 2022), and more progressive candidates successfully made reproductive rights a central part of their campaigns (Goldmacher and Glueck 2022).

Although the *Dobbs* decision "accelerated" deep ideological divisions (Weisman 2022), the evidence in this book suggests that we need to think more broadly

FIGURE 8.1   A 2022 Election Billboard in a Farm Field in Rural Ohio Advocating Women to Vote for Democrats Who Support Reproductive Freedom

Source: Author.

about how the gender revolution influences elections. Voters are demanding that women have control over their own lives, and support for reproductive freedom represents one important aspect of this broader demand for self-determination. Commentators support this perspective; as Young (2022) said,

FIGURE 8.2 A Reproductive Freedom Lawn Sign in Michigan Linking the Late Supreme Court Justice Ruth Bader Ginsburg with the 2022 Election

Source: Author.

Women for whom abortion is the dominant issue tend to frame it not as a matter of their own right to get an abortion but as a "war on women" in which abortion opponents are motivated primarily by fear and hatred of female autonomy.

As Kamarck and Galston (2022) put it, "Central to the story of the 2022 midterms, then, is an issue central to women's lives, powerful enough to snatch victory from the Republicans, and durable enough to send a message about the future." Voters, even conservative women, were "not willing to compromise our rights and our personhood" (Hesse 2022). For example, in a number of Michigan counties, the majority of voters simultaneously supported Republican candidates and reproductive freedom.

Political polarization is highly gendered. Voters' perspectives on gender roles are connected with political party alignment, and some research suggested that the partisan gender gap is much larger than the partisan racial gap (Edsall 2022). According to exit polls, the gender gap in party choice was a whopping 22–23 percentage point gap from 2018 to 2022 (McCormack 2022). There have also been signs of changes in culture, such as a surge in readership in progressive digital publications aimed at women (Robertson 2022). And a culture of women speaking out has affected other arenas. For example, the congressional hearings on the January 6, 2020, attack on the Capitol featured women, some of whom lacked power, coming forward to challenge threats to democracy that were largely carried out by men (Karni and Haberman 2022).

Thus, the gender revolution—uneven, a work in progress—is a force among us, whose ideas, behaviors, and even identities have spread into everyday life. Resistance may be powerful but so are innovators. As average people become innovators and innovative perspectives diffuse widely, culture and society will continue to shift, even at times when resistance gets the upper hand. The gender revolution will continue and helps us to envision something new.

The Future of the Gender Revolution

Although transformations happen slowly and unevenly and face resistance, the social and cultural changes that have already taken place in everyday life suggest that a more egalitarian future has the potential to emerge. To create deeper and lasting changes, transformations in laws and policies will continue to solidify the cultural transformations already underway. On the U.S. legal front, more states are considering adopting an affirmative consent legal standard and are placing limits on nondisclosure agreements, which have silenced survivors. Legislation has already been enacted to improve rape kit testing and extend the statute of limitations for civil lawsuits. Internationally, the International Labour Organization Convention on Violence and Harassment Treaty went into legal effect under international law, codifying some of the demands of the #MeToo movement.

We expect that transformations will continue in workplaces and educational settings. In workplaces around the country, we have already witnessed the development and expansion of sexual harassment policies, trainings, and consequences for violators. Although studies suggest that mandatory training is not always effective (Banner et al. 2022), we expect that training will expand and improve over time. We also expect more "belief" in the words of survivors, especially those who are among the most disadvantaged.

Some skeptics might argue that having a greater representation of women in politics by itself typically cannot remove gender inequality. Certainly, we have seen real obstacles and challenges to instituting important policy changes around issues like LGBTQ rights, paid family leave, and abortion rights. Although social change can be swift, the American political system is designed to be incremental, to pull politics toward the center, and to change slowly. Many of the bold initiatives put forward on the campaign trail often become watered down when first brought into the political system.

And yet despite the stubbornness of political and institutional change, social and cultural transformations are often more rapid. In fact, real change has occurred in people's everyday lives and identities. These cultural shifts are important and have transformed gender relations. All the same, change needs to go further: Ideally, we need to expand the critical mass of people who view gender inequalities in electoral politics and sexual misconduct within a *collective* rather than an individualized framework. We need to move away from accepting power differences and a lack of self-determination as legitimate or natural, and instead put greater emphasis on how inequalities—encompassing race and class—connect within a broader social structure. Despite significant gains and the potential to transform the future, the current gender revolution is still very much in progress.

Although the gender revolution has been uneven and stalled at times, it will continue to have profound effects. As boys and men continue to be held accountable for their actions, they will continue to learn that abusive behaviors will not be tolerated. As more innovators, women, LGBTQ individuals, and people of color take on positions of political power, they will continue to transform our social and political institutions. The court of public opinion matters. Innovators will not go back to outdated, traditional arrangements without a forceful fight. Despite clear signs of contestation and resistance, including not only "false" accusation discourses but also bitter confrontations over abortion and LGBTQ rights, agency and self-determination are deeply embedded within the public imagination. As innovators are powerfully connected to, and have deeply absorbed, a belief in their own self-determination, they will continue to propel society and culture forward, toward further equality. After all, these ideas have been planted, have been spread, and have grown strong roots.

References

ABC Action News. 2022. "Ron DeSantis 2022 Florida Governor Race Victory Speech." Retrieved November 11, 2022 (www.youtube.com/watch?v=vDJtCCpeXNE).

Aronson, Pamela. 2017. "The Dynamics and Causes of Gender and Feminist Consciousness and Feminist Identities." pp. 335–353 in *The Oxford Handbook of U.S. Women's Social Movement Activism*, edited by Holly J. McCammon, Verta Taylor, Jo Reger, and Rachel L. Einwohner. New York, NY: Oxford University Press.

Aronson, Pamela. 2008. "The Markers and Meanings of Growing Up: Contemporary Young Women's Transition from Adolescence to Adulthood." *Gender & Society* 22(1):56–82.

Associated Press. 2021. "#MeToo Poll: Many in US More Willing to Call Out Misconduct." *ABC News*. Retrieved September 13, 2022 (https://abcnews.go.com/US/wireStory/metoo-poll-us-call-misconduct-80596932).

Astor, Maggie. 2022. "Elected to House in 2018, Most Democratic Women Are Hanging On." *New York Times*. Retrieved November 17, 2022 (www.nytimes.com/2022/11/09/us/politics/women-midterms.html?smid=nytcore-ios-share&referringSource=articleShare).

Banner, Francine, Lisa Martin, Pamela Aronson, Grace Bradley, Islam Jaffal, and Maureen Linker. 2022. "Can Respectful Citizens Create Equitable Institutions? Promoting a Culture of Respect in the #Metoo Era." *Feminist Criminology* 17(3):315–321 https://doi.org/10.1177/15570851211062577.

Blinder, Alan. 2022. "University of Michigan Will Pay $490 Million to Settle Abuse Cases." *New York Times*. Retrieved November 16, 2022 (www.nytimes.com/2022/01/19/sports/ncaafootball/michigan-abuse-settlement-robert-anderson.html).

Bokat-Lindell, Spencer. 2022. "Is the #MeToo Movement Dying?" *The New York Times*. Retrieved September 13, 2022 (www.nytimes.com/2022/06/08/opinion/depp-heard-me-too.html).

Bowley, Graham, Lauren Herstik, and Douglas Morino. 2022. "Bill Cosby Loses Sex Assault Lawsuit and Must Pay Damages." *The New York Times*. Retrieved September 13, 2022 (www.nytimes.com/2022/06/21/arts/television/cosby-verdict-sexual-assault-damages.html).

Bruni, Frank, Jonathan V. Last and Mallory McMorrow. 2022. "'We May Have Reached the Limit of Crazy That Will Be Tolerated.'" *New York Times*. Retrieved November 17, 2022 (www.nytimes.com/2022/11/09/opinion/2022-midterm-elections.html?smid=nytcore-ios-share&referringSource=articleShare).

Center for American Women and Politics. 2022. "2022 Election Results Tracker." Retrieved November 16, 2022 (https://cawp.rutgers.edu/election-watch/2022-election-results-tracker).

Chandra, Giti and Irma Erlingsdóttir. 2020. "Introduction." pp. 1–23 in *The Routledge Handbook of the Politics of the #MeToo Movement*, edited by Giti Chandra and Irma Erlingsdóttir. New York, NY: Routledge.

Closson, Troy. 2022. "R. Kelly, R&B Star Who Long Evaded Justice, Is Sentenced to 30 Years." *The New York Times*. Retrieved September 13, 2022 (www.nytimes.com/2022/06/29/nyregion/r-kelly-racketeering-sex-abuse.html).

Cohn, Nate. 2022a. "Trump's Drag on Republicans Quantified: A Five-Point Penalty." *The New York Times*. Retrieved November 17, 2022 (www.nytimes.com/2022/11/16/upshot/trump-effect-midterm-election.html).

Cohn, Nate. 2022b. "Kansas Result Suggests 4 out of 5 States Would Back Abortion Rights in Similar Vote." *The New York Times*. Retrieved September 13, 2022 (www.nytimes.com/2022/08/04/upshot/kansas-abortion-vote-analysis.html).

Cottom, Tressie Mcmillan. 2022. "Citizens No More." *The New York Times*. Retrieved September 13, 2022 (www.nytimes.com/2022/06/28/opinion/citizens-no-more.html).

DeVise, Daniel. 2022. "Young Women Broke Hard for Democrats in the Midterms." *The Hill*. Retrieved November 17, 2022 (https://thehill.com/homenews/campaign/3731564-young-women-broke-hard-for-democrats-in-the-midterms/).

Donegan, Moira. 2022. "The Amber Heard-Johnny Depp Trial Was an Orgy of Misogyny." *The Guardian*. Retrieved September 13, 2022 (www.theguardian.com/commentisfree/2022/jun/01/amber-heard-johnny-depp-trial-metoo-backlash).

Edsall, Thomas B. 2022. "How You Feel About Gender Roles Can Tell Us How You'll Vote." *The New York Times*. Retrieved September 13, 2022 (www.nytimes.com/2022/07/20/opinion/gender-gap-partisanship-politics.html).

Fitzgerald, Madeline. 2022. "Why the 2022 Elections Are Historic for Women." *U.S. News and World Report*. Retrieved November 17, 2022 (www.usnews.com/news/elections/articles/2022-11-07/woman-vs-woman-2022s-record-breaking-governors-races).

Fossett, Katelyn. 2022. "What Was Really at Stake in the Depp-Heard Trial." *POLITICO*. Retrieved September 13, 2022 (www.politico.com/newsletters/women-rule/2022/06/03/what-was-really-at-stake-in-the-depp-heard-trial-00036985).

Goldberg, Michelle. 2022a. "Amber Heard and the Death of #Metoo." *The New York Times*. Retrieved September 13, 2022 (www.nytimes.com/2022/05/18/opinion/amber-heard-metoo.html).

Goldberg, Michelle. 2022b. "The Future Isn't Female Anymore." *The New York Times*. Retrieved September 13, 2022 (www.nytimes.com/2022/06/17/opinion/roe-dobbs-abortion-feminism.html).

Goldmacher, Shane and Katie Glueck. 2022. "Why Abortion Has Become a Centerpiece of Democratic TV Ads in 2022." *The New York Times*. Retrieved September 13, 2022 (www.nytimes.com/2022/08/14/us/politics/abortion-midterms-2022-ads-democrats.html).

Hesse, Monica. 2022. "A 'Red Wave' Swept in. Just Not the One Expected." *Washington Post* and *Bloomberg Opinion*. Retrieved November 17, 2022 (https://replica.startribune.com/infinity/article_popover_share.aspx?guid=85a11352-6132-4eb1-89be-9f146fd59fff).

Jasper, James M. and Francesca Polletta. 2018. "The Cultural Context of Social Movements." pp. 63–78 in *The Wiley Blackwell Companion to Social Movements, Second Edition*, edited by David A. Snow, Sarah A. Soule, Hanspeter Kriesi, and Holly J. McCammon. Hoboken, NJ: John Wiley & Sons Ltd.

Kamarck, Elaine and William A. Galston. 2022. "It Wasn't Just 'the Economy Stupid'—It was Abortion." *Brookings*. Retrieved November 17, 2022 (www.brookings.edu/blog/fixgov/2022/11/10/it-wasnt-just-the-economy-stupid-it-was-abortion/).

Karni, Annie and Maggie Haberman. 2022. "In Jan. 6 Hearings, Gender Divide Has Been Strong Undercurrent." *The New York Times*. Retrieved September 13, 2022 (www.nytimes.com/2022/07/23/us/politics/jan-6-hearings-women-witnesses-committee.html).

Katz, Jackson. 2022. "Media Coverage Misses the Gender Issues at the Heart of School Shootings." *Ms. Magazine*. Retrieved September 13, 2022 (https://msmagazine.com/2022/06/06/media-coverage-of-uvalde-misses-the-gender-issues-at-the-heart-of-school-shoo tings/?fbclid=IwAR1hX7aOJzDwCLSeEQm13NjD95Lq8i9HXFA6TXZq7ms 3NS6I3Ya8Zu1bUTQ&fs=e&s=cl).

Kazin, Michael. 2022. "Even If Republicans Outlaw Abortion, Americans Will Soon Rebel." *The New York Times*. Retrieved September 13, 2022 (www.nytimes.com/2022/07/11/opinion/republicans-abortion-prohibition.html).

Knoll, Carina and Mtich Smith. 2022. "My Main, Core Issue': Abortion Was the Driving Force for Many Voters." *New York Times*. Retrieved November 16, 2022 (www.nytimes.com/2022/11/10/us/abortion-ballot-midterm-elections.html?smid=nytcore-ios-share&referringSource=articleShare)

Lavietes, Matt. 2022. "As Florida's 'Don't Say Gay' Law Takes Effect, Schools Roll out LGBTQ Restrictions." *NBCNews.com*. Retrieved September 13, 2022 (www.nbcnews.com/nbc-out/out-news/floridas-dont-say-gay-law-takes-effect-schools-roll-lgbtq-restrictions-rcna36143).

Lerer, Lisa. 2022. *"Abortion on the Ballot."* *New York Times*. Retrieved November 16, 2022 (www.nytimes.com/2022/11/10/briefing/abortion-midterm-elections.html).

Lerer, Lisa and Elizabeth Dias. 2022. "How Democrats Used the Abortion Debate to Hold Off a Red Wave." *New York Times*. Retrieved November 16, 2022 (www.nytimes.com/2022/11/10/us/politics/abortion-midterm-elections-democrats-republicans.html?smid=nytcore-ios-share&referringSource=articleShare).

McCormack, John. 2022. "Gender Gap Holds Steady From 2018 to 2022." *National Review*. Retrieved November 17, 2022 (www.nationalreview.com/corner/gender-gap-holds-steady-from-2018-to-2022/).

New York Times. 2022. "Abortion on the Ballot." *New York Times*. Retrieved November 16, 2022 (www.nytimes.com/interactive/2022/11/08/us/elections/results-abortion.html).

Paris, Francesca and Nate Cohn. 2022. "After Roe's End, Women Surged in Signing Up to Vote in Some States." *New York Times*. Retrieved November 16, 2022 (www.nytimes.com/interactive/2022/08/25/upshot/female-voters-dobbs.html).

Reger, Jo. 2012. *Everywhere and Nowhere: The State of Contemporary Feminism in the United States*. New York, NY: Oxford University Press.

Robertson, Katie. 2022. "After Roe v. Wade Reversal, Readers Flock to Publications Aimed at Women." *The New York Times*. Retrieved September 13, 2022 (www.nytimes.com/2022/08/14/business/media/abortion-womens-media.html).

Rochon, Thomas R. 1998. *Culture Moves: Ideas, Activism, and Changing Values*. Princeton, NJ: Princeton University Press.

Shepherd, Katie, Rachel Roubein and Caroline Kitchener. 2022. "1 in 3 American Women Have Already Lost abortion Access. More Restrictive Laws are Coming." *The Washington Post*. August 22. Retrieved September 13, 2022 (www.washingtonpost.com/nation/2022/08/22/more-trigger-bans-loom-1-3-women-lose-most-abortion-access-post-roe/).

Shure, Natalie. 2022. "Stop Trying to Extract Larger Lessons From the Amber Heard—Johnny Depp Trial." *The New Republic*. Retrieved September 13, 2022 (https://newrepublic.com/article/166501/amber-heard-johnny-depp-trial).

Solnit, Rebecca. 2022. "Women's Rights have Suffered a Grim Setback. But History is Still on Our Side." *The Guardian*. Retrieved February 23, 2023 (https://www.theguardian.com/commentisfree/2022/jul/03/abortion-roe-v-wade-womens-rights-rebecca-solnit).

Swidler, Ann. 1986. "Culture in Action: Symbols and Strategies." *American Sociological Review* 51(2):273–286.

Taub, Amanda. 2022. "A Wider Lens on the Metoo Backlash: Who Pays for Societal Change?" *The New York Times*. Retrieved September 13, 2022 (www.nytimes.com/2022/06/08/world/asia/depp-heard-metoo-women.html).

UN Women. 2022. "The Shadow Pandemic: Violence Against Women During Covid-19." Retrieved September 13, 2022 (www.unwomen.org/en/news/in-focus/in-focus-gender-equality-in-covid-19-response/violence-against-women-during-covid-19#facts).

The Washington Post. 2020. "Read the Transcript of Kamala Harris's Victory Speech in Wilmington, Del." Retrieved September 13, 2022 (www.washingtonpost.com/politics/2020/11/07/kamala-harris-victory-speech-transcript/).

Weber, Kirsten M., Tisha Dejmanee, and Flemming Rhode. 2018. "The 2017 Women's March on Washington: An Analysis of Protest Sign Messages." *International Journal of Communication* 12:2289–2313.

Weisman, Jonathan. 2022. "Spurred by the Supreme Court, a Nation Divides Along a Red-Blue Axis." *The New York Times*. Retrieved September 13, 2022 (www.nytimes.com/2022/07/02/us/politics/us-divided-political-party.html).

Weisman, Jonathan and Katie Glueck. 2022. "Republicans Begin Adjusting to a Fierce Abortion Backlash." *The New York Times*. Retrieved September 13, 2022 (www.nytimes.com/2022/08/05/us/politics/republicans-abortion-kansas.html).

Young, Cathy. 2022. "Blame All the Single Ladies." *The Bulwark*. Retrieved November 17, 2022 (www.thebulwark.com/blame-all-the-single-ladies/).

Zamarro, Gema and M. J. Prados. 2021. "Gender Differences in Couples' Division of Childcare, Work and Mental Health during COVID-19—Review of Economics of the Household." *SpringerLink*. Retrieved September 13, 2022 (https://link.springer.com/article/10.1007/s11150-020-09534-7).

APPENDIX 1

Research Design: How We Study the Gender Revolution

Focus Group Participants' Demographic Information

Here, we provide additional details about our sample and research design. As mentioned in the introduction, one of the strengths of our study is that it captures the experiences of a diverse sample. The sample had significant racial and ethnic diversity: Only 27 percent (n = 20) were white (non-Hispanic/Latinx and non-Middle Eastern/North African). There were some racial and ethnic differences by gender: Women were more likely than men to classify themselves as Black (45.5 versus 7.5 percent), whereas men were more likely to classify themselves as white, Middle Eastern or North African, Hispanic/Latinx, or Asian American (see Table 1).

TABLE 1 Distribution of Racial and Ethnic Background by Gender

	Women	Men	Nonbinary	Total
White	7	13	0	20
Middle Eastern or North African	3	7	0	10
Hispanic/Latinx	2	3	0	5
Black	15	3	0	18
Asian American	2	10	0	12
Multiracial	3	2	1	6
Unknown	1	2	0	3
Percent (n)	44.6% (33)	54.1% (40)	1.4% (1)	100% (74)

Note: χ^2 (12, N = 74) = 28.597, p < .01

Comparing the sample's racial and ethnic background with those of people in the local county and the educational institution is complicated because neither the Census Bureau nor the university collects information on Middle Eastern or North African background. As a result, people with this background are typically classified as white. All the same, county-level Census data (Wayne County including Detroit and a portion of its surrounding suburbs) suggest that 49.2 percent are white (non-Hispanic/Latinx), 38.4 percent are Black, 6.5 percent are Hispanic/Latinx, 3.6 percent are Asian American, 2.8 percent are multiracial, and 0.5 percent are American Indian and Alaska Native (Census Bureau 2022).[1] Likewise, institutional data suggest that the student population was distributed as follows in both fall 2018 and fall 2019: 64 percent white (including Middle Eastern or North African), 6 percent Hispanic/Latinx, 8 percent Black, 8 percent Asian American, and the remainder multiracial, "nonresident alien," or unknown. Thus, it appears that our sample had a somewhat smaller proportion of Black interviewees than was present in the county yet a higher proportion of Black interviewees than was present in the institution. Although it is difficult to arrive at direct comparisons as a result of the way race and ethnicity are defined by the Census and university, our sample overall reflects the diversity of the area from which it was drawn.

About one-third (n = 29) were first-generation college students. There were some differences in social class by gender, with women about twice as likely as men to be the first in their families to attend college (see Table 2). The household income level is very close to the median household income of the county in which it rests, which had a median income of $49,359 in 2021 (Census Bureau 2022).

TABLE 2 Distribution of Parents' Education and Household Income by Gender

	Women (n)	Men (n)	Nonbinary (n)	Total (n)
First-Generation College Student	54.5% (18)	27.5% (11)	0	32.9% (29)
Parents Have Bachelor's Degree or Higher	45.5% (15)	60% (24)	100% (1)	54.1% (40)
Unknown Education	0	12.5% (5)	0	6.8% (5)
Low Income*	54.5% (18)	45% (18)		48.6% (36)
Middle to Higher Income*	42.4% (14)	45% (18)	100% (1)	44.6% (33)
Unknown Income	3% (1)	10% (4)		6.8% (5)
Percent (n)	44.6% (33)	54.1% (40)	1.4% (1)	100% (74)

* Low income is defined as household income near the median household income in 2018. The median household income in Michigan was $56,697. Middle to higher income is above this median income.

[1] The Census Bureau (2022) population listings by race and ethnicity do not add up to 100 percent.

Table 3 illustrates that men and women had similar ages: Slightly more than 70 percent were between 18 and 24 years old and slightly over a quarter were over 25 years old (see Table 3). As students at a commuter campus, they had a wide range of life experiences, work backgrounds, and family situations. The sample was generally evenly split in whether or not interviewees were currently in a relationship (see Table 4). Women interviewees were twice as likely as men to have children, although the number with children was quite small (12.2 percent, n = 9; see Table 4). Among the interviewees, women were more likely to be currently employed than men (78.8 percent, n = 26 versus 55 percent, n = 22; see Table 5). Nearly 84 percent of all genders were registered voters (see Table 5).

TABLE 3 Distribution of Age by Gender

	Women (n)	Men (n)	Nonbinary (n)	Total (n)
18–24	66.7% (22)	72.5% (29)	100% (1)	70.3% (55)
25 and Older	33.3% (11)	22.5% (9)	0	27.0% (20)
Unknown	0	5% (2)	0	2.7% (2)
Percent (n)	44.6% (33)	54.1% (40)	1.4% (1)	100% (74)

TABLE 4 Distribution of Relationship and Family Status by Gender

	Women (n)	Men (n)	Nonbinary (n)	Total (n)
Single, Divorced or Widowed	12	18	0	30
Cohabiting, Married or in a Relationship	15	12	1	28
Unknown Relationship Status	6	10	0	16
Parent	6	3	0	9
Non-Parent	27	35	1	63
Unknown Parental Status	0	2	0	2
Percent (n)	44.6% (33)	54.1% (40)	1.4% (1)	100% (74)

TABLE 5 Distribution of Employment and Voting Status by Gender

	Women (n)	Men (n)	Nonbinary (n)	Total (n)
Employed	78.8% (26)	55% (22)	0	64.9% (48)
Not Employed	21.2% (7)	40% (16)	100% (1)	32.4% (24)
Unknown Employment Status	0	5% (2)	0	2.7% (2)
Registered to Vote	84.8% (28)	82.5% (33)	100% (1)	83.8% (62)
Not Registered to Vote	15.2% (5)	10% (4)	0	12.2% (9)
Unknown Voting Status	0	7.5% (3)	0	4.1% (3)
Percent (n)	44.6% (33)	54.1% (40)	1.4% (1)	100% (74)

Interview Guide

Given the sensitive nature of our topic, we followed all ethical guidelines from the Belmont Report in our research. For example, although published after we conducted our research, our data collection and analysis were consistent with the principles outlined by Campbell et al. (2019: 4769) when they said: 1) "Understand and be prepared to hear a wide variety of traumatic experiences, coping mechanisms, and continuing impacts after the trauma," 2) "During debriefing, offer information and referrals to local, culturally competent trauma services," 3) "Emphasize participants' rights to refuse participation in the study or opt out of the study at any time with no loss of benefits/incentives," and 4) "Data collection: Use active listening techniques during interviews to demonstrate empathy for survivors' feelings and choices." Furthermore, as these authors recommended (Campbell et al. 2019: 4473), we never asked "detailed questions about participants' previous sexual assault experiences." Instead, we asked, "Do you think that there's confusion about how to define sexual consent?" Although our questions sought to understand general attitudes toward the rise of women in politics, consent, and the #MeToo movement, many participants chose to share deeply personal experiences. Our interview guide included the following questions:

Women in Politics:
1. How do you think gender impacted the 2016 election?
2. What did you think about the 2018 election?
3. Who did you support in the governor's race: Gretchen Whitmer, Bill Scheutte, or someone else?
4. Do you think the obstacles that men and women candidates face are different? Why or why not?
5. How do you feel the media represents male and female candidates—similarly or differently?
6. More women ran for office and were elected in 2018 than in prior elections. Why do you think this happened?
7. Which of the 2018 election races interested you the most?

#MeToo Movement: Introduction: One issue we have been hearing about a lot in the media and politics is sexual assault and harassment. These next set of questions are focused on this issue and the #MeToo movement. In case you haven't heard of it, it is a movement around giving voice to private experiences with sexual assault and harassment.
1. What did you think about Supreme Court Justice Brett Kavanaugh being accused of sexual assault?
2. How big of a problem are harassment and assault?
3. Do you think there is confusion about how to define sexual consent? How so? Do you think we have commonly agreed upon definitions?

4. Do men and women think about consent, harassment, and assault differently? How so?
5. How do you feel that public cases—like Trump, Nassar, or R. Kelly—have changed how men and women interact and communicate with each other?
6. Do you think sexual assault and harassment are accurately reported? Why or why not? Do you think more occurs than we actually hear about or is it less reported than actually happens?
7. What do you think about the #MeToo movement?
8. Do men and women view the #MeToo movement differently? Why or why not?
9. What do you think of feminism? Do you consider yourself to be a feminist? What is your definition of feminism?
10. Is there anything you would like to add?

References

Campbell, R., R. Goodman-Williams, and M. Javorka. 2019. "A Trauma-Informed Approach to Sexual Violence Research Ethics and Open Science." *Journal of Interpersonal Violence* 34(23–24):4765–4793. doi:10.1177/0886260519871530.

Census Bureau. 2022. "QuickFacts, Wayne County, Michigan." Retrieved February 25, 2023 (www.census.gov/quickfacts/waynecountymichigan).

APPENDIX 2

Study Participants at a Glance

Pseudonym	Gender	Age	Race/Ethnicity	Age of Child(ren)	Relationship Status	Household Income Range	Perspective
Aaron	Man	Unknown	Unknown	Unknown	Unknown	Unknown	Resister
Adam	Man	22	Hispanic/Latinx	–	Single	$30,001–$50,000	Resister
Adnan	Man	21	Middle Eastern or N. African	–	Relationship	Less than $15,000	Innovator
Ahmad	Man	21	Middle Eastern or N. African	–	Single	$15,001–$30,000	Resister
Alex	Nonbinary	21	Multiracial	–	Relationship	$50,001–$70,000	Fused
Alexandra	Woman	38	Black	6, 13	Married	$30,001–$50,000	Fused
Alyssa	Woman	29	Black	–	Relationship	$15,001–$30,000	Innovator
Amelia	Woman	20	Multiracial	–	Married	$50,001–$70,000	Fused
Amy	Woman	19	Asian American	–	Single	Over $90,000	Fused
Angel	Woman	54	Black	18, 30, 32	Divorced	$15,001–$30,000	Fused
Anthony	Man	35	Black	–	Relationship	$15,001–$30,000	Fused
Aran	Man	20	Asian American	–	Unknown	Over $90,000	Fused
Aria	Woman	21	Unknown	–	Married	Less than $15,000	Innovator
Brianna	Woman	21	Black	–	Single	Over $90,000	Innovator
Bryson	Man	31	White	–	Married	$15,001–$30,000	Resister
Caleb	Man	21	White	–	Single	$30,001–$50,000	Fused
Cam	Man	18	Asian American	–	Single	Over $90,000	Resister
Carter	Man	21	Middle Eastern or N. African	–	Relationship	Less than $15,000	Fused
Charlotte	Woman	23	Multiracial	–	Relationship	$50,001–$70,000	Innovator
Christina	Woman	36	Black	13, 14, 20	Married	$15,001–$30,000	Fused
Christopher	Man	19	Hispanic/Latinx	–	Single	$15,001–$30,000	Resister
Damien	Man	18	Black	–	Single	$50,001–70,000	Fused
Derek	Man	22	White	–	Relationship	$70,001–$90,000	Innovator
Deven	Man	20	Asian American	–	Relationship	$15,001–$30,000	Fused
Dominic	Man	20	White	–	Unknown	Over $90,000	Fused
Don	Man	58	White	26, 30, 34	Unknown	Less than $15,000	Resister

(Continued)

(Continued)

Pseudonym	Gender	Age	Race/Ethnicity	Age of Child(ren)	Relationship Status	Household Income Range	Perspective
Ethan	Man	28	White	1.5	Married	$70,001–$90,000	Resister
Gabriel	Man	23	Asian American	–	Single	Over $90,000	Fused
Grayson	Man	22	Middle Eastern or N. African	–	Single	Over $90,000	Resister
Harper	Woman	23	Multiracial	–	Relationship	$15,001–$30,000	Fused
Hunter	Man	22	White	–	Single	Less than $15,000	Fused
Isabella	Woman	21	Hispanic/Latinx	–	Relationship	$50,001–$70,000	Innovator
Isiah	Man	24	Asian American	–	Single	Unknown	Innovator
Jack	Man	Unknown	Unknown	–	Unknown	Unknown	Resister
Jada	Woman	18	Black	–	Relationship	Over $90,000	Innovator
Jasmine	Woman	40	Black	18, 21	Single	Unknown	Innovator
Jeremiah	Man	36	Multiracial	6	Married	$70,001–$90,000	Resister
Jin	Man	21	Asian American	–	Single	$50,001–$70,000	Fused
Joel	Man	20	White	–	Unknown	Over $90,000	Innovator
Jonah	Man	20	White	–	Unknown	Over $90,000	Fused
Kayla	Woman	21	Black	–	Single	$15,001–$30,000	Innovator
Khalid	Man	21	Middle Eastern or N. African	–	Relationship	$30,001–$50,000	Resister
Kiara	Woman	18	Black	–	Single	$50,001–$70,000	Innovator
Kim	Woman	27	White	–	Single	Over $90,000	Innovator
Laila	Woman	43	Black	24	Unknown	$15,001–$30,000	Innovator
Lakin	Woman	22	Black	–	Relationship	Less than $15,000	Innovator
Leo	Man	18	Asian American	–	Single	Less than $15,000	Fused
Li	Man	18	Asian American	–	Single	$70,001–$90,000	Resister
Ling	Woman	29	Asian American	–	Married	Less than $15,000	Innovator
Luke	Man	22	White	–	Relationship	Over $90,000	Resister
Malik	Man	19	Middle Eastern or N African	–	Single	Over $90,000	Fused
Maram	Woman	21	Middle Eastern or N. African	–	Single	$30,001–$50,000	Innovator

Meghan	Woman	22	White	—	Unknown	$30,001–$50,000	Innovator
Mia	Woman	20	White	—	Relationship	$70,001–$90,000	Innovator
Michelle	Woman	19	White	—	Relationship	$15,001–$30,000	Innovator
Mark	Man	31	White	—	Married	Less than $15,000	Fused
Mahmud	Man	18	Middle Eastern or N. American	—	Unknown	Unknown	Resister
Mitchell	Man	20	White	—	Single	$30,001–$50,000	Innovator
Nadine	Woman	20	White	—	Unknown	Over $90,000	Innovator
Nia	Woman	49	Black	24, 28, 29	Single	$30,001–$50,000	Fused
Noah	Man	33	Multiracial	—	Single	Less than $15,000	Resister
Olivia	Woman	27	White	—	Single	$30,001–$50,000	Innovator
Riley	Woman	18	Black	—	Unknown	Over $90,000	Innovator
Rima	Woman	20	Middle Eastern or N. African	—	Single	$15,001–$30,000	Innovator
Sang	Man	19	Asian American	—	Unknown	Over $90,000	Resister
Sarah	Woman	20	White	—	Unknown	$50,001–$70,000	Innovator
Sasha	Woman	20	Black	—	Relationship	Over $90,000	Innovator
Sofia	Woman	21	Hispanic/Latinx	—	Single	Unknown	Innovator
Taylor	Woman	18	Black	—	Unknown	Over $90,000	Innovator
Terrell	Man	25	Black	—	Single	Less than $15,000	Resister
Thiago	Man	25	Hispanic/Latinx	—	Cohabitating	$70,001–$90,000	Resister
William	Man	18	White	—	Single	$70,001–$90,000	Fused
Xiu	Man	22	Asian American	—	Unknown	$15,001–$30,000	Resister
Zainab	Woman	32	Middle Eastern or N. African	—	Divorced	$30,001–$50,000	Innovator

APPENDIX 3

Timeline of Key Gender Revolution Events

Year	Month	Event
2006	October	Tarana Burke coined the phrase "me too."
2016	October	Release of *Access Hollywood* video, in which Donald Trump bragged about sexual assault. Millions of survivors posted their own stories of sexual assault on social media.
2016	November	Election of President Donald Trump. Defeat of Hillary Clinton, first woman to run for U.S. president on a major party ticket.
2017	January	Inauguration of 45th President Donald Trump.
2017	January	Millions of people around the world take to the streets to protest the inauguration of President Donald Trump.
2017	October	The *New York Times* exposes a 30-year history of rape, sexual assault, and sexual abuse committed by Harvey Weinstein.
2017	October	Apparently unaware of the connection with Burke's phrase "me too," Alyssa Milano popularized #MeToo as a hashtag on social media, referring to her experiences with Harvey Weinstein.
2018	January	In the first high-profile case to emerge in the #MeToo movement, Larry Nassar was sentenced to 40 to 175 years in prison for sexual assault. Nassar used his position in sports medicine to abuse hundreds of women and girls and Judge Rosemarie Aquilina encouraged over 150 of his survivors to speak out about their experiences.

(Continued)

(Continued)

Year	Month	Event
2018	September	U.S. Senate confirmation hearings for Supreme Court Justice Brett Kavanaugh; Kristine Blasey Ford testified at these hearings that Justice Kavanaugh sexually assaulted her when she was at a high school party; Protests against Kavanaugh's nomination swayed public opinion but did not block his confirmation.
2018	September	Actor Bill Cosby convicted of three counts of aggravated indecent assault.
2018	September	Comedian Aziz Ansari was accused of sexually assaulting a woman on a date.
2018	October and November	Focus groups conducted.
2018	November	Midterm elections.
2019	January and February	Focus groups conducted.
2019	June	Debate 1 of the 2020 Democratic Primary for President at The Adrienne Arsht Center for the Performing Arts in Miami, Florida.
2019	July	Debate 2 of the Democratic Primary for President at Fox Theatre in Detroit, Michigan.
2019	September	Debate 3 of the Democratic Primary for President at Texas Southern University in Houston, Texas.
2019	October	Debate 4 of the 2020 Democratic Primary for President at Otterbein University in Westerville, Ohio.
2019	November	Debate 5 of the 2020 Democratic Primary for President at Tyler Perry Studios in Atlanta, Georgia.
2019	December	Debate 6 of the Democratic Primary for President at UCLA Luskin School of Public Affairs in Los Angeles, California.
2020	January	Debate 7 of the Democratic Primary for President at Drake University in Des Moines, Iowa.
2020	February	Weinstein sentenced to 23 years for sexual assault and harassment.
2020	February	Debates 8, 9 and 10 of the Democratic Primary for President at St. Anselm College in Manchester, New Hampshire; Paris Theater in Las Vegas, Nevada; and the Gaillard Center in Charleston, South Carolina.
2020	March	COVID-19 pandemic hit the United States, causing widespread closures of schools, government, and industry.
2020	September	First Presidential Debate at Case Western Reserve University in Cleveland, Ohio (the University of Notre Dame in South Bend, Indiana withdrew as a host as a result of the pandemic).

Year	Month	Event
2020	October	Vice-Presidential Debate at the University of Utah in Salt Lake City, Utah.
2020	October	Second Presidential Debate was cancelled.
2020	October	Final Presidential Debate at Belmont University in Nashville, Tennessee.
2020	November	Joe Biden elected president and Kamala Harris elected vice president.
2021	January	Attack on the Capitol challenged U.S. democracy.
2021	January	Kamala Harris sworn in as the first Black woman vice president.
2021	January	Studies find that the pandemic deepened gendered wage disparities and inequalities in the gendered household division of labor.
2021	June	Cosby was released from prison; a judge ruled that his due process rights had been violated.
2022	January	The largest settlement ever reached by an American university to compensate survivors of sexual assault, in which of the University of Michigan will pay $490 million to 1,050 claimants alleging abuse by Dr. Robert Anderson.
2022	March	Florida's governor, Ron DeSantis, signs the "Don't Say Gay" bill into law, prohibiting discussion of sexual orientation or gender identity in young elementary classrooms.
2022	May and June	Amber Heard and Johnny Depp trial and hearings. Jury in a defamation trial awarded $10 million to Johnny Depp and $2 million to his ex-wife Amber Heard. Heard had accused Depp of domestic violence.
2022	June	R. Kelly sentenced to 30 years in prison for sex trafficking and racketeering. Most of his victims were teenage girls.
2022	June	Jury found Cosby guilty of sexually assaulting a 16-year-old in 1975 and awarded $500,000 compensatory damages. This case offered public vindication when the *Constand* case was overturned on due process grounds.
2022	June	Supreme Court's decision in *Dobbs v. Jackson Women's Health Organization* overturned *Roe v. Wade*, which had guaranteed women's right to abortion for nearly a half century.
2022	June	Fiftieth anniversary of Title IX, which prohibited exclusion from participation or discrimination on the basis of sex under any education or program with federal funding.
2022	June and July	Congressional hearings on the January 6, 2020 attack on the Capitol.

(*Continued*)

(Continued)

Year	Month	Event
2022	August	First ballot referendum shocked the nation as otherwise conservative voters in Kansas turned out in unprecedented numbers to support abortion rights by a wide margin.
2022	November	In the midterm elections, about one-third to three-quarters of voters in Michigan, Vermont, and California voted to amend their state constitutions to protect reproductive freedom, while over half of voters rejected ballot initiatives in Kentucky and Montana that would have eroded abortion rights.
2022	November	Exit polls and interviews suggested that voters from all parties were motivated by their support for abortion rights.
2022	November	Donald Trump announced his candidacy for president in 2024.
2023	February	R. Kelly, already serving 30 years for sex trafficking, was sentenced to 20 years for federal charges of child pornography.
2023	February	Weinstein, already serving a 23-year prison sentence, was sentenced to 16 years for rape and sexual assault.

INDEX

Note: *Italic* page number refer to *figures* and **Bold** page number refer to **tables**.

Made in the USA
Middletown, DE
10 October 2023

40560145R00157